New Directions in Counselling

Counselling is currently going through a period of rapid growth and change. Increased demand for services, national and European legislation and pressures from within the field are pushing counselling towards greater professionalism and accountability. *New Directions in Counselling* examines key issues for the present and future development of the profession.

Part one considers various aspects of counselling as a profession, including accreditation, the influence of National Vocational Qualifications (NVQs), developing Codes of Ethics and evaluating effectiveness. Part two looks at developments in counselling practice in terms of the interventions being used to treat common problems, such as smoking and depression; the settings in which counselling is being practised; and advances in counselling techniques, such as the use of narratives. Part three discusses issues affecting training, raising crucial questions such as whether there are myths surrounding counselling which still need to be challenged and how central a feminist perspective should be.

New Directions in Counselling makes a timely response to questions affecting all counsellors, whether in training or in practice.

The editors all work at the University of East London. **Rowan Bayne** is Senior Lecturer in Counselling and Psychology. **Ian Horton** is Senior Lecturer in Counselling and Psychotherapy. **Jenny Bimrose** is Head of the Centre for Training in Careers Guidance.

New Directions in Counselling

Edited by Rowan Bayne, Ian Horton
and Jenny Bimrose

London and New York

First published 1996
by Routledge
11 New Fetter Lane, London EC4P 4EE

Simultaneously published in the USA and Canada
by Routledge
29 West 35th Street, New York, NY 10001

Routledge is an International Thomson Publishing company I(T)P

Typeset in Times by Harper Phototypesetters Limited
Printed and bound in Great Britain by Clays Ltd, St Ives PLC

British Library Cataloguing in Publication Data
A catalogue record for this book is available from the British Library

Library of Congress Cataloguing in Publication Data
New directions in counselling/edited by Rowan Bayne, Ian Horton
and Jenny Bimrose.
    p.   cm.
  Includes bibliographical references and index.
  1. Counseling. 2. Counseling – Practice. 3. Counselors – Training
  of. 4. Psychotherapy. I. Bayne, Rowan. II. Horton, Ian, 1940– .
  III. Bimrose, Jenny, 1949– .
BF637.C6N48   1996
361.3'23–dc20   95–50080 CIP

ISBN   0–415–13142–1 (hbk)
ISBN   0–415–13143–X (pbk)

Contents

Illustrations

Contributors

Michael Barkham is Senior Lecturer in Clinical Psychology, University of Leeds and Deputy Director, Psychological Therapies Research Centre, University of Leeds.

Judith Baron is General Manager, British Association for Counselling and Former Chair of the British Association for Counselling.

Rowan Bayne is Senior Lecturer in Counselling and Psychology, University of East London.

Jenny Bimrose is Head of the Centre for Training in Careers Guidance, University of East London.

Tim Bond is Staff Tutor in Counselling, University of Durham and Chair of the British Association for Counselling.

Cary L. Cooper is Professor of Organisational Psychology and Deputy Chairman of the Manchester School of Management, University of Manchester Institute of Science and Technology.

Graham Curtis Jenkins is Director, Counselling in Primary Care Trust.

Delia Cushway is Lecturer in Clinical Psychology, University of Birmingham.

Windy Dryden is Professor of Counselling, Goldsmiths College, University of London.

Hetty Einzig is Development Officer, Parenting Education and Support Forum and Research Director, Artemis Trust.

Colin Feltham is Senior Lecturer in Counselling, Sheffield Hallam University.

Alan M. Frankland is Principal Lecturer in Counselling and Psychotherapy, Nottingham Trent University and Chair of the British Association of Counselling Individual Accreditation Scheme.

Paul Gilbert is Head of Adult Mental Health, Kingsway Hospital, Derby and Professor of Clinical Psychology, University of Derby.

J. Carolyn Highley is an independent business psychologist specialising in the audit and evaluation of workplace counselling programmes (including EAPs) and also provides general consultancy in this area.

Ian Horton is Senior Lecturer in Counselling and Psychotherapy, University of East London.

Francesca Inskipp is a freelance counsellor, supervisor and trainer.

Marcus Lefébure is Assistant Director of Wellspring, an independent counselling co-operative, Edinburgh and Book Reviews Editor, *Counselling*.

John McLeod is Lecturer in Counselling and Director of the Centre for Counselling Studies, Keele University.

John Mellor-Clark is Clinical Evaluation Co-ordinator, Psychological Therapies Research Centre, University of Leeds.

Andy Parrott is Reader in Psychology, University of East London.

Janice Russell is Associate Tutor in Counselling, University of Durham and an independent consultant in counselling, supervision, research and training.

Moira Walker is Head of the Counselling Service, Leicester University.

Acknowledgements

We would like to thank all the people who have contributed to this book, especially Susamma Ajith for word-processing skilfully and treating us calmly and positively. She has the wonderful quality of grace under pressure.

Figure 12.1 first appeared in *Addiction*, 1995, *90* and is reprinted here with the permission of Carfax Publishing Company.

Introduction

This book is for practitioners and students in the field of mental health, most obviously counsellors and trainee counsellors. Psychotherapists, applied psychologists and health professionals whose work includes counselling may also find it useful. It gives ideas, evidence and arguments about some of the main new directions which counselling is taking in the UK. Counselling's main current concerns – professionalism, multiculturalism, brevity, accountability, effectiveness and integration – are all represented (cf. Dryden 1994; Horton *et al.* 1995).

The book is in three broad and inevitably overlapping parts: counselling as a profession, counselling practice, and counsellor education and training. In the first part, Chapter 1 provides a broad context and conveys the muddle and frustration experienced by many counsellors about what is and is not going to become of counselling as a 'profession', and about their place, if any, within it. The other chapters explore different facets of the increasing – and seemingly unstoppable – professionalisation of counselling.

The second part focuses first on counselling in the workplace and in primary care, then on selected problems, techniques and areas of work. Several other topics which could have been included here are reviewed in Lindsay and Powell (1994) such as eating disorders and alcoholism.

The third part explores six areas of counsellor education and training in which significant developments are taking place or, the authors argue, are needed. These chapters too have implications for practice, but are more concerned with training and less with what counsellors in various settings actually do with clients.

Each chapter is self-contained, so that the book can be used to gain an overview of new directions in UK counselling or as a specialist resource. We hope it will contribute to useful discussions and good decisions at a particularly exciting and volatile time for counsellors.

REFERENCES

Dryden, W. (1994) Possible future trends in counselling and counsellor training: a personal view. *Counselling 5* (3) 194–7.

Horton, I., Bayne, R. and Bimrose, J. (1995) (eds) New directions in counselling: a roundtable. *Counselling 6* (1) 34–40.

Lindsay, S.J.E. and Powell, G.E. (1994) (eds) *The Handbook of Adult Clinical Psychology*. London: Routledge. 2nd edn.

Part I

Counselling as a profession

Chapter 1

Who will count as a counsellor?
Gleanings and tea-leaves

Marcus Lefébure

INTRODUCTION

This chapter's title may well seem obscure, but, when duly interpreted, it is meant to sum up the series of convictions out of which the chapter is written: that the emerging profession of counselling and psychotherapy is undergoing rapid and profound developments of both substantive and organisational orders; that even the organisational changes will affect each one of us, to the extent, at the worst, of depriving us of the right to exercise our profession legally; that we can no longer afford to be ostriches; that we therefore need to inform ourselves better of these developments; that the relevant information is not readily available; that the most important elements can nevertheless be *gleaned* – hence the first part of the chapter's subtitle – from two of our main professional journals, *Counselling* and the *British Journal of Psychotherapy;* but that even after such a diligent search the shape of the future can still at this stage be only guestimated, by a process rather dismayingly but fascinatingly like that of interpreting *tea-leaves* – hence the second term of the subtitle; that we have no option but to hazard such a guestimate, but that any such guestimate will be reliable in proportion to its being informed.

This chapter is, therefore, in two main parts: selectively gathering and presenting the main elements of information available to the best of my ability, and then, on that basis, hazarding a few guesses about the future and its corresponding impact on counsellors.

GLEANINGS OF INFORMATION

Since I write as a counselling therapist, the total field of psychological care seems to me to be dominated by my chief representative body, the British Association for Counselling (BAC), which is, however, flanked, on the one hand, by the United Kingdom Council for Psychotherapy (UKCP, as the UK Standing Conference on Psychotherapy became at the beginning of 1993, after years of difficult struggle and debate), but also, on the other, by the Association for Counselling at Work (a division of BAC), the British Psychological Society (BPS) and, as from 1 April 1993, counselling in the context of the government's reforms of community care (see Robertson and Tudor 1993).

I draw particular attention to the BPS and the news that it has established a Diploma in Counselling Psychology and a Division of Counselling Psychology, in so far as this marks the bringing to bear of the more than one hundred years of the scientific tradition and credibility of the BPS on counselling and therefore the entry of another very powerful player onto the field. And I put the last three groupings together because they do not, I think, generally figure large in the consciousness of the average counselling therapist, which is all the more of a defect of vision for these groups being, in my opinion, destined to be ever more important players on the therapeutic scene as a whole. Reddy (1993), for example, states that 'The centre of gravity of the counselling universe is moving inexorably to the workplace.' As for the UKCP, I shall say no more for the present beyond noting that, without any government intervention or legislation, it has already set up a national register of psychotherapists, which will therefore surely have an ever-increasing moral and de facto authority only just short of full legal authority – and that this register does *not* include counsellors (Deurzen Smith 1993).

Granted, however, that this suffices as a first approximation to a view of the whole scene, and that the BAC thus occupies a mid-position, this middle ground is far from being an undisturbed island. On the contrary, BAC seems in the early 1990s to have become more and more jostled and challenged from within and without. And I go on therefore to suggest the nature of this disturbance, in terms of what I see as the four main factors: (1) European pressure and opportunity; (2) the development of National Vocational Qualifications (NVQs); (3) the move towards a National Register of Counselling; and (4) the issue of a single body for counselling and psychotherapy.

The single European market: pressure, politics and opportunity

For practical purposes, the story begins in 1991, shortly before the coming into force of the single European market in 1993. The Management Committee of BAC set up a small working party to consider the Association's response to the single European market and in particular to European Economic Community (EEC) regulations which might affect the practice of counselling in Britain and the other member states. After widespread consultation, BAC decided to work towards taking a lead role in establishing a European network for those concerned with counselling and psychotherapy (*Counselling* 1991, *2* (4) 123).

Even prior to this, however, there had been what seems to have been a powerful stimulus to this initiative in the shape of the keynote address given at the 1991 training conference (Deurzen Smith 1991). This really put the subject on the map and indicated its main contours. Speaking with the inside feel of her Dutch and French background, with the authority of many years' involvement with the subject in the UKSCP, and with the overview of an 'applied philosopher' (existentialist), Emmy van Deurzen Smith began by referring to the would-be reassuring statement of the then general manager of BAC, Elizabeth Davies, that 'there are no European directives that mention either counselling or psychotherapy', but went on to say that by dint of 'reading between the lines' of the emerging directives and policies, much could be descried. She then went on to point out that there were already two relevant 'directives' from Brussels.

First, the 1st Diploma Directive (89/48/EEC), already in force, and being implemented through the Department of Trade and Industry, governs all professions for which at least three years' full-time education and training at university or the equivalent level are required – as is the case for most psychotherapy training courses – and 'protects the rights of a person qualified in a particular profession in one EEC country to practise that profession in another EEC country without having to retrain'. But the monitoring of the equivalence of forms of training requires the existence of a so-called 'designated authority' in each country, which is in turn easily established where there is already a 'competent authority' for that profession, that is, a national body that sets standards and controls the awards of diplomas for the profession in question. And this is precisely what the UKCP has expressed its intention to become for the field of psychotherapy. In other words, in the UK the pressure for a national 'competent authority' for psychotherapy has come in the first place from within the country and not from Europe, but this would-be competent authority has thus been ready to fit into the European legislation when it comes into being.

The process is the reverse in the case of diplomas that do not require graduate entry, such as those in some areas of counselling, because there is nothing like a 'competent authority' for the whole range of counselling bodies. Moreover, the relevant directive here is not yet in force. But the grand political reasons for working towards intra-European mobility and the mutual recognition of qualifications across member states obtain at least as much for counselling as for psychotherapy. And there is in fact a second directive in draft (being actively processed by another government department, the Department of Employment) – the 2nd Diploma General Directive (COM(90)389 Final). Therefore there is pressure in the field of counselling too towards inter-state equivalence of training and so towards a national 'competent authority' for counselling (see too *Counselling* 1992, *3* (4): 3 of the 'Stop Press' section). It is just that here there is, as it were, European legislation in search of a due competent authority, whereas in the case of psychotherapy it was a case of a competent authority in search of due legislative recognition (and see *Counselling* 1992, *3* (2) 64).

In the same article, Deurzen Smith (1991) made a powerful plea for an overall, umbrella body to represent both psychotherapy and counselling. This idea of a single authority for the whole gamut of therapy was one that was to have an independent future, as we shall have occasion to see later in this chapter.

Lest the idea of a single authority seems to be rather academic, let me point out that the kind of representation there is to be is a political matter. This is because the experience of counselling is very variable within the Western countries, strong in the Anglo-American tradition, weak to the point of non-existence in countries like Italy. This, however, carries the corollary that there is a risk that the non-Anglo-American countries will require any counselling that does emerge to be in their own national image and so to be restricted to medically trained people – unless the countries with wider traditions of counselling can make their counter-influence felt: the process that was later elegantly named 'power-broking' (see *Counselling* 1992, *3* (4) 3 of 'Stop Press', and 1993, *4* (2) 72), power politics by any other name. That this is not chimeric is shown by the fact that there have already been two attempts to launch a European association for psychotherapy, restricting membership to medically or psychoanalytically trained people (see *Counselling* 1991, *2* (4) 134, and 1993, *4* (2) 72). And this, of course, is but the pan-European equivalent of a group of so-called 'conservative' or strict training institutes in Great Britain restricting psychotherapy to their kind (see *Counselling* 1991, *2* (4) 134 and 1993, *4* (2) 72; *British Journal of Psychotherapy* 1993, *9* (4) 514, 515–16).

It also happens that part of this involvement truly 'at the heart of Europe' is cross-fertilisation with the work towards the so-called National Vocational Qualifications:

National Standards development and European Development for BAC has [*sic*] a sibling-like relationship, their growth appears to be developing hand in hand. It is not possible to analyse one in isolation from another. It is vital that a strong cohesive national voice is presented in order to have any influence in the development of counselling and psychotherapy within the single European market.

(*Counselling* 1992, *3* (2) 64)

This is, therefore, a suitable point at which to turn to my second factor: NVQs.

National Vocational Qualifications (NVQs)

The concept of NVQs has been born of a government initiative that seems to constellate a number of aims: to develop a flexible vocational training system for a skilled workforce in the 1990s and beyond; to respond to the EC idea of mobility of labour and therefore of mutually recognised qualifications; to give a new place to work experience as distinct from traditional education in the acquisition of qualifications, therefore to bring providers and users of education and training into closer collaboration; and so to institute the notion of progression in qualifications and thus to the concept of national (and Scottish) vocational qualifications (NVQs and SVQs) organised into levels (of which there are so far four, with a fifth – professional – level well under way).

From the beginning it was envisaged that this new structure should apply to all areas of employment. It was therefore to include whatever could be considered to be counselling. But at first there were no NVQs in that field. The government, therefore, acting through the Department of Employment, soon turned to BAC to fill this gap. And BAC responded to such effect that it was first asked to manage the initial project to differentiate between advice, befriending, guidance, counselling skills and counselling, and so to inform the appropriate 'lead body' (the Lead Body on Advice, Guidance and Counselling), and finally secured a sizeable representation on this lead body. This was formally launched on 8 October 1992. The task of the lead body seemed to be threefold: to differentiate between advice, befriending, guidance, counselling skills and counselling; to identify the different standards of competence required by each activity; to match competencies with appropriate qualifications.

The result of BAC's involvement in the development of the National Council for Vocational Qualifications seems to be double-edged. On the one hand, by being so effectively recognised to be the, or at least a, leading representative of counselling, BAC has extended its influence deep into the world of ordinary skilled work. On the other hand, it may thereby have contributed to digging its own grave. For by lending its authority to the differentiation of advice, befriending, guidance and 'counselling skills' prior to what might be called core or therapeutic counselling, and to the articulation of four levels, it has inevitably raised the idea of integrating such counselling 'proper' into the whole emerging structure of progressive competencies as the fifth level. But this has already provoked a strong reaction from those who see such a development of counselling as a threat to the emergent 'separate and identifiable professional activity having parity with other professional qualifications' (*Counselling* 1991, 2 (4) 1 and 4 of 'Stop Press').

However, apart from the fact that those reacting in the way indicated

beg the question whether their justifiable concern for professional counselling status could not be met within the very context of the NVQs, the
idea of such a grand integration is organisationally and politically very
appealing and potent. And in fact *Counselling* reported in May 1993 that
'Included in the action plan [of the Lead Body on Advice, Guidance and
Counselling] to develop standards and establish NVQs and SVQs will be
further work on the production of a function map to *encompass
psychotherapy*' (*4* (2) 71, italics added). And this in turn raises the question of an even grander, overall structure of some integration of the whole
field from the lowest mooted level of advice, through counselling
'proper', to psychoanalysis, what Deurzen Smith (1991: 134) called 'the
national and European stratification of the profession of counselling with
that of other professions that cover a similar terrain'.

However, it also takes us into the dimension of what I called at the
beginning 'guestimation', whereas we are at this point still fact-finding. I
should, therefore, like to suspend further discussions of this issue until
this fact-finding is complete. Suffice it to say that BAC has here put its
future on the line. Nor is this the only way in which it has done so. It has
put itself on the line in the very way in which it has come to participate in
the project of a so-called 'National Register'. We come therefore to my
third factor.

A National Register

The first mention of a National Register came in BAC's *Annual Report* for
1992/93:

> A verbal report at last year's conference indicated that BAC alongside
> the Westminster Pastoral Foundation (WPF), Relate and the
> Confederation of Scottish Counselling Agencies (COSCA) had begun
> to explore the possibility of setting up a single National Register.
> During the year we have identified, through means of a questionnaire,
> which of our member organisations might already fulfil most of the
> criteria for a Register and by the time of the Annual Conference this
> year will have met this larger group for the first time. This is where the
> discussion will really begin. It will be important, as this work develops,
> that BAC is open in its negotiations as to the form the Register might
> take. At the same time we must maintain standards we have already set
> and make sure the Register is professional in all senses.
> (BAC Annual Report 1992/93: 2; and see *Counselling* 1992, *3* (4) 3
> of 'Stop Press'; 1993, *4* (2) 70, and 1993, *4* (3) 154)

This statement is charged with explosive implications:

1 The very fact that there is no mention of the psychotherapeutic organisation of the UKCP and its register (see above) and that it takes it for granted that the newly projected register is about a 'single, national, government recognised system of professional self-regulation for *counselling* which might eventually lead to some form of legal recognition' (*Counselling* 1993, *4* (3) 154, italics added) leaves open the questions of the de facto division of the therapeutic profession as a whole into two main groupings (psychotherapy and counselling), of their mutual relationship, and of a possible umbrella organisation.

2 The fact that, even within the field of counselling alone, BAC recognises such well-established and powerful players as the national networks of the WPF and Relate, puts itself forward as only an 'equal partner', and declares itself 'open' to the processes of negotiation – all this expresses BAC's relative and possibly transitional position.

3 Then, as regards what is a sub-topic within counselling, but a critical one – that of accreditation – the final two sentences indicate a tension between the existing emphasis given by BAC to 'standards' (in fact interpreted rather quantitatively) and the progressive notion of 'competence', taken over from the system of NVQs and SVQs by the still young but independent-minded and so potentially challenging COSCA.

This leaves the last of the four factors.

A single umbrella organisation for the whole of psychological care

In her keynote speech at the BAC Annual Conference in 1991, Emmy van Deurzen Smith made a powerful plea for a single, over-arching organisation to reassure the public, strengthen the profession within the country, and speak for Britain and the Anglo-American tradition of psychological care in Europe:

> Isn't it true that to provide a full service to clients, ranging from counselling skills and different levels of counselling through counselling psychology and a variety of therapeutic approaches to specialist psychotherapy or psychoanalysis, we do need to simplify and rationalise levels of training and practice?

(1991: 134)

In the summer 1993 issue of the *British Journal of Psychotherapy* she called this idea '*stratification* of the entire field' (1993: 516, italics added). Now this is a controversial notion, which seems to have receded somewhat from view, and in any case belongs to the future and what I called at the beginning 'guestimation'. So let us turn at last to interpretation.

INTERPRETING THE TEA-LEAVES

The motto here must surely be:

> If you can look into the seeds of time,
> And say which grain will grow and which will not,
> Speak then to me.
>
> *(Macbeth*, I, iii: 58–9)

From among the various forces now in play in some such manner as indicated above, which will prevail and which subside? To begin with what seems the clearest evidence, this is surely that the pressure of the European idea and of its attendant apparatus, quite apart from the inner dynamic of existing organisations, is such that the momentum towards national organisation and therefore professionalisation of psychological care is unstoppable.

As to how this is likely to come about, most of the work in the field of psychotherapy strictly so called has been done by the UKCP. It also seems to me that, as a matter of another hard political fact, it is highly unlikely that the UKCP will admit any counselling organisation into any process of renegotiation at this to them late stage, since this would be to risk letting ten years of hard work unravel. No, the logic of events is surely towards the development of a separate branch of psychological care comprising counselling as distinct from psychotherapy in the strict sense – at most a sister (younger?) organisation.

This, then, leaves the question of how the equivalent development is to take place in the field of counselling. Now here I think that it is again a matter of plain political realism to recognise that already there are a number of established, about equally powerful and virtually self-regulating bodies, including BPS, Relate and WPF as well as BAC – to which must now certainly be added COSCA, and even the Association for Counselling at Work, at present a division of BAC, in so far as this might wax on the lines indicated by Reddy (1993) and perhaps declare effective UDI from BAC.

Granted this, the question is how a (national) 'competent authority' (precursor, it will be recalled, to a 'designated authority') for counselling will emerge from all these counselling organisations. Theoretically, they could be left to fight it out. There is, however, a more honourable and British alternative: to negotiate a power share (which might not be without an element of horse-trading). I think, therefore, that the way forward might well be in two stages. In the first, there could be a mutual recognition of equivalence of standards and procedures, and therefore the establishment of a series of parallel routes to an equivalent diploma of counselling or counselling psychology (rather as at present roughly equal degrees can be obtained via a variety of universities). Such a phase of development could then, in due course, lead into a phase of a common register.

At this point the alert reader might well blink and object that this is not how things were in fact going. For according to the report in the November 1994 issue of *Counselling*, negotiations towards a national register had advanced so far that it could already be said: 'It is intended that the structure for the Register will be in place early in 1996', and 'There will be a system of *dual entry* to the Register' (1994: 252–3, italics added). The truth is that the paragraph at which the alert reader blinked dates from the first version of this chapter, but I have left it in order to illustrate by its very falsification at once the hazards of divination and the dynamic of actual developments.

At the same time, partially falsified forecaster as I have proved to be, I do seem to have been on the right track. For, on the one hand, people will under this scheme be able to proceed to registration not only via BAC's own established and refined route but via as many sponsoring agencies as the Founding Group of 'fifteen organisations and a number of individuals' and its successors allow, so that there will indeed be many routes to quali- fication. This will acknowledge the pluralism that has developed in the UK. On the other hand, since 'Those registered will hold either BAC or COSCA individual membership', thus making BAC and COSCA the (double) gate-keeper, the proposal also affects the principle of national co-ordination and representation required by the European directives. In terms of power, since the bodies listed as participants in the founding process include most of those I had already identified as powerful players in the counselling world (such as WPF, Relate and COSCA, but, interest- ingly, not BPS or the Association for Counselling at Work: why?), BAC is formally conceding power to those who already have its substance. On the other hand, by securing its role as gate-keeper to registration, it has also perpetuated its own central role.

What is more, by allowing for a 'minimum training' and stepped 'training increases' and therefore for a progression in training and, implic- itly, a gradation of training institutes, this proposal from the Founding Group writes into the very structure of registration, as well as into its process, the government-initiated and supported concepts of 'compe- tence' and 'progression in qualifications', as exhibited in the system of NVQs and SVQs and advocated especially by COSCA. It therefore further propels the dynamic towards an ever-wider integration and system of progressive levels.

Already this concept of progressive, experience-based competence seems to be the main engine for the simultaneous progress towards several convergent aims: providing a language for collaboration between the British government, European governments and independent professional bodies; complementing traditional, more academic formation with modern, practice-based training; at once meeting European policies and promoting the Anglo-American tradition of counselling within Europe; integrating counselling skills and counselling proper into an overall organisation of counselling and related activities, if not, eventually, psychotherapy too. In fact, I predict that the nationally and internationally political and organisational attraction of this dynamic will eventually be such as to include even UKCP and all the by then mutually integrated counselling skills and counselling bodies into one overall organisation of what I am calling 'psychological care'.

That such a development is likely is supported by two facts: it is essentially the pattern foreseen by Emmy van Deurzen Smith – who, it will be remembered, was the first chair of the pivotal body UKCP; it is also very similar to the pattern envisaged in the very lucid consultative paper drawn up earlier on by the National Register Working Party (UK), comprising representatives of BAC, Relate, WPF and COSCA, and circulated to all organisational members of BAC. The paper envisages a development from multiple registers, through a single national register, on to a UK government-recognised national register, and concluding with EEC acceptance of UK government recognition and even chartered status. This, however, is limited to counselling, whereas Emmy van Deurzen Smith's vision, like my own, ultimately integrates psychotherapy and counselling.

CONCLUSION AND QUERIES

There is, it seems to me, a now unstoppable momentum towards the professionalisation of counselling and psychotherapy, at least separately and probably together in due course; towards the subdivision of the generic profession of psychological care into two main parts; and towards the corresponding development of at least two national registers, possibly one somehow amalgamated national register, outside of which it will become illegal to practise as a psychotherapist/counsellor. This poses problems for counsellors and trainee counsellors individually and for any group we may be in. The following questions occur to me:

- Are we even individually prepared for these developments?
- Do we have, or are we on the way to acquiring, relevant qualifications?
- Amidst the proliferation of claims to accreditation, are any qualifications which we have or are acquiring likely to be professionally recognised?
- Do we have the necessary knowledge to make at least an informed guess?
- Will groups of counsellors be able legally to continue with mixed qualifications, or will they need to find some other status?

There are no doubt many more questions, as there are probably more items and nuances of information to be integrated. I make no claim to either infallibility or completeness. All I want to do is to sound the alarm, begin the process of gathering intelligence, and stimulate a more informed debate.

REFERENCES

Deurzen Smith, E. van (1991) 1992 and all that. *Counselling 2* (4) 133–4.
Deurzen Smith, E. van (1993) UKCP and the National Register for Psychotherapy. *British Journal of Psychotherapy 9* (4) 513–17.
Reddy, M. (1993) The counselling firmament: a short trip round the galaxy. *Counselling 4* (1) 47–50.
Robertson, G. and Tudor, K. (1993) Counselling in the context of community care. *Counselling 4* (3) 188–90.

Chapter 2

The emergence of counselling as a profession

Judith Baron

INTRODUCTION: THE NEW DIRECTION

In March 1993 the British Association for Counselling (BAC) Management Committee, after wide consultation, decided to support counselling as a profession actively and that all activities of the Association should be professional in approach. This was done in the knowledge that some of the members of the Association do not wish to describe themselves as professional counsellors and that the Association needed to address these members' needs too. It was acknowledged that such a move could significantly alter the structure of the Association and the face of counselling to the outside world over the coming decade and beyond. There was also a desire to try to influence the structure of this emergent profession in a way that is congruent with BAC's codes of ethics and practice for counselling and related activities, taking account of new forms of a profession that are apparent in the twentieth century, and avoiding as many as possible of the problems that more established professions have had to face in an age of increased technology and widely available access to knowledge (Watkins *et al.* 1992).

The title of this chapter immediately poses the question, 'What is a profession?' It assumes that there are some characteristics of a profession which are so easily recognisable that one can say 'counselling has arrived'. If only that were the case. Furthermore, if counselling is emerging as a profession, is this desirable or should one be beating a hasty retreat?

Sociological theorists, particularly from the 1940s and beyond and those with an interest in functional analysis, occupational classification and class structures, have attempted to define the essential characteristics of a profession. The Monopolies and Mergers Commission in 1970, commenting on 'the supply of professional services', suggested that the professional may possess some or all of the following characteristics to some degree (Monopoly and Mergers Commission 1970):

- a specialist skill enabling a specialist service;
- an intellectual and practical training in a well-defined area of study;
- detachment and integrity in exercising personal judgement on behalf of the client;
- a direct personal relationship with a client, based on confidence, faith and trust;
- a collective sense of responsibility for maintaining the competence and integrity of the profession;
- certain methods of attracting business (or the professional may be requested to have these);
- an affiliation with a body, which may have government recognition, which provides the mechanism for testing competence and regulates standards of competence and conduct.

A further survey of the literature suggests more attributes for defining the professional. He or she:

- has more allegiance to his or her profession than to his or her setting or employer;
- has a broad theoretical base to his or her work;
- sees work as more than a means to earn a living;
- has a higher level of educational qualifications and an ability to learn and amass knowledge;
- has intellectual skills which can grasp events and respond effectively and creatively;
- has discretion in the workplace and can take on multiple responsibilities and autonomous working.

What appears to be basic to those working as a professional is a trust relationship between them and the client and, in the twentieth century, a growing requirement for accountability to the client and society, and for standards to test work against.

It would be helpful here to cast an eye over the history of the groupings of occupations. It is suggested that such groupings reflect the knowledge base of the time and the differentiation of tasks undertaken. In pre-industrial society lawyers, the clergy and doctors held eminent places in society. This is reflected in literature, and one is reminded of the characters in Chaucer's *Canterbury Tales*, many of whom were ridiculed for not reaching the expected ethical standards of the time. In the eighteenth and nineteenth centuries there was the emergence of the Industrial Revolution. Engineers, chemists and accountants, to name a few, began to achieve eminence and recognition. From 1900 onwards the post-industrial and information technologies have come to the fore. There has been an expansion in the status available to people of enterprise and heading small and large businesses. The growth of access to education and understanding of human behaviour has led to credit and status for knowledge workers.

In the Standard Occupational Classification, under Major Group 2, the following professionals are listed:

- natural scientists;
- engineers and technologists;
- health professionals;
- legal professionals;
- business and financial professionals;
- architects, town planners and surveyors;
- librarians and related professionals;
- miscellaneous professionals, such as clergy, psychologists and social workers.

For the clergy, it seems an absolute claim to status is receding. For others, there is a chance to establish themselves, at least for now. Do counsellors wish to appear on this list?

A closer consideration of the characteristics of a profession leads one to believe that it is justified and appropriate to put counselling on this list for the following reasons. First, the BAC Code of Ethics and Practice for Counsellors, which has developed considerably since 1984, places an obligation on members of BAC to establish a relationship of faith and trust with clients on a basis that does not tilt the balance of power in favour of the counsellor. Second, the privacy of the setting in which counselling takes place demands integrity and the need for the individual counsellor to exercise judgement. Third, there is a requirement that counsellors take account of their allegiance to their employer as well as to the Codes, and it is becoming increasingly understood by employers that allegiance to the Codes of BAC (BAC 1984–95) overrides the demands of the workplace.

The development of BAC Recognised Counsellor Training Courses has embraced the requirement for practical and intellectual skills and a broad theoretical base to the work of its students (BAC 1988b). This requirement is also reflected in the criteria for individual counsellor accreditation. The BAC Codes of Ethics and Practice for Counsellors also lay down requirements for the maintenance of competence, advertising, and the monitoring of multiple responsibilities and relationships, as well as clear statements on responsibilities towards colleagues and other professionals. Finally, all this is backed by a rigorous complaints procedure to regulate the activities of BAC members (BAC 1986, 1992, 1994).

Such attributes were taken into account by the VAT Tax Tribunal, which sat in public on 13 December 1993, and which had to consider whether BAC could be classed as a professional association or an association whose primary purpose is the advancement of a particular branch of knowledge or the fostering of professional expertise. In the light of the broad membership with a broad practice and interest base, BAC did not postulate that it is a professional association but was clear that there is a professional expertise based on knowledge.

The tribunal was satisfied that BAC has the primary purpose of fostering the expertise of its individual members who are practising counsellors. It did not follow that this expertise was in a profession one of whose characteristics is the application of a specialist skill. However, having regard to the contemporary role of counselling, it was considered that accredited members could be said to practise professionally. It would thus seem that, at least in some legislative form, experienced counsellors with a history of training in theory and practice will be recognised as 'professional' counsellors, with a career and training route to that position. The steady rise in applications for accreditation and the imminent arrival of a United Kingdom Register of Counsellors is further evidence that the professionalisation of counsellors is under way.

The tribunal findings stated: 'Taking into account the evidence we heard on the academic courses on counselling and the level of the articles in the Journal of the Association for Counselling we have no difficulty in concluding that counselling is a branch of knowledge for this purpose.' This purpose is the advancement of a particular branch of knowledge connected with the past or present professions or employments of its members.

The ruling goes on to say that the representative of the Commissioners of Customs and Excise submitted that counselling 'was simply an advanced form of communication skill'. The panel members reported that this may be one way of describing it, but neither

> that description, nor the fact that it may be a form of knowledge or skill that can be acquired to a high level by intelligent people through practice and the normal experience of life, precludes it from being an area, form or branch of knowledge that can clearly be more deeply, and probably much more quickly, learnt with proper teaching and instruction.

Furthermore, they felt that:

> that teaching will be more effective the more it is based in relevant aspects of human behaviour. How people will react to different crises and how they will or may thereafter respond or relate to other persons adopting different approaches in an attempt to help them seems to us to raise very complex questions of the study and teaching of which can readily be described as the advancement of a branch of knowledge.

This ruling ably addresses the twentieth-century dilemma of addressing the growth and availability of knowledge. Knowledge is now available to all. No one person has sole access to it. It is the nature and control of its application which would seem to be the essence of a twentieth-century profession.

THE IMPETUS

This has come from many sources, internal and external. In the 1970s, the individuals and organisations that came together to form the Standing Conference for the Advancement of Counselling (SCAC) were concerned to set boundaries on the varying activities that were described as counselling, some of which made claims to cure that could not be substantiated, and used methods of working that might put clients at risk. One could say the motive for organising joint activity was enlightened self-interest, in that the early movers in the field wished to establish themselves as 'respectable'.

Hans Hoxter, a Vice President of BAC and the prime mover in the establishment of SCAC and BAC, has spoken of his desire to find a way of working with individuals in need which did not rely on psychoanalytical principles alone and was thus much more widely available to clients and usable by counsellors who had a wider variety of trainings. He travelled widely in America and brought ideas back which resulted in the establishment of counsellor training in a number of university settings in the 1960s. Here we see a training and knowledge base being established in the academic world.

Through the 1970s, 1980s and beyond, the statutory services, under economic and political pressure, have redefined the services that can feasibly be on offer within budget constraints. Probation services and social services have less time and freedom to offer a counselling service. Religious leaders have looked to sources other than doctrine to meet the needs of their congregations. The medical profession, in its wide sense, is managing rapid technological advance and choice of treatments for patients, which has led to consideration of who does what best. Many doctors believe that they can serve their patients best by administering the medicine and technology, whilst others with different trainings and skills can help people manage the life changes which follow diagnosis and treatment. BAC's Membership Survey of 1993 (BAC 1993) suggests that counsellors have moved into work which fills the gap left by others and related professions, in the process coming into their own as a recognisable grouping of practitioners. It is interesting to imagine what a survey will reveal in ten years' time.

There has been a massive increase in the number of students on counsellor training courses, the numbers of courses available, and interest in BAC Course Recognition, as well as the establishment of undergraduate and postgraduate courses in counselling and psychotherapy, and the establishment of Chartered status for Counselling Psychologists. All these developments offer a career path for counsellors and a more informed and politically able group of workers looking for a recognised place in the job market. They are unlikely to differ from the rest of the workforce in seeking such things as security, self-respect, status and autonomy along with personal growth and development, which are themselves some of the cornerstones of counselling.

There are external factors too which have affected the field. In particular, I see a growing demand from the public, which includes clients and employers, for value for money, for accountability in terms of competence, for contracts and for definitions of skills, benefits and knowledge that the counsellors will bring to the place of work. This is reflected in the work on the development of National Vocational Qualifications (NVQs) in counselling. The initiative was one led not by counsellors but by government, which wants a workforce with recognised qualifications as it moves into the competitive workplace of the European Union (EU). It is employer led and looks for transferability of skills and qualifications. In many ways it reflects an anti-professional movement which sees professionalism as elitist and exclusive. The reaction to this is to combine to fight to justify professionalism and the benefits it can bring, such as codes of ethics and practice, disciplinary procedures and accountability of peers, knowledge, research and commitment to the client. Counselling, as an emerging profession, can be seen as having taken an initiative in the area of NVQs in that it has recognised these external late twentieth-century demands, and is working with them to see how best they can be absorbed into a new professional structure. It is interested in the process for the wide variety of its membership but particularly for levels 4 and 5 of NVQs, which can be viewed as describing attributes of autonomy and discretion in the workplace.

Another major external factor has been the establishment of the EU and the potential impact on counsellors, and on those providing counselling services, of regulations which might affect the practice of counselling in Britain and the member states. In particular these are currently the 1st Diploma Directive (89/48/EEC) and the 2nd Diploma General Directive (COM(90)389 Final) for vocational trainings. In order to move one's qualifications freely across transparent borders it will be necessary to have these qualifications recognised in some special way by one's own government. There is a requirement for equivalence of forms of training, and this in turn requires the existence of a designated authority in each country, which will be more easily established if there already exists some national body or association that sets standards and controls the work in question. There is an enormous incentive to establish an organisation to be such an authority, or to align with an existing organisation to be so recognised. If NVQs are to be the recognised European ticket to transferability and movement in the labour force, and this appears to be the case, it would seem foolish not to embrace the process.

Counselling has sought to provide its own answers to these outside factors. The two major initiatives have been to assist in an active way the formation of the European Association for Counselling (EAC), which was registered in Belgium in June 1993, and the part played in establishing a United Kingdom Register of Counsellors. The first move came in 1991, with BAC establishing a European Working Group to consider BAC's reaction to European Economic Community (EEC) regulations. There was also a concern that there were moves in some European countries to restrict the provision of psychotherapy to medically qualified people, and that where psychotherapy appeared to be synonymous with counselling as understood in Britain, in some European countries counselling as practised in Britain would be unacceptable. Where can the concept of lay counselling/psychotherapy be found in Europe? Where were the people delivering equivalent services to that provided by counsellors in Britain? Many have been found, and 1994 saw the establishment of national counselling associations in the Netherlands and Italy, with embryos in Greece, Spain, France, Hungary and Poland, to stand together with that of Ireland and the United Kingdom to assert the professional nature of counselling in Europe.

The move to work with and for the establishment of a United Kingdom Register of Counsellors grew not only from the need for a focal point for counsellors and for government special recognition with regard to Europe, but also from widespread public demand for more visible accountability for counsellors. The initiative was undertaken with BAC as an equal player in the field with other counselling organisations – initially Relate, the Westminster Pastoral Foundation (WPF) and the Confederation of Scottish Counselling Agencies (COSCA). BAC saw itself as having a register of some kind by virtue of its accredited counsellors, and was aware that if registers of many counselling agencies were to combine, then many were relinquishing a part of themselves and this had to be acknowledged. The question has to be asked whether or not this undermined BAC's position as the counselling association and voice of the emerging profession in the United Kingdom. The ability to manage diversity and change and to respond to the needs of members and counselling clients, and the fact that BAC is one of the largest (in terms of population size) associations worldwide, and strengthening its position, would indicate this was a risk worth taking. In January 1996, BAC individual membership was 12,964 and organisational membership was 766. With the laying down of minimum criteria for entry to, or sponsorship onto, the register, counselling will be establishing an entry point into what is increasingly called 'a profession'.

THE FUTURE

Not everyone is enthusiastic about the professionalisation of counselling. Professionalism in general has its critics (Illich *et al*. 1977). It can be said

that such a move fosters restrictive practice, stifles initiative and is motivated by money, status seeking and bargaining power, which in turn are
out of line with the values of counselling and those roots which are in
'voluntaryism'. The steps, or hurdles, on the way to full recognition as a
professional can be seen as limiting career opportunities for minority
sections of our society, because money and access to educational estab-
lishments are less likely to be available.

The embryo of the EAC is fragile and may have some difficulty in
asserting the multinational acceptance of counselling as a professional
activity. This is not because of lack of enthusiasm or purpose, but because
of lack of financial and political resources at this moment. It may well be
that it will be the growth of national associations for counselling in
Europe that will add credibility to any claim for counselling in Britain to
be seen to be a professional activity.

How does counselling as a profession sit with the claims of
psychotherapy and counselling psychologists to be professions? Over 50
per cent of BAC members in its membership survey said they used
psychotherapeutic models of counselling (BAC 1993). Membership of
BAC and UKCP (United Kingdom Council for Psychotherapy) overlaps
considerably. The British Psychological Society (BPS) is an active
supporter and member of BAC yet retains its own identity and register,
and there is a considerable amount of dual individual membership of BPS
and BAC. It may be there is a place for a generic profession, with colleges
of particular interest or therapeutic models. Marcus Lefébure in Chapter 1
suggests these bodies might not fight but might confederate through a
process of rapprochement, in what appears to be an unstoppable
momentum towards the professionalisation of the disciplines.

CONCLUSION

As a person who has had considerable involvement in the establishment
and development of BAC, I am surprised by the innocence of the journey
towards professionalisation, which has probably been inevitable with the
establishment of the Codes of Ethics and Practice in all their forms, the
Complaints Procedure, accreditation of individual counsellors, and a
research interest. The early chairs of the Association, of which I was one,
strove hard to get structures and a supportive staff in place. Members and
counsellors then learnt to believe in themselves and their service, organise
themselves into categories and interest groups, and finally, under the leadership of chairs since 1991, have moved into the public arena with confidence and political acumen.

On the whole this has not been a journey of self-interest but one which
puts clients first. It differs in one significant way from the traditional
description of a profession, in that counsellors do not exercise personal

judgement on behalf of a client. As in other true products of the twentieth century, where the accent has been on the growth of individualism and liberty, the core value of client autonomy has been preserved.

REFERENCES

BAC (1984, 1990, 1992, 1993) Codes of Ethics and Practice for Counsellors. Rugby: BAC.
BAC (1985) Code of Ethics and Practice for Trainers. Rugby: BAC
BAC (1986, 1992, 1994) Complaints Procedure. Rugby: BAC.
BAC (1988a) Code of Ethics and Practice for the Supervision of Counsellors. Rugby: BAC.
BAC (1988b) Recognition of Counsellor Training Courses. Rugby: BAC.
BAC (1989) Code of Ethics and Practice for Counselling Skills. Rugby: BAC.
BAC (1993) Membership Survey, Individuals. Rugby: BAC.
BAC (1995) Code of Ethics and Practice for Trainers in Counselling and Counselling Skills. Rugby: BAC.
Illich, I., Zola, I.K., McKnight, J., Kaplan, J. and Shaiken, H. (1977) *The Disabling Professions*. Boston: Marion Boyars.
Monopolies and Mergers Commission (1970) *The Supply of Professional Services*. London: Monopolies and Mergers Commission.
Watkins, J., Drury, L. and Preddy, D. (1992) *From Evolution to Revolution: The Pressures on Professional Life in the 1990s*. Bristol: University of Bristol.

Chapter 3

Accreditation and registration

Alan M. Frankland

INTRODUCTION

To agree to write a chapter like this is to take on writing history without the benefit of hindsight: what we are trying to chronicle is still going on. In an attempt to get some element of distance on recent debates and discussions about Accreditation and Registration I have considered some forty-four relevant contributions (editorials, letters and articles) to *Counselling*, the journal for the British Association for Counselling (BAC), over the last eleven years (August 1983 to August 1994), as well as reflecting on discussions, in committees and at conferences, on these issues over this period.

The most obvious development of the past decade has been the establishment of a number of different schemes for the accreditation and registration of counsellors and psychotherapists – and initially this chapter will describe and analyse these schemes. Some counsellors believe that the shortcomings that this analysis will identify, and some of the divisions evident in the current systems, will be resolved by the development of National Vocational Qualifications (NVQs) and qualifications based on them. However, I will argue that NVQs (and similar 'competence'-based systems) are fundamentally flawed. Finally, I will explore the possibility of a unified and unifying accreditation system for the counselling/psychotherapy profession as a whole.

THE SCHEMES

There are five schemes for accreditation or registration worth considering here. These are the accreditation schemes run by the Association for Student Counselling (ASC) and BAC; the registration scheme developed by the United Kingdom Council for Psychotherapy (UKCP); the scheme whereby counselling psychologists may become chartered members on the professional register of the British Psychological Society (BPS); and the United Kingdom Register of Counsellors, which, at the time of writing, is still in gestation.

I will consider the first two of these together because they have inter-twined roots. Subsets of what is now BAC began to contemplate accreditation schemes in the 1970s. Much of the thinking that went into these schemes, particularly those of the Association for Pastoral Care and Counselling and the ASC, became the foundation on which the BAC accreditation scheme was built. For a number of reasons ASC has maintained a separate accreditation scheme for student counsellors, which could therefore lay claim to being the oldest extant national accreditation scheme for counsellors. The generic scheme offered by BAC got off the ground in the early 1980s, and was extensively reviewed in the mid-1980s (this was a condition of its original acceptance, but also reflected concerns about how the original scheme was working). It has grown consistently ever since that review, and has achieved considerable acceptance as setting sound standards for professional counselling. The numbers of BAC accredited counsellors are still relatively small in relation to the membership as a whole (approximately 6 per cent of total membership, or 8 per cent of those who consider themselves to be counsellors), and the debates about details of the system within BAC are sometimes still passionate and even vituperative.

The UKCP (which evolved from the Rugby Conference via the United Kingdom Standing Conference for Psychotherapy) developed a less centralised and potentially more inclusive system for the recognition of a range of professional (psycho)therapists through a system of voluntary registration, influenced by the potential for European regulation, and the possibility of moving to statutory controls in the UK. Their first register was published in May 1993 and contained the names of approximately two thousand therapists. Many of the UKCP constituent bodies (whose approved professional membership make up the register) have recognised a debt to the pioneering work of BAC in setting standards and creating systems for assessing suitability for accreditation, and there seems to be a significant level of cross-membership between accredited counsellors and those on the UKCP Register.

The most recent scheme to get up and running is that for chartered counselling psychologists. BPS received a charter to set up a professional register of psychologists as a whole in December 1987, the first register being published in 1990. This register is open to those who, in the view of the society, are professionally qualified to offer psychological services. Eligibility for registration as a chartered psychologist is demonstrated mainly through academic or professional qualifications acceptable to the society as a whole and to the relevant professional divisions.

Although there were a number of psychologists who were counsellors, and others who identified as counselling psychologists when the register was set up, there was, at that time, no professional Division of Counselling Psychology, so no direct access to the register for such psychologists, and therefore no such thing as a chartered counselling psychologist. The registration and professionalism arguments for counsellors whose primary identification is as psychologists have thus not been about the desirability or otherwise of a register per se (because the register existed already), but about the reshaping of their interest group within BPS to become a professional division and the development of their accreditation system (subsumed under the society's notion of a Professional Diploma examination). By May 1994 all such steps were complete, giving existing counselling psychologists with acceptable qualifications and experience access to the register. Numbers of *chartered* counselling psychologists are currently small, but the Division as a whole has grown very fast (in excess of 1,200 members, of whom some 14 per cent are fully accredited practitioners), and is already a major subdivision of the Society.

The scheme that is still in gestation – the UK Register of Counsellors – is an ironic reflection of the failure to build on the commonality of the issues around accreditation and registration, and an illustration of the division of the occupational community into factions which compete (sometimes quite bitterly) not just about theory or points of ethical difference but for the right to do the work at all – as if there was only one way to work or not enough work for all to do. It is ironic because historically BAC has maintained that there is no clear division between counselling and psychotherapy and has sought to be a broad church welcoming the widest possible membership. However, BAC has also been extremely diffident about making a clear claim to any part of the territory of psychotherapy, so when participants in the United Kingdom Standing Conference for Psychotherapy began to work towards ideas of accreditation and registration BAC allowed itself to become separated from the main body, and gradually excluded itself from the conference, of which it had been a founding member. (For some further exploration of the reasons for this see Charles-Edwards 1993: 7). Thus when the first UKCP register appeared, BAC members, even those who were accredited, had no direct access on to it through their own accrediting organisation, which might reasonably have been seen as the logical standard bearer for therapeutic counselling as one form of psychotherapy.

Even before the UKCP register appeared, the weakness of BAC's position became evident to many of its members, and there has consequently been a strong push for an equivalent (but separate) register for counsellors. Initially the push did not come from central management or individual members, but from a number of counselling organisations some of which may have found the requirements for individual accreditation with BAC too stringent for the majority of their counsellors but nevertheless wished to see some acknowledgement of their capabilities and training. The matter was not initially widely debated, and there were no conceptual discussion papers published in the BAC journal before the time when the membership was informed that their management group was committed to facilitating discussions aimed at generating a register for counsellors.

At the time of writing it seems likely that a register of counsellors will appear in 1996, facilitated/managed by BAC and with two types of entry: one for individual practitioners, registered in their own right on the basis of their accreditation by BAC (or parallel Scottish accreditation) as counsellors; and one for counsellors within counselling services who are registered to work within an agency which guarantees that they have met certain minimum standards of training and induction, and that they are provided with appropriate supervision and ethical management, including an accessible complaints procedure for clients, etc.

COMMON FEATURES AND KEY DIFFERENCES OF THE SCHEMES

It might well appear that these schemes represent very different approaches to the recognition/accreditation issues, but I see them as really quite similar for three reasons: all are seeking to solve the same problems associated with standards and professionalisation; there are historical links between the schemes; and many of these conceptual and historical links are mediated through both formal and (much more frequently) informal links and exchanges of personnel. What I find surprising and dismaying is that with all this commonality we have ended up with separate schemes encouraging workers to pretend that they are engaged in different occupations, rather than recognise that they approach the same occupation with only slightly different sets of theories and assumptions.

A comparative scrutiny of the schemes (Frankland 1995: 55) makes clear that there is a degree of agreement about what is to be assessed. All the schemes consider professional commitment, capacity and standing from a number of different sources of evidence, which vary in kind as well as in focus. These include:

- induction;
- experience;
- probity;
- practice assessment;
- theoretical understanding;
- continuing development;
- use of supervision.

Other professional accreditation/induction schemes (in related areas including nursing, social work and clinical psychology) consider some or all of the following as well:

- general education;
- research capabilities;
- the capacity to work as a colleague;
- understanding of the social context of professional work.

It is quite startling to note that although counselling is apparently a liberal profession, none of the counselling accreditation schemes pays much attention to its members' capacity to work with others, or their understanding of the social context of their work. Whilst blatant prejudice against people with different abilities, sexism or racism, etc., would be accounted for in the assessment of an applicant's probity in any of the schemes, none of them features a clear requirement for training in issues surrounding equal opportunities or for demonstrated practice of an anti-discriminatory nature.

There are, of course, also some interesting differences between schemes in both criteria and operation. The BPS Diploma in Counselling Psychology is clearly constructed as a postgraduate professional qualification with considerable emphasis on academic skills, including research. The BAC scheme allows for the possibility that an induction into practice, theory and appropriate values may be achieved wholly through the experience of reflexive (that is, supervised) practice over a considerable period. Some routes to registration insist that there can be no adequate induction into the practice of counselling/therapy without an extended experience as a client (BPS and some UKCP schemes), whilst others do not agree that this experience is essential (BAC and ASC). Some schemes rely heavily on the judgements of counselling/therapy trainers and supervisors to clarify the applicant's grasp and integration of theory and ethics into their practice (ASC and BPS), whilst others (BAC) require evidence to be presented directly to assessors in the form of case studies, etc.

Essentially these are differences of detail. Viewed from some distance, it is clear that the schemes are assessing much the same things, often in similar ways, and that, at least in the realms of ethics and practice, they are aiming at similar levels of functioning. All the schemes also have the common feature that their processes are at one remove from the actual work of their applicants with clients. That is to say that these are all *inferential* schemes: inferring that a standard has been achieved and will be maintained from largely indirect evidence, such as the quantity of applicants' supervised practice experience, reports of their work, their capacity to explain themselves theoretically, and their ability to explore their work to the satisfaction of a supervisor, etc.

THE ASSESSMENT OF COMPETENCES: NVQS

Two factors are now leading us towards discussion of NVQs and the notion of competences as a basis for professional qualifications. First, there is a belief that the assessment systems set up for accreditation and registration rely too heavily on indirect, inferential evidence. Although not much is published, there is clearly considerable discussion within the schemes of ways in which real work may be sampled, through tapes, interviews and vivas, role-play exercises, etc. NVQs are predicated on the apparently straightforward notion of directly assessing whether people can actually do what the job requires them to do, so this difficulty in the current systems leaves the door open for the NVQ initiative.

Second, counsellors' discourse about professionalisation has developed over the years and the ground being fought over has changed somewhat. Initially, it might have been fair to characterise the struggle as being between, on the one hand, those who saw any kind of professionalisation as taking counselling away from its voluntaristic, egalitarian ideals in order to meet the needs of the counsellors (to make a living, manage resources, etc.), raising issues of elitism and social control; and, on the other, those who saw professionalism as defending actual and potential clients by seeking to raise standards. More recently the argument has tended to be about which system of professionalisation is the most effective and egalitarian *for the counsellors* seeking registration, etc. Although both sides constantly invoke the interests of clients, the energy of the dispute now quite often centres on the interests of the counsellors: elitism is bad not so much because it moves counsellors away from their common ground with their clients, but rather because it may operate to exclude some counsellors and include others. The progressive pattern of interlocking qualifications that NVQs seem to present appears as a sound resolution to this issue.

The government's drive to create NVQs has stimulated a great deal of activity in the counselling/psychotherapy world. There are some who sincerely believe that it will bring real benefits to clients and practitioners alike, but I am constantly surprised that so many educated and intelligent people have been carried along, apparently uncritically, by the rhetoric of 'competence'. There are fundamental questions to be asked about this discourse and its origins, and no sound reason to sweep away more traditional systems without firm evidence that 'competence'-based qualifications do indeed, and over time, meet the fundamental purpose of all qualifications – that of quality assurance.

I am not clear quite why we have been so open to this rhetoric. Perhaps the absence of a substantial critique is simply a sign of professional insecurity and the kind of uncertainty that so many counsellors seem to feel in the face of authoritative or academic criticism. Instead of holding to what we know and feel, and putting our case strongly to confront this hostile attempt to reshape our activities and organisations, too many counsellors seem to have backed off and defended themselves against the pain and loss of the integrity of our potential profession by the process of identification with the aggressor.

Most of the factors historically considered in the registration of other professions such as social work, education and nursing can be grouped into three areas. Counselling too has:

1 a knowledge base, determined by rational argument as well as professional tradition to be relevant to effective practice, and assessed in a variety of ways, in writing and in practice;
2 a skills base, determined by both tradition and analysis, and assessed by observation, self-report, etc., and by other pragmatic measures of effectiveness including patients continuing to live, students passing exams, etc.;
3 the execution of the professional role, including adherence to the ethics and attitudes underlying the profession's ideal of service, and assessed through observation and report, in relationships and in writing.

Whilst it has to be admitted that any traditional evolutionary approach carries some risk of inertia, it must be recognised that it also requires practitioners to engage with the subtlety and uniqueness of their professional culture.

With the arrival of NVQs we are being asked to replace this rich tapestry of understanding in depth with an assessment of so-called 'competences', which are distilled from a particular style of statistical analysis of *behavioural* output known as occupational mapping. The fundamental question here is whether what counsellors are engaged in is an activity that is really amenable to a reductionist analysis. I do not see that this has been demonstrated and, in consequence, prefer, for the time being at least, to stay with a system of quality assessment that is multi-dimensional, and thus more likely to be sensitive to the complex of knowledge, activities and attitudes that come together to make up our professional engagement in counselling and therapy.

It is possible that those who have espoused occupational mapping and the creation of competences for counselling and psychotherapy see themselves as engaged in creative consultations and dialogue; that they have intellectually resolved the issues of reductionism and for them the take-over bid is to be conceived as a merger, colonisation as for the good of the people. They may really believe that this essentially behaviourist approach will provide powerful measures of an individual's capacity to deliver effective help.

As we have seen, current systems of accreditation are inferential – assessors infer from evidence of experience or induction into areas of knowledge, skills and values that practitioners will be able to deliver an effective professional and ethical service in the future. The standards that derive from occupational mapping are seductive because they seem to provide for *direct* observation of that service delivery, and thus would seem to give a firm and rational basis for assessment, which is lacking in current systems.

That justification is fundamentally flawed. First, there is so much evidence that it is non-specific, relational factors that differentiate between effective and ineffective helpers; second, it is not generally true that the assessment of skills and professional functioning in traditional systems is only based on self-report or other indirect evidence; and third, even direct observations can only be of a sample of behaviour and are therefore themselves also inferential. It is not the case that because I have seen you do X once or twice I *observe* that you can do X. I merely make the generalising inference that you can do X. It is a reasonable inference, as are inferences based on other kinds of evidence, but it is not logical to regard it as pre-emptively powerful and able to replace all other evidence.

I have no doubt that in the training and accreditation of counsellors and psychotherapists we are attempting to develop and assess not only outcomes and technical skills but relational, wholistic subtleties like workers' way-of-being, their attitudes and intentions, and their capacity to select appropriate actions and change them in response to feedback (some of which will not necessarily be observable to a third party). In my experience there are very few counsellors and psychotherapists who would be prepared to stand by the assertion that effective helping is no more than a series of observable behaviours that are completely amenable to verbal description. And yet many counsellors and psychotherapists seem to be preparing to deliver their professional qualification, registration or accreditation procedures to a methodology which can *only* extract the observable and clearly definable elements of effective helping activities. The Training Agency defines competence as 'the ability to perform activities within an occupation' (itself a narrow and conservative concept), but sets up systems for deriving and testing for the presence of competence as if the definition were 'the ability to perform *behaviours* within an occupation' (Nicholychuk 1992: 63).

The Lead Body for Advice, Guidance, Counselling and Psychotherapy has had to recognise the necessity of taking attitudes, values and knowledge into account in order to write sensibly about any kind of complex helping activity. In doing so it has been forced to distort the apparently straightforward methodology of 'competence' to try to include increasingly abstract elements that can only be assessed indirectly. Russell and Dexter (1993: 266) celebrate the attempt being made to 'integrate equality of opportunity within the standard setting process' and advocate the need for candidates 'to demonstrate awareness of issues . . . and knowledge appropriate to equal opportunities practice', and of course I have no quarrel with this; but they fail to realise that setting standards which can only be expressed and assessed in terms of awareness or knowledge actually undermines the essential reductionist logic of the whole NVQ methodology, and hence the claim to provide better evidence than current systems.

It seems likely that, in time, the lead body will have so compromised its fundamental methodology with such additions as values and knowledge criteria that it will create a version of what we already have. We will, however, be offered not a familiar wheel but a 'hub-supported rotary transport device'. This will not justify the funding, time and energy taken up in the 'consultative' process which could have gone in to developing, refining and co-ordinating the existing systems.

There is a political agenda to consider here too: it is arguable that NVQs are not really intended to inform and supplement current systems, by a process of organic development, but to discredit and supplant them. To welcome them as a progressive revolution is to fail to take account of the history of these projects in a conscious political attack on the traditions of the liberal professions.

Despite the apparent boom of the 1980s and the evident strength of competitive materialism, the Conservative government seemed dismayed to find a continuing growth of liberal humanist and anarchic tendencies within our society. Alongside raves and travellers, green politics and by-pass protests, counselling and therapy continued to grow, counterbalancing that government's stated desire to move the middle ground of social values clearly to the right. If liberal humanism were to be halted then the supports for such values, in education, counselling and therapy, the professions and the arts would have to be changed. NVQs are an excellent vehicle for doing this; and if trainers and practitioners in counselling, as in other trades and professions, can be persuaded to adopt them for themselves, the political nature of the changing value frame can be disguised.

The new jargon, the shifting frames of reference and the timetable-driven development schedule all work to undermine the critical capabilities of those who feel uncomfortable about this self-styled progress. It is hard to criticise something that you do not understand, especially if it is being presented as almost a fait accompli by consultants who *are* at ease with the jargon (they created it), with warnings that if you do not come on board soon it will be too late, and that if you decide not to be involved at all then some less scrupulous operator will take it over and act against your best interests.

It seems crazy to oppose 'progress' – and the notion of Britain becoming more skilled, with more open advancement through staged training opportunities, *seems* entirely progressive. But the assessment of competences is really about doing the job as it is currently defined, which is essentially conservative; and the reduction of the influence of educators and academics from the developmental process (in the name of workplace realism and keeping the competitive edge) is actually an unnecessary slur on a generation of college and further education teachers and trainers, who have never been funded to create a skills-rich society. It leads to a reduction in a scholarly and questioning approach to education and training, which is clearly not progress at all.

In any case, the arguments about progression through levels of skills assessments are spurious if there is to be no more money for training. NVQs will not create the skilled workforce that we are told will allow us to catch up with our competitors in the world market. Recognising skills that already exist in a workforce, of itself, adds nothing to the skill level of that workforce.

I have sometimes been urged to omit political themes from discussions about NVQs. It seems that counsellors and psychotherapists are unwilling to see a party political dimension to this debate, or that they believe that academic arguments should be above such discourse, and that to raise the possibility of political malice is to be polemical and vitriolic, and undermines the strength of other arguments that may be made against the NVQ/occupational mapping approach. I have carefully considered the possibility that my hostility to NVQs is the product of unreasonable anxiety in the face of change, driven by my vested interests as an academic and as chair of one of the current accreditation systems; but I have concluded that rejection of the NVQ approach is based on a rational understanding of the conceptual weaknesses of the system *and* a reasoned appreciation of its political motivation, so I continue to present both elements for consideration. Whilst accepting that there are flaws in the present systems, it is clear to me that NVQs simply cannot meet the paradoxical challenge of satisfying a public need for standards without distorting the subtlety of the processes of counselling and therapy.

AN ALTERNATIVE NEW DIRECTION?

I remain hopeful that the threat and waste of the NVQ system can be neutralised before it does much more harm, or that when it crumbles under the weight of its own inconsistencies the profession will not have been too horribly debilitated, so that we can get on with developing the best of our current systems and begin to move them towards convergence.

Although there is not much in the literature on this in relation to accreditation and registration schemes, there is some recent work which calls for an end to divisive posturing between the various sub-groups of the counselling and psychotherapy profession in Britain. In keynote addresses to consecutive BAC conferences, eminent speakers have made their position on the competitive past clear, and correspondence following the conferences seems to have agreed that it is time to set aside the 'dismal quest for difference' (Thorne 1992: 244) because 'this is the time for co-operation in an effort to look for overlap and similarity' (Deurzen Smith, 1991: 133).

I am disappointed to find no published account of continuing discussion at a conceptual, theoretical or organisational level about what will be entailed in bringing the profession together around one set of accreditation or registration standards. The UKCP, however, is beginning to promote discussion on this front, and I notice in discussions in committees, meetings, seminars and conferences that people do keep talking informally about greater co-operation, about the need to get accreditation and registration schemes more formally aligned and to move towards cross-recognition procedures and then on to integration.

Paradoxically, there is sometimes also a sense that alignment is impossible at the moment; but there is no clear understanding of why this should be so. My own view is that this is, at least in part, because innovative energy is being syphoned off to NVQs – but I have said enough about that already. There are also continuing anxieties about the possibility that some 'key' group will opt out. I think there are always going to be some individuals who are going to stand out for separation, and there may ultimately be whole groups that decide not to come in on a joint scheme. UKCP 'lost' some of the analytic groups in the process of creating its register; perhaps some of these would move back into a broader amalgamation, but presumably others are so wedded to schism that they will choose to wander beyond the pale in the name of purity forever. An incomplete spectrum within a broad profession will undoubtedly be a real loss, but as Deurzen Smith (1991: 133) pointed out, 'it cannot be right to let large professional bodies be held to ransom by powerful but small interest groups'.

CONCLUSIONS

In this chapter I have described the five main systems for accreditation and registration to which counsellors might relate, and argued for their essential similarity. I have tried to show that occupational standards, derived from reductionist occupational mapping strategies, cannot be expected to encompass counselling and psychotherapy fairly or accurately, because of their conceptual and political origins. In concluding, I have argued that there are faint signs in recent articles and possibly a stronger feeling in informal discourse that the process of differentiation that has produced a diversity of accreditation/registration schemes has gone far enough, and that counsellors and psychotherapists need to be pulling the systems together, working for the creation of a more unified although technically diverse profession. I believe that integration of the richer and more subtle 'traditional' systems ultimately offers a much better hope of delivering to clients a united, skilful and ethical profession with common and comprehensible standards, to the benefit of us all.

REFERENCES

Charles-Edwards, D. (1993) Correspondence: Counselling and psychotherapy. *Counselling 4* (1) 7.

Deurzen Smith, E. van (1991) 1992 and all that. *Counselling 2* (4) 133–4.

Frankland, A. (1995) An invitation to accreditation – steps towards an emerging profession. *Counselling 6* (1) 55–60.

Nicholychuk, L. (1992) National Vocational Qualifications development. *Counselling 3* (2) 63–4.

Russell, J. and Dexter, G. (1993) Ménage à trois: accreditation, NVQs and BAC. *Counselling 4* (4) 266–9.

Thorne, B. (1992) Psychotherapy and counselling: the quest for differences. *Counselling 3* (4) 244–8.

Chapter 4

Counsellor competence

John McLeod

INTRODUCTION

The question of counsellor competence has emerged as a pivotal issue in recent years. As counselling services have become more accountable to third party funding agencies, there has grown a need to demonstrate that their employees are capable of providing a professional service. Concerns over accountability have been exacerbated by rare but widely reported episodes of therapist abuse of clients. The proliferation of training courses has raised questions about how to define and assess the levels of knowledge and skill necessary for licensed practice. In Britain, there is now a government-funded body for establishing national standards for vocational qualifications in the field of counselling. Finally, the realisation that many counsellors do not operate in sufficiently supportive organisational environments, or may suffer burn-out at some point in their career, has introduced an awareness of the importance of contextual and developmental factors in the maintenance of therapist competence.

In practice, these concerns translate into a set of key counsellor competence questions:

- What qualities, skills and competencies should training courses be aiming to develop in their students?
- What competencies should trainees already possess before beginning a course?
- What level of competence should constitute the pass/fail cut-off point on a counsellor training course?
- What methods and techniques can best be used to assess competence?
- How can accreditation bodies appropriately evaluate the competence of candidates for professional status?
- How can potential clients assess the competence of a therapist whose name they find in a directory?
- How can an employer assess the competence of someone applying for a counselling job?

• How can counsellors themselves judge the limits of their competence, for example when agreeing to work with a new client group?

The nature of counsellor competence is a complex matter, and there are substantial problems involved in arriving at satisfactory answers to the questions listed above. There has been relatively little systematic research into counsellor competence. The existing knowledge base is dominated by the writings and observations of clinicians and trainers. While the beliefs and collective wisdom of experienced practitioners undoubtedly possess a great deal of validity, it is also necessary to acknowledge the limitations of the views of 'experts'. Counsellor trainers and supervisors have a particular perspective on competence. Trainees and supervisees typically select or filter the data they present for scrutiny. For example, it makes sense to regard competence as a continuum that ranges from creative and 'transformative' interventions at the one end to abusive, exploitative or damaging interventions at the other end. Trainees are likely to attempt to conceal from their tutors examples of the latter type of work. Also, even the most experienced trainers only possess detailed information on a relatively limited number of trainees. Most serious of all is the fact that it is seldom possible for supervisors to take the views or experiences of clients into consideration. As a result, it is essential that practical knowledge about competence is approached critically and supplemented by the findings of appropriately designed research studies.

Two quite different strategies have been applied in the pursuit of knowledge about counselling competence. These are: (1) defining competence in terms of adherence to a treatment manual; and (2) developing taxonomies of skills. The treatment manual approach defines competence as the ability to deliver a specific type of therapy to a specific type of client. The skills taxonomy model is based on an assumption that there exists a set of 'core skills' applicable to all counselling situations.

TREATMENT MANUAL APPROACHES TO COUNSELLOR AND THERAPIST COMPETENCE

Randomised controlled trials and comparison group studies have been widely used to evaluate the outcomes of counselling and psychotherapy (McLeod 1994). One of the features of more recent studies of this type has been a high degree of methodological sophistication, often characterised by an intention to ensure that clients receive a 'pure' form of the 'treatment'. This is achieved by developing a training manual that specifies in great detail the types of intervention to be implemented during the form of therapy in question. Then therapists participating in the study are trained to follow the manual. Finally, when the study is under way the adherence of the therapists to the manual is assessed through ratings of tapes of sessions, or through on-going clinical supervision. The degree to which a therapist follows the manual can therefore be regarded as an indication of his or her competence in that particular brand of therapy (see Lambert and Ogles 1988; Shaw and Dobson 1988). Examples of therapies that have been 'manualised' include time-limited dynamic psychotherapy (Strupp and Binder 1984), cognitive therapy for depression (Beck *et al.* 1979) and experiential therapy (Greenberg *et al.* 1993). This approach to competence represents a sophisticated technique for answering the question: 'Can this counsellor/therapist apply *this* kind of intervention to *this* type of client?'

However, while the use of treatment manuals is clearly valuable in outcome research, and also produces knowledge relevant to theory and training (for example, through consideration of what is involved in the creation and use of a manual), it has limitations as an approach to under-standing competence. The key point is that competencies defined in manuals reflect a relatively narrow range of technical operations conducted by the therapist, rather than the potentially much broader set of personal qualities and values, generic interpersonal skills and contextual factors that might be understood as necessary for competence in its fullest sense. Further, the competencies studied within such an approach are only those specified by a particular model, and therefore lack cross-theoretical generalisability. Another problem with this approach is that therapist competence defined in this way may have little demonstrable relationship to outcome, as in the situation where 'the operation was a success . . . but the patient died'. Manual-based ratings only indicate whether or not the counsellor has carried out an intervention in the manner prescribed by the manual, *not* whether this intervention has actually helped the client. Finally, manual-based competency studies are likely to be of marginal relevance to the majority of therapists who describe themselves as eclectic or integrationist in orientation.

TAXONOMIES OF COUNSELLOR SKILLS

Many attempts to understand counsellor competence have concentrated on the construction of lists or taxonomies of counsellor skills, and then on developing methods for assessing levels of these skills. This work has been associated with the *microskills* approach (Ivey and Galvin 1984), which has influenced the design of many skills training programmes. Two recent examples of skills taxonomies, which have built on the early work by Ivey and his colleagues, are the models proposed by Crouch (1992) and by Larson *et al.* (1992). Information about other skills taxonomies and inventories can be found in Ponterotto and Furlong (1985) and Scofield and Yoxheimer (1983).

For example, the Larson *et al.* (1992) Counselling Self-Estimate Inventory (COSE) is derived from a survey of a wide variety of counsellor skills models, including those of Ivey and Egan, and is designed to assess the degree of 'self-efficacy' experienced by counsellors – the extent to which they judge themselves capable of performing in counselling situations. The COSE is a 37-item questionnaire comprising statements about counselling competence, using a response format with a six-point scale ranging from 'strongly disagree' to 'strongly agree'. Table 4.1 displays sample items from the COSE. The authors of this inventory have carried out a number of procedures to establish its validity and reliability. The inventory yields scores on five factors: 'microskills', 'process', 'difficult client behaviours', 'cultural competence' and 'awareness of values'.

Skills taxonomy models have mainly been used in the context of initial counselling training courses. In many ways, in making it possible to assess counselling performance in a structured fashion, they fulfil the same function as manual-derived rating scales. However, there are two important differences between skills taxonomies and manual-based rating scales. Skills taxonomies assess global performance rather than directly sampling in-session counselling behaviour, and are trans-theoretical or integrative rather than being grounded in a specific theoretical approach. Thus, skills taxonomies/inventories are less precise measures of technical counselling skills than are manualised scales, but are more widely applicable and more economical to use. There are, however, a number of limitations to the skills taxonomy strategy for assessing competence, and these will be briefly summarised.

First, this perspective on competence employs a reductionist strategy of breaking down a complex area of human performance into a set of component parts. The difficulty here, as with any attempt to dissect human action, is that, in the end, the whole may add up to less than the sum of the parts. In other words, a trainee may have successfully worked through every exercise in the training programme, but at the same time fail to grasp the 'spirit' of what is required. The microskills approach is similar to any behavioural methodology in focusing on discrete areas of behaviour while avoiding any engagement with wider meaning.

A second drawback to the taxonomy approach is that it can lead to the generation of ever-longer lists of skills and competencies that must be trained and assessed. For example, both the Larsen *et al.* (1992) list and the one developed by Crouch (1992) include items on cross-cultural knowledge and awareness. Sue *et al.* (1992) have produced a list of 31 cross-cultural competencies that they believe should be included in counsellor training. There is a danger here that counselling competence could end up being specified through an extremely detailed list of items. Yet how can information of sufficient quality be collected on each item without turning the assessment of counsellors into a stultifying, bureaucratic exercise?

Table 4.1. Sample items from the Counselling Self-Estimate Inventory

Microskills

> I am confident that the wording of my interpretation and confrontation responses will be clear and easy to understand.

> I feel I will respond to the client in an appropriate length of time (neither interrupting the client or waiting too long to respond).

> I am confident that I will be able to conceptualise my client's problems.

Process

> * I am worried that my interpretation and confrontation responses may not over time assist the client to be more specific in defining and clarifying the problem.

> * I am worried that the types of response I use at a particular time – that is, reflection of feeling, interpretation, etc. – may not be appropriate.

> * I am afraid that I may not understand and properly determine probable meanings of the client's non-verbal behaviours.

Difficult client behaviours

> * I do not feel I possess a large enough repertoire of techniques to deal with the different problems my client may present.

> * I am unsure as to how to deal with clients who appear non-committal and indecisive.

> I feel competent regarding my abilities to deal with crisis situations which may arise during the counselling sessions, such as suicide, alcoholism, abuse, etc.

Cultural competence

> I will be an effective counsellor with clients of a different social class.

> * In working with culturally different clients I may have a difficult time viewing situations from their perspective.

Awareness of values

> * I am likely to impose my values on the client during the interview.

> I feel confident that I have resolved conflicts in my personal life so that they will not interfere with my counselling abilities.

Note: *Negatively phrased items, where agreement indicates perceived lack of skill
Source: Larson *et al.* 1992

A final weakness of the taxonomy strategy is that, so far, these lists of counsellor competence have not been derived from observations of what effective counsellors actually do. This situation can be contrasted with studies from areas such as the assessment of managerial potential (Klemp and McClelland 1986) and general 'expertise' (Glaser and Chi 1988).

David McClelland and his associates have studied the attributes of highly successful managers in a wide variety of organisations. Their research strategy has involved finding 'outstanding' and 'average' performers, and using a type of critical incident interview to gather information about the kinds of generic competency that are particularly associated with effective or outstanding role performance. Over several groups of managers, they found several generic competencies which appeared in 80 per cent of cases, such as planning/causal thinking, diagnostic information seeking, conceptualisation, concern for influence, directive influence, collaborative influence, symbolic influence/setting personal example, and self-confidence. In a similar set of studies, Raven (1984) identified other important generic competencies such as willingness to use feedback, ability to monitor performance, values clarity, willingness to learn without instruction, and ability to exercise self-control.

In a different field of applied psychology, considerable research has been carried out into the characteristics of expertise. In this research, expert performers are usually asked to provide a sample of their behaviour, by responding to a case vignette, recalling complex material, or thinking aloud while solving a problem. Glaser and Chi (1988) suggest that there are consistent findings from studies that have examined the generic competencies associated with expert performance in domains such as chess, medicine, science and judicial decision making. In comparison with novice performers, experts tend to: perceive large meaningful patterns, perform faster, make fewer mistakes, have superior memory for information, represent problems at a deeper level, spend more time analysing the problem qualitatively before suggesting solutions, and monitor themselves more effectively.

It is instructive to compare these studies of managerial and other expertise with the work on counsellor microskills. Treatment manuals and skills taxonomies describe what counsellors do. The competencies identified in expertise research, on the other hand, would appear to represent the qualities or abilities that would enable someone to do counselling *well*. There are some hints from the therapy research literature of where counsellor expertise comes from; what is involved is not merely possessing a repertoire of technical skills, but additionally having a capacity to employ them to good effect and with sensitive timing.

For example, in a series of studies carried out by Combs (1986, 1989), counsellors (and members of other helping professions) in training were asked to write about episodes or incidents in which they had helped another person. These accounts were coded in terms of ratings of 'person-centred beliefs' (see Table 4.2). The degree of 'person-centredness' of the subject's belief system was found to correlate significantly with independent assessments (by trainers) of their counselling effectiveness. These findings were replicated by McLeod and McLeod (1993) in a study of

Table 4.2. Person-centred beliefs held by competent counsellors

Beliefs about significant data

Good helpers are people-oriented, and attend to internal personal meanings rather than external behavioural data.

Beliefs about people

Effective helpers seem to hold more positive beliefs about the people they work with than do less effective helpers. They see them as trustworthy, able, dependable and worthy.

Beliefs about self

Effective helpers possess a positive view of self, confidence in their abilities, and a feeling of oneness with others.

Beliefs about purposes or priorities

Effective helpers view the world in terms of 'wider' purposes and meanings.

Source: Combs 1986, 1990

British counsellors in training. A particularly interesting aspect of these findings was that person-centred beliefs assessed *before* commencing a training course were predictive of success on the course.

There have also been some studies that have suggested that therapist effectiveness is associated with underlying attributes such as cognitive flexibility (Lutwak and Hennessey 1982; Whiteley *et al.* 1967), ability to conceptualise (Kivlighan and Quigley 1991; Martin *et al.* 1989), openness to personal experiencing (Allen 1967), and clinical memory (Shaw and Dobson 1988).

NEW DIRECTIONS IN THEORY AND PRACTICE

What are the important new directions in our understanding of competence in counselling? Treatment manuals and skills taxonomies give us knowledge about the extent to which a counsellor has mastered technical and relatively superficial aspects of the work. However, it has been argued that there exists a more fundamental set of generic competencies, similar to those displayed by experts in other fields, that need to be defined for counselling. Being clear about the distinction between technical and generic competencies is therefore critical to new developments in this area.

The generic–technical distinction presupposes that generic competence is mediated and *amplified* through the application of technical competencies. There are several ways in which this process can be demonstrated, for example when the therapist makes a technical mistake or error. A therapist or counsellor may engage in inappropriate non-verbal behaviour, such as touching a client who is covertly terrified of physical contact. The client might withdraw from meaningful therapeutic work following such an event. If the therapist is sensitive enough to what has happened (generic competency), this rupture in the therapeutic alliance can become an opportunity for useful learning and insight. If, on the other hand, the therapist perseveres with technical procedures (lack of generic competence), the client may quit therapy.

Research into the comparative effectiveness of professional, highly trained therapists and non-professional, minimally trained volunteers contributes to an understanding of the differing roles of technical and generic competencies. It can be assumed that lay counsellors rely mainly on generic competence, while professional therapists possess, in addition to their generic competence, a repertoire of technical skills and knowledge. Several studies have shown (Strupp and Hadley 1979; Wills 1982) that professional and non-professional therapists tend to be equally effective in helping clients. In interpreting the results of these studies, some writers have pointed out some of the disadvantages of technical expertise (Dumont 1991; Wills 1982) in practising counselling and psychotherapy. For example, the self-esteem of a client may be enhanced by the belief that he or she is valued by the counsellor. It is quite possible that, with a non-professional counsellor, the client is more able to accept the valuing as genuine, whereas with a professional therapist the client may attribute valuing as arising from other factors: 'she has been trained to say that', 'he is only saying that because I am paying him'.

The generic–technical distinction can be applied to many situations in counsellor training and supervision. In selecting people for counsellor training programmes, it is essential to assess the repertoire of generic competencies they bring with them. Most counsellor trainers have an intuitive idea of what they are looking for in this area, but most trainers will admit that they get it wrong more often than they would like. Research is needed both to map the generic competencies relevant to therapeutic work, and to evaluate the efficacy of different techniques (for instance, interviews, group discussions, references, questionnaires) for gathering data on these qualities. Selecting on the basis of generic competence is important, because there is no evidence that these attributes can be trained. Again, systematic research evidence is lacking, but anecdotal and observational evidence suggest that the elements of training courses that address generic competencies (personal therapy, experiential groups) are on the whole most helpful to those trainees who are already personally 'sound'. Those whose life experiences or personal development have left them with gaps in their array of generic competencies will almost always hide or conceal this in the group, since to embark on the kind of reappraisal of self that would be necessary to make a difference would be massively disruptive to participation in the course.

During a training course, there are times when the balance of attention needs to be shifted in the direction of technical competencies. People in training workshops need to have opportunities to acquire the ability to carry out the specific technical procedures being taught. In a workshop environment, where the trainee is practising new skills on other trainees or volunteer clients, he or she must lay aside the normal wish to help the other (generic competence) and be willing to make mistakes, to be unhelpful, in order to learn. In supervision, by contrast, theorists such as Hawkins and Shohet (1989) have stressed the importance of developing supervision contracts and styles that encourage counsellors to seek consultations on both the personal/generic and technical aspects of their work.

Counselling competence can be viewed as encompassing a continuum that ranges not merely from 'high' to 'low' levels of competence but from abuse and cruelty at one end to artistic creativity at the other. An adequate theory of counsellor competence needs to include a model of *incompetence*, viewed not merely as the possession of low levels of either generic or technical competencies, but as a kind of 'anti-competence' or 'negative helpfulness' (see Heron 1976, 1990). Descriptions of negatively competent therapists can be found in Allen (1990) and Bates and Brodsky (1989). These therapists were individuals who appeared to be locked into fixed patterns of destructive behaviour in relation to all of their clients. However, it is probably true that any counsellor or psychotherapist will from time to time be negatively helpful for some of his or her clients. This process is not well researched or understood. The dynamics of therapist 'failure' are a painful topic for inquiry. It is similarly important to accumulate more research on the existence of the therapeutic 'genius' who can offer the rest of us the equivalent of the musical 'master class'.

Counsellor competence is socially constructed. Therapy can be understood as constituting a form of discourse that is not widely legitimated in Western society. If people as a whole were able to talk to significant others as they learn to do with their therapist, they would have no need to see the therapist. The therapeutic metanarrative, the story the therapist constructs about his or her life and work (Omer and Strenger 1992), is a narrative existing in tension with the main stories of everyday life, and to remain in existence must be continually retold by members of the community of therapists. Technical competencies also rely on a constant process of social construction. This happens so much that therapists are not aware that they are doing it. Simply, the client giving feedback on whether a particular intervention or approach has been helpful is engaging in social construction. Consulting a supervisor or colleague is another example of social construction. In other words, *all* counsellor competencies are embedded in social relations, and are influenced by considerations of how power and authority are exerted in these relationships.

The existence of different perspectives on therapist competence was emphasised by McLeod (1992), who argued that the skill or ability of a therapist can be perceived from six distinct perspectives: those of the client, of the therapist himself or herself, of the supervisor or trainer of the therapist, of his or her peer group, of the manager of a counselling agency, or of an external assessor such as a researcher or accreditation examiner/ gate-keeper. Individuals in each of these roles possess their own unique set of experiences and observations in relation to the performance of the therapist. An influential piece of research which illustrates this point is the study by Chevron and Rounsaville (1983), which found low levels of agreement between competence ratings made by therapists, peers, trainers, supervisors and clients.

A social constructionist perspective on counselling competence has serious implications for training and practice. In assessing trainees, the evaluations made by staff running the course provide only one part of the picture. Self- and peer assessment can often yield quite different appraisals of competence. Despite this, in most training courses, pass/fail decisions are made only by those in positions of authority. In practice, the competence of a counsellor will often depend on the supportiveness of the environment in which he or she operates. This fact is explicitly acknowledged by those working in the family therapy tradition, which employs a team approach.

The most critical implication of a social constructionist view of competence is that it highlights the views of the client. In the end, competent counselling is that which brings benefit to the client: 'the operation is only a success if the patient gets better'. However, although there have been hundreds of studies of the effectiveness of *therapies* (Smith *et al.* 1980), there have been relatively few studies into differential success rates of individual *therapists*. When such studies have been carried out (Crits-Christoph *et al.* 1991; Lambert 1989; Luborsky *et al.* 1985), they have demonstrated clear individual differences in effectiveness, even when the therapists included in the studies have received uniformly high levels of training and supervision, and have been treating clients matched in severity of presenting problem. These research studies are costly to set up. Clients receive standardised assessments pre-therapy, at termination and at follow-up. Only a tiny minority of counsellors will ever participate in such a study. For the majority of counsellors, client feedback is either informal or by means of a brief end-of-counselling satisfaction questionnaire. It is known that methods of assessing benefit to clients in terms of perceived satisfaction produce much higher success rates than do studies that compare pre- and post-counselling scores on standardised measures of depression or anxiety (Berger 1983). There is therefore often a sense of deep insecurity in counsellors, brought about by the lack of knowledge of how helpful they have been.

CONCLUSIONS

In this chapter, ways of gathering information about competence in counselling have been discussed in terms of skills taxonomies, treatment manuals and outcome data from clients. These are the formal, scientific, 'operationalised' techniques for gathering data on competence. However, anyone assessing a counsellor would also use these strategies in an informal way, by asking questions such as: 'what can she do?' or 'where are the gaps in her awareness?', 'is his work anchored in a coherent model?' or 'can we see him delivering the model we adopt in our agency?', 'what evidence is there that she has helped people?' or 'do I feel as though she might be able to help me, if I were her client?'.

Returning to the list of competence questions raised at the beginning of the chapter, it can be seen that in any practical setting, such as assessing students on a course or choosing a candidate for a job, all these strategies might be utilised. McLeod (1992) has identified some of the techniques available for collecting information about counsellor competence. There is a wide variety of tools that can be applied, including rating scales, questionnaires, role-play, learning journals, analysis of tapes, computerised simulations and written examinations. However, the effective use of these assessment techniques relies on an informed appreciation of the nature of competence and the complex set of issues involved in making sense of it.

In conclusion, the review of current trends carried out in this chapter indicates four main emergent themes in the study of competence in counselling. First, there is the crucial distinction between generic competencies, conceived as broad-band personal qualities and attributes, and technical competencies, conceived as skills applied in specific domains of counselling activity. Second, any adequate model of competence must include a developmental perspective. There are different challenges to competence at different stages in the career of a counsellor. Third, competence ranges along a continuum that stretches from creative mastery through to damaging abuse. Fourth, judgements about competence in counselling are socially constructed and defined. Each of these themes leads toward significant practical implications. Further research and theory are clearly needed in this area. Most important of all is research and practice that incorporate the client's perspective on what is, or is not, competent counselling.

REFERENCES

Allen, L. (1990) A client's experience of failure. In D. Mearns and W. Dryden (eds) *Experiences of Counselling in Action*. London: Sage.

Allen, T. (1967) Effectiveness of counselor trainees as a function of psychological openness. *Journal of Counselling Psychology 14* 35–40.

Bates, C.M. and Brodsky, A.M. (1989) *Sex in the Therapy Hour: A Case of Professional Incest*. London: Guilford.

Beck, A.T. *et al.* (1979) *Cognitive Therapy of Depression: A Treatment Manual*. New York: Guilford Press.

Berger, M. (1983) Toward maximising the utility of consumer satisfaction as an outcome. In M.J. Lambert, E.R. Christensen and S.S. DeJulio (eds) *The Assessment of Psychotherapy Outcome*. New York: Wiley.

Chevron, E. and Rounsaville, B. (1983) Evaluating the clinical skills of psychotherapists. *Archives of General Psychiatry 40* 1129–32.

Combs, A.W. (1986) What makes a good helper? *Person-Centred Review 1* 51–61.

Combs, A.W. (1989) *A Theory of Therapy: Guidelines for Counselling Practice*. London: Sage.

Crits-Christoph, P., Baranackie, K. and Kurcias, J. (1991) Meta-analysis of therapist effects in psychotherapy outcome studies. *Psychotherapy Research 1* 81–91.

Crouch, A. (1992) The competent counsellor. *Self and Society 20* 22–5.

Dumont, F. (1991) Expertise in psychotherapy: inherent liabilities in becoming experienced. *Psychotherapy 28* 422–8.

Glaser, R. and Chi, M. (1988) Overview. In M. Chi, R. Glaser and M. Farr (eds) *The Nature of Expertise*. Hillsdale, NJ: Lawrence Erlbaum.

Greenberg, L.S., Rice, L.N. and Elliott, R. (1993) *Facilitating Emotional Change: The Moment-by-Moment Process*. New York: Guilford Press.

Hawkins, P. and Shohet, R. (1989) *Supervision in the Helping Professions*. Milton Keynes: Open University Press.

Heron, J. (1976) A six-category intervention analysis. *British Journal of Guidance and Counselling 4* 143–53.

Heron, J. (1990) *Helping the Client*. London: Sage.

Ivey, A.E. and Galvin, M. (1984) Microcounselling: a metamodel for counseling, therapy, business and medical interviews. In D. Larson (ed.) *Teaching Psychological Skills: Models for Giving Psychology Away*. Monterey, CA: Brooks/Cole.

Kivlighan Jr, D. and Quigley, S. (1991) Dimensions used by experienced and novice group therapists to conceptualize group process. *Journal of Counselling Psychology 38* 415–23.

Klemp, G. and McClelland, D. (1986) What characterises intelligent functioning among senior managers? In R. Sternberg and R. Warner (eds) *Practical Intelligence: The Nature and Functioning of Intelligence in the Everyday World*. Cambridge: Cambridge University Press.

Lambert, M. (1989) The individual therapist's contribution to psychotherapy process and outcome. *Clinical Psychology Review 9* 469–85.

Lambert, M. and Ogles, B. (1988) Treatment manuals: problems and promise. *Journal of Integrative and Eclectic Psychotherapy 7* 187–204.

Larson, L.M. *et al.* (1992) Development and validation of the counselling self-estimate inventory. *Journal of Counselling Psychology 39* 105–20.

Luborsky, L. *et al.* (1985) Therapist success and its determinants. *Archives of General Psychiatry 42* 602–11.

Lutwak, N. and Hennessey, J. (1982) Conceptual systems functioning as a mediating factor in the development of counselling skills. *Journal of Counselling Psychology 29* 256–60.

Martin, J. *et al.* (1989) Conceptualizations of novice and experienced counsellors. *Journal of Counselling Psychology 36* 395–400.

McLeod, J. (1992) What do we know about how best to assess counsellor competence? *Counselling Psychology Quarterly 5* 359–72.

McLeod, J. (1994) *Doing Counselling Research.* London: Sage.

McLeod, J. and McLeod, J. (1993) The relationship between personal philosophy and effectiveness in counsellors. *Counselling Psychology Quarterly 6* 121–9.

Omer, H. and Strenger, C. (1992) The pluralistic revolution: from the one true meaning to an infinity of constructed ones. *Psychotherapy 29* 253–61.

Ponterotto, J. and Furlong, M. (1985) Evaluating counselor effectiveness: a critical review of rating scale instruments. *Journal of Counselling Psychology 32* 597–616.

Raven, J. (1984) *Competence in Modern Society: Its Identification, Development and Release.* London: H.K. Lewis.

Scofield, M. and Yoxheimer, L. (1983) Psychometric issues in the assessment of clinical competencies. *Journal of Counselling Psychology 30* 413–20.

Shaw, B. and Dobson, K. (1988) Competency judgements in the training and evaluation of psychotherapists. *Journal of Consulting and Clinical Psychology 56* 666–72.

Smith, M., Glass, G. and Miller, T. (1980) *The Benefits of Psychotherapy.* Baltimore, MD: Johns Hopkins Press.

Strupp, H.H. and Binder, J.L. (1984) *Psychotherapy in a New Key: A Guide to Time-Limited Dynamic Psychotherapy.* New York: Basic Books.

Strupp, H.H. and Hadley, S.W. (1979) Specific vs. non-specific factors in psychotherapy – a controlled study of outcome. *Archives of General Psychiatry 36* 1125–36.

Sue, D.W., Arredondo, P. and McDavis, R.J. (1992) Multicultural counselling competencies and standards: a call to the profession. *Journal of Counselling and Development 70* 477–86.

Whiteley, J. *et al.* (1967) Selection and evaluation of counselor effectiveness. *Journal of Counselling Psychology 14* 226–34.

Wills, T.A. (1982) Nonspecific factors in helping relationships. In T.A. Wills (ed.) *Basic Processes in Helping Relationships.* New York: Academic Press.

Chapter 5

Future developments in ethical standards for counselling

Tim Bond

INTRODUCTION

Ethical standards are not fixed and unchanging, and I will argue that counselling is at a particularly crucial stage in the development of them. There are issues of identity which are fundamental to determining such standards. Unless the boundary of what is and, perhaps more importantly, what is not counselling is demarcated, the process of producing them is frustrated. It is much easier to develop clear and relevant ethical standards which are focused on the needs of clearly identifiable professions/groups. If the group is too wide ranging in its interests and ill focused, the ethical standards are forced to become little more than abstract and generalised statements of intent rather than concrete and specific requirements.

We are approaching some crucial decisions about the future identity of counselling, which parallel decisions which have confronted other professions in the development of ethical standards. These relate to the future shape of the profession and are considered in the first section of this chapter, which suggests that there is much to be gained from collaboration rather than competition between subdivisions of the talking therapies. I will argue that there is a significant risk of tribalism within counselling, which would be best avoided. The tribalism within talking therapies is clearly present, but difficult to explain or justify outside those who are directly involved. As this is associated with the choice of name for divisions within the talking therapies, in the next section I ask 'what is in a name?'.

In the third section I discuss new opportunities to address the perennial problem of minimising malpractice in order to protect clients and to improve on weaknesses in the current systems. However, just in case this all seems too easy and straightforward, I conclude with a section which sets out some of the radical critiques of current assumptions about ethical standards which our profession will need to consider, regardless of the way it resolves the current issues around identity. It will be apparent from what I say that the development of ethical standards is a combination of analysis of the problems and political activity in order to effect solutions. Neither of these tasks looks very straightforward as we approach the turn of the century. These are exciting but challenging times for anyone who is interested in the ethical standards of counselling.

THE SHAPE OF THINGS TO COME?

Counselling is approaching a crucial developmental phase in its credibility with the public and related professions. At the moment, 'counselling' is only one of several labels applied to what might be generically termed the 'talking therapies'. Counselling, counselling psychology, psychotherapy and psychoanalysis all have many characteristics in common. We all offer a facilitation of changes in feeling, thinking and behaviour by skilled listening and talking, informed by a shared pool of theory. However, we are divided at an organisational level between the British Association for Counselling (BAC), the British Psychological Society (BPS), the United Kingdom Council for Psychotherapy (UKCP) and a variety of psychoanalytic organisations. This raises the question about whether the current infrastructure for 'talking therapies' is adequate for the future. Do the organisational differences correspond with significant differences within the talking therapies? Perhaps the best way of approaching this question is to examine the significance of the different labels that we have adopted for our work, by a procedure known as role differentiation.

There are a range of possible outcomes from any role differentiation exercise. Roles may be readily distinguished and those distinctions may correspond to functional and, therefore, socially valued differences. These roles can be considered as clearly differentiated. Intermediate levels of differentiation may arise where it can be demonstrated that there is much in common between roles as well as significant differences with regard to some functions but not all. Role differentiation is not established if the differences between roles are merely semantic or matters which are of marginal significance to the role. For the purposes of role differentiation, it seems sensible to compare the roles at the basic entry point to practitioner status, which in this case corresponds to accredited, chartered or recognised practitioner level rather than the general membership of the key organisations involved. This is the basic standard for practice that each professional group has articulated as that to which its members aspire in order to be recognised as a practitioner by peers. It is reasonable to conclude that in the future the majority of members in their respective organisations will have achieved this status or will be in the process of doing so, as all the organisations are trying to increase the proportions of the membership who have done this.

A comparison of functions between counselling, psychotherapy and counselling psychology reveals that there is much in common. All aim to produce changes in behaviour, feelings or thinking which enhance the well-being of the person concerned. All operate according to ethical principles which place client autonomy as a high priority. In a general sense, counselling, counselling psychology and psychotherapy draw on a shared pool of knowledge, although there may be differences of emphasis within that shared pool; for example, between psychodynamic, humanistic and behavioural/cognitive-behavioural theory. However, these differences of emphasis are not central to the choice of role title, because representatives of each of these orientations are to be found within counselling, counselling psychology and psychotherapy. Overall, it is difficult to detect any indications of a clear differentiation of function between the roles.

Is there any difference at the point of entry into recognised practitioner status in terms of training requirements and the required professional standards? A comparison of published statements is summarised in Table 5.1. This reveals a considerable similarity in approach and concern about key issues. At first sight, counselling psychology has the most demanding criteria for training. The main issues are as follows:

- Graduate status: a major difference in the basis for acquiring accredited status relates to being a graduate, which is required in counselling psychology and psychotherapy, but not counselling. Counsellors have considered that there is a valued place for people with other professional qualifications or life experience in their midst. For counsellors to insist on graduate status would seem unnecessarily restrictive and perhaps alienate some counsellors from their client groups, where similarity in social experience is essential. In order to be a counselling psychologist, a degree in psychology is considered essential, whereas the kind of degree is not specified for psychotherapy. None the less, 63 per cent of counsellors who were members of BAC in 1993 were graduates (BAC 1993b).
- Experience as a client: only counselling psychology specifically requires that the practitioner should have had experience of being counselled. Some have seen this kind of formal requirement as incompatible with the voluntary nature of counselling and psychotherapy, and have avoided making such a strict requirement. None the less, experience and anecdotal evidence suggest that most counsellors and psychotherapists will have received personal counselling or therapy.
- Research: psychology emphasises research by practitioners, and counselling psychologists are following this tradition, making it a requirement to achieve chartered status. Research is becoming a higher priority in counselling and psychotherapy but is not considered an essential requirement for all practitioners. None the less, in 1993, 26 per cent of the membership of BAC held a masters degree or higher, which will

Table 5.1 Comparison of professional requirements for eligibility to recognised practitioner status

	Counselling	Counselling psychology	Psychotherapy
Basis for recognised practitioner status:			
Postgraduate		✔	✔
Training	✔	✔	✔
Required training:			
Theory	✔	✔	✔
Experiential skills	✔	✔	✔
Personal development	✔	✔	✔
Experience of being a client		✔	✔
Counselling research		✔	
Length of required training (hours)	450	230+	Varies
Length of required supervised practice (hours)	450	450	Varies
Required professional standards:			
Accuracy of any statements about qualifications	✔	✔	✔
Observance of code/guidelines of ethical standards	✔	✔	✔
Compliance with complaints procedures	✔	✔	✔
Duty to report colleague's misconduct	✔	✔	✔
Supervised practice	✔	✔	Varies
Sources of information	BAC 1993a, 1993b, 1994a, 1994b	BPS 1993, 1995a, 1995b	UKCP 1993a, 1993b

have been acquired by conducting research. Comparable figures with regard to psychotherapy have not been collected to date.

• The duration of training: at first sight, it would appear that counselling has the longest requirements for training, but there are good grounds for not leaping to this conclusion. Counselling psychology requires the completion of a psychology degree, which would usually (but not necessarily) include components which constitute part of the training for counselling and psychotherapy. There are different lengths of training required within psychotherapy. Psychoanalytically oriented psychotherapists must have received 500 hours exclusive of clinical work and an introductory year of unspecified contact time in order to be registered (UKCP 1992a: nos 1–5). In contrast, humanistic and integrative therapists must have 900 hours tutor-contact time and 450 hours supervised client-contact time (UKCP 1992b). This appears to be the most demanding of all training requirements measured by contact time. However, it may be that the whole concept of required training times will prove to be a rather indirect way of determining training requirements. One of the strengths of National Vocational Qualifications (NVQs) is that they require the demonstration of specific competencies regardless of how long (or short) a period of time it takes someone to acquire them. NVQs are in the process of being identified for each of these groups, and it may be easier to compare trainings when this process has been completed. At the moment any differences in training requirements may be in approach to stating the requirements rather than substantive ones in the actual training. There is a need for a detailed comparison of actual trainings to look behind the different ways the requirements are stated.

There are some areas of uncertainty about the comparability of requirements for eligibility to recognised status in counselling, counselling psychology and psychotherapy. But there is no unequivocal evidence of significant and substantive differences. There is no such difficulty over professional standards, which are strikingly similar. A more detailed breakdown than space permits would reveal that this similarity extends beyond the broad headings used in Table 5.1 to quite a considerable level of detail, but this would be another study in its own right. Such differences as do exist tend to be differences in emphasis or, to put it another way, differences in degree rather than of kind. The unique omission of a requirement of on-going supervision beyond training for the registration of psychoanalytic psychotherapists should probably be viewed as an important exception in shared standards. But, in practice, many therapists within this tradition seek on-going supervision.

So far it has proved impossible to sustain the idea that there are substantive role differentiations between counselling, counselling psychology and psychotherapy with regard to function, training requirements or professional standards. So what is the significance in our use of different labels to describe ourselves?

WHAT IS IN A NAME?

The absence of significant differences in function, training and professional requirements between the three professional roles raises the question about why these differences of identity are considered significant. Dorothy Rowe (1989: 8) has observed: 'Psychiatrists do psychotherapy, so do psychologists, nurses, social workers and occupational therapists. If people feel that "psychotherapy" is too pretentious a word to apply to what they do, they describe what they do as counselling.' The pretensions appear to relate to status and the competition for work. Status is important with regard to levels of remuneration and control over others. Jenifer Elton Wilson (1994: 7), writing from the viewpoint of counselling psychology, regards 'a recent rush of "How to" books about counselling by senior psychotherapists' as an illustration of 'the tendency of psychotherapists to maintain an elite position which differentiates counselling practice from psychotherapy, while adopting the mantle of teachers of counselling practice'.

It may be that counselling psychology, with its more wide-ranging formal training requirements, is positioning itself above counselling in the pecking order of 'talking therapies'. This reveals the ambiguity of statements of difference. Sometimes differences relate to standards, but statements may equally and perhaps more importantly encode claims to differences in status. In this respect, claims to particular labels of group identity may be more akin to membership of particular tribes in a way which is analogous to academic tribalism (Becker 1989). An outsider may be struck by the similarity in rules, the methods of self-regulation and general culture between tribes which share the same territory. Minor differences may be detectable, but appear to carry greater significance to tribal members than seems immediately justifiable. From the inside, these differences are thrown into sharp relief and define allegiances.

The introduction of metaphorical tribalism highlights the choice which faces the future development of counselling and psychotherapy. I will elaborate the choice in the form of a fable:

> Once upon a time, there was an island which kept growing in size as the sea deposited sand and earth on its shores and its inhabitants worked to bring the new land into cultivation. The island provided a reasonable living for three tribes, each of which organised itself around a special name inherited from its ancestors. These names had symbolic importance in the initiation rituals and served to maintain a sense of tribal identity, especially in moments of conflict. However, visitors to the island reported that they were unable to discern much difference between the tribes. They all seemed to do much the same range of things in rather similar ways. But the names were obviously important to the inhabitants, and were the focus of periodic discussions. Visitors would be startled by public cries of 'What's in a name?' followed by a rush of tribal representatives to a public arena, where a vigorous dispute over meanings and significance would take place. Encoded within claims to meaning were claims to which tribe should have highest status, the right to oversee other tribes or a larger share of the

new land. These debates were often followed by a period of friction between tribal leaders, but visitors reported that most of the islanders seemed uninterested and continued to rub along with each other regardless of tribal identity.

Indeed, there seemed to be an air of disappointment with the tripartite system of government. There was a general feeling that an island of plenty could be better organised to mutual advantage. Sometimes the divisiveness between the tribes meant that everyone lost out to people on other islands, who subordinated tribal differences to an over-arching system of cultural identity and organisation. There was always a nagging doubt that a skilled rival could provoke such competition between the tribes that they could be divided against one another and thus more easily conquered.

This fable attempts to encapsulate the earlier discussions about relationships between counselling, counselling psychology and psychotherapy and therefore needs little deciphering. We seem to be in a state of an almost unstoppable growth in the volume of actual and potential work, which probably defuses some of the potential tensions between our professional tribes. None the less, the fable casts into sharper relief an awareness of the wider context and the dangers of remaining organisationally separate in comparison to other, better co-ordinated professions.

Others have reached similar points in their development. The medical profession was divided by its disciplines, but nearly a century and a half ago united to mount a concerted attack on quacks or unqualified practitioners. During this century, nurses, midwives and health visitors joined together to form a united voice to advocate the enhancement of nursing standards. More recently, professions supplementary to medicine formed into a single system of regulation, which has enhanced their status to such an extent that they are currently collaborating to create their own professional identity in ways which are not defined as being supplementary to another profession. It seems to me that all the major contributors to the talking therapies are faced with similar decisions. Should we find a way of bringing our national organisations together to form a shared basis of standard setting and regulation? For example, it is possible to envisage a United Kingdom and ultimately a European Council for Counselling, Counselling Psychology and Psychotherapy. Such a council could hold the register of practitioners. Although this is only one of a possible number of outcomes of coming together, it seems highly desirable that we *should* join together, regardless of the preferred method of achieving this.

There are alternative views about the choice of names within the talking therapies. One is based on concepts of progressive levels of expertise from counselling skills through counselling to psychotherapy. Jenifer Elton Wilson (1994: 7) used to argue for the existence of a continuum between counselling and psychotherapy with counselling psychology falling in the middle, thereby inserting counselling psychology into the established hierarchy, which is primarily used within psychodynamically oriented therapies. This approach suffers from two major shortcomings.

First, it has proved extremely difficult to demarcate the roles in a way which bears close examination by client or therapist. It is sometimes suggested that the progression relates to the depth of working, with counselling being focused on issues arising in the present with a practical component, and psychotherapy working with the presenting past and the structure of personality. Another distinction is based on the idea that counselling is concerned with cognitive problems and psychotherapy with affective problems. However, Brian Thorne (1992: 245) has debunked this way of thinking:

> I would suggest that it takes only a moment's reflection to reveal the uselessness of such distinctions. Clearly cognition and affect are both involved in all behaviours. No choice, for example, can ever be simply logical and rational. What is more a serious personality problem usually brings with it many situational and environmental dilemmas and a situational problem may well have its source in a personality disturbance. It would, of course, be highly convenient if problems could be categorised and circumscribed so neatly but to suggest that they can is to fly in the face of the facts.

The second major objection to a hierarchy running from counselling skills to psychotherapy relates to the concept of progressive expertise. Using counselling skills requires great expertise in situations where there may be no formal clarification of roles, agreement about duration, or even agreement to meet again. In my work and personal life, I have watched skilled nurses use counselling skills to considerable effect to elicit what was frightening a mother-to-be during labour or, in other circumstances, a doctor breaking the news of a terminal illness to a single parent with a view to eliciting her wishes about arrangements for her surviving children. These are 'one-chance' opportunities whilst working under pressures which are seldom as acute within the counselling or psychotherapy room. My own view is that within each of the roles of counselling skills, counselling, counselling psychology and psychotherapy, there are levels of expertise. These levels work from novice via trainee to accredited, senior and consultant levels. My choice of terminology may not be the one which would be adopted by the relevant professional groups, but the idea of progressive levels of expertise within the roles is clear.

As a counsellor, I find this approach attractive because it separates role descriptions from claims to status and therefore makes dialogue between peers, regardless of professional label, more accessible. As an academic I consider that this is a more accurate representation of the professional roles which avoids entrenching a historical accident. I have written else-where about the first uses of 'counseling' by Frank Parsons (Bond 1993: 18) and how the term was adopted by Carl Rogers. As a psychologist he was not allowed to use the term 'psychotherapist', which was restricted to medically qualified practitioners, and therefore he adopted the term 'counsellor'. For him, the terms 'counseling', 'psychotherapy' and aspects of 'psychology' were interchangeable. The current vogue for hybridising them into 'therapeutic counselling', 'counselling psychology', 'psycho-therapy psychology' and 'psychoanalytic counselling' seems to put a nail in the coffin of any attempt to maintain clear role distinctions, even if this were desirable. At most, it is possible to say that the personal choice of title may indicate a personal preference for a particular tradition. One title has a tendency to emphasise empowerment of individuals within their social context (counselling). Another stresses the importance of under-standing and perhaps changing character or personality (psychotherapy). A third attaches importance to adopting a discriminatory approach to theory and practice, informed by empirical research (psychology). However, none of these traits is unique to the group which emphasises it. All are present in the others.

The length of this discussion about 'what is in a name?' is indicative of the importance of this issue for the future development of talking thera-pies. It is too early to anticipate the actual outcomes of this kind of debate. That will be determined by political process within the professional groups and between them and the government. However, I would wish to sound a cautionary note. A debate about role differentiation and status will inevitably turn attention inwards within the profession, but I think the most important gaze will be outwards. We need to end up with arrange-ments which are easily understood by the public and the media. We do not have these now. The current distinctions are not well understood by trained practitioners of 'talking therapy' and cannot be easily explained to the public. Almost as important as the outcome of the debate will be the manner in which it is conducted. The talking therapies will have much greater claim for credibility and esteem with the public if we are seen to be capable of overcoming our structural divisions in a spirit of collabora-tion, rather than replicating the divisiveness of the market place in a quest for status and power relative to one another. Greater collaboration between us will help with another major concern shared by practitioners and the public alike: the prevention of malpractice.

PREVENTION OF MALPRACTICE

The ease with which people can set themselves up as therapists, and the relative lack of sophistication of the talking therapies over how they regu-late themselves, comes as a great surprise to many. For example, it is possible for someone to walk out of prison after serving a sentence for fraud or sexual assault and to set up as a counsellor or therapist on the same day, with a view to attracting potential victims. Fortunately, so far as I know, this has never occurred in practice. However, the profession has struggled over how to respond effectively in order to discipline a small number of people who have repeatedly exploited their clients, and to prevent any recurrence of this kind of activity. It is worth considering the present arrangements for dealing with breaches of ethical standards, before suggesting how these arrangements could be improved by collaboration between professional groups and by other measures.

Anyone who has been involved with complaints against the members of any profession, including counsellors, will be struck by the emotional and practical obstacles facing a conscientious complainant. There is the natural and sometimes healthy desire to leave behind a painful and exploitative experience rather than invest further time, effort and emotional upset in correcting someone else's misconduct. Sometimes the potential complainant feels that he or she may have, however unwittingly, contributed to the exploitation, especially in the case of sexual or financial matters. This sense of guilt may compromise the desire to make a formal complaint. Perhaps the greatest obstacle is retaining sufficient trust in a profession's own complaints system after having just been exploited by a member of that profession. The fear that the exploiter may be typical of the profession is a powerful disincentive to initiating a complaint. Similarly, the sense of being an individual taking on the full weight of a profession which will provide the adjudicators from within its own ranks is also a disincentive, because of the potential for a profession's inbuilt bias towards protecting its own. These obstacles are such that the talking therapies will need to continue to develop new approaches to minimise the disincentives to legitimate complaints. Perhaps the greatest step forwards would be the introduction of adjudicators from outside the profession, so that it is no longer a matter of a profession being seen as judging its own. This will not be as easy to achieve as it sounds. It would almost certainly require the co-operation of a number of different professions in the recruitment and training of potential adjudicators, in order to ensure that sufficient people would be available from outside the profession to form adjudication panels.

Another way of reducing the disincentive for complaints would be to develop alternative approaches to quasi-judicial hearings. For example, an ombudsman for the talking therapies existing independently of, or in conjunction with, a mediation service would be a useful alternative. It is probable that the talking therapies are now sufficiently large to be able to afford such a development if they shared the cost across several national organisations.

Counselling psychology and psychotherapy are well into the process of establishing national registers of practitioners. Counselling is further behind but, as I write, the preparation of a national register for counsellors is well advanced and has proved that a number of national organisations such as BAC, the Confederation of Scottish Counselling Agencies (COSCA), Relate, Westminster Pastoral Foundation (WPF), Cruse and others can collaborate successfully to provide a form of self-regulation for counsellors. Over time, the new register seems likely to become an important means of enhancing the ability of the profession to police itself. To the public, membership of a register will be seen as a hallmark of quality assurance. To a large extent the register will enhance the quality assurance of counselling, but it will be much more effective if there is collaboration between organisations with registers concerning the talking therapies, so that they all benefit from each other's experience. It may be that a joint statutory register for closely related roles within the talking therapies would be the best possible means of quality assurance for the public. The requirements of statutory registration may be at the cost of creating a cumbersome and relatively expensive bureaucracy, but it is a clear expression of counsellors being willing to be accountable to the public.

Whether or not counselling adopts statutory registration, it is apparent that there will be considerable pressure on counselling to look outwards to its relationships with other professions and the public. This may involve some reconsideration of the interplay between professional and national culture. Current trends in the wider culture may require some radical rethinking of the established, current ethical standards applicable to this profession.

QUESTIONING THE BASIS OF COUNSELLING ETHICS

The current basis of counselling ethics is the enhancement of individual integrity and respect for individual autonomy. This is exemplified by the stress on the voluntary nature of counselling (BAC 1993b), negotiation of a clear contract (BAC 1993b; BPS 1995b) and on the counsellor's responsibility for managing the process of the counselling rather than the outcome, which remains the responsibility of the client (Rowan 1983: 172). The management of confidentiality is an important corollary of this principle, because it marks the boundary between the counselling and the client's control of the outcome in other aspects of his or her life. Respect for the principle of individual autonomy – literally self-government – is not limitless. It requires the capacity to act autonomously, which may not be present in the very young, the severely disturbed, the extremely distressed and those acting under the influence of intoxicants or duress. There is also a widely acknowledged limitation on people's rights to act autonomously when their actions would harm the autonomous actions of others. In common with other professions, counsellors have had to consider the implications of these limitations, especially with regard to young people, suicidal clients, and clients threatening physical harm to others. I have considered these issues elsewhere (Bond 1993). However, it seems probable that the use of concepts of individual autonomy as the basis for a professional ethic may become more questionable in the future. The challenge comes from two sources. Cross-cultural and gender awareness have exposed the limitations of the concept of autonomy. I will consider each of these in turn.

In some cultures, the locus of responsibility is not placed on the individual as the fundamental unit. Instead, the extended family may be the basis for all ethical decision making. The exact way that this is expressed will vary between cultures. Sometimes the fundamental responsibility will rest with the head of the family and be exercised in conjunction with a community leader. Therefore any concept of confidentiality between counsellor and client which did not also include these people could be seen as destroying the traditional infrastructure of the community and a denial of the social context. On the other hand, if the counsellor co-operates too readily with a family or community view of what is appropriate, there may be a cost to an individual client who finds this oppressive and who wishes to be seen as an autonomous individual.

I am told that counsellors in New Zealand have encountered the issue in a particularly acute form. Most Maoris think of themselves in terms of family groups. 'You hurt my brother and I hurt' is one of the sayings reported to me. The strength of their feelings of interconnectedness is so all-pervading in their language and thinking that the prevailing ethic used by counsellors, with its emphasis on respect for individual autonomy, is inappropriate in a Maori culture. The search for an ethical base which can be shared by both Caucasian and Maori counsellors in New Zealand is under way but proving difficult. This is a vivid example of a dilemma which may be going unnoticed in the search for ethical standards within Britain. The multicultural nature of our population poses a parallel challenge, but one that seems to be less commented on.

A parallel critique of concepts of autonomy has emerged within studies of gender differences, which suggests that there may be contrasting gender-based approaches to ethics. Feminists have argued that male theorists consistently mistake their experience of social, political and moral life for the totality of experience. They suggest that women simply do not fit the liberal description of the independent, abstract citizen who freely enters into contracts on the basis of personal choice. It is suggested that because women are symbolically, and most are actually, living within the realm of the family, they have a greater sense of the interrelatedness of people. It is also suggested that they have a pre-formed status which defines them in relationship to others, particularly the provision of services to men (Gatens 1995: 19). This status limits the ability of women to enter into social contracts in comparison to men, or changes the nature of these contracts. This social context has ethical implications. The ethical thinking which has its origins in female experience is identified as an ethic of care (Gilligan 1982), which is characterised by three important features: (1) resolving ethical dilemmas by reference to the social context and taking emotional aspects of experience into account; (2) moral attitudes being formed in the context of dependent relationships, particularly the mother–child one, but with other kinds of relationship also being significant in the development of a sense of self and values; (3) responsibilities and duties of care to others being the focus of the care stance.

In contrast, the ethic of justice (Rawls 1971), as the name suggests, is concerned with: (1) determining appropriate principles of justice; (2) the importance of independence from both the circumstances and emotional relationships when applying the principles of justice; (3) the emphasis on the rights of the individual. The compatibility of these two approaches is a matter of debate. It is possible to polarise them so that they are seen as incompatible and requiring two separate approaches to ethical standards, including for counsellors. On the other hand, it can be argued that this polarisation is a consequence of a history of men's abuse of power over women. But in practice most people employ aspects of both the care and justice ethics in familial, work and friendship settings, and the concepts are conceptually compatible (Friedman 1993).

I have drawn attention to this debate because it invites a review of ethical standards for counsellors in terms of the appropriate balance of ethics of care and of justice. Where does the division of responsibility truly lie within the counselling relationship? Are the current divisions inadvertent replications of a male and somewhat detached concept of relationship, or are they essential to the counselling relationship? We are invited to re-examine the concepts of relationship which inform our understanding of the theory and methodology of counselling and their implications for developing ethical standards. However, could counselling also have a contribution to make to the wider debate, from ideas about relationship and the centrality of relationship to the formation of concepts of self and values which neither gender can escape?

I find it difficult to anticipate the outcome of the influence of multicultural and gender-based experience on the future development of counselling ethics. My intuition is that concepts about the quality and integrity of the counselling relationship will become more important, with an increased emphasis on the social and cultural context in determining what this means in practice. For example, the emphasis on counsellors operating according to respect for the client's control of the outcome of counselling may need to be modified, to constructing a relationship and process of working which the counsellor and client have agreed as appropriate to the personal, social and cultural context. This need not be a radical break with existing ethical standards, because it could grow out of the existing emphasis on client consent. However, it would involve a change in the factors considered relevant to that consent, with a greater emphasis on the social and cultural context. The client's own understanding of these additional factors would be extremely important, but not to the exclusion of the counsellor's responsibility for self-development with regard to cross-gender and cross-cultural issues.

CONCLUSIONS

Predicting the future is always risky. Some major event may intervene which will create a different set of dynamics, away from those that I have envisaged. Notwithstanding such an event, I consider that the extent to which counsellors can collaborate with others in similar roles to face the many challenges before them is fundamental to the future of ethical standards. A major conflict between closely related roles within the talking therapies would be a supervening event which could adversely affect the future development of ethical standards. Collaboration provides the best way of minimising malpractice within our roles and of facing the complex challenges of ethical standards in a diverse social context.

REFERENCES

Becker, T. (1989) *Academic Tribes and Territories – Intellectual Enquiry and the Culture of Disciplines*. Buckingham: Open University Press.

Bond, T. (1993) *Standards and Ethics for Counsellors in Action*. London: Sage.

BAC (1984) Code of Ethics and Practice for Counsellors. Rugby: BAC.

BAC (1993a) Membership Survey 1993 – Individual Members and Organisations: A Short Summary of Results. Rugby: BAC.

BAC (1993b) Code of Ethics and Practice for Counsellors. Rugby: BAC.

BAC (1994a) Accreditation Criteria. Rugby: BAC.

BAC (1994b) Complaints Procedure. Rugby: BAC.

BPS (1993) Code of Conduct, Ethical Principles and Guidelines. Leicester: BPS.

BPS (1995a) Regulations and Syllabus for the Diploma in Counselling Psychology. Leicester: BPS.

BPS (1995b) Guidelines for the Professional Practice of Counselling Psychology. Leicester: BPS.

Elton Wilson, J. (1994) Current trends in counselling psychology. *Counselling Psychology Review 9* (4) 5–12.

Friedman, M. (1993) *What Are Friends For? Feminist Perspectives on Personal Relationships and Moral Theory*. Ithaca, NY: Cornell University Press.

Gatens, M. (1995) Between the sexes: care or justice. In B. Almond (ed.) *Introducing Applied Ethics*. Oxford: Blackwell.

Gilligan, C. (1982) *In a Different Voice: Psychological Theory and Women's Development*. Cambridge, MA: Harvard University Press.

Rawls, J. (1971) *A Theory of Justice*. Oxford: Oxford University Press.

Rowan, J. (1983) *The Reality Game – A Guide to Humanistic Counselling and Therapy*. London: Routledge.

Rowe, D. (1989) Foreword. In D. Masson *Against Therapy*. London: Collins.

Thorne, B. (1992) Psychotherapy and counselling: the quest for differences. *Counselling 3* (4) 244–8.

UKCP (1992a) Criteria for Psychoanalytic Psychotherapy Trainings. London: UKCP.

UKCP (1992b) Humanistic and Integrative Psychotherapy Section Criteria and Guidelines (Amended). London: UKCP.

UKCP (1993a) Ethical Guidelines. In *Directory of Members – General Information and Training Courses*. London: UKCP.

UKCP (1993b) Training Requirements. In *Directory of Members – General Information and Training Courses*. London: UKCP.

Chapter 6

Sexual exploitation in counselling

Janice Russell

INTRODUCTION

Although it is only recently that the issue of sexual exploitation within counselling and psychotherapy has started to be named in the therapeutic world (Russell 1993; Rutter 1990), it is not new or specific to modernity. As far back as the practice of mesmerism, we can discover an awareness that such exploitation is a possibility. In this case it was conceptualised as gender specific. Chertok and de Saussure (1979: 10–11) cite an observation made in the late eighteenth century that:

> The woman is always magnetized by the man . . . whatever the nature of the illness, it does not divest us of our own sex, nor does it entirely remove us from the power of the other sex . . . It is not surprising that the senses are inflamed.

Thus, there was within the practice of mesmerism an understanding of the influential nature of the relationship, with the acknowledgement that 'All the greatest abuses . . . may follow from this influence which you acquire over your patients' (1979: 14). Themes of eroticism, power, influence and complaisance in helping relationships were recognised two centuries ago. They were framed in gender-specific ideology, and were raised to awareness primarily to alert practitioners for their own protection.

Since then, there have been several instances of renowned therapists having sexual encounters with their clients, with Fritz Perls perhaps being suggested as the most notorious (see Shepard 1976). A more recently controversial disclosure in the therapeutic world is that of Brian Thorne, a prominent client-centred counsellor who justifies his being naked with a client and acknowledging the erotic feelings present for them both as a legitimate aspect of ultimately client-centred practice (Thorne 1991). The disclosure is provocative, and clearly the practice is open to debate, if only in terms of 'is this counselling?'.

There are many ways in which the development of psychology and sexuality are intrinsically linked in terms of theoretical development, from Freudian theories to the advent of sex therapy. Suffice it to note this for now, and to reiterate that the issues pertinent to this chapter are not entirely new within the therapeutic discourse.

WHAT IS SEXUAL EXPLOITATION WITHIN COUNSELLING?

The British Association for Counselling (BAC) Code of Ethics declares that 'Counsellors must not exploit their clients financially, sexually, emotionally or in any other way. Engaging in sexual activity with the client is unethical' (BAC 1990: 2.2.6). An amendment to the code in 1992 suggested that there should be a twelve-week 'cooling off' period after the termination of the counselling relationship, and an advisory note added that we might wish to consider a lifetime ban on sexual relationships between erstwhile counsellors and client. Clearly, this raises contentious issues, particularly around whether all relationships have the same depth, whether the resolution of the counselling is complete, and what the nature of the motivation for the relationship might be. It may also be argued that two adults who have ended a contractual relationship, given maturity and mutuality, are perfectly capable of making appropriate decisions for them-selves, and that each situation must be looked at uniquely (Wilkins 1993).

The tension lies between attempting to offer reasonable and ethical guidelines for professional practice, and recognising the autonomous rights and abilities of human beings. There is after all a paradox operating if we profess that 'once a client, always a client', while espousing the notions of self-determination and self-actualisation. The first statement may imply that the counselling enterprise has not achieved its objectives. The philosophical debate is worthy of much more attention. For now, it is perhaps sufficient to note it and to suggest that we need to distinguish between the concepts of 'sexual' and 'sexually exploitative', and to try to identify some of the factors which make the difference.

In order for a practice to be non-exploitative, it is first necessary to investigate that which makes it exploitative, and to know why it has adverse effects. To this end, a major concern of my research into this area has been to gather information on the construct of sexually exploitative behaviour within counselling. The findings discussed in the rest of this chapter are reported in detail in Russell (1993). They are based on a series of interviews with people who considered themselves sexually exploited in counselling or therapy, and with people who were students on courses where sexual exploitation was experienced or observed.

One thing which becomes clear is that the behaviours and experiences which may be identified as sexually exploitative are wide ranging. They may be loosely classified as physical and non-physical. The first group includes clear physical assault (women told of being grabbed, shaken or struck in 'intimate' areas), episodes of stroking, kissing, sexual touch which was justified as a diagnostic tool, such as stroking of the inner thighs, oral sex, erotic touch when the client was distressed, sexual intercourse in or outside of the consulting room. Non-physical behaviours may include inappropriate verbal responses, such as a 'so what, the guy was having a wank' when one woman described an obscene phone call, explicit sexual overtures or expressions of flattery, inappropriate dress, the failure to deal with eroticised elements of the relationship where the client had expressed sexual attraction to the therapist, the sexualisation of the client's material, or else a denial of sexual issues by the therapist. People who have experienced sexually exploitative behaviour in counselling stress that the events took place within a subtle process where boundaries were repeatedly broken. This made identification of exploitative behaviour somewhat elusive. As one woman observes, 'this kind of issue begins at a very subtle level, it's not just somebody full of lust'.

American research on the subject suggests various ideas as to what constitutes sexually exploitative behaviour. Nancy Gartrell *et al.* (1986: 1126) use sexual contact to refer to contact which is intended either to 'arouse or satisfy sexual desire' in either party. Adams talks about 'pressured sexual situations . . . in which someone in a subservient position is used for another's gratification, profit or lust' (1987: 61). Rapp makes a more forceful definition, introducing the power dynamic and the notion of informed consent: 'an abuse of power to obtain sexual gratification that one would not otherwise obtain' (1987: 193), and likens it to rape situations where 'a consent of a sort is obtained by false pretences'.

None of these definitions incorporates all the experiences identified by the participants in my own research (Russell 1993). Coleman and Schaefer (1986) seem to show a more useful understanding of the complexities in using a continuum model with polarised extremes to categorise 'psychological, covert and overt abuse'. Covert abuse includes 'sexual hugs', 'professional voyeurism' and 'sexual gazes', whereas overt abuse ranges from 'sexualizing remarks' to 'sexual intercourse' (1986: 342–3). Psychological abuse represents interventions that serve the psychological needs of the therapist rather than the client. I assume that this would include the distancing response identified as exploitative within my research.

While acknowledging the difficulties inherent in this subject, given that sexuality may itself be seen as a construct relevant to experiences of the self, it nevertheless becomes possible to elicit some guidelines as to what is *appropriate* behaviour in the therapeutic situation. This will be behaviour where the counsellor:

• takes responsibility for setting and maintaining clear boundaries;
• does not exploit the client either covertly or overtly for his or her own gratification;

- sees the client's psychological needs as being paramount in the relationship;
- has an awareness and an understanding of the intentionality of his or her own actions and is able to communicate that intention to the client;
- has a clear understanding of the possible consequences of those actions.

Currently, it is my experience that although some of these prescriptions are embedded in professional codes of ethics, some counselling is made 'mystical'. The counsellor may be inappropriately interpretative, and demonstrate poor communication skills which rely heavily on the assumption rather than the demonstration of clear understanding. Given that sexuality is a complex area, it is understandable that some counsellors may not be experienced enough to deal constructively with sexual feelings within the relationship. Moreover, there is some level of ignorance about the possible effects of sexually inappropriate or exploitative behaviour on the client group. How are these effects perceived by people who feel that they have been sexually exploited by counsellors?

EFFECTS ON CLIENTS

My own research investigated people's experience as clients. As far as I know it is unique in this respect in Britain, and indeed most of the American research is based on counsellors' accounts or surveys. In considering the effects of sexually exploitative behaviour on clients, it is apparent that these may be reconstrued over a period of time. Feelings at the time might be positive or ambivalent, and only later construed as harmful. The process of reconceptualising events, after the therapeutic encounter has concluded, may be lengthy. In many of the interviews which I have carried out, participants used the terminology of therapy, such as 'transference' and 'countertransference', in their attempt to make sense of what had happened. It must also be noted that the language of therapy may be used by authorities to dismiss the client's experience – 'it was just the transference' – and to trivialise the events.

Emotional effects may be summarised as follows. In some instances, the first emotional reaction is that of feeling special to the counsellor. In a sense, this may be seen as a false sense of specialness in that it implies an expectation that cannot professionally be lived up to. Such specialness may be initially experienced as positive – 'I thought, oh gosh, this is lovely, I love this feeling and to get all this attention.'

A second possible effect is that of dependency, which is encouraged by some counsellors, so that clients might feel helpless without the special attention they thought they were receiving.

Every person I have met who has felt himself or herself exploited within counselling has described experiencing difficulties with the issue of trust. This shows in three ways. First, they lose a sense of trust in themselves. The words of one woman are telling: 'The worst thing about all of this is that it made me unsure of my own feelings, it made me mistrust my own feelings . . . until other people named it for me.' Second, there is the sense of betrayal of trust by the counsellor. Third, there is the question of who can be trusted to hear about the experience and to help make sense of it.

A fourth emotional reaction is guilt. This has two main edges, in that many people who are exploited as clients may feel guilty about the experience, as if the exploitation had been their fault. Further guilt may then be felt on disclosure, as if they are betraying the counsellor. Anger, too, seems to be a pivotal emotion, and many people who are exploited experience a deep sense of rage. Anger of course can be experienced in a highly destructive sense, as it may be turned inward or displaced. Those who had felt able to direct their anger appropriately felt empowered by the experience.

Many other people I have spoken to, however, expressed a sense of frustration and helplessness when they felt unable to warn other people about their counsellors. It is not uncommon to experience such feelings when an incident is difficult to disclose, and when to make public statements is to be vulnerable to libel charges. As one woman said, 'I felt I had to tell or else I would be colluding in him abusing, yet I didn't feel able to.'

Those who are exploited in counselling may therefore be left with very mixed feelings, both about the counselling they have received and about the counsellor. Some feel that they have made gains within the counselling. Such ambivalence must be respected as a part of the reintegrative process, and it is important to allow people to retain their sense of agency in the process even though they may now believe that the counsellor should have acted more responsibly.

Other effects which I have observed include poor or distorted self-concept leading to self-blame, and isolation because there seems to be nowhere to go with the problem. People in my research either did not know about complaints procedures, or felt that these would be contaminated – that is, serving the interests of the profession before the interests of the clients in a sort of wall of professional silence – or sexist. One woman said, 'My big fear was that they would say, Oh God, another hysterical woman, and bin it.'

Several specific and idiosyncratic effects were described by participants as attributable to the confusion of the exploitative experience. The most marked of these were violence to others or to self, as in self-harm and suicide attempts, and in the case of one woman, the compounding of a depression which she felt resulted in her children being taken into care. In addition, subsequent counselling proved problematic for those who sought it.

Undoubtedly, the type and severity of effect must be located within the context of the previous experience of the client's and in how they personally construe their world. Many of the participants I interviewed had experienced previous sexual abuse, and felt that the 'therapeutic' exploitation compounded the effects of this, or reinforced negative patterns of behaviour already in place.

COUNSELLORS

Little work has been done in Britain on 'offending counsellors'. As far as I am aware, there is at present only one completed piece of research available (Garrett 1992), although I recognise that this is an expanding area of interest and research, particularly within the British Psychological Society (BPS). Tanya Garrett carried out a survey of 300 clinical psychologists and found that 4 per cent admitted to sexual intimacy with current or former clients, 22 per cent had treated clients who reported sexual intimacy with previous counsellors, and 40 per cent knew of offending counsellors through other sources. A literature review of research available in the States, coupled with my own experience as a counsellor and a researcher, suggests that there is something of a 'wall of silence' on the issue, often coupled with the belief that 'it couldn't happen here'. Many people who are concerned about the problem are unsure to whom misgivings should be reported.

My research was concerned with the clients' perspective and was therefore of a qualitative rather than a quantitative nature. I did discover, however, that counsellors reported as sexually exploitative included those from the disciplines of general practice, marriage guidance, community psychiatric nursing, Jungian counselling, psychoanalysis, psychosynthesis, Gestalt counselling, bioenergetic counselling, person-centred counselling, re-evaluation counselling and 'eclectic' counselling. I have also been approached by several counsellors who knew someone who had exploited clients, and by students on courses who have witnessed exploitation and harassment of other students, or who had personal experience of it. There is also some conflict around reporting, with one pole of the debate being that such behaviour should always be reported, and the other that it should never be reported because of client confidentiality. My personal perspective is that client confidentiality is a concept which seeks to serve client interest, and is not to be used as a strategy for collusion in unethical practice. Clearly, there are difficulties when the client does not want to report unethical practice but subsequent counsellors are privy to compromising information. Each extreme poses not only ethical problems, but dilemmas concerned with client empowerment.

My own analysis suggests that 'offending counsellors' do not, on the whole, fit the stereotypical view of the abuser. It seems unlikely that they are made up of evil opportunists, setting out to lure and abuse clients, although this end of the spectrum does exist. It seems equally inaccurate to see them as people who will abuse only at certain low points when actually they are in need of counselling, as some of the American literature suggests.

My position is more complex. At one end of the scale, I would accept some form of deliberate opportunism, here as in any walk of life. I would also accept some level of distressed practitioners. But I am also suggesting that there is some exploitative practice by people who are neither skilled nor experienced enough to be doing the job, and who lack self-challenge and awareness. It seems most helpful to locate the problem as one of boundary transgression or blur. Since sexuality is a powerful aspect of the human condition, it is no surprise that some boundary transgression is of a sexual nature. And of course a great deal of the behaviour under review reflects sexist, heterosexist and exploitative attitudes which are common to the society in which counselling is practised, and to some of the theoretical foundations of some approaches.

That boundaries will be transgressed is a notion reflected by the existence of codes of ethics which specifically ban exploitation: as Rock (1973) suggests, if there have to be statute laws, then the social rules have lost their potency. If we apply this to professional codes of ethics, it suggests that there is recognition in their very creation that they will be transgressed.

SEXUALITY

A brief word must be said on the notion of sexuality itself. My position here, informed by the work of Michel Foucault (1981), Frigga Haug (1987) and Jeffrey Weeks (1986), is that sexuality is itself a social construct which is a part of the reflexive project of self. It is clearly too simple to reduce sexuality to the physiological or essentialist view of sex. Our understanding of sexuality is culture bound, and differs between individuals, depending on their experience and view of the world. It is not appropriate to expand this here (see Russell 1993), but suffice it to say that such a view makes it difficult to make specific bans within the therapeutic relationship.

On the other hand, it must also be recognised that we operate within a specific Western culture, so that it would be reasonable and ethically desirable to concede to the norms of that culture. It might then be reasonably expected that any behaviours which involve either primary or secondary sexual characteristics will be experienced as sexual. All behaviour which is motivated by the sexual urge or gratification of the counsellor will also be seen as sexual, and will by its nature be exploitative. And any behaviour which stimulates the client into any kind of eroticised response must be acknowledged as sexual. To have no recognition of these issues or prohibitions allows a relativistic position to obscure the possibility of firm guidelines, which are essential to good practice and to inform clients' rights.

POWER

Another concept central to the issues under review is that of power. Again, while it is not appropriate to enter the full debate here, one or two points are worthy of mention. The first is that I would challenge the purely patriarchal analysis espoused by Rutter (1990) on the grounds that it is too simplistic. Rutter's research documents exploitative practice by a range of professional helpers, within male helper–female client dyads. My own research, where two of the participants were men who felt exploited by women, demonstrates that women may sexually exploit when they are in a position of power or trust. This is substantiated by the American literature where dyads have been female–male, or same gender, and by some of the contentions of lesbian women on lesbian counselling in Britain (Kitzinger and Perkins 1993). We may conclude that gender is only one variable to be considered in analysis, albeit as a primary focus.

It seems to me that power abuse is at least partly situational. Power itself is conceived not as a static commodity but as a dynamic force between two or more parties. Power is ascribed as well as taken. It would seem that in counselling, many clients allow counsellors to have power over them, some counsellors exercise power over their clients, and some abuse power in relation to their clients. This seems at least partly related to the structure of the situation. It is useful also to glance at the dimensions of authority, influence and force.

I would suggest that authority is ascribed because of status or perceived knowledge. It carries the notion of power invested in someone in order to fulfil particular objectives. Authority is invested in those who claim expertise. In counselling, this entails a double edge in that not only is the individual claiming expertise, but so are the theories which inform the practice. The discourse of psychology claims the authority that not only can we assert that there is such an entity as the mind, but that the discipline of psychological counselling can tell us about the state of that mind, its mechanisms, its imperfections, its flaws, and what it should ultimately look like. A powerful position indeed.

Another aspect of manifestations of power is influence. Influence is the ability to change, modify or control people's behaviour or attitudes without the use of overt power or force. Counsellors claim and carry this influence, and clients respect their claims to do so; indeed they often want to be influenced in some way to effect personal change. It must be remembered that power can be a positive energy: we speak of fulfilling potential, and becoming empowered. To enable this process, a whole host of theoretical perspectives, attitudes and techniques must enter the counselling arena. Indeed, the counsellor is implicitly asking the client to take these on trust. The potential for sexual exploitation is immediately in place.

A third aspect of power is that of force, which may be seen as operating along a continuum from coercion – as in the case of one person who feared not complying with her counsellor lest she should be dismissed from the course where she was student and he tutor – to overt physical force, as when a woman was physically assaulted.

We may then see power as entailing a set of relations between people, places and things. It is enabled and transmitted through language, ideas, images, practices and beliefs. Within counselling, these include therapeutic techniques and the ideologies of therapeutic discourse. Therefore, to analyse the abuse of power, we need to look much wider than simple gender relations, without denying that gender is a central variable in both the theory and practice of psychological counselling, and within the structures of the discipline.

The 1993 Annual General Meeting of BAC passed a further amendment to the Code of Ethics on the issues of sexual exploitation, which acknowledges that it is perhaps the power aspects which should inform whether the counselling relationship could ethically change its nature. The amendment is an important guideline, suggesting that 'The decision about any change(s) in relationship with former clients should take into account whether the issues and power dynamics present during the counselling relationship have been resolved and properly ended.' Ambiguities will remain, and living with these while creating practice of the highest ethical standard will remain a central challenge for the professionalised counselling world.

CONCLUSIONS AND NEW DIRECTIONS

Sexual exploitation within counselling represents a major challenge to the profession. It can be seen that the effect of such behaviour is invariably harmful, and can be likened to that found in other sexually abusive experiences, with the added dimension that counselling is specifically set up to help.

This raises ethical dilemmas which need urgent and on-going attention. Issues of reporting and collusion need to be addressed. Although ethical codes and directives exist, they are not always supported by the structure of the organisations involved. And reparative work needs to be available for those who feel that they have been sexually exploited within counselling. The context is wider than this, of course, and raises questions about the standard and the level of ethical practice to be found on training courses. Indeed, I believe that this issue raises many others related to competence, training, supervision, and the challenging of sexist and heterosexist practice within counselling.

As I said earlier, I deliberately made no detailed gender analysis in my research because of the nature of the contracts made with the participants. So far, a straightforward patriarchal perspective like that of Peter Rutter leaves too much unanswered. Undoubtedly gender is a key variable in exploitative practice, and there is also the 'dripping tap' notion of sexual harassment present in the counselling world. But counselling is one arena where women can be very powerful in the eyes of the client, and where they can become 'gurus' to a whole counselling community. On a structural level, however, the theory and research of counselling psychology remain a predominantly male domain. This needs exploring further (see Chapter 18).

Counselling is in a comparatively early stage of its own professionalisation. My personal views on this are ambivalent, but *if* it is to claim professional status, then it seems necessary that the following areas are addressed in more detail.

Training and supervision

Training and supervision of counsellors need to incorporate much more work on awareness raising and challenging sexually exploitative practice. There is an increasing literature on the subject which is helpful in this respect. It is of central importance that practitioners know the possible effects of sexually exploitative behaviour, and that these may be reconstrued over time.

Awareness raising also encompasses the development of an honest self-awareness of our own sexual and boundary issues. While this is implicit in the self-determination philosophy of counselling courses, it is currently possible to achieve masters degree status in counselling with no obligation to consider aspects of our own sexual development or sexual needs. It remains an 'open-by-choice' area.

Supervision is well integrated into the ethos of counselling, and is an obvious forum for the airing of uncertainties around this area. Supervisors and supervisees need to make clear contracts so that they know at what stage, if any, the supervisor would consider taking reporting action if a counsellor is sexually involved with a client. Supervisors need to be able to help counsellors explore threatening or difficult areas, with the client's welfare paramount. I have illustrated my own model of supervision with an example of how it may be useful for such issues elsewhere (Russell 1993). Honesty and clarity are key features of such a supervisory process.

Ethical committees

Professional ethical committees need to be more genuinely accessible to the public. It would be useful to have regional contacts available for clients/students/supervisees to discuss situations which give them cause for concern. It would also be useful to have some measure of independent arbitration and/or support available to the ethical committees. Much very positive work has been done through the professional organisations which exist, and their efforts deserve recognition. At this period, I have no doubt that there is tremendous goodwill and motivation to meet values of empowerment and justice. Structurally, there are moves to have registration of practitioners, so that erring counsellors can at least be struck off. While there are many aspects of registration which concern me, it is an advantage for the profession that there might be sanctions available to it. One of the frustrations of those who have had their exploitation investigated and validated is that currently, perpetrators may simply carry on practising.

Codes of ethics

Organisations such as BAC have given considerable time and effort to developing a code of ethics which maximises client safety while being respectful of the notions of autonomy and integrity. Currently, however, the BAC Code of Ethics is extraordinarily vague and 'on the fence'. To suggest that each case must be treated individually, presumably at the discretion of the counsellor, creates a massive loophole which is a gift to the exploitative counsellor. Who is to decide when the power dynamics in a relationship are properly ended? It seems to me that there needs to be much more clarity *if* there is to be a professional stance which is seen to be professional when held up to the light.

A professional code of ethics needs to give clear guidelines not only for its membership, but for the public whom it serves. Clients need to know what they might reasonably expect or not expect. My personal preference is that there should be clear stipulation of at least some of the following points.

Counsellors should never conduct a sexual relationship with current clients. While sexuality may be a dynamic of a counselling relationship, it should never be explored or used for the arousal or gratification of the counsellor. My personal preference is to make this quite explicit in the early stages of contracting, in clearly stating that this is a professional relationship which is different from that of a friend or a lover.

Counsellors should never terminate a counselling relationship expressly to change it to a sexual relationship. It is too easy for this to occur with protests of 'I referred her/him to another counsellor.' This sticks only to the letter of the current code, certainly not to the spirit.

Where there is any likelihood of a personal relationship of *any* kind developing between counsellor and client after the termination of the counselling contract, this should be totally in the control of the ex-client, while boundaries are clearly set and maintained by the counsellor. I would suggest that there should be a period of at least six months before any contact may be established. Six months is not an arbitrary time span, nor is it a 'cooling-off' period. Sexual ardour is not an irresistible urge which is purely time controlled: flames must be fanned to make a fire, and the bellows may be applied to the embers at any time. Rather it recognises a period of grief within which a 'healthy griever' of a separation may start to recover sufficiently to make some kind of informed choice. This is extremely necessary to the client, and gives the counsellor time to review the situation honestly with sensitive supervision.

If contact is then established, it should be at the instigation of the former client, with the counsellor now in the responsive role. If contact is attempted before this time span, the counsellor should refuse it. I realise that this is not flawless, but it seems to me crucial that another aspect of our guidelines is that the counsellor never pursues contact with the former client. It seems clearer to ensure the counsellors know this when they enter the profession, and the clients know it when they enter the counselling relationship, than to have the rather retrospective process which occurs currently. I fail to see how counselling can claim professional status without some clear stipulation of boundaries and guidelines.

Collusion and reporting

Some forum for concerned professionals to address issues of collusion and reporting would be useful. As stated, over the last five or six years, many people have approached me to voice their knowledge of other professionals who transgress the sexual boundaries, either within counselling or training. Some express their knowledge as a piece of gossip which they have never considered reporting. I say this without criticism, as an observation of the lack of awareness of the possible level of seriousness of the situation. Others are deeply concerned but apprehensive and unsure of where to go 'without hard evidence'.

And for users of counselling much more information needs to be available about what they should and should not expect, about whom they can go to informally if they are unsure what is happening. Much work has been done in this area. Support groups do exist for people who have felt exploited, some exclusively for women. Some authorities have clients' charters, which are a beginning but which, like policies of equal opportunity, are only as useful as the commitment, structure and resources to implement them.

Counsellors' self-challenge and education

At the end of the day, the profession of counselling will only be as ethical as its practitioners. It is useful as counsellors to consider the following questions:

* Can I imagine being sexually attracted to my client?
* What if my favourite film actor/fantasy figure walked through the door as my client?
* What if my client recounted my favourite sexual fantasy as a piece of his or her personal material?
* How would I feel if my client declared his or her love for me?
* Whom would I turn to if I imagined myself falling in love with my client?
* How would I react if a client made me a sexual proposition?
* Have I ever encountered sexual feelings within the therapeutic relationship?
* Whom could I talk to honestly and without censure should any of the above occur?

Counsellors are human beings and are likely to encounter any or all of the above at some point in their practice, with the probable exception of the film actor's appearance! It is crucial to react from a professional and a personally congruent position. We ask a lot of ourselves. Sexual interest is exciting and flattering, but it is important to override our own vanity and to treat such interest as an aspect of the situation, which is, first and foremost, a therapeutic one within a structure which demands the highest possible ethical standards. A tall order for us mere mortals, but crucial if counselling is to become a worthy profession.

REFERENCES

Adams, C.D. (1987) Sex with patients: is it malpractice? *Trial 23* 58–61.

BAC (1990) Code of Ethics and Practice for Counselling. Rugby: BAC.

Chertok, L. and de Saussure, R. (1979) *The Therapeutic Revolution: From Mesmer to Freud*. New York: Brunner, Mazel.

Coleman, E. and Schaefer, S. (1986) Boundaries of sex and intimacy between client and counsellor. *Journal of Counseling and Development 64* 341–4.

Foucault, M. (1981) *The History of Sexuality. Vol. 1*. Harmondsworth: Penguin.

Garrett, T. (1992) Survey of sexually intimate behaviour with clients among clinical psychologists. MSc dissertation, University of Warwick.

Gartrell, N. *et al.* (1986) Psychiatrist–patient sexual contact: results of a national survey. 1: Prevalence. *American Journal of Psychiatry 143* (9) 1126–31.

Haug, F. (ed.) (1987) *Female Sexualization*. London: Verso Press.

Kitzinger, C. and Perkins, R. (1993) *Changing our Minds*. London: Onlywomen Press.

Rapp, M.S. (1987) Sexual misconduct. *Canadian Medical Association Journal 173* (3) 193–4.

Rock, P. (1973) *Deviant Behaviour*. London: Hutchinson.
Russell, J.M. (1993) *Out of Bounds: Sexual Exploitation in Counselling and Therapy*. London: Sage.
Rutter, P. (1990) *Sex in the Forbidden Zone*. London: Mandala.
Shepard, M. (1976) *Fritz*. New York: Bantam Books.
Thorne, B. (1991) *Person-Centred Counselling: Therapeutic and Spiritual Dimensions*. London: Whurr.
Weeks, J. (1986) *Sexuality*. London: Ellis Norwood.
Wilkins, P. (1993) Sexual relationships between counsellors and ex-clients: can they ever be right? *Counselling 4* (3) 206–9.

Chapter 7

Evaluating counselling

John Mellor-Clark and Michael Barkham

INTRODUCTION

This chapter attempts to present a synthesis of the 'new directions' in counselling evaluation by tying current thinking into practical and experiential learning gleaned from implementing evaluation in a national counselling organisation, namely Relate (Relate Marriage Guidance). Relate is the largest relational counselling organisation in the voluntary sector (Lewis *et al.* 1992). Yet in terms of evaluating counselling outcomes, until recently only one substantial study had been conducted in over fifty years of counselling practice (Hunt 1985). The literature contains many explanations for such a paucity of evaluation, and Lewis *et al.* (1992), in their critical analysis of marriage guidance, present a synthesis which emphasises scepticism and constraint. Specific examples cited include the following: the availability of valid frames of reference (Wallis 1968) and appropriate measures (Heisler 1977); the preoccupation with theory development over empirical evaluation (Hooper 1985); anxiety about breaches of confidentiality (Tyndall 1985); and the tendency for research activity to slip down the list of priorities in the face of pressures to maintain a service (Tyndall 1993). Lewis *et al.* (1992: 254) conclude by maintaining that 'on the whole, client-centred approaches were not seen to lend themselves to or invite evaluative research'.

But 'new directions' in the domains of socio-political context, evaluation methodology and quantitative instrumentation show such evaluation is not only feasible, but positively beneficial. To present these developments, this chapter utilises a question-driven framework, adopting a literature-led, practical and experiential stance. Evaluation is broken down into a sequence of questions anticipated as offering not only a general 'theoretical' understanding, but a 'feel' for the complex interaction of factors which makes such a task appear so daunting to so many. This is then summarised through a practical, experientially based, progressive stage model for implementing evaluation research, derived from a continuing involvement in evaluating services across the continuum of psychological interventions. In conclusion, we propose 'future directions' which might begin to map a 'road to research-mindedness' as advocated by Hicks and Wheeler (1994: 31):

> The road to research-mindedness, research knowledge and experience can be tortuous and/or exciting. It is a road worth taking to help the discipline of counselling become more valued and recognised as a profession continually striving towards higher standards, quality of service and conscious of the need for monitoring and evaluation at all levels.

EVALUATION: ART OR SCIENCE?

Evaluation is concerned with judging merit (Milne 1987) and, to some, is not constrained by having to adhere to the canons of scientific rigour inherent within research. Barker *et al.* (1994) maintain there is a long-standing debate over whether evaluation is an art or a science. The 'science' camp argue for scientific rigour in methodology, whilst the 'art' camp maintain that evaluation should be tailored to the specific circumstances under evaluation. The compromise proposed by Barker *et al.* (1994) suggests that evaluation should be as systematic as possible within the practical and organisational constraints inherent in service settings. Conceptualised within such a framework, it is best to consider evaluation and research as existing on a continuum rather than being dichotomous. At one end is 'pure', 'traditional' or 'laboratory' research while at the other end is 'applied', 'naturalistic' or 'field' research. So what are the essential characteristics of evaluation which distinguish it from research?

Drawing on Milne's (1987) distinctions, Barker *et al.* (1994) maintain that evaluation differs from research in the following features:

- Its primary aim is to assist decision making rather than to add to an existing body of knowledge.
- It is done on behalf of a decision maker, often a manager, who may be distinct from the evaluator.
- It takes place in a naturalistic setting rather than the more controlled academic research environment.
- It is intended for immediate use and is usually done under considerable time pressure.
- It is often written up for purely local consumption, rather than wider consumption in academic journals.

However, these characteristics create very practical tensions for evaluators, often pulling them in incompatible directions. To attract funding for their evaluative research they are required to show that their work is scientifically respectable within the canons of the experimental, applied medical research tradition. But to demonstrate the relevance of their findings to practitioners, they need to acknowledge the non-scientific, educational, reformist or redemptionist dimensions of counselling therapy (McLeod 1994).

Having defined the characteristics and tensions of evaluation, it is important to highlight that it is not a unitary concept. Rather, it has a multiplicity of foci and activities: service audit, quality assurance, effectiveness, and assessment of cost-benefit, cost-efficiency and cost-effectiveness. There is often considerable overlap between these activities and they should not be considered to be mutually exclusive. In the Relate illustration, the above features of evaluation were pivotal in both design and utility. But is evaluation the domain of external 'experts' or is it something the counselling community needs increasingly to be turning its attention to?

CONTEXT AND IMPETUS: DO WE ALL NEED TO EVALUATE OUR COUNSELLING?

The British Association for Counselling (BAC) reports considerable growth in both accreditation and membership. To date, over a thousand counsellors have been accredited. However, given that accreditation is a lengthy process, many practising counsellors compromise by simply joining BAC. Since 1987, membership has grown from 3,541 members to 12,964 (January 1996), with a further 766 organisation members. Alongside such growth in counselling provision, there continues a parallel growth in counselling demand. One example is the growth of counselling in the primary care sector. Corney and Jenkins (1993: 1) report GPs as identifying the need for help with managing the psychosocial component of their workload as their second most important priority. The authors estimate that over one-third of all patients who consult their GPs are likely to be seeking help with psychological difficulties. Similar increases are reported across most of the national counselling organisations. Naturally, such an increase in supply and demand is not without ramifications.

There is increasing impetus for all services to evaluate practice, and this is reflected in the current literature (for example, Barker *et al.* 1994; McLeod 1993, 1994; Parry 1992, in press; Tyndall 1993). There is a growing consensus that, in a climate of increased accountability and limited resources, it is critical for service agencies to prove their worth in order to survive potential wholesale cuts, and there are strong indications that funding may increasingly become contingent on proven effectiveness. Consequently, it seems essential to move towards knowledge-based practice – that is, practice based not on intuition and gut feeling, but on objective observations of the facts (Hicks and Wheeler 1994). Such views are epitomised by Parry (1992: 14) in her review of research, audit and evaluation when she states that 'unmonitored service is no longer defensible'. In summary, current thinking suggests that there is an urgent need for *all* counselling service providers to begin to evaluate their services. Thus the question is not *whether* to evaluate, but *how* to evaluate.

None the less, given the anxiety that traditionally accompanies evaluation, is it plausible to conceptualise many counselling services as viewing evaluation to be the task of services which are better resourced or more specialist than themselves (such as those attached to university departments, services within the new research-aware NHS, or services specifically funded to conduct evaluative research)? McLeod (1993) reports that one of the important outcomes of the early evaluative studies (for example, Sloane *et al.* 1975) is that they proved to be difficult to organise and expensive to implement and, as a result, they have tended to be carried out in 'elite' therapy institutions, such as university psychiatric, psychological or counselling clinics. Consequently, the therapists involved have tended to be highly trained, skilled and experienced. In response, McLeod (1995) maintains an urgent need for more evaluative studies (including case studies and client experience studies) to be carried out into the effectiveness of the work done in agencies that are less well resourced, and that may well serve a more 'front-line' activity for clients who present with a wider range of problems or have less counselling sophistication.

In 1991, the Department of Social Security agreed to fund the costs of external research consultants for a pilot study to assess the feasibility of collecting reliable evaluative information from Relate clients and write a report on the findings (Shapiro and Barkham 1993). The aim was to devise a 'system' that would allow Relate to monitor a representative sample of its work continuously. With the guidance of the external consultants, Relate set about the task, and with considerable success demonstrated that systematic evaluative research was not only feasible, but could deliver highly useful data: profiling clients, describing impacts of counselling, and quantifying associated benefits.

A recent presentation and discussion of the results of the Relate counselling evaluation at the first BAC Research Workshop (held at the University of Birmingham in 1995) may begin to redress the balance through positively promoting the feasibility and utility of evaluation. So what can be passed on to help others hoping to implement evaluation in their own counselling services?

RESEARCH DESIGN CONSIDERATIONS: WHO, WHAT, WHEN AND WHERE SHOULD WE MEASURE?

There are several texts dedicated to a thorough exploration of the design and measurement aspects of research, audit and evaluation: Sanders and Liptrot's (1993) *Incomplete Guide to Basic Research Methods and Data*

Collection for Counsellors; McLeod's (1994) *Doing Counselling Research*; Barker *et al.*'s (1994) *Research Methods in Clinical and Counselling Psychology*; and Parry's (in press) chapter on 'Service evaluation and audit methods' in *Behavioural and Mental Health Research: A Handbook of Skills and Methods*. In this section, the focus will be on highlighting some of the practical considerations and, through the example of the Relate experience, some of the decisions required in designing and implementing evaluation.

The 'who' of evaluation is identified in the methodology literature as comprising the 'sample' (population) and the 'n' (target). The first addresses the population selected to participate, whilst the latter concerns the actual target number identified as a realistic sample size. Of the sample population, there are three primary participative information sources within counselling practice: the client, the counsellor, and a counsellor/client mix. Third party sources such as GP and/or referrer, partner, family, social workers, etc., should be considered as supplementary information sources. In Relate the decision was to collect information from both clients and counsellors in order to assess the potential of each for enhanced and extended implementation throughout the remainder of the organisation.

The 'what' of evaluation is best conceptualised as the data or the measures used to collect information. Barker *et al.* (1994), Barkham and Barker (in press) and McLeod (1994) offer specific accounts of current available measures. Here, as a preliminary step to identifying what measures may be pertinent, it is suggested that it may be very useful to think about the information which is wanted from the evaluation exercise. Horowitz (1982) recommended 'gaming-out' in advance the various possible patterns of data that a study might obtain. The purpose here is to maximise the yield of the evaluation by ensuring that no collected information is uninformative. Gaming-out offers scope for questions to be refined in the light of the likely yield of the available methods, as well as for the methods to be modified to answer the questions more fully.

Whilst the primary purpose of the Relate study had been to assess the feasibility of implementing counselling evaluation, it was an obvious opportunity to collect informative data capable of enhancing counselling provision and practice. Thus information-exchange meetings between the consultants and Relate management concentrated on gaming-out in advance the information likely to have the greatest utility. Questions identified at this early consultative stage addressed such issues as client sociodemographic representativeness in order to examine the belief that Relate served a predominantly white, middle-class population. Orientation to and expectation of counselling were considered crucial in order to explore potential reasons for high attrition rates. Conversely, for those completing counselling contracts, clinical items measuring changes in psychological health and relationship quality were considered critical as measures of effectiveness. Finally, specific counselling achievements and client satisfaction were thought to offer considerable insight and merit.

The identification of the required measures inherently shaped the evaluation design, and it was considered critical in meeting the identified needs to use instruments that would collect information before, during and after counselling. Thus the core elements of the 'when' were determined by the identification of the evaluation interests. However, this could only be considered a first-level solution, as residual issues such as administration, information, consent, confidentiality, access and equity would all impact on the eventual design of the evaluation.

Finally, concerning the 'where', issues abound about the identification of participating sites in a multicentred counselling service. Here, the focus was on pragmatics, representativeness and feasibility. Pragmatically, it made sense to the consultants to choose a geographical region giving them ready access to participants. Thus Relate's north-east region was selected as being the closest to their academic base. In terms of representativeness, given that the consultants were remitted to assess the feasibility of collecting reliable evaluative information from Relate clients, it was imperative to ensure that those sites chosen to participate could be considered representative of Relate counselling centres more generally. To this end it was important to draw up a taxonomy of centres using criteria based on factors such as size (reflected in volume of work recorded), population served (urban vs. rural catchment) and organisation (single vs. amalgamated site). Having secured representativeness, the final consideration was one of feasibility: were the resources at the identified sites sufficient (with assistance) to meet the demands of the study?

These planning considerations might then be considered a first step towards implementation, but how might we best operationalise progression to secure commitment and engage the wider service?

IMPLEMENTING EVALUATIVE RESEARCH: HOW DO WE GO ABOUT IT?

Implementing counselling evaluation is a messy, politicised affair, inevitably likely to generate considerable tension within any service setting. Various texts specifically address some of the problems associated with operationalising the implementation of evaluation (for example, Firth-Cozens 1993; Hardy 1995; Milne 1987). Moreover, several practice-based commentators attest to a variety of associated problems (Shapiro and Barkham 1993; Shipton 1994; Tyndall 1993). The common element among these and other texts and commentaries is that evaluation appears to impose an immense threat to those participating by raising anxieties about intrusion, resentment about the use of limited resources compromising service delivery, fears about the use (or misuse) of results, and frustrations and irritations that the evaluation criteria may not capture important service aspects. So what can we do at the outset to make it appear less threatening and promote more positive feelings?

Shipton (1994), in recounting her experience of implementing an evaluative study in a university student counselling service, concludes that there appear to be many similarities between engaging clients in therapeutic work and setting up an evaluation project with colleagues. Time and effort need to be dedicated to creating a solid framework for the research, which allows resistance to emerge and be worked through, or to be taken into account in the operation of the research activities. Indeed, Shipton (1994) maintains the skills required in setting up evaluation are not new and unfamiliar, but incorporate the normal, routine strategies counsellors use to work with clients. These include the following: listening skills; interviewing; dealing with fragmentation, anxiety and resistance; communicating clearly and resolving ambiguities or conflicting messages; and a knowledge base for understanding interpersonal relationships, group behaviours and hidden agendas. So, how does this work operationally?

Returning to the Relate example, at the outset, concentration was focused on identifying the organisational pressures and constraints initiated through a bi-monthly consultative group consisting of a representative selection of Relate management. Functional groups started work on creating a shared vision by identifying 'hopes and fears' consequent on involvement. Whilst 'hopes' focused substantially on service development, not unnaturally, in a voluntary organisation increasingly having to meet escalating demands and expectations with diminishing resources, 'fears' focused on practical resource constraints and anticipated counsellor resistance. Field management, working closely with counsellors, predicted that in the absence of a research-minded culture, practitioners would be highly anxious about clients evaluating their experience of counselling. Clearly, for the research to succeed within Relate's federated structure, with its largely autonomous centres, voluntary workforce and fragmented accountability, apprehensions had to be not only identified but also eased.

Throughout the initial information-gathering period, the research consultants worked 'therapeutically', helping management stakeholders to identify sources of apprehension, working them through, and building a solid and trusting relationship. Explicitly, it was soon recognised that Relate was not being offered a tightly packaged definitive method, but rather options and choices, as the consultants put it: 'a creative compromise based on explicit understanding of the implications of the choices made'. What transpired was a generalisable, exploratory, naturalistic approach rather than the confirmatory tradition of applied research that had been expected. Choices were made, ramifications and angst were worked through, and core topics for inclusion in the instrumentation were identified. Six months later an unprecedented research initiative was presented to the next tier of participants – the identified research sites.

Four Relate centres were selected to be invited to take part. As stated, those selected were believed to be representative of the work of the administrative region within which the consultants were based. This was a pragmatic choice designed to maximise efficient communication between the consultants and Relate personnel working under guidance as imple-mentationists. In much the same way as the national organisation had worked through choices in the 'grand design', participating centres now had the opportunity to shape the process of implementation which was most suitable for them. To this end, an inaugural workshop presented the 'package' to date and set up working parties in each of the four centres. These were designed to secure commitment to a shared vision by working through more practical hopes and fears, addressing the specific details for local implementation.

What followed was a very difficult period with high levels of anxiety for all concerned. Issues of ownership and lack of empowerment were abundant as the boundaries of traditional autonomy were tested. Regional management staff felt increasingly exhausted, learning 'on the hoof' about the complexities of research and prioritising their already over-stretched time. Predicted counsellor anxieties were realised. Some were confused as to why evaluative research needed to take place at all. Several claimed to know their effectiveness because clients rarely complained, attended repeatedly, expressed their innermost feelings and even recommended others to the service. Others felt that clients would be put off attend-ing because they would find the questionnaires intrusive, invasive and insensitive. Administrative staff felt that the burden of co-ordinating research was more than they could handle. Finally, to many, the antici-pated benefits appeared nebulous and simply 'pie-in-the-sky'. However, identified problems were worked through methodically within a climate of determination, which resulted in high levels of commitment from participants.

In summary, the crucial elements that can be ascribed to the success of the Relate evaluative initiative were the consultants' academic credibility, clinical skills, and the attention to the organisational dynamics of Relate. Together, these led to an immense commitment by all 'stakeholders' to be engaged in the study. The groundwork, undertaken over an eight-month period, was exhaustive in identifying the context within which the research would take place, shaping its content in terms of research aims, procedures and practicalities, and designing a process that was congruent with all the information gathered from the myriad of agendas.

The pilot evaluation that eventually transpired invited over six hundred new clients attending for counselling to complete a number of question-naires at different stages of their counselling. Data collected from clients included demographics, relationship history, expectations of counselling, pre-/post-measures of mental health and relationship state, individual session impact ratings, and retrospective evaluations of specific aspects of counselling. From counsellors, routinely collected information was gath-ered on psychodynamic-oriented demographics (familial relations, etc.), presenting problems, perceived outcomes and client trajectories.

MEANING, CONTEXT, UTILITY AND DISSEMINATION: WHAT DO WE DO WITH THE FINDINGS?

Having collected data, the first step in preparing for dissemination is to consider the interlocking factors of meaning, context and utility. As suggested earlier, preparatory work could have gamed-out the central issues that the data would seek to address, and questions posed in designing the instrumentation should now act as a useful guide to the core task of analysis. Some of this might be straightforward descriptives (that is, frequency counts and percentiles) such as client profile, orientation to counselling, and satisfaction with the service. Other data might be comparative (such as pre-/post-counselling measures), requiring mean-ingful change to be determined. What is paramount is that data should be in the service of a particular argument (utility) and thus used in context, not isolation. Barkham (1993) and Barker et al. (1994) provide texts with specific sections addressing the general areas of interpretation and presen-tation in detail.

One example of a method which has been successfully used in several evaluative studies (including Relate's) and which might emphasise the concepts of context and utility, is to present an exploratory analysis of data to participants, obtaining comments and feedback. Such a method has two distinct advantages. First, it allows hands-on exploration of the data by those responsible for collection. This will help in identifying necessary caveats through consideration of extraneous variables (such as unmea-sured events) which may impact on determinants of change. Second, it will add considerable weight to the final report to have experiential commentary on the study: where it was successful, where it was problem-atic, how the design might be improved, etc. For Relate, such an early feedback event allowed the strengths and weaknesses of the research method and the instrumentation to be assessed to see whether the study could claim to have met its objectives and whether the interpretations the researchers wished to ascribe to the data were defensible.

In total, over a thousand pieces of information were collected for each of the Relate clients participating in the study. The consent rate was in excess of 90 per cent, and commentary from participant administrators suggested that clients had valued the questions asked of them and were impressed at the opportunity to give their views of their counselling experience. For participant Relate staff, the general consensus was one of gratification, stimulation and pride in achieving what had been thought to be unachievable. Staff and clients of the four participating centres, to their credit, by-passed the scepticism traditionally expressed and demonstrated the capacity to collect useful evaluative information profiling the clientele, describing the impacts of counselling, and quantifying the benefits to relationship quality and associated mental health. Following the delivery of the consultants' report to the funders (Shapiro and Barkham 1993), Relate went on to publish the headlines of the study for internal consumption ('Relate clients: who they are and what they tell us'), presenting the findings as the highlight of their 1994 Annual General Meeting.

THE EVALUATION CYCLE: ONCE WE'VE DONE IT, IS THAT IT?

As outlined in the first section, evaluation, unlike research, is central to the process of quality assurance in any service delivery system, and the socio-political arena is suggesting that contingent funding may increasingly become the norm. This leads us to two propositions. First, from a practical perspective, evaluation should not be a one-off event but something inherent in the monitoring of service quality. Second, from a more theoretical stance, it is unlikely that any service evaluation is going to get it right first time. The best way to increase the validity of findings is to replicate them in other settings and, where necessary, to improve instrumentation, enhancing sensitivity and reliability. Often studies reveal, with the benefit of hindsight, that the questions gamed-out could have been better formulated, the methods could have been more finely tuned, or the methods and instrumentation showed sufficient promise to be expanded and/or applied more broadly.

Although preliminary, the initial findings of the Relate study suggested considerable promise for a more substantive study investigating the level of severity in relationship and mental health problems presented by clients on referral, and the substantial improvements achieved by those completing counselling. Many lessons had been learnt from the pilot phase of this project. Of primary importance was the realisation that it was eminently feasible for a voluntary organisation such as Relate to gather substantive data to help manage and supervise counselling services, select and train practitioners, and explain to clients, funders and others the kinds of service Relate offers and its potential benefits. All stakeholders were optimistic, and the confidence of the DSS was demonstrated through the recommendation to the Home Office to provide Relate with the funding it had requested to conduct a more substantive evaluative research project.

Currently, Relate is adding to a corpus of data containing over 2,600 clients tracked through counselling and followed up at intervals of both six and twelve months after counselling. Implementation has been substantially smoother and consequently less time-consuming, as new research sites experience considerably reduced apprehension in the knowledge that the new substantive endeavour had a highly successful precedent. Collaboration in the preparation of consent information and instrumentation has been enhanced, and there exists a greater feeling of mutual ownership for all stakeholders. Additionally, the management and co-ordination of the research have shifted from reliance on expert consultants to using the valuable operational knowledge gained by personnel involved in the pilot. In short, research has been whole-heartedly taken on board as an invaluable, necessary and prioritised on-going endeavour.

SUMMARY: A PROCESS MODEL FOR COUNSELLING EVALUATION

This chapter has attempted to pass on experientially gained knowledge of implementing counselling evaluation so as to promote evaluation as not only feasible, but enjoyable, informative and, most importantly, highly relevant to sustaining practice. Relate is but one example of implementation experience. University student counselling services, counselling services in primary care settings, clinical psychology services, community mental health teams and both NHS and private psychotherapy services are other settings adding to the evolving knowledge of best implementation practice. In summary, we present and operationalise in Table 7.1 an evolving process model for evaluation pertinent to a variety of service settings.

CONCLUSIONS: FUTURE DIRECTIONS FOR COUNSELLING EVALUATION

In conclusion, we present three ways in which we might begin making inroads on enhanced, knowledge-based, monitored counselling practice, proposed as the future directions for counselling evaluation.

The first is to share experiences so as to hone evaluation methodology. Too often, as is characteristic of evaluation, findings are reported for local consumption and seldom disseminated into the wider counselling community. We share our evolving experience through the process model summarised in Table 7.1.

The second way in which we can move towards knowledge-based, monitored counselling practice is to take up the challenge of evaluation, taking the initiative and helping to shift the culture of counselling practice towards incorporating evaluation as part of service design and delivery. In

Table 7.1 Process model of counselling evaluation

Event	Content
Management information exchange(s)	Define the organisational and socio-political context
	Game-out the questions
	Identify the sample, attend to pragmatics, representativeness and feasibility
Inaugural workshop for service participants	Introduce the rationale for conducting evaluation
	Work in small groups to identify, at a fairly abstract level, 'hopes and fears', addressing potential/anticipated impacts on clients, counsellors and service delivery
	Identify participants representative of the service personnel and willing to form a working party group. This should include representation from practitioners, management, administration and possibly (if applicable) service funders and/or evaluation sponsors
Working party meeting(s)	Introduce the aims of the working party group: • To motivate and support one another in pursuing the shared vision of carrying out the requirements of the evaluation • To identify and resolve particular operational issues relating to implementation
	Readdress the 'hopes and fears' identified in the inaugural meeting and attempt to identify concrete operational 'hurdles' to implementation
	Once concrete 'hurdles' have been identified, work towards identifying potential solutions and, where necessary, set tasks for specific individuals to investigate and address in a subsequent pre-implementation workshop
Evaluation administration meeting(s)	Prior to data collection commencing, anticipate and discuss potential administrative problems, such as clients arriving late, dealing with distressed clients, clients with reading/writing difficulties, clients withdrawing participation, etc.
Evaluation monitoring meeting(s)	Once data collection has started, establish a monitoring group to hold regular meetings to review progress, discuss any problems arising, note potential modifications, etc.

continued opposite

Table 7.1 (continued)

Feedback and debriefing workshop(s)	Once all data has been collected, present and discuss findings, identify caveats, potential extraneous variables and mitigating cause–effects relations, and obtain experiential data on participation
Dissemination	Report the findings of the evaluation and disseminate as widely as resourcing will allow
Enhancement and progressive implementation	Enhance and improve methodology and instrumentation in the light of findings, and (where appropriate) trial in other sites

this respect, Relate has been forward-thinking in initiating organisational change (in terms of both resource and culture) conducive to conducting evaluation as part of routine practice. Aware of the priorities of funders, it has looked to service provision based on information derived not from intuition, speculative estimates or gut feelings, but from consideration of consumer-provided evaluative data. As a consequence, client-dependent evaluation has both facilitated development and suggested that clients think well of the organisation for considering their views to be important. Ultimately, this can only increase confidence for all stakeholders associated with this counselling practice and, by example, hope to move others towards similar endeavour.

Finally, in looking to future directions, there is an urgent requirement to reach a consensus in identifying the most sensitive, relevant and consumer-friendly measures to enable information to be pooled across the continuum of counselling-therapy centres, practitioners and clientele. Aveline *et al.* (1995) call for the development and field testing of treatment–effect measures: a core battery of key outcomes tapping, amongst others, general health, quality of life, interpersonal relationships, and enhanced criteria for clinically significant change. This would begin to help mitigate the need for traditional methodological rigour (such as using control groups and/or placebo treatments) through the utilisation of well-validated standardised scales, capable of defining and/or demonstrating people as being and/or moving from being symptomatic to asymptomatic.

Collectively, these three considerations of 'future directions' aim to offer insights into how practices and practitioners might start out on this hopefully less tortuous and more exciting road to research-mindedness (Hicks and Wheeler 1994).

REFERENCES

Aveline, M., Shapiro, D.A., Parry, G. and Freeman, C. (1995) Building research foundations for psychotherapy practice. In M. Aveline and D.A. Shapiro (eds) *Research Foundations for Psychotherapy Practice*. Chichester: Wiley.

Barker, C., Pistrang, N. and Elliott, R. (1994) *Research Methods in Clinical and Counselling Psychology*. Chichester: Wiley.

Barkham, M. (1993) Understanding, implementing and presenting counselling evaluation. In R. Bayne and P. Nicolson (eds) *Counselling and Psychology for Health Professionals*. London: Chapman and Hall.

Barkham, M. and Barker, C. (in press) Evaluating counselling psychology practice. In R. Woolfe and W. Dryden (eds) *Handbook of Counselling Psychology*. London: Sage.

Corney, R. and Jenkins, C. (1993) *Counselling in General Practice*. London: Routledge.

Firth-Cozens, J. (1993) *Audit in Mental Health Services*. Hove: Lawrence Erlbaum.

Hardy, G.E. (1995) Organisational issues: making research happen. In M. Aveline and D.A. Shapiro (eds) *Research Foundations for Psychotherapy Practice*. Chichester: Wiley.

Heisler, J. (1977) Client–counsellor interaction. *Marriage Guidance* Jan./Feb., 233–8.

Hicks, C. and Wheeler, S. (1994) Research: an essential foundation for counselling, training and practice. *Counselling 5* 38–40.

Hooper, D. (1985) Marital therapy: an overview of research. In W. Dryden (ed.) *Marital Therapy in Britain. Vol. 1*. London: Harper and Row.

Horowitz, M.J. (1982) Strategic dilemmas and the socialization of psychotherapy researchers. *British Journal of Clinical Psychology 21* 119–27.

Hunt, P. (1985) *Clients' Responses to Marriage Counselling*. Rugby: NMGC.

Lewis, J., Clark, D. and Morgan, D. (1992) *Whom God Hath Joined Together: The Work of Marriage Guidance*. London: Routledge.

McLeod, J. (1993) *An Introduction to Counselling*. Buckingham: Open University Press.

McLeod, J. (1994) *Doing Counselling Research*. London: Sage.

McLeod, J. (1995) Evaluating the effectiveness of counselling: what we don't know. *Changes 13* (3) 192–200.

Milne, D. (1987. *Evaluating Mental Health Practice: Methods and Applications*. Beckenham: Croom Helm.

Parry, G. (1992) Improving psychotherapy services: applications of research, audit and evaluation. *British Journal of Clinical Psychology 31* 3–19.

Parry, G. (in press) Service evaluation and audit methods. In G. Parry and F.N. Watts (eds) *Behavioural and Mental Health Research: A Handbook of Skills and Methods*. Hove: Lawrence Erlbaum. 2nd edn.

Sanders, P. and Liptrot, D. (1993) *An Incomplete Guide to Basic Research Methods and Data Collection for Counsellors*. Manchester: PCCS Books.

Shapiro, D.A. and Barkham, M. (1993) *Relate – Information Needs Research*. Unpublished report to Department of Social Security.

Shipton, G. (1994) Swords into ploughshares: working with resistance to research. *Journal of the British Association for Counselling 5* 38–40.

Sloane, R.B., Staples, F.R., Cristol, A.H., Yorkston, N.J. and Whipple, K. (1975) *Psychotherapy vs. Behavior Therapy*. Cambridge, MA: Harvard University Press.

Tyndall, N. (1985) The work and impact of the National Marriage Guidance

Council. In W. Dryden (ed.) *Marital Therapy in Britain. Vol 1*. London: Harper and Row.

Tyndall, N. (1993) *Counselling in the Voluntary Sector*. Milton Keynes: Open University Press.

Wallis, J.H. (1968) *Marriage Guidance: A New Introduction*. London: Routledge and Kegan Paul.

Part II

Counselling practice

Chapter 8

Counselling in primary care

Graham Curtis Jenkins and Hetty Einzig

INTRODUCTION: A HISTORICAL PERSPECTIVE

Over the centuries, doctors have noted the emotional and psychological aspects of their patients' maladies. Galen in AD 200 estimated that at least six in every ten people who consulted him for a seemingly 'physical' complaint actually had an underlying psychological problem. This is still the case (Schild and Herman 1994), and patients who somatise are now at last being recognised as a major problem in the National Health Service (Royal College of Physicians and Royal College of Psychiatrists 1995), in particular by general practitioners traditionally trained in a biomedical model that was until recently essentially dualistic and reductionist. Doctors with better training are now beginning to understand the multidimensional aspects of their patients' presenting symptoms, seeking to develop a more holistic approach to their work, and starting to explore the therapeutic implications of such an approach.

The developments which have led to the current situation can be dated back to 1910, when Stevens in *Medical Diagnosis* used the word 'interrogation' to describe for the first time the process of discovering the patient's history. The new psychologies which developed in the early part of this century hastened the process. By 1938 Cabot gave a whole chapter to 'History taking' in his widely read *Manual of Internal Medicine*. The concepts of the 'pathological lesion' and 'the clinical sign' were still paramount, but gradually it came to be recognised that the patient needed to be listened to and at the same time had a life outside the consulting room.

Through the 1940s and 1950s the sophisticated approach of Balint (1964) was starting to influence a generation of general practitioners. Balint argued that the detective-like search for the 'pathological lesion' was only part of the task of clinical practice, and that the general practitioner needed to attend to the ever-present but often unrecognised 'neurotic illness', especially so when this presented in patients who, for instance, were high users of medical services but who had a paucity of medically categorisable disorders (now often called 'fat folder' or 'heart sink' patients) (Mathers *et al.* 1995). Making interconnections between feelings, symptoms and social context, Balint stressed, often allowed doctors to see that the 'lesion' caused only a small fraction of the patients' problems. In addition, Balint stressed over and over again the urgent need for doctors to acknowledge their powerful placebo effect on patients, and the nature of 'compliance cure'.

With the development of this new perspective, general practitioners began to learn the necessity for effective communication within their consultations and to consider the psychotherapeutic dimension in their work with patients. Today most general practitioners acknowledge the importance of communication and counselling skills in their practice. Moreover, vocational training programmes, mandatory since 1977 for all doctors who wish to enter general practice, have also ensured that those who have entered practice after this date have had at least a modicum of communication skills. By 1997 it is planned that all general practitioner trainees will be specifically examined in this area of their practice to ensure they possess these skills before they can become general practitioners.

The idea of employing a counsellor did not begin to really gain ground until the late 1970s, when reports from general practice began to appear in the medical literature (Waydenfeld and Waydenfeld 1980). Although many studies reported benefit, there were few controlled trials. Nevertheless, general practitioners discovered for themselves how valuable a competent counsellor could be to their work. Through the 1980s the process quickened, and with the new NHS contract for general practitioners in 1990 and the sudden availability of Health Promotion Clinic money to pay counsellors, the number of counsellors working in general practice grew rapidly. The sudden withdrawal of Health Promotion Clinic fees in July 1993 put a stop to this increase. However, many more general practitioners had now discovered the value of counsellors in their practices, and despite violent opposition in some quarters from managers and professionals in different disciplines, who saw the perils of losing patients to this 'new' health professional, the growth of counsellors working in general practice continued and accelerated.

In 1995, 36 per cent of all general practices in England and 65 per cent of fund-holding general practices employed counsellors at least on a part-time or sessional basis (Corney 1995a). A counselling service in the practice can serve many patients more appropriately who would otherwise be referred to community mental health teams and psychiatry and psychotherapy services. Patients are usually seen more quickly within the practice, and without feeling the stigma often created by referral to the secondary-level mental health services (Corney 1995b). In addition, the gain of circumventing long waiting lists makes it likely that patients are seen before their distress becomes severe or chronic, and its alleviation is easier. This reduces both inappropriate and overall referrals to these services.

EVIDENCE FOR COUNSELLOR EFFECTIVENESS

It is now clear that trained counsellors with sufficient experience and appropriate supervision, who have learned to integrate their work with the rest of the primary care team, can achieve the following outcomes: between 80 per cent and 90 per cent of patients referred to a counsellor by the gate-keeping general practitioner are seen on average four to six times, and 80–90 per cent of patients report that they find the experience helpful or very helpful (Curtis Jenkins 1995; Boot 1994). In one study (Harvey 1995), up to 70 per cent of patients referred by general practitioners to counsellors were taking psychotropic drugs when seen by counsellors, which indicated the severity of the distress, and no less than 41 per cent of patients were assessed by the very experienced counsellors as requiring referral to secondary services. Many referral protocols presently in use are meant to forbid referral of patients with 'psychiatric illness', but nearly every study reports that it is rarely possible to stick to the protocols or guidelines given the degree of distress, the inability of the general practitioners to contain it, and the inadequacy or non-availability of secondary-level services.

After receiving counselling, many patients report that they have either discontinued or reduced their psychotropic medication (Ives 1979). This might suggest (but not prove) that the medication was being taken to alleviate psychological distress and pain rather than for strictly 'psychiatric' reasons, and that the counselling intervention was found by patients to be as effective or more effective than drugs alone. Some studies also report that between 2 per cent and 6 per cent of patients subsequently increase the dose of their prescribed drugs (Spiers and Jewell 1995), which could be interpreted as increasing compliance with appropriate therapy. Consultation rates with general practitioners often fall and are reduced for sometimes as long as six months after the counselling intervention.

In fund-holding general practices with more sophisticated audit and evaluation processes, it is now increasingly reported that there are falls in referrals to out-patient departments of psychiatry, to psychotherapy, to community mental health teams and psychology departments, and even to other out-patient hospital services – gastroenterology, cardiology or general medical and surgical departments (Thomé 1995). This is natural when it is realised that up to half of all patients referred to hospital out-patient departments have a psychological problem as well as a physical one (Royal College of Physicians and Royal College of Psychiatrists 1995). Achieving such outcomes depends on the availability and acceptability of services, on the skill and expertise of general practitioners, and on the general practitioners and the trained, competent counsellors learning how to work together to produce these outcomes.

There is evidence which suggests that general practitioners tend to employ counsellors when there is a lack of credible local mental health services (Sibbald *et al.* 1993). This should come as no surprise. In addition, the changing work patterns of community psychiatric nurses (CPNs), who are now being forced to withdraw from their general practice positions to spend more of their time caring for the severely mentally ill in the community, are having a dramatic effect on the workload of practice counsellors and general practitioners. Both CPNs and liaison psychiatrists have been working in a fifth of all general practices for some years. Their withdrawal is likely to cause some problems in practices which referred most of their psychiatric problems to them and so lost some of their own skills in managing their patients (Jenkins 1995).

THE FUTURE

Although the number of counsellors working in primary care is rising rapidly, we do not know how general practitioners view counsellors who work with them in their practices. However, general practitioners anecdotally report that they 'wonder how they ever managed without', particularly when the counsellors are employed for sufficient hours to have a noticeable impact on the working of the practice – that is more than 30 hours per 10,000 patients at risk. In Britain and in the USA, experience suggests that the optimal hours counsellors need to work in general practices are approximately 36 per week per 8,000 patient population, with 65 per cent of the time spent seeing clients. The rest of the time is divided between administration, consultation with team members and supervision. Too few hours of counsellor availability invariably mean that the service is not seen as credible or immediately useful by the referring general practitioners, who tend in this situation to think of alternatives to referral to the counsellor, like drug treatment or referral to psychiatry out-patients or to community mental health teams. Curtis Jenkins and White (1994) explored the sometimes problematic relationship between general practitioners and counsellors and tried to find ways of improving it. The study found that counsellors and general practitioners are able to establish collaborative ways of working and can identify the necessity to integrate their different belief systems and models of work, but that there are many obstacles to understanding action.

The medical model of cure and salvation, and the counselling model of search for meaning, sometimes seem to hold the two professions apart. For effective patient care, both counsellor and general practitioner need to have a clear understanding of these apparently alternative but actually complementary points of view, and to use the interface between them therapeutically. General practitioners, it is said, too often see counsellors as the dumping ground for difficult patients or as soft-edged support for their more 'weepy' patients. However, our research did not demonstrate this. Counsellors did sometimes report that they found the general practitioner mechanistic and ignorant of the counselling process, 'holding the power' and belittling the counsellors' work. When counsellors and general practitioners were working collaboratively, such attitudes were rare. However, counsellors' feelings of inferiority or of vulnerability were commonly reported, and when faced with the powerful and hierarchical structure of the medical profession it could be seen as natural for counsellors to feel overawed or threatened at times.

TRAINING AND DEVELOPMENT

We have recently carried out two in-depth, qualitative studies to find out how counselling training is organised and how counsellors feel about their work and their training requirements. Our first study (Einzig *et al.* 1992) looked to see whether twenty-five of the national counsellor training organisations were meeting the training needs of counsellors working in primary care. Our research showed that they were not doing so. Training organisations did not see the importance of preparing counsellors particularly wishing to work in primary care. They were, for the most part, not teaching counsellors about psycho-pharmacology, brief counselling models or the structure of the National Health Service – all of which are vital if the counsellors are to understand the context of general practice and to meet the demands of the workplace.

Second, Einzig *et al.* (1995), in an in-depth, semi-structured qualitative study of twenty-five experienced counsellors working in primary care, explored what counsellors actually wanted from their training in the light of their current experience in primary care. The counsellors identified four core areas of knowledge: working collaboratively in the primary health care team, understanding medical models of health and illness, time-limited ways of working, and professional and personal development. The information gained has been invaluable in constructing the syllabus for the one-year postgraduate diploma programme for counsellors working in primary care, which started in five universities and colleges in January 1995, to be supported by bursaries from the Counselling in Primary Care Trust for the first three years.

WORKING IN GENERAL PRACTICE: CHALLENGES AND SOLUTIONS

When counsellors start working in NHS practice, the immediate challenge they face is the shift from seeing 'clients' to seeing 'patients'. A general practice patient is less likely to be self-reflective than individuals who seek private counselling. Patients come to the general practitioner for help: they want doctors, nurses and counsellors to provide answers to and help with their problems (Savage and Armstrong 1990). The person-centred or 'non-directive' approach of counsellors is at times seen by patients to be alien, unwelcome, threatening or simply unhelpful. Patients from other cultures and ethnic groups also sometimes find non-directive counselling styles inhibiting and puzzling (Mpofu 1994). Patients arrive at the general practice counsellor's door with varying degrees of psycholog-ical distress: fear, sadness, anger, loneliness and despair are commonly present. Patients have often failed to identify these feelings correctly. When this occurs they are likely to express them somatically, so counsel-lors need to develop an understanding of disease processes, and to learn how to work with patients behaving in this way.

Counsellors also find that they need to tailor their counselling approach to include, if necessary, guidance and information giving, even though these ways of working may well have been frowned upon during their training. In their work, they also need to combine facilitation for the search for meaning (if patients indicate that this might be what they seek) with action-oriented problem-solving skills. Patients have often learned from previous health care experiences to expect to receive practical help rather than support or long-term self-exploration. Patients also often come and go after one session with the counsellor, taking what they want and returning when they think it necessary (Talmon 1990). This upsets coun-sellors not used to working in this way, but it is important for them to be aware of patient expectations and be willing to meet these. When this is done it sometimes becomes possible to educate the patient, if appropriate, into the 'counselling culture' of person-centred ways of working, but only if this is what patients say they want or need.

Counsellors who work in general practice also learn the importance of considering the context of their patients' lives. For instance, a general practice in a middle-class urban area will have a very different patient clientele from one in an area of urban deprivation or in an isolated rural area. The needs of the elderly and young people, as well as ethnic minori-ties, should be recognised by counsellors and must be always taken into account. This affects approaches to history taking, contract making, and the counselling process itself. Many counsellors report that sensing the moment when they reach their level of 'conscious incompetence' is vital to prevent them being caught up in situations where they get out of their depth.

In our research (Einzig et al. 1995), pressure of time was mentioned frequently by counsellors, and often unnerved the counsellor new to general practice. Counsellors we interviewed cited the pressure of having to learn how to work briefly with patients who have no prior experience of counselling. Managing often long waiting lists caused many counsellors concern. However, most counsellors in our study with sufficient experience demonstrated that they had learned to manage their workload with considerable skill. They were clear about which patients were suitable for counselling and avoided becoming involved in areas not relevant to their skills (such as social work, medication, or areas covered by the practice nurse or health visitor).

A powerful influence that affects the counselling process in general practice, and one that counsellors always need to take into account, is the psychodynamic implications of the triadic relationship between general practitioner, counsellor and patient, as opposed to the dyad of counsellor and client in private practice. Unless the influence is acknowledged and understood, it causes problems when one of the relationship triad consciously or unconsciously is adversely influenced by the process (Small and Conlon 1988). Sabotage is not too powerful a word to use to describe the effects that some general practitioners and counsellors have reported.

Counsellors have found solutions to many of the problems that arise in offering a service with inadequate resources. Some counsellors successfully manage long waiting lists by offering a first contract of three sessions with further sessions as and when needed weeks or months later. Patients can find this appropriate to their needs, and there is no indication that the effect of the therapeutic intervention is any the less profound or less long-lasting. However, this does cause problems to some counsellors working within a different frame of reference, thinking long-term in order to provide the psychodynamic 'holding' context for the patient and yet, because of the time constraints, unable to do so. When they discover for themselves that they need to work short-term in a ·skills-oriented way, underpinned with, for instance, the core counselling qualities of empathy, warmth and genuineness, their task is greatly eased and patients still report high levels of satisfaction. An acceptance of uncertainty and a high tolerance of 'no change' in their patients are also required. This can reduce counsellors' anxiety when faced with distressed patients who nevertheless seem quite unresponsive to their interventions. These same patients often do return weeks, months or years later to continue the process started at the unsatisfactory (from the counsellor's point of view) first session (Budman and Gurman 1988: 14).

Advocacy is another useful concept for counsellors to adopt. Being an advocate for patients entails having a working knowledge of and a willingness to use, or refer on to, a broad range of other services, and sometimes to work to ensure that their patients receive the help from other agencies by guiding them through the bewildering array available. A good referral network is the primary care counsellor's most useful tool, and many practices have excellent local resource directories. Building this up by meeting and collaborating with professionals in social services and in mental health services can pay dividends. The general practitioners' confidence in the counsellor increases if the counsellor demonstrates that he or she shares the 'caring' ethos of the rest of the practice team. By attending practice meetings, nursing or reception staff help cement their relationships with other team members.

There are other problems caused by the working environment that can be a challenge to a counsellor. For example, the intrusive data collection now demanded by NHS managers on health promotion activities, consultations and prescribing, in a search for value for money in the NHS market place, sits ill with counselling's tradition of total confidentiality. The threats come from many quarters; for instance, insurance companies sometimes penalise patients with a counselling referral entered in their medical notes, which the general practitioner is obliged to mention when completing a medical report for a life insurance proposal. Access by patients to their medical and counselling notes written since the change in the law in November 1991 is also affecting practice.

Maintaining appropriate levels of confidentiality is already difficult for counsellors when they are asked for progress reports by general practitioners about their patients, or when asked by a receptionist 'Is Mrs Jones better?' Wise counsellors ensure that everybody they work with understands their ethical position in relation to confidentiality, which is quite different from the ethos of shared confidentiality held by the other members of the primary health care team. But as a result of the present state of general practice, triggered by the ill-thought-out new contract of 1990, which has created intolerable workloads and low morale in general practice, counsellors often report that general practitioners cannot even find time to meet them frequently enough to enable a collaborative working pattern to develop, or for them to even have time to explain their position *vis-à-vis* ethics and confidentiality.

Just as counsellors need clarity about their work and its goals, so general practitioners need to be clear about why they are employing counsellors in the first place. The parameters and boundaries of counsellors' roles should be clear: what they can or cannot do, how to identify appropriate patients who would benefit from counselling, how individuals can be helped, and what that might mean – not just for the impact on prescription rates and general practice consultation rates but for the patient as an individual. It is important that general practitioners and counsellors agree on the need for audit and evaluation. They are essential to demonstrate the usefulness of counselling, and to ensure that counsellors are effective in their work and are achieving the agreed aims and objectives written into their contracts (waiting list length, follow-up, case mix, outcomes and patient satisfaction), but it is obvious that none of this can happen if the general practitioner and counsellor fail to meet regularly to discuss these issues.

There are other factors that need to be taken into account; for instance, skill mix. In larger practices two or three counsellors are often working with identical groups of patients. A better solution would be for the practice to employ counsellors with differing skills and areas of work. Working as a team they share the workload, cross-referring to their colleagues with special areas of expertise as necessary, and even to other practices.

Individual general practices are now beginning to plan how to meet more fully the psychological and emotional needs of their patients, and involving counsellors in planning and implementation. Counsellors need to be quite clear about their boundaries; they also need to negotiate and establish their working practices, such as the ratio of client contact hours to administration (as already mentioned, ideally no more than 65 per cent of a counsellor's time should be spent working with clients, the rest being spent carrying out administrative tasks, consultation liaison and supervision), and a proper payment for fulfilling roles such as practice team development, meeting facilitation, and running stress management courses for staff or patients. All these tasks call for great skill. Supervisors too need to be well versed in the culture of general practice to help counsellors struggling with such issues.

Other problems arise when the counsellor becomes drawn into a dysfunctional primary health care team. General practice morale is low at the moment, and high levels of stress are reported by individual members of the primary care team. It is easy in this situation for an individual counsellor to fall in with the culture of over-work. Counsellors can feel responsible for trying to play their part in rescuing patients and even other distressed team members.

Counselling in general practice is here to stay. As mentioned above, a postgraduate diploma in counselling in primary care was launched by the Counselling in Primary Care Trust at five universities and colleges in January 1995, to be extended to other sites over the following two years. By 1998 nearly five hundred counsellors already working in general practices will have undertaken this further training, especially tailored to develop their expertise. The course design, influenced by our discoveries of what counsellors want in training, will evolve and change over time, and be responsive to the changing needs of general practice counsellors. Participants on the diploma programme already report that they are being greatly helped to understand and work in general practice, with its demands for audit, evaluation, and research into effectiveness, and to respond to the particular demands of patients from other ethnic and racial groups and those with disabilities.

The diploma is setting standards of competency and is encouraging participants to learn how to use brief therapy approaches derived from the best available models here and abroad. It is encouraging eclecticism and integrative and pragmatic models of counselling, and the successful integration of counselling with medical care. All this needs, of course, to be based on a sound core of prior counselling training. Research and research methodology are also being taught.

General practitioners too need information and help to work effectively with counsellors, and many practices are using induction programmes for counsellors joining their teams in an endeavour to gain understanding of each other's role. By employing appropriately trained and supervised counsellors, general practitioners quickly appreciate how to develop and extend the work of counsellors in their teams. But this can only happen if a continuous dialogue can be maintained.

CONCLUSIONS: RESEARCH

What are the new research directions for counselling in primary care? Studies in the United States (Cummings *et al.* 1993) have focused on targeting specific groups of patients to receive counselling interventions; for example, patients suffering from diabetes, asthma or heart disease. It has been shown that the use of specific, focused counselling interventions can have a potentially major impact on improving the quality of patient care, with inevitable cost containment and often reduction in total health care costs, yet producing a health gain that can be quantified and accompanied by high levels of patient satisfaction.

These studies need to be replicated in general practice in the UK. We need to evaluate primary care counselling interventions in specifically targeted groups of patients with chronic illness and acute post-traumatic stress disorder, who are usually seen in secondary care where waiting lists have ensured the condition has become chronic by the time the patient is seen. Clinical psychologists, to whom they are often referred, commonly report waiting lists of up to one year. There are now well-established ways of helping these patients, and counsellors are demonstrating their ability to learn and use them in primary care. Solution-focused ways of working and cognitive-behavioural modification are just two of the new ways of working that counsellors are beginning to use.

Patients with severe mental illnesses who refuse to use existing psychiatric services are a constant part of general practice. They prefer to obtain most of their health care from within primary care, and counsellors in the future, with appropriate training and adequate safeguards, will be drawn into helping this group of patients. The Hearing Voices movement in North America and the UK has brought to the attention of doctors and counsellors alike the valuable work that can be done with patients with psychotic illness accompanied by auditory hallucinations.

Patients with severe chronic depression, who often sap the will and resolve to help of all who care for them, are another group that could be targeted by counsellors who have learned to work effectively with these patients, preventing relapse and allowing them to maintain a normal existence in their families and communities (Frank *et al.* 1991). Infants and young children exhibiting difficult behaviours are another special group: their problems can often be nipped in the bud with appropriate counselling intervention (often brief and concentrated) in the safe and accessible context of general practice, with the counsellor working alongside the general practitioners and health visitors. The advantage of early intervention is to prevent the behaviours from becoming entrenched and thus damaging the child's emotional and educational development.

Counsellors working in general practice are at the forefront of the development of different models of working: many counselling trainers and theorists are learning too of the depth and effectiveness of brief ways of working, developed through necessity in general practice (Curtis Jenkins 1995). Primary care may be the ideal place to challenge the assumption that long-term work is the only truly effective vehicle for psychological change, and for longitudinal in-depth research into different models and lengths of brief counselling to be undertaken.

The foundations are now firmly in place for the evolutionary growth of counselling in general practice. Training, competence, supervision and models of collaborative working are some of the areas of research and development for the next decade. Demonstrating that counselling is cost effective is not the same as demonstrating that counselling 'works' (Curtis Jenkins 1995).

The future growth of counselling in general practice depends on the counselling profession being bold enough to seize the initiative, and flexible enough to embrace the environment of general practice in a way that makes them indispensable to patients and other members of the primary health care team alike.

REFERENCES

Balint, M. (1964) *The Doctor, His Patient and the Illness*. London: Pitman. 2nd edn.

Boot, D. (1994) Evaluation of short term impact of counselling in general practice. *Patient Education and Counselling 24* 79–89.

Budman, S. and Gurman, A. (1988) *Theory and Practice of Brief Therapy*. New York: Guilford Press.

Corney, R.H. (1995a) Personal communication.

Corney, R.H. (1995b) Mental health services in interprofessional issues in community and primary health care. In P. Owen, J. Carrier and J. Horder (eds) *Interprofessional Issues in Community Health Care*. London: Macmillan.

Cummings, N., Dorken, H., Pallak, M.S. *et al.* (1993) Medicaid managed behavioural health and implications for public policy. Health care: utilisation and cost series. *Health Care Utilisation and Cost Series for the Foundation of Behavioral Health 2* 3–23.

Curtis Jenkins, G. (1995) Does counselling work? *Update* 1 April, 413–14.

Curtis Jenkins, G. and White, J. (1994) Action learning, a tool to improve inter-professional collaboration and promote change: counsellors, general practitioners and the primary care team. *Journal of Interprofessional Care 8* (3) 265–73.

Einzig, H., Basharan, H. and Curtis Jenkins, G. (1992) The training needs of counsellors working in primary medical care: the role of the training organisations. *CMS News, Quarterly Journal Counselling in Medical Settings Division of British Association for Counselling 33* 9–13.

Einzig, H., Basharan, H. and Curtis Jenkins, G. (1995) The training needs of counsellors in primary medical care. *Journal of Mental Health 4* 205–9.

Frank, E., Kupfer, D., Wagner, E., McEachran, A. and Comes, C. (1991) Efficacy of interpersonal psychotherapy as maintenance treatment for recurrent depression. *Archives of General Psychiatry 48* 1053–9.

Harvey, I. (1995) Counselling in General Practice: The Results of a Randomised Controlled Trial. Report to South Glamorgan Family Health Services Authority.

Ives, G. (1979) Psychological treatment in general practice. *Journal of Royal College of General Practitioners 29* 343–51.

Jenkins, R. (1992) Studies of the effectiveness of counselling in general practice. In R.H. Corney and R. Jenkins (eds) *Counselling in General Practice*. London: Tavistock/Routledge.

Jenkins, R. (1995) Personal communication.

Mathers, N., Jones, N. and Hannay, D. (1995) Heartsink patients: a study of their general practitioners. *British Journal of General Practice 45* 293–6.

Mpofu, E. (1994) Counsellor role perceptions and preferences of Zimbabwe teachers of a Shona cultural background. *Counselling Psychology Quarterly 7* (3) 311–26.

Royal College of Physicians and Royal College of Psychiatrists (1995) The Psychological Care of Medical Patients. Report.

Savage, R. and Armstrong, D. (1990) Effect of a general practitioner's consulting style on patients' satisfaction: a controlled study. *British Medical Journal 301* 968–70.

Schild, P. and Herman, J. (1994) Somatic fixation revisited. *Family Systems Medicine 12* (1) 31–6.

Sibbald, B. *et al.* (1993) FHSA and DHA Policy regarding Counselling Services within General Practices. Report to the Counselling in Primary Care Trust.

Small, N. and Conlon, I. (1988) The creation of an inter-occupational relationship: the introduction of a counsellor into an NHS general practice. *British Journal of Social Work 18* (2) 171–87.

Spiers, R. and Jewell, J.A. (1995) One counsellor, two practices: report of a pilot scheme in Cambridgeshire. *British Journal of General Practice 45* 31–3.

Talmon, M. (1990) *Single Session Therapy*. Oxford: Jossey Bass.

Thomé, C. (1995) Personal communication.

Waydenfeld, D. and Waydenfeld, S. (1980) Counselling in general practice. *Journal of Royal College of General Practitioners 30* 29–33.

Whitmore, D. (1995) In I. Horton, R. Bayne and J. Bimrose (eds) New Directions in Counselling: A Round Table. *Counselling 6* (1) 34–40.

Chapter 9

Counselling in the workplace

J. Carolyn Highley and Cary L. Cooper

INTRODUCTION

In recent years, a new dimension has been added to counselling: that of workplace counselling. There has been a rapid expansion of employee counselling services, which are aimed at helping employees (and some-times their families) deal more effectively with personal, family and work-related problems. The sudden growth is the result of a number of influences, including the recognition of stress as a real phenomenon within organisations, and more recently the increase in the likelihood of stress litigation, relating to stress caused by the workplace (Earnshaw and Cooper 1991, in press).

It is widely recognised that stress is a major contributor to sickness absence, lack of mental well-being, alcoholism and other problems in the workplace (Cooper and Payne 1988; Cartwright and Cooper 1994). The Confederation of British Industry (CBI) estimates that eighty million working days are lost to mental illness every year, and MIND claims that 30–40 per cent of all sickness absence from work is attributable to mental or emotional disturbance. Organisations are thus becoming increasingly aware that they can ill afford the cost of reduced effectiveness and increased turnover amongst their workforce (Cooper and Williams 1994).

Whilst the concept of 'employee counselling' itself is not a new one, the particular form of these services is unique because of the association with employee assistance programmes (EAPs). Indeed, EAPs are often seen as synonymous with employee counselling services. However, there is very little consensus about what an EAP is (Highley and Cooper 1994).

The research reported in this chapter focuses on EAPs. There are two main themes. First, there is a real need to ensure that workplace coun-selling programmes have an organisational orientation, and are not purely personal counselling services which are paid for by an organisation. Second, the sudden expansion in workplace counselling programmes has resulted in a great many counsellors looking to such services as a source of work. However, the skills required to carry out short-term counselling with an organisational perspective satisfactorily are very different from those required for personal counselling.

The chapter is based on the findings of a recently completed Health and Safety Executive commissioned research project (Highley and Cooper 1994). The aim of our research was to highlight the main characteristics of EAPs in the UK, from the perspective of the EAP providers, the organisations that use them and the counsellors who interface with the client-employee (and the providers). Since very little is known about UK EAP providers, and their numbers have dramatically increased over recent years, it was decided that we needed to know a great deal more about who they were, what kind of counsellors they employed, and how they were trained (1) before commencing EAP work and (2) since joining a provider. To answer these questions, interview and survey data were collected from EAP providers, the purchasing organisations of these providers, and a sample of the counsellors working for EAP providers.

We interviewed 10 EAP providers and 4 external workplace counselling providers in-depth, and surveyed an additional 16 providers, plus 168 organisations that provide an EAP or workplace counselling service for their employees. In addition, in-depth interviews were carried out with a further 21 organisations (10 had EAPs, 2 had external counselling services, 4 had a combination of internal and external provision, and 5 had in-house counselling services). Finally, we interviewed 10 workplace/EAP counsellors and sent questionnaires to another 78.

The chapter focuses on three main issues:

1 the workplace perspective, including identifying organisational sources of stress and in-house versus external services;
2 the qualities and skills of workplace counsellors, including problem areas, understanding the organisation, short-term counselling training and experience, recruitment, and counsellor qualifications and training;
3 working as a workplace counsellor, including client-company information, supervision and case management.

THE WORKPLACE PERSPECTIVE

Workplace counselling has an added dimension: the workplace perspective. Traditionally, workplace counselling programmes have tended to concentrate on individuals with personal problems. However, it is unlikely that such services will mitigate stress-related claims, unless some attempt has been made by the organisation to identify and, where possible, tackle sources of stress within the organisation. Whilst helping individuals to cope with personal problems is obviously fundamental to an employee counselling service, in terms of both their personal happiness and their work performance, stress at work is caused by a complicated combination of both personal and work-related issues. Thus, in order to be really effective, counselling programmes at work must address both personal and workplace issues.

Using workplace counselling in the traditional way can lead to the responsibility for employee mental health being shifted from the company on to the individual employee. If a counselling programme operates purely at the individual level, then clearly the organisational sources of stress are not being tackled, and the organisation can conveniently 'forget' such organisational problems on the grounds that 'we provide a counselling service to help employees cope'. The organisation is in effect distancing itself from the programme, and hence from the need to address structural problems of stress within the organisation. Any EAP or workplace counselling programme should identify such sources of stress, and advise the organisation on appropriate resources to help them deal with these. We should not see EAPs and workplace counselling programmes as short-term, individual-based, 'sticking-plaster' solutions, but rather as a way of feeding back problems to the organisation (within the bounds of confidentiality) and empowering that organisation to help itself (Hopkins 1994).

Identifying organisational sources of stress

Cooper and Cartwright (1994) assert that it is necessary to broaden the conceptualisation of stress-management interventions (including employee counselling programmes), because activities aimed solely at individuals' reactions to stressful circumstances, and not also targeted at modifying the circumstances themselves, will not be sufficient to avoid the negative legal ramifications highlighted earlier. Workplace counselling has an important part to play in extending the individuals' psychological and physical resources, but its role is essentially one of 'damage limitation', often addressing the consequences rather than the sources of stress, which may be inherent in the organisation's structure and culture (Cooper and Cartwright 1994).

In a recent article, Murphy (1995: 44) suggests that 'EAPs provide very limited feedback to the organisation. Usually feedback is restricted to information about how many employees were seen by the EAP and the general types of problems encountered.' He goes on to point out that EAPs have tended to focus on characteristics of employees, not characteristics of the job or organisation, which may be causing employee stress. Further, he addresses the issue that counsellors have not been formally trained in organisational behaviour – they are not usually occupational psychologists, for example – and may therefore not appreciate the effects of job/task factors and management practices on employee health and performance. He concludes by saying that we must adopt strategies that target the organisation, as well as the individual, for change.

Cartwright and Cooper (1994) agree with Murphy (1995) and point out that occupational stress is likely to present a major threat to the financial health and profitability of organisations. Organisational preoccupation with the outcome of the stress process has tended to detract from the more proactive approach of addressing the source or causal factors. Rather than focusing exclusively on what the organisation can provide for employees to help them cope with stress more effectively, organisations would be well advised to consider what the organisation can do to eliminate or reduce workplace stressors (Cartwright and Cooper 1994).

Any workplace counselling programme needs to be positioned in order to maximise the value of the benefits in the human resource and organisational areas. The service needs to function as an integral, yet independent part of the organisation, and needs to ensure that it offers support to all involved in change and other company developments.

There is also a need to consult with the organisation, where developments and events impact on the well-being of employees, and to respond promptly to requests for counselling programmes to address organisational needs. The service should report any relevant organisational trends, distilled from problems presented by its users to a key person in the organisation, and be proactive in suggesting steps that a public/private sector company might take to reduce or at least minimise the adverse impact of organisational change.

The problem here is that once the decision to introduce a counselling service has been made, responsibility for the service is usually passed down to someone in a non-senior position within the company. This is not really the most appropriate level at which feedback could lead to action. Someone in a senior position is far better placed to institute changes as a result of feedback. Indeed, the recently published Employee Assistance Professionals Association (EAPA) Standards state that:

> The EAP needs to be positioned at an organisational level where it can be most effective and where it will gain support and endorsement from all levels of management, including the Board Directors. The EAP should establish working relationships with a variety of internal departments including Human Resources, Occupational Health etc.
>
> (EAPA 1994: 37)

In-house versus external services

One of the main advantages of providing an in-house counselling service may well be that the counsellors know the company culture, and if problems are identified it is easier for internal counsellors to influence managers, whether to help the employee affected, or, if appropriate, to modify their own behaviour or the company's practice. Companies with

EAPs generally expect to be told less than companies with internal coun-selling services. However, this tends to lead to a lack of organisational feedback from EAP providers, even though such feedback does not in any way compromise confidentiality. In this respect EAP providers do not really live up to the EAPA's Standards with regard to the issue of organisa-tional feedback: 'EAPs consult with the organisation where developments and events impact on the well-being of employees and fall within the EAP professionals' areas of expertise' (EAPA 1994: 35).

Services which combine the best of internal and external provision are likely to function most effectively in this sense. A good combination appears to be an internal company counsellor, who has the back-up of an external service, either for cases he or she feels unable to deal with, or in some cases for employees to contact directly, if they wish.

However, a different type of service, not seen in the recent survey (and not really prevalent in the UK as yet), could well be the best option. This type of counselling service would operate in the following way: a company pays an external counselling provider to supply them with their own dedicated company counsellor/s. This counsellor regularly visits the company and gets to know its culture, policies, procedures, etc. However, the clinical responsibility is held by the external provider, thereby ensuring confidentiality and quality. In addition to combining the positive aspects of internal and external provision, this type of service would also address the negative aspects associated with external provision (such as lack of integration with the company) and those of internal provision (such as lack of perceived confidentiality). One of the key aspects of this type of service would be the ability of the counsellor to give effective feedback to the organisation on issues which might need addressing.

Thus, it has been argued that any workplace counselling service is likely to develop into an organisational change consultancy. 'This posi-tion reflects in many ways the Tavistock Institute's philosophical position, in which fundamental organisational interventions are required to make the individual therapeutic work anything more than peripheral tinkering' (Berridge and Cooper 1993: 98). Indeed, at least one study has found that few organisations have in reality adopted such a role for their counselling service (Swanson et al. 1991), and one reason for this may be to do with the fact that counsellors' training gives them little or no appreciation or skills in the business arena (Afield 1989). It is to this topic that we now turn.

THE QUALITIES AND SKILLS OF WORKPLACE COUNSELLORS

As more and more organisations have seen the benefit of counselling, so the need for well-qualified professionals has increased and will continue to do so. The irony is that there are few professionals available who have the wide range of skills necessary to help organisations. What is needed is an individual who has professional counselling training and experience as well as an experience and understanding of organisational behaviour. As discussed above, sources of stress acting on a particular individual at work can stem from a number of organisational sources. While it is important to help and counsel a distressed person on a one-to-one basis, it is also crucial to get at the root of the problem. In some cases, the sources of difficulties are internal or rooted in the client's past, but in many others they are linked to the way in which a job is organised or a work group is structured, or the way in which bosses treat their subordinates. Thus, we need a new breed of professional who can not only utilise counselling skills but also understand organisational behaviour (Cooper 1986).

In the UK, opportunities are increasing all the time for counsellors to work in a variety of workplace and employee assistance settings. However, in the future these will only be open to individuals who can satisfy the training, professional and business requirements which will be demanded by workplace counselling and EAP providers and their customer organisations. Assistance offered by EAPs (and most other work-based programmes) will by its very nature be short-term (eight sessions maximum), so counsellors need to demonstrate the skills of focused, short-term, problem-solving approaches. They also need to be comfortable with assessment techniques which are designed to elicit information about issues as diverse as alcohol and drugs, mental health and suicide risk, and equally familiar and comfortable with referring clients to specialist services (Galliano 1994).

In addition, counsellors must be able to appreciate the pressures that both employees and organisations are under, and not lose sight of the workplace counselling perspective. An individual's personal difficulties are more likely than not to impact on work performance, and a workplace counsellor is asked to address these, even if they are secondary issues (Galliano 1994).

Problem areas

In the UK, the most common categories of 'problem area' in workplace counselling are debt, health, marriage, general emotional disturbance and, especially, anxiety. Alcohol and drug dependency account for only 5 per cent of presenting problems (though the proportion rises when underlying issues are also assessed). General personal distress, plus marriage and family conflict, account for around 50 per cent of the counsellor's daily task. Job pressures are the primary source of stress in 22 per cent of cases, and are probably implicated in many more. Financial and legal worries account for 18 per cent of problems being dealt with by EAPs (Highley and Cooper 1994).

Only a tiny proportion of those who use counselling services would be diagnosed as mentally ill.

> What most counsellors are dealing with are 'excesses' in one of a number of key areas. In one or the other – often in two or three at the same time – people have overspent their 'capital', their credit, their resources and are, so to speak, temporarily running in the red. This is most obvious in the case of financial resources. It is, however, just as tempting for many to 'overspend' in other areas e.g. physical resources, social resources, psychological resources, skills resources.
>
> (Reddy 1991: 51–2)

Thus, today many clients of workplace counsellors are receiving help for problems that do not reflect the same degree of severity as many counsellors are used to dealing with. Problems are likely to be universal problems of living, which call for different techniques and models of assistance. Counsellors must have a 'person-in-situation' perspective which emphasises the need to understand the situational contexts of the problems people experience (Cunningham 1994).

Understanding the organisation

Although most EAP clients refer themselves for non-work-related problems, the work environment may be having a major impact on clients in ways that are significant. EAP and workplace counsellors cannot ignore issues of work. For counsellors to remain alert to potential work factors in their clients' problems, it is necessary for them to have a dynamic understanding of the employing organisation – its structure, policies, personnel, and current stresses, and how these fit into some historical perspective.

A unique feature of workplace counselling is the dual responsibility that counsellors should have towards both the companies they work for, either as paid employees or contractors, and the individual employees who become their clients. At times the counselling service can intervene in the organisation to bring about changes in attitudes that are undermining the welfare of both the company and its employees.

Many counsellors will not have worked in a private employment context, and should be aware that every counsellor–client contact is likely to have organisational implications (Megranahan 1994). The counsellor who is accustomed to seeing a client on a one-to-one basis needs to see the client in an organisational context, and anticipate any problems others may have with the counsellor's assessment and recommendations for treatment. Counsellors need to be familiar with organisational structures and channels of communication if they are to be able to influence management to make changes.

Short-term counselling

So, the work of an EAP or workplace counsellor is very different from any other form of counselling, requiring not only that the individual has recognised qualifications, but also experience of the world of work and workplace counselling. In addition, workplace counsellors need to be well qualified in short-term counselling, because workplace counselling is essentially short-term, and can range from as little as three to a maximum of eight sessions. The counsellor, in many instances, is called upon to make an initial assessment of the client and to make a decision about the type of therapy the client needs. The counsellor then has to decide whether or not he or she has the ability to work with the client, and whether to refer the client on for some alternative therapy.

The vast majority of EAP providers (over 90 per cent) in our research offer services with a session limit of about six, the aim being to try and help the client to resolve the problem – that is, short-term counselling. Relatively few providers use a three-session assessment and referral model. However, some workplace counselling providers do not set session limits, because it is not seen as ethically or clinically acceptable to impose a limit on the number of counselling sessions a client may receive. This may well be the viewpoint of individual counsellors, and if so, then working for a conventional EAP provider may not be a good move. Even if counsellors do feel happy with the notion of session limits, then it is for each individual counsellor to decide what session limit he or she feels is appropriate, and to work only for providers who feel the same way.

Training and experience

When EAP and workplace counselling providers were surveyed about whom they employ to carry out their counselling and on what basis, it was found that 70 per cent of the providers' counsellor networks consist of 'counsellors', with only a minority being professionally qualified in some other profession (such as clinical psychology). Only 10 per cent of those who work for the providers are actually employed, with 90 per cent being affiliates who are paid on a sessional basis, with no guarantee as to how much work they may be given (Highley and Cooper 1994). It is thus clear that 'counsellors' are by far the group most favoured by providers of workplace counselling, and hence the possibility of obtaining some additional (but not steady or secure) work from this quarter is high.

The training and experience providers require of their counsellors varies widely, with some providers requiring all their counsellors to be eligible for British Association for Counselling (BAC) accreditation, and others requiring very little in the way of formal training. Providers report that counsellors do need to be experienced in short-term counselling, but that experience of workplace counselling is not essential. Providers believe that the ability to work on a short-term basis is crucial to workplace counselling programmes, because client companies cannot, or are unwilling to, afford extended counselling. However, the picture is again very cloudy in terms of exactly what constitutes training and experience in short-term counselling, and the only way to find out is to approach individual providers. The issue of workplace counselling experience is also an important one. Only 25 per cent of EAP providers believe that experience of workplace counselling is necessary for an EAP counsellor. (Current levels of training and experience are summarised later in this chapter.)

However, most do expect counsellors to be able to demonstrate an understanding of the workplace. Worryingly, there was a tendency for some providers to feel that because most problems being brought to the EAP are non-work-related, experience of workplace counselling is not necessary and could in fact cloud the issue. The view tended to be that workplace counselling experience is rarely relevant and that services are usually put in to provide independent counselling provision.

Recruitment

The recruitment procedures for counsellors are extremely varied. Some providers have comprehensive assessment procedures (including case studies), check the counsellor's suitability for short-term work with their supervisor, and where appropriate inspect the counsellor's premises. In contrast to this, there are some providers who recruit counsellors solely on the basis of a CV.

Some of the problems associated with counsellor qualifications and training may well be a reflection of the poor recruitment procedures which some providers have. According to the providers, the general method of recruitment for network counsellors is the interview (in 63 per cent of cases), although this may only be conducted over the telephone. Indeed, 50 per cent of the surveyed counsellors were selected, by EAP providers, only on the basis of an informal interview, with 18 per cent having no interview. Of the counsellors who were either not interviewed or only had an informal interview, 27 per cent stated that their assessment and diagnostic skills were judged on their qualifications and experience. A number were actually recruited solely on the recommendation of a third party, and 27 per cent stated that they were uncertain as to how their assessment and diagnostic skills were judged.

When providers are questioned about the subject of judging counsellors' assessment and diagnostic skills, some interesting comments arise. Some providers attempt to do this by initially interviewing and taking up references, and then monitor counsellors through in-depth supervision. Other providers point out that it is actually very difficult to judge the assessment and diagnostic skills of counsellors, but this can be achieved to some extent by conducting rigorous checks on qualifications, supervision and case notes. Most providers believe that the best way of ensuring that counsellors are 'up to scratch' is initially to supervise their work carefully, and then by on-going case management. Providers tend to verify a counsellor's supervision arrangements unless the policy is for all counsellors to be supervised via the provider.

Whilst the prime responsibility for counsellor qualifications and training must lie with the provider, it is also counsellors' responsibility to ensure that they have the relevant skills to do the job, according to the EAPA Standards: 'Individual EAP counsellors are responsible for recognising the limitations of their competencies and making certain that all work is performed within those limitations' (EAPA 1994: 18). Most counsellors commented on the differing standards of EAP providers with regard to selection procedures, level of feedback, supervision, training, and the number of sessions allocated.

The providers also say that it is rare (31 per cent) that all counsellor premises have been inspected, and this is backed up by the counsellors, because 50 per cent of the counsellors surveyed said that they do use their own premises for counselling, but these have never been inspected by the EAP providers they work for. This is despite the fact that, in some cases, it is in their contract that the provider will visit their premises before they carry out any EAP work. Eighty per cent of providers say that they train counsellors once they have been recruited, but this varies in terms of content and depth, and one of the two areas which overall seems to cause the most dissatisfaction with providers, from the counsellors' point of view, is training. Forty-five per cent of counsellors rate the amount of training they have received from providers as only about 1 out of 6 (on a 6-point Likert-type scale), with a further 36 per cent rating it as approximately 3 out of 6. Neither of these scores can be seen as good.

Providers in general report that they do not give counsellors information about client companies as a matter of course, but do so only if this information is necessary. However, a few providers ask counsellors to visit client companies to meet key personnel, and others ask client companies to provide a 'brief for counsellors'. These few providers feel that it is essential for counsellors to know all about the company, and that this should be standard where workplace counselling programmes are concerned.

Counsellor qualifications and training

Our research suggests that the quality of counsellors is basically good, but that there is a minority of counsellors involved in workplace counselling and EAPs who are not properly qualified. The findings do not support the recommendations put forward by the EAPA Standards document with regard to the minimum levels of qualifications and experience that an EAP counsellor should have. The results revealed that 10–20 per cent of counsellors are being recruited without formal counselling qualifications and/or appropriate experience.

The EAPA Standards document states that: 'Each EAP shall retain counsellors qualified to perform their duties. The quality of provision depends on the professional qualification, training and experience of its counsellors' (EAPA 1994: 18). The Standards go on to explain that staff competence is critical to programme success and that depending upon the types of service provided, various levels of experience, professional training and supervision may be required. However, the work of an EAP counsellor is basically that of crisis intervention, assessment and short-term counselling. The EAPA also states that: 'The minimum professional Standards for EAP counsellors are: training and experience to a level required by the registration and accreditation systems of the different professional bodies e.g. BAC, BPS [British Psychological Society]' (EAPA 1994: 18).

However, of those counsellors who were surveyed, 11 per cent held no formal counselling qualifications, and a further 11 per cent held only a basic Certificate in Counselling. A number of these counsellors were actually working for between 10 and 40 hours per week, carrying out EAP counselling, despite having no formal counselling qualifications. In addition, a number of counsellors said that they were concerned about the levels of qualifications and experience of some counsellors. They were also concerned about the dangers for the client when faced with an inexperienced counsellor. Their view was that clients should be made aware that they can complain if they are not satisfied with the standard of counselling they receive.

Counsellors who lacked counselling qualifications were quite open about this, and tended to explain it by stating that they had experience of counselling within the workplace (for example, personnel or welfare). In our view they were simply using 'counselling skills'. Further, counsellors in general revealed that they are often faced with an individual who has been referred with a fairly minor issue which is not the underlying one, and only through training and experience can the counsellor effectively assess and deal with the client's problems. Thus, a 'counsellor' who has no formal counselling training is unlikely to be appropriate for EAP work. It is extremely disturbing that some providers are recruiting individuals on the strength of their workplace experience only.

Another standard relates to the fact that: 'EAP counsellors should have training and experience in work-related and organisational issues, and EAP practice' (EAPA 1994: 18). This has to be an essential component, along with recognised training in brief counselling and experience over a certain period of time. 'An EAP counsellor must be trained in short-term counselling and problem management' (EAPA 1994: 31). Whilst providers report that counsellors do need to be experienced in short-term counselling, they feel that experience of workplace counselling is not essential. However, 18 per cent of the counsellors surveyed said that they did not have any previous experience of short-term counselling prior to working for EAP providers. One of the areas which caused these counsellors the most dissatisfaction was resolving work-related problems.

We found that counsellors with only basic training and experience in workplace counselling were somewhat out of their depth, and had genuine difficulty defining what approach they used when carrying out their counselling. EAP providers who are recruiting unqualified counsellors are to a certain extent undervaluing the training and experience of 'good' counsellors who have undertaken extensive training, and they are also potentially endangering clients.

WORKING AS A WORKPLACE COUNSELLOR

Client-company information

Most providers, worryingly, do not give counsellors information about client companies as a matter of course. This only happens if it is felt necessary for some reason. However, only a minority of counsellors expressed any concern about the lack of information provided to them about client companies. These counsellors stated that they are not prepared to work with a provider unless thorough information about the client company is provided. They also tend to insist upon a contact name within the company, so that if faced with a potential work problem they know whom to speak to. However, the majority of counsellors felt that there is no need for any information about the client company, as they see their role as being to work with the individual, and any external information as possibly hindering this process. Counsellors said that they do not need such background information because they go by what the client tells them about the organisation. They tend to feel that if one has information about the organisation then one has a prejudice or perception about the client. It is the client's interpretation of the problem which is important, according to most counsellors.

Importantly, in-house workplace counsellors were believed to have a better appreciation of the organisation's procedures, policies and culture than EAP counsellors (Highley and Cooper 1994).

Supervision

The EAPA Standards clearly state that: 'Every EAP counsellor must receive regular professional supervision from a senior counsellor trained in supervision' (EAPA 1994: 20). Professional counsellor supervision serves to protect the clients' interests, to assure the quality of client services, and to respond to the EAP counsellors' skills and effectiveness. The EAP provider must ensure that each EAP counsellor receives professional supervision which is equivalent to that recommended by BAC.

Whether in-house or external, counsellors themselves need regular supervision. According to BAC (1988), supervision is necessary in order to enhance the therapeutic effectiveness of the relationship between counsellor and client; enable the counsellor to develop his or her professional identity through reflection on his or her work; clarify the relationship between counsellor, client, supervisor and organisation; and ensure that ethical standards are maintained. Clearly this is not always the case. Some providers expect the counsellor to arrange their own suitable supervision, and whilst this may be a reasonable request, providers should be checking that this is taking place.

Case management

Another key area addressed by the EAPA Standards is that of case management: 'Case management is distinct from counselling supervision, in that it focuses principally on the role the EAP plays in supporting individual clients. Case management is essential where clients are seen by freelance affiliates contracted by the EAP provider' (EAPA 1994: 21). After initial assessment, the EAP counsellor and his or her case manager need to consider whether the individual can benefit from short-term counselling, or whether referral is more appropriate.

This clearly does not happen in some cases, because counsellors say that they only have to report back to the provider after counselling has ended, not after initial assessment. However, there are some providers who clearly have very detailed and systematic case management procedures, where the counsellor is required to feed back to their case manager after every counselling session.

CONCLUSIONS

In the UK, counselling in the workplace has suddenly expanded over the last few years. However, these programmes have tended to be employee rather than organisation directed, with the focus being on changing the behaviours of the individuals and improving their lifestyles and/or stress-management skills (Cooper 1993). The interactionist approach (Cox 1978; Cooper *et al.* 1988) depicts stress as being the consequence of a 'lack of fit' between individuals and their environment, in this case the workplace. However, most workplace interventions (including workplace counselling programmes) emphasise improving the adaptability of the individuals to the workplace. This is often described as the 'band-aid' or inoculation approach, the implicit assumption being that the organisation will not change and will hence continue to be stressful, so the individuals must be helped to strengthen and develop their resistance to stress. There seems to be much less concern with adapting the organisation to 'fit' the individual. One reason for this may be that the professional 'interventionists' – the counsellors, etc. – are more comfortable with changing individuals than with changing organisations (Ivancevich *et al.* 1990).

There are thus a number of key areas which need addressing and have been discussed in this chapter. First, there is a need for workplace counselling programmes to become much more of a business tool and to help organisations to address sources of stress within the company. This obviously requires a different set of skills from that which counsellors traditionally may have. The second area which needs addressing, therefore, is that of training and qualifications for workplace counselling. Such counselling is characterised by short-term, focused counselling and needs a workplace perspective.

It is hoped that counsellors, together with organisations and providers, will play their part in helping to raise the standard of all workplace counselling programmes further to one which can be seen as a real help to organisations as well as individuals.

REFERENCES

Afield, W.E. (1989) Running amok: employers losing control of EAP costs. *Business Insurance 23* 27–30.

BAC (1988) Code of Ethics and Practice for the Supervision of Counsellors. Rugby: BAC.

Berridge, J. and Cooper, C.L. (1993) Stress and coping in US organisations: the role of the Employee Assistance Programme. *Work and Stress 7* (1) 89–102.

Cartwright, S. and Cooper, C.L. (1994) *No Hassle: Taking the Stress out of Work*. London: Century Books.

Cooper, C.L. (1986) Job distress: recent research and the emerging role of the clinical occupational psychologist. *Bulletin of the British Psychological Society 39* 325–31.

Cooper, C.L. (1993) Finding the solution – primary prevention (identifying the causes and preventing mental ill health in the workplace). In R. Jenkins and D. Warman (eds) *Promoting Mental Health Policies in the Workplace*. London: HMSO.

Cooper, C.L. and Cartwright, S. (1994) Stress-management interventions in the workplace: stress counselling and stress audits. *British Journal of Guidance and Counselling 22* (1) 65–73.

Cooper, C.L. and Payne, R. (1988) *Causes, Coping and Consequences of Stress at Work*. New York: Wiley.

Cooper, C.L. and Williams, S. (1994) *Creating Healthy Work Organisations*. New York: Wiley.

Cooper, C.L., Cooper, R.D. and Eaker, L.H. (1988) *Living with Stress*. London: Penguin.

Cox, T. (1978) *Stress*. London: Macmillan.

Cunningham, G. (1994) *Effective Employee Assistance Programs – A Guide for EAP Counselors and Managers*. London: Sage.

EAPA (1994) UK EAPA Standards of Practice and Professional Guidelines for Employee Assistance Programmes. London: EAPA.

Earnshaw, J. and Cooper, C.L. (1991) Workers' compensation in stress-related claims. *Work and Stress 5* (3) 253–7.

Earnshaw, J. and Cooper, C.L. (in press) Employee stress litigation: the UK experience. *Work and Stress*.

Galliano, S. (1994) Counsellor criteria for EAPs. *ACW Journal – Counselling at Work* Summer, 13–14.

Highley, J.C. and Cooper, C.L. (1994) An Assessment of Employee Assistance and Workplace Counselling Programmes in British Organisations. Report for the Health and Safety Executive. Unpublished.

Hopkins, V. (1994) Who is the client? Unpublished paper.

Ivancevich, J.M., Matteson, M.T. and Richards, E.P. (1990) Worksite stress interventions. *American Psychologist 45* 252–61.

Megranahan, M. (1994) Counselling in the workplace. In W. Dryden, D. Charles-Edwards and R. Woolfe (eds) *Handbook of Counselling in Britain*. London: Routledge.

Murphy, L.R. (1995) Managing job stress: an employee assistance/human resource management partnership. *Personnel Review 24* (1) 41–50.

Reddy, M. (1991) Counselling – its value to the business. In R. Jenkins and N. Coney (eds) *Prevention of Mental Ill Health at Work – A Conference*. London: HMSO.

Swanson, N.G., Sauter, S.L. and Murphy, L.R. (1991) Mental health counselling in industry. In C.L. Cooper and I.T. Robertson (eds) *International Review of Industrial and Organisation Psychology*. Chichester: Wiley.

Chapter 10

Working with abuse survivors
The recovered memory debate

Moira Walker

INTRODUCTION

Abuse of children and adults has a long history, recorded in both literature and historical documentation through the ages. Wherever there has been a power imbalance, whether because of age, class, culture, gender, religion or politics, abuse of some of the weaker by some of the stronger has occurred. Violence and abuse may be positively sanctioned or tacitly allowed by the ruling regime of the time: the treatment of slaves throughout history, and the torture and rape that quickly occur in any war, are examples. We only have to look at the current levels of child prostitution in some countries to see that the sexual abuse of children is not always hidden away; and, of course, it is often wealthy Western businessmen who are exploiting these children. Hitting children has a long and acceptable history. The degree of violence and damage caused may be a question of debate, but the act of hitting itself has in many cultures been deemed acceptable child care practice. Abuse of children needs to be understood in the context both of society overall and of the psychology of the individual – it does not exist in a vacuum. It is part of a world in which violence, torture and uncontrolled aggression are sadly commonplace.

What is more recent is the acknowledgement of abuse as a serious social and psychological problem that has long-term and often devastating consequences. Given its long history, it is interesting that only in recent years has it been given rather more consistent and serious notice by clinicians and others. Certainly, concern over the well-being of children is not new: the philanthropists of late nineteenth-century Britain fought to get children out of the factories and into schools. There was a growing awareness of children as having special needs and rights. The NSPCC was founded, and the work of Freud emphasised the existence of childhood in its own right as a significant stage in the development of the person.

Freud's early acknowledgement of the existence of sexual abuse and the on-going controversy over the degree to which he retracted from this position cannot be discussed in detail here, but it is clear that he was not entirely alone in recognising the possibility of the real abuse of children. Indeed, Helene Deutsch, the first leading woman member of Freud's Vienna Society, was herself brutally treated by her mother and sexually abused by her older brother Emil. However, this personal trauma was not to be reflected or utilised in her own work: it did not inform her theoretical or clinical understanding. She went on to write of the little girl's 'desire to be castrated by her father' (Deutsch 1973: 141) and saw this as an explanation of the frequent rape fantasies of little girls. She quotes as an example to support this view a patient reporting a dream in which she is forcibly penetrated by a male doctor with obstetric forceps while Deutsch watches, telling her she should not struggle. Her own experience of being sexually abused did not provide her with another possible explanation of these phenomena. It seems as if she successfully repressed or split off this aspect of her own childhood experiences. Melanie Klein, highly influential in the development of psychoanalysis in this country, emphasised the inner experience and fantasies of the child, and did not explore the possibility or likelihood of real traumas as being significant. However, the Hungarian psychoanalyst Ferenczi, in his paper 'Confusion of tongues between adults and the child', written in 1932 although unpublished until the 1950s, clearly recognised the existence of sexual abuse in childhood and the severity of consequences for the child and the adult (Ferenczi 1955).

In the wider world, greater attention was being given to the plight of children. The development of late nineteenth-century philanthropy was followed by two world wars which also gave rise to enormous concern over the health and well-being of children as well as adults. Following the Second World War, Britain saw the politics of state care and responsibility for its citizens put firmly in place through the burgeoning welfare state, tragically now eroded; and with this a key feature was legislative measures designed to protect children. Society has had the rights of children somewhere on the agenda for a long time, but sadly this has neither prevented their abuse nor meant that their needs in this respect have been consistently addressed.

THE DIFFICULTY OF BELIEVING

Although the last hundred years have seen a growing awareness and concern over the treatment of children, recognition of the abuse that many experience in their own homes or places of care belongs to the last few decades. Nowadays the term 'abuse' is often taken to mean sexual abuse, but it is crucial to recognise that neglect and physical and emotional abuse can be equally damaging. In fact, it was the physical abuse of children – 'baby-battering' – that first attracted public attention in the UK; recognition of sexual abuse came some time later. The shock that faced society in the light of deaths caused by physical abuse was matched in later years by the recognition that children were also being abused sexually, and that the real danger was not from strangers but from those very people children are told they can trust.

The reality of abuse is a harsh one, shattering many popular myths. Not surprisingly, one defence against facing such horrors is to question the truth of the victims' stories; not believing avoids facing terrible reality. Another is simply not to hear or notice. As Judith Herman (1992: 7) points out, it is 'very tempting to take the side of the perpetrator. All the perpetrator asks is that the bystander do nothing. He appeals to the universal desire to see, hear and speak no evil.' Herman has commented on what she describes as the 'episodic amnesia' that characterises the history of inquiry into psychological trauma, a concept that is particularly apposite for any discussion of the recognition of child abuse. She points out (1992: 7) that:

> This intermittent amnesia is not the result of the ordinary changes in fashion that affect any intellectual pursuit. The study of psychological trauma does not languish for lack of interest. Rather, the subject provokes such intense controversy that it periodically becomes anathema. The study of psychological trauma has repeatedly led into realms of the unthinkable and foundered on fundamental questions of belief.

Abuse continually poses a challenge to what we are able to think and believe of our fellow humans. The pathway to the recognition of abuse has been consistently rocky: a process of societal resistance and denial, interspersed with periods of recognition and acknowledgement. It is a painful process, and resistance is understandable as people are continually being asked to believe what they deeply need to consider unbelievable: that parents can intentionally and repeatedly harm their small children physically; that men sexually assault little girls; that they organise together, and plan elaborately in order to hurt, torture and sometimes kill children; that older children abuse younger; that women can be abusers; that boys as well as girls are victims; that the places children should be safest can be the most dangerous; that abuse can be ritualistic or satanic. The list is endless, and in writing it, and perhaps for those reading it, the question may be – what next?

However, for the counsellor, therapist or other helper involved in working with the survivors of childhood abuse, the escape routes of denial and disbelief are less possible, as they are for the survivor. They have had to face the uncomfortable fact that large numbers of children are abused physically, emotionally or sexually, and that it is not unusual for children to experience all three forms. Although increased media reporting has focused public attention on the realities of the horrors many children encounter, for many the shock is transitory, and the horror portrayed today is forgotten by the next, in a process similar to the 'episodic amnesia' referred to by Herman. If you work in this field this cannot be the case. Abuse is not a transitory phenomenon, quickly forgotten. It has to be worked with and responded to. Working with abuse survivors is experienced by practitioners as a huge responsibility. There is a recognition that abuse can cause long-term and serious difficulties, and that some survivors will have had previously unhelpful experiences with the caring professions. Practitioners wish to be helpful but recognise the complexities of so doing. They also know that they work in an area surrounded by quarrels and controversy, itself an anxiety in an already potentially anxiety-provoking situation. Recently, the recovered memory debate has intensified the level of concern and anxiety for many working in this field.

THE RECOVERED MEMORY DEBATE

A very recent controversy, and one that is still raging, relates to issues of the repression of memory, of subsequent recovered memories, and of whether false memories can be created in their clients by counsellors and therapists. This causes great concern to survivors of abuse, to those who work with them, and to families who believe themselves wrongly accused of abuse. Potentially it may also, dangerously, prove to be a perpetrator's escape route. As Herman (1992: 8) points out:

> In order to escape accountability for his crimes, the perpetrator does everything in his powers to promote forgetting. Secrecy and silence are the perpetrator's first line of defence. If secrecy fails, the perpetrator attacks the credibility of his victim.

Some readers may wonder why the chapter is entitled '*recovered* memories' rather than the often-heard '*false* memories'. This reflects my view that serious and proper debate is needed on this subject and that all too often a highly emotive presentation prevents this from happening. The term 'false memory' is in itself emotive, suggesting that the memories referred to *are* false. When, as often happens, the term 'syndrome' is also attached, a pseudo-scientific validity is implied, which is neither accurate nor helpful. To place the discussion in this chapter in context, some of the history relating to this area will be briefly discussed.

The term 'false memory' was originally coined in the USA after a woman, Jennifer Freyd, recovered memories of childhood sexual abuse whilst in therapy. Her parents disputed the accuracy of her memories and, in conjunction with Ralph Underwager, started the False Memory Syndrome Foundation (FMSF). They believe that otherwise healthy families are being destroyed by ill-trained therapists who may actively seek to discover in therapy, particularly by the use of hypnosis and 'truth drugs', repressed memories of abuse that are essentially false.

Dr Ralph Underwager was well known in the USA, before his involvement with this group, for acting as a defence witness in over two hundred cases of child sexual abuse. In a study carried out by Anna Salter, and supported by the New England Commissioners of Child Welfare Agencies, she studies the accuracy of his 'expert testimony' and examines the literature he refers to which apparently strongly supports his arguments (Salter 1989). She discovers many inaccuracies, including research referred to that is inaccurately quoted; minor findings quoted out of context which, if taken in context, would not have supported the position; extrapolating beyond the limitations of the data; and ignoring contrary evidence. Underwager (1993) has also published an interview in the Dutch magazine *Paidika, The Journal of Paedophilia* in which he is asked if choosing paedophilia is a responsible choice for the individual. He replies:

> Certainly it is responsible. What I have been struck by as I have come to know more about and understand people who choose paedophilia is that they let themselves be too much defined by other people . . . Paedophiles spend a lot of time and energy defending their choice. I don't think a paedophile needs to do that.
>
> (1993: 3)

Readers will decide for themselves how appropriate it is for any group seriously involved with questions relating to the abuse of children to have had as a founder member someone who holds these views. Following the publication of this article, Underwager resigned from the FMSF. The group has rapidly gained momentum in the USA, with people taking up strongly adversarial positions on both sides of the argument. It is worth noting for therapists and counsellors working in the UK that a very different legal system operates in the USA: there therapists are legally required to report any allegations of sexual abuse, and litigation related to such allegations is frequent.

The British False Memory Society was set up in 1993 by Roger Scotford, who had been accused by his two daughters of sexually abusing them in childhood. This group is also adamant that unscrupulous and undertrained practitioners are able to plant false recollections in their clients, and that the lives of innocent families are being ruined as a result of the consequent accusations made against them. Much of the attack from the False Memory Society is against therapists, who (they argue) strongly suggest to their clients that they have suffered childhood abuse. As in the USA, debate has become heated and has attracted enormous media attention. Some readers may feel that this is somewhat out of proportion compared to the smaller publicity given to the huge numbers of children known to be abused, and to the numbers of adults presenting for help with horribly clear recollections, often with no wish to accuse anybody, or to take legal action, but with a desperate need to try to heal their pain.

The concept of false memory has received considerable publicity. Given the discussion above regarding resistance to believing in abuse, it can be understood as an appealing idea for many: abuse is not so wide-spread, the argument could run, unscrupulous counsellors and therapists are the problem after all. This is not to dispute that many of those involved in the false memory group are undoubtedly convinced they have been falsely accused. And it is important to recognise that false allegations of abuse are possible and do occur. However, the concern of some working in the field is that it could be a convenient abusers' charter. It is well known that perpetrators of abuse are highly likely to deny their offences, and will continue in this denial after conviction (Kennedy and Grubin 1992).

The British Psychological Society (BPS) report on recovered memory (BPS 1995) reviewed the relevant literature, surveyed its members, and scrutinised the records of the British False Memory Society. The report notes that most public attention is concerned with memories recovered in therapy, but in fact most clinicians working in this field are counselling survivors who come with memories of abuse, and for many the abuse has been verified by another person. The BPS survey gives some indications of actual occurrence. Of those questioned, 90 per cent had seen clients in the last year who had reported child sexual abuse. A third of those questioned said clients had recovered memories before therapy, and about 20 per cent had seen at least one client who had in the previous year recovered a memory of abuse. What is not clear from this figure is whether or not this 20 per cent presented with some existing memories of abuse.

An interesting result from this survey is that a third also reported clients recovering a memory of a traumatic experience other than abuse. In the BPS analysis of the ninety-seven cases recorded by the British False Memory Society, only half gave enough information to allow crude statistics to be extracted. In half of these there was explicit mention of memory recovery from total amnesia – that is, a quarter of the total.

The BPS survey is a sensible document and avoids the over-dramatic and sensationalising approach of much that has been more popularly written. As a research document it has limitations, in that it is a relatively small-scale study of only one professional group, but it provides a useful and thoughtful framework for further and more detailed investigations and discussion. Its guidelines for practitioners are sound and careful. However, it is typical of the nature of the debate on recovered memory that a very rapid response and challenge came from the journal *The Therapist*. In the editorial comment, which accompanies an article by Weiskrantz (1995) challenging the content and conclusion of the BPS report, the headline is 'The British Psychological Society needs its head examined'. Sadly, these inflammatory and insulting words are more fitting to the tabloid press than a serious journal. In his article Weiskrantz comments with regard to the BPS report that 'I fear that some of its statements, quite unnecessarily, will further polarize and add heat to the debate, which many of us have tried to avoid' (1995: 5). If this concern is genuine, it is indeed inappropriate that his article is placed next to the statement quoted above.

The debate continues to rage in the United States and is reflected in the recent lengthy exchanges in the *New York Review*. In his two-part article 'The revenge of the repressed', Frederick Crews (1994) offers a detailed critique of some aspects of recovered memory. Whilst he offers some valid criticisms, he falls into the same trap that he accuses others of: he strays away from actual empirical evidence and distorts theoretical concepts in an attempt to prove his point. At times the language of his articles is intemperate, derogatory and emotive:

> Until the recovered memory movement got properly launched in the later 1980s most Satanism charges were brought against child care workers who were thought to have abused their little clients for the devil's sake. In such prosecutions, which continue today, a vengeful or mentally unhinged adult typically launches the accusations, which are immediately believed by police and social workers. These authorities then disconcert the toddlers with rectal and vaginal prodding with invitations to act out naughtiness on anatomically correct dolls with bloated genitals and, of course, leading questions that persist until the child reverses an initial denial that anything happened.

It is interesting to note that although the concept of repression of memory that Crews challenges has been the subject of on-going theoretical and clinical discussion in other contexts, it has not always evoked this degree of controversy and vitriolic feeling. However, when it becomes attached to the issue of recovered memories of abuse, hackles rise, insults abound, and reasoned debate rapidly descends into something more primitive. It does raise the question of what this is about. Reading some of the debates in detail suggests that very primitive parts of the self are not only being encountered but somehow rudely assaulted in a way that cannot quite be contained.

Crews continues in praise of the False Memory group: 'Above all, steady progress has been forged over the past two and a half years by the False Memory Syndrome Foundation most of whose members are themselves slandered relatives of survivors.' In a letter of reply, Theresa Reid (1995), Executive Director, American Professional Society on the Abuse of Children, remarks that: 'When Crews refers to the members of FMSF as "slandered relatives of survivors" he claims an access to wisdom that Solomon himself would envy.' She continues by commenting that:

'Crew's vitriol against professionals is hard to understand, and his depiction of zealous incompetence as the rule is indefensible.' At this point, the way this debate will resolve is hard to predict, but it seems set to stay with us for some time.

CAN MEMORIES BE REPRESSED AND RECOVERED?

As has been noted, a central question in this debate surrounds the concept of the possibility of the repression of memory. This is in itself a major field, and the following can only be a brief summary of some of the relevant findings. We know that in multiple personality, different personalities are amnesic to each other's experiences. A woman with multiple personality explains this:

> I have six children and I think I remember their childhood but, even so, when they are together and talking there is so much I don't remember. I have lost an awful lot of time. I feel I've got to this age in my life and I've lost half of it. As far as I'm concerned everyone seems to know more about me than I do, because when the other personalities come through it's the therapist they're talking to. I know nothing about it. The therapist has to tell me what's been said. I've no idea. It's very odd and embarrassing.
>
> (Walker 1992: 124)

Sargant (1967) reported that during World War II there were many cases of what he called acute hysterical losses of memory. Research by Herman and Schatzow (1987) found that 64 per cent of women with self-reported histories of sexual abuse, most of whom had corroboration from other sources, had incomplete or absent memories of their abuse at some time in their past. The more violent the abuse the greater the degree of memory impairment. The authors comment that:

> Marked memory deficits were usually associated with abuse that began early in childhood, often in the preschool years, and ended before adolescence. In addition, a relationship was observed between frankly violent or sadistic abuse and the resort to massive repression as a defense.
>
> (1987: 5)

A significant study has been carried out by Linda Meyer Williams (1992) into women's memories of childhood sexual abuse. Its particular significance is that it studied 129 women with previously documented histories of sexual victimisation in childhood. In other words, abuse had been proved to have taken place. In detailed interviews about their abuse histories, a large proportion of the women did not recall the abuse which had been reported seventeen years earlier. Women who were younger at the time of the abuse and those molested by someone they knew were more likely to have no recall of the abuse. In one case a woman told the interviewer that she was never sexually abused as a child, and she repeatedly and calmly continued to deny any such experiences throughout the detailed questioning. In fact her uncle had sexually abused her when she had been 4, as well as her cousin aged 9, and her friend also aged 4. In addition to the research, survivor accounts give further weight to the argument for amnesia in respect of childhood abuse. An example of complete repression of a traumatic and painful childhood is found in Matthews (1986).

The question arises: 'If memories can be repressed, what is it that allows them to surface?' Clinical experience suggests many factors may be at work here: one is that the individual's tolerance level increases if his or her external world becomes safer and more secure. A male survivor of sexual abuse I interviewed explained this:

> I had genuine friends, something I hadn't had before and I had a steady partner. I was being allowed to be me and I was being supported. So all this support and I think somewhere inside myself I'd recognised that the time was right to let these memories resurface. It was safe enough to feel unsafe. I remember sort of crawling round on my hands and knees for three days not knowing when the next one was going to hit me. It was like there were more and more of these images coming at me. There was everything waiting in my head. It was like an explosion. Before it had all been completely and utterly blocked. I had assumed it was like that for everyone, that memories were second hand, given you by someone else saying do you remember such and such and so on.

It should also be noted that these memories surfaced after the abuser had died. Contrary to one of the arguments of the false memory groups, who see recovered memory as a weapon against the family, this pattern of recall after the abuser has died and cannot therefore be directly accused or prosecuted is not unusual. It has been noted that repeated or extended severe trauma or abuse is more likely to lead to extreme amnesia than single episodes. This is certainly so in the example above: the abuse had been systematic, extensive and exceedingly brutal. Violence and sexual abuse towards others had also been witnessed. Other frequently cited triggers for remembering are the birth of a child; a child reaching the age where the abuse began; other major life events; or further traumas or losses. As with the example above, clinical experience suggests that abuse survivors can experience periods when trauma-related memories intrude into consciousness and cannot be blocked or stopped.

CLINICAL IMPLICATIONS

Although the concept of repression of experiences and the consequent remembering of events in later life may be controversial, the existence of traumatic forgetting has been well documented. In many instances this can be confirmed by other family members, by other victims and occasionally by the perpetrator. Little convincing research has yet taken place into whether therapists or others can implant 'false' memories, but it is known that those who have suffered childhood abuse may be more suggestible. It would seem sensible to assume that as a consequence of this the possibility of false memories being induced can exist, and that counsellors and therapists need to exercise care in particular aspects of their practice – this will be discussed below.

However, a balanced view must be maintained. In the same way as false allegations of abuse can be made, false memories may be a possibility. Research on false allegations made by children suggests these are a small number (Goodwin *et al.* 1978; Jones and McGraw 1987), and false memory can most usefully be regarded similarly. That is, it is a possibility that must be taken seriously but must not be allowed to overwhelm and cloud the real issue: that of the abuse of children in larger numbers than we are ever likely to know, and the severity of the consequences for the adult population. There is a danger of the 'false' memory issue becoming a therapeutic red herring, something that, once again in the history of abuse, acts as a block and defence to facing its appalling extent and effects. And it must always be remembered that perpetrators and denial go hand in hand. Undoubtedly the false memory group will include some genuinely distressed and falsely accused families. However, inevitably they will also act as a magnet for perpetrators searching for another psychological line of defence against acknowledging to themselves or their victims their responsibility for their violence.

As there is a danger of the real issue being subsumed and side-tracked into this debate, so there is a danger of counsellors becoming so intimidated that they will back off from work with abuse survivors. Survivors are often so alone and alienated from the world around them that to revert to one traditional approach that argues that malevolent persecutors are an internal fantasy rather than an external reality would be to do them a grave injustice, when they have already suffered from so many. As Bettelheim (1980:113) says: 'It is so unjust, so unreasonable, that of all people the survivor should have to struggle, all by himself, with some of the greatest psychological difficulties imaginable.' Patrick Casement is referring to satanic abuse when he says: 'Not to believe someone who has actually been a victim of such abuse leaves that person still alone in the torment of their own experiences' (1994: 23). But the same is true of all who bring stories of their abuse: if they are disbelieved, their abuse and their pain are once again reinforced and intensified.

To work effectively with abuse survivors, counsellors do need to be resilient and have sufficient confidence in their therapeutic skills. As I have written elsewhere:

In order for counsellors and therapists to work effectively with abuse
survivors they need to be able to encounter, work with and contain
material that can be of a deeply disturbing nature. They have to be able
to make contact at a deep level whilst remaining intact themselves.

(Walker 1992: 197)

There is a danger that this ability to work with disturbing material will be
undermined by counsellors' fear of having allegations of implanting false
memories made against them. This would be counter-productive for both
the counsellor and the client, and raises the question of what counsellors
and therapists need to do, or not do, to ensure they work professionally,
ethically and responsibly with abuse survivors.

First, it should never be assumed that those presenting with issues other
than abuse have been abused just because the clinical material may
suggest this as one possibility. An example would be clients who present
with eating disorders. Although research has shown (Oppenheimer 1985)
that two-thirds of women with bulimia had been sexually abused before
the age of 15, and others have presented evidence linking anorexia with a
history of childhood abuse, nevertheless abuse cannot be diagnosed or
assumed on the basis of presenting symptoms such as an eating disorder. It
may provide the counsellor with a tentative hypothesis that can be held in
mind and checked against other evidence as it emerges: it should not be
leapt at as an explanation or shared with the client. Similarly, lack of
recall of childhood events may suggest abuse, but is not the only explanation.

Second, counsellors nowadays are quite rightly very aware of the
numbers of clients presenting as survivors of childhood abuse, and as
more is written and researched they have more knowledge of how this
might be manifested. But as with all knowledge it must be used with care
and with the recognition that knowledge is never absolute. There is a twin
risk: one is that counsellors deny the level of abuse and its effects, particularly when abuse is severe and horrifying. The other is that the counsellor,
in an anxiety to create certainty in the midst of chaos and confusion, may
over-emphasise or wrongly interpret certain aspects of the client's experience in order to provide a definite explanation that both may want and
need.

A clinical example illustrates this. A young woman in great distress
went to a counsellor. She was depressed, agitated and desperate to find a
cause for her unhappiness. She felt that if only there was a reason to attach
to this to she would somehow feel better. In fact her story as it was later
told to me was such that her symptoms were altogether understandable in
terms of a chaotic and uncontained family, which was at times violent,
where boundaries were very blurred and secrets abounded. It was unfortu-
nate, to say the least, that this first counsellor, in a first session, told this

client that her feelings indicated a strong possibility of sexual abuse. She also quite correctly told the client she was not experienced enough to work with her, but damage was undoubtedly done by this suggestion of sexual abuse. This client's agitated anxiety made her very suggestible, and the experienced counsellor who took over working with her had to struggle to contain her. In the work with her, nothing transpired to suggest sexual abuse, and it seemed as if the client's readiness to accept this first explanation was in part a resistance to looking at what actually had happened in her family, and to facing how devastating it had been. She also had a desire to find a definite and specific reason for her acute unhappiness.

Although in this instance there was good reason for the client to feel as she did in terms of her already remembered history, in other instances this may not be the case. Sometimes counsellors and therapists need to help their clients to find a way of coming to terms with the reality that there are parts of their life that may never be clear, never tidied away, and never fully understood. For instance, clients who have been abused at a very young age may always have patchy, incomplete and vague memories. And in some families patterns of interaction are deeply dysfunctional and disturbing. They create great unhappiness in a way that cannot be specifically located. It is the whole process of being in that family that has been disturbing, rather than specific traumas. To help clients cope with this, counsellors themselves have to be able to tolerate and work with uncertainty, ambiguity and chaos. Although the example quoted above may be a rare one, the possibility and reality of this type of clumsy and unprofessional practice has to be recognised. Supervisors should take great care to challenge and not collude with these instances when they occur.

Third, counsellors need to recognise the strength of language – the word 'abuse' is a powerful one with very particular connotations currently. It should not be used unless the client uses it. The pace of the work should always be set by the client; if he or she is using phrases such as 'things weren't easy when I was little', or 'bad things happened to me', this is also the level at which the counsellor should respond. To reframe these types of comment in terms of the client having had abusive experiences before the client recognises them as such – if he or she ever does – is invasive and inappropriate; but it does happen. The client *can* be asked, for example, whether they want to tell the counsellor a little more about things not having been easy, but this should also be accompanied by reassurance that he or she can take his or her own time in whatever he or she wants to talk about. If a client has been abused, this may take time and courage to tell, and can only occur in the context of a trusting relationship. Many abuse survivors disclose hesitantly and gradually, otherwise it can be too much to bear.

Fourth, although most abused clients come with some memories and recall more as they begin to deal with the abuse, and some come because they have recently recovered memories, there will be those who do recover memories in counselling. This can be deeply shocking for the client and for the counsellor, and it is important to respond calmly. There are particular memories that act like a log-jam – once dealt with and the fear removed, the client may be free to recall others. In this way a retrieved memory can start a whole process of remembering. This is neither comfortable nor easy: there can be great resistance, as enormous pain is likely to be encountered and threatening instructions in the past not to tell have often been well internalised.

Fifth, if the client is wanting to act on these memories by taking legal action or by confronting the perpetrators, counsellors can encourage the client to take his or her time with these major decisions. If it is sufficiently acknowledged that recovering traumatic memories is a disturbing experience, clients are often able to recognise for themselves that rapid responses may not be advisable, and may be self-destructive and self-defeating. In the same way as counsellors normally help someone to think through the consequences of confronting abusers, this needs to be especially carefully undertaken when memories are recovered. If a client is seriously considering legal action, it is essential that he or she consults lawyers. Counsellors should not advise on this; it breaks the boundaries of the work and is beyond their expertise.

Finally, the use of hypnosis to aid the recovery of memories is a fraught and emotive debate. I have worked with a client who recovered memories under hypnosis when the training of the hypnotist had been limited to a correspondence course and two weekend workshops. She had no idea how to work with the material or the regressive state that emerged. There is a reality that has to be acknowledged that too many people practise as counsellors with too little experience. In fact in this case the recovered memories were not entirely accurate; some detail was distorted, but in essence they were true and were verified by an older family member. On the other end of the scale, some very experienced clinicians regard hypnosis as a means of reintegrating dissociated parts of the self, and it is recognised that those with dissociative difficulties are very open to hypnosis. There is a huge difference between experienced and highly trained clinicians employing this as one tool amongst many, and those who are inexperienced dabbling with what is a powerful technique. The rule of thumb should be that unless a counsellor is highly trained both as a hypnotherapist *and* in working in abuse survival, he or she should not use hypnosis. My own perspective is that I work with recovered memories if they emerge, and I work with regression similarly, but I do not use techniques actively aimed at precipitating these. It is worth repeating that the client must set the pace.

CONCLUSIONS

My own clinical experience in this field suggests that the proportion of clients being seen who recover memories, having started from a base of no memories, is small. However, gaps in memory of varying degrees of severity are commonly reported amongst those who have suffered abuse in childhood, and those who have experienced other forms of trauma. It should be noted, therefore, that the amount of publicity given to memories totally recovered in psychological treatments may not bear much relationship to the actual incidence of this occurrence. There is clearly a real concern that there is at least a possibility that false memories can be induced in the therapeutic setting, particularly when certain techniques are employed, and this must be taken seriously. The volatility of some of those who are most actively involved in forwarding this notion is not helpful, and counsellors need to address the issue without becoming caught up in highly emotional arguments. As in all their client work, counsellors should not be suggestive; they should not jump to rapid conclusions; and, perhaps most importantly, they should be able to tolerate and work with uncertainty. It is essential that this controversy is not allowed to distract us from our work with survivors of childhood abuse, or undermine us in so doing. The history of the denial of abuse is worrying in its power and its tenacity. This debate must not validate and encourage the deepening of denial.

REFERENCES

Bettelheim, B. (1980) Trauma and reintegration. In *Surviving and Other Essays*. London: Vintage Books.

BPS (1995) *Report on Recovered Memory*. Leicester: BPS.

Casement, P. (1994) The wish not to know. In V. Sinason (ed.) *Treating Survivors of Satanic Abuse*. London: Routledge.

Crews, F. (1994) The revenge of the repressed. *New York Review* 17 November and 1 December.

Deutsch, H. (1973) *Confrontations with Myself*. New York: Norton.

Ferenczi, S. (1955) Confusion of tongues between adults and the child. In *Final Contributions to the Problems and Methods of Psychoanalysis*. London: Hogarth Press.

Goodwin, J., Shad, D. and Rada, R. (1978) Incest hoax: false accusations, false denials. *Bulletin of the American Academy of Psychiatry and Law* 6 269–76.

Herman, J.L. (1992) *Trauma and Recovery*. New York: Basic Books.

Herman, J.L. and Schatzow, E. (1987) Recovery and verification of memories of childhood sexual abuse. *Psychoanalytic Psychology* 4 1–14.

Jones, D. and McGraw, J. (1987) Reliable and fictitious accounts of sexual abuse to children. *Journal of Interpersonal Violence* 2 27–45.

Kennedy, H. and Grubin, D. (1992) Patterns of denial in sex offenders. *Psychological Medicine* 22 191–6.

Matthews, C. (1986) *No Longer a Victim*. Canberra: Acorn Press.

Oppenheimer, R. (1985) Adverse sexual experiences in childhood and clinical eating disorders: a preliminary description. *Journal of Psychiatric Research 19* 357–61.

Reid, T. (1995) Victims of memory: an exchange. *New York Review* 12 January.

Salter, A. (1989) Accuracy of Expert Testimony in Child Sexual Abuse Cases: A Case Study of Ralph Underwager and Holida Wakefield. New England: Commissioners of Child Welfare Agencies.

Sargant, W. (1967) *The Unquiet Mind*. London: Heinemann.

Underwager, R. (1993) Interview: Holida Wakefield and Ralph Underwager. *Paidika, The Journal of Paedophilia 3* 1.

Walker, M. (1992) *Surviving Secrets: The Experience of Abuse for the Child, the Adult and the Helper*. Buckingham: Open University Press.

Weiskrantz, L. (1995) Comments on the report of the working party of the British Psychological Society on 'recovered memories'. *Therapist 2* 4.

Williams, L.M. (1992) Adult memories of childhood abuse: preliminary findings from a longitudinal study. *APSAC Advisor*.

Chapter 11

Working with the depressed person

Paul Gilbert

INTRODUCTION

Depression is well known to be a very common problem. It is estimated that there may be in excess of a hundred million people suffering from it in the world today. Some studies suggest lifetime rates for depression (including bipolar depression, major depression and dysthymia) are about 8.2 per cent, but there are variations from country to country and from place to place within countries (Jenkins *et al.* 1991; Weissman and Klerman 1994). Urbanisation and industrialisation seem to increase risk. For major depression women are more at risk, in the order of 3:1. More worrying still is the evidence that rates of depression, especially in younger cohorts, have been increasing steadily since the turn of the century (Fombonne 1994; Weissman and Klerman 1994). Not only can depression occur in a relatively pure form but it is also the most common difficulty accompanying other disorders such as anorexia, social anxiety, schizophrenia and alcoholism.

In the last thirty years there has been an enormous expansion in both the psychological theories of depression and types of therapy. The main thrust of these have been:

- cognitive (Abramson *et al.* 1989; Beck 1967; Beck *et al.* 1979; Young *et al.* 1993; Williams 1992);
- behavioural (Ferster 1973; Lewinsohn 1974; Rehm 1988, 1989);
- interpersonal (Klerman *et al.* 1984; Klerman and Weissman 1994);
- interpersonal and family therapy (Gotlib and Colby 1987; Beach *et al.* 1990);
- self-psychology (Deitz 1988, 1989; Kohut 1977);
- Gestalt and emotion-focused therapy (Greenberg and Safran 1987; Greenberg *et al.* 1990);
- attachment theory (Bowlby 1980; Guidano and Liotti 1983; Gut 1989; Liotti 1988, 1993);
- interpersonal cognitive therapy (Gilbert 1992b; Safran and Segal 1990);

- more recently, social ranking theory (Gilbert 1992a; Price *et al.* 1994; Sloman *et al.* 1994).

These approaches have been reviewed in detail elsewhere (Gilbert 1992a).

In general psychotherapy practice there are increasing efforts to integrate different approaches and models of working (Newman and Goldfried 1992). As Karasu (1990) points out, in treating depression, one often needs a mixture of approaches that speak to different aspects of the depressive experience; one cannot be a one-club golfer. Thus, one may need to work with cognitions and evaluations, emotions and feelings, specific behaviours, interpersonal style and also past trauma. In this chapter various of the above approaches are touched on; including the role of past (early) relationships, core-self and other emotional schemas, dysfunctional beliefs, social behaviour and critical events (see Gilbert 1992a for a more comprehensive review). Nowadays my own approach tends to be integrationist but within a constructivist (Mahoney 1990) and interpersonal framework. After discussing how one might conceptualise a case I shall outline one particular case example. For those who would like a more detailed, step-by-step list of specific approaches the writers noted above can be consulted.

CONCEPTUALISATION OF CASES

Although not all therapeutic approaches work with the life history of the patient, there is increasing recognition that the person's past history is important, at least for case conceptualisation. The cognitive interpersonal approach, which will be the main focus of this chapter, suggests that case conceptualisation requires the exploration of (at least) five different domains: past relational patterns, core-self and other emotional schemas, dysfunctional attitudes and rules for living, social roles, and critical events.

Past relational patterns

These are elicited from exploration of the patients' past and early relationships. Key themes are: the degree of love and care (emotional warmth) they experienced in early life; the degree of neglect and abuse; and the types and qualities of core conflicts. One can explore these by asking about the significant relationships they had in the past; for example, 'What was your relationship like with mother, father, siblings and peers?' The patients' interpretation of the early relational style is important. For example, one patient, whose siblings were much older, thought that he had been a mistake and his parents resented him. Another thought that the harsh discipline she received was because she was a 'difficult' child. It is also worth exploring how conflicts ended and how people reconciled their differences (such as the tendency for parents to sulk, withdraw love, create bad atmospheres, generate strong guilt and shame feelings, demand the child submit and apologise, etc.). From reports of these early experiences the therapist can build up a view of the typical self–other schema, life rules and habitual styles of social relating. Sometimes this can be done fairly quickly, at others it can be more complex, especially in abuse cases. There is of course concern about how accurate these memories may be, but research suggests that while distortion may occur it is less than is often suggested (Brewin *et al.* 1993). Layden *et al.* (1993) have given some very helpful suggestions for both exploring early life history and working with this material, especially in imagery.

Core-self and other emotional schemas

Emerging from early relating patterns, people develop a number of 'working models' (Bowlby 1980) or schemas (Gilbert 1992b; Young *et al.* 1993) about themselves and others. In cognitive interpersonal therapy it is the *emotional core* of these schemas that it is crucial to understand. These arise from previous, direct emotional experiences and are key to the sense of one's core identity. When they are activated they give rise to direct emotional experiences within the self (Guidano and Liotti 1983) and may not be easily coded into language. This does not mean that core emotional schemas arise only before language, as some suggest (such as Young 1994); it can also be their direct emotional quality (as in trauma and shame) which is important.

Research has shown that the way the caregiver and infant interact has a significant effect on the maturation of the infant's nervous system, emotions and sense of self (see Schore 1994 for a major overview). When the non-verbal communication of parent and child is attuned (baby smiles, mother smiles; baby gestures, mother gestures) the infant experiences positive emotions. Misattuned behaviours (for example, baby smiles but mother presents a blank face) produce negative emotions. Various reciprocal interactions between child and parent, as the child seeks recognition for his or her talent, abilities, lovability and general sense of goodness, are crucial for developing positive core-self emotional schema. Indeed, many core emotional experiences of the self arise out of what is called social referencing (Schore 1994).

To clarify this aspect, consider the following scenario. Jane, a 3-year-old, sits quietly doing some drawings. Then suddenly she jumps up, rushes to Mum and proudly holds up the drawing. Mum responds by kneeling down and saying, 'Wow – that's wonderful. Did you do that?' (Jane nods proudly). 'What a clever girl', says Mum. Now in this encounter Jane not only experiences her mother as proud of her, she also has emotions *in herself, about herself* – she feels good about herself. Psychoanalytic and self-psychologists would call that a good self-object experience (Kohut 1977). I have argued that these are conditioned emotional experiences and responses and fit well with classical conditioning theory (Gilbert 1992a). In any event Jane experiences positive mirroring, or what we could call a positive core-self emotional experience. But suppose that when Jane goes to Mum with her drawing Mum responds with, 'Oh God not another of those drawings. Look I'm busy right now. Can't you go off and play?' Clearly, the way Jane will experience her mother, the interaction between them, and the *feelings in herself, about herself*, will be quite different. In this case Jane is unlikely to have good feelings in herself and may have a sense of disappointment, a deflation of (the hoped for) positive affect, and possibly shame (Nathanson 1992). Her head goes down and she slinks away. She will also experience the mother (the significant other) as unavailable and uninterested. Thus, the lack of recognition and dismissal of the self, when the self tries to display something attractive to others, can produce negative and shamed core-self and other emotional experiences that over time will form the nucleus of a core-self emotional schema.

As discussed elsewhere (Gilbert 1992a, 1992b) there are various themes of core-self emotional experiences, such as lovability, trust in self and others, a sense of goodness or badness, a sense of personal efficacy or personal inferiority. Recently, Young *et al.* (1993) and Young (1994) have outlined a number of what they call Early Maladaptive Schemas. These are grouped into six domains: instability and disconnection, impaired autonomy, undesirability, restricted self-expression, restricted gratification, and impaired limits. In Young's approach there is less stress on the emotional schemas of others (such as others as unavailable, uninterested, hostile, powerful). Whether or not this type of listing is borne out by research remains to be seen. Others have suggested schemas derived from Eriksonian developmental theory (for example, Layden *et al.* 1993). These kinds of listing provide a useful hybrid of many different ideas and approaches. Patient and therapist can work together to identify and challenge specific schemas (for example, for unattractiveness). However, some of these schemas may be secondary to more primary core-self emotional experiences that cluster around shame (Kaufman 1989; Gilbert 1992a, 1992b; Lewis 1992; Nathanson 1992). Moreover, there are other experiences that are key to depression, such as envy, idealisation, injustice and entrapment, which are activated in relationships (Gilbert 1995).

Dysfunctional attitudes and rules for living

At times cognitive therapists can use the idea of self-schema and belief interchangeably. However, in the cognitive interpersonal approach, dysfunctional attitudes and rules for living need not, in themselves, be coded in affective structures but are adaptations from core-self emotional experiences. For example, if someone has a core-self emotional experience that they are unlovable then this might lead them to form rules for living and attitudes of, 'I can only form a close relationship if I make sure I am what the other person wants me to be.'

Rules for living and attitudes can be spoken of as if one is speaking of a personal philosophy (such as, 'I believe people should help each other', 'One is a second-rate person if one makes mistakes'). Core-self emotional experiences, however, are nearly always voiced in how the self feels inside ('I feel I am bad, a loser, a victim, empty, disconnected, unlovable'). Sometimes these feelings are difficult to put into words and become 'I just feel upset or bad.' Generally, working with core-self emotional experiences requires more empathy from the therapist, especially if there is a strong sense of shame and the educative, rational aspects are engaged in slowly and gently.

Social roles

Those researching attachment theory suggest that there are a number of styles for close relating:

- secure attachment, where the person feels relatively comfortable with closeness and distance;
- anxious attachment, where the person is anxious about abandonment and aloneness;
- avoidant, where the person is uncomfortable with closeness and maintains a certain distance in intimate relationships;
- ambivalent, where the person oscillates between needing closeness and then wanting distance.

These styles are also noted in the therapeutic relationship (Holmes 1993; Liotti 1988, 1993).

The interpersonal cognitive approach focuses on typical interpersonal style and social patterns of behaviour. We are interested in how people seek out (or avoid) certain types of relationship and how they act in relationships. A person who (for example) always felt inferior to a sibling might become highly competitive and avoidant in his or her relational style. In social situations he or she has to act in such a way as to avoid being placed in inferior positions, has to win, or has to prove his or her self-worth continually via achievement. Such people relate to others in a narcissistic way, can be exploitative and only interested in others in so far as the other will continually admire them. These social styles of relating can cause difficulties (Gilbert 1992a, 1992b; Horowitz and Vitkus 1986). For example, Sandra was very shame prone. In conflict situations with lovers she would experience overwhelming feelings of shame, anger and anxiety. Her social response was to withdraw quickly, sulk or end the relationship. She would then look back, feel more depressed and blame herself for being alone. This experience of shame needed to be brought into the therapy by helping her relive the details of what actually happened in such situations and connect this with earlier experiences from childhood.

Another aspect to social roles is that some of the roles we play can be seen (and named) as *parts of the self*. For example, a therapist and patient might identify the 'internal critical bully', 'the rescuing hero', 'the martyr' or 'the lost child' (Rowan 1990). It is then possible to set up a dialogue with these part selves (say) by using the two-chair approach. The patient can play the role of, for example, the lost child or bully in one chair and then explore the feelings and possible responses in another chair.

In many cases of depression one finds that there are key interpersonal styles that repeat. Key relationships might activate these social roles of (say) 'rescuing hero' or the 'lost child'. And there can be internal conflicts in the roles we try to enact. Moreover, these styles can be noted in how the patient relates to the therapist. Some patients will be highly submissive and accommodating, others competitive and avoidant.

Once patients are depressed, and sometimes before, their interpersonal style is very unrewarding to others, and this is one reason they can be rejected (Segrin and Abramson 1994). However, it is also the case that some depressed people can come from abusive and neglectful families and their negative behaviour arises from such abuse and secondarily from the depression. In either case social skills training (for example, assertive training), or just exploring the impact their behaviour might have on others, can be helpful. But one needs to be cautious here, because sometimes being more assertive in the context of an abusive relationship can lead to more abuse.

Critical events

Beck (1967) pointed out that many depressogenic schemas are latent when a person is not depressed but can be triggered by life events. Indeed, it is often some crisis in social relationships that brings people into therapy. The life event research of Brown and his colleagues (Brown *et al.* 1986, 1987, 1988; Brown and Harris 1978) has made the important distinction between vulnerability factors and life events. It is only events that have long-term consequences that trigger depression (such as finding that one's spouse is having an affair or is about to leave). Vulnerability factors include: low self-esteem, reduced opportunities for confiding relationships, being in a shaming and neglectful relationship, and being trapped in the home (Brown *et al.* 1995).

The critical events are normally the focus of the first stages of the therapy: why did the patient come to therapy and what are the current problems in the here and now? But in the long term one also wishes to work with vulnerability factors; those factors that may be chronic and present even before the onset of the first depression (such as core-self emotional schemas and rules for living).

These life events often trigger a style of thinking and automatic thoughts that maintain the depression; for example, negative views of the world ('life is full of insurmountable obstacles'), the self ('it's all my fault', 'I can't succeed') and the future ('things will never improve'; Beck *et al.* 1979). These negative thoughts, expectations and attributions, according to Beck, produce many of the symptoms of depression. Beck *et al.* (1979) also argue that as depression takes hold people become more global and negative in their styles of evaluation. These styles include, for example, personalisation (blaming the self), overgeneralisation and black-and-white thinking. Thus, the more negatively the patients see the self, the future and the world, the more depressed they feel and they less they do – and the more depressed they become, the more negative their thinking. Hence, they spiral downwards. Therapy is aimed to break into this spiral by disputing negative thoughts and encouraging new behaviours

ENGAGING IN THERAPY

Having reviewed some of the main areas for conceptualisation of a case, we can now briefly explore a case example. As noted above, there are many models of therapy, but in general most have some structure around bonds, tasks and goals. The bonds reflect the therapeutic relationship that the patient and therapist develop. In interpersonal cognitive therapy great stress is placed on the role of empathic attunement, getting in touch with core-self emotional experiences, and helping the patient feel understood. Moreover, as will be indicated in the case below, the emotional sharing and quality of the relationship, especially at critical moments in the session, can be a major factor in the patient being able to use (internalise) the therapy. This can be crucial in situations of shame, perhaps one of the most common depressogenic difficulties (Kaufman 1989). The tasks are the things that will be the focus of the therapy, such as illuminating styles of thinking, challenging, problem solving, facing shame. The goals are the targets or aims of the therapy.

Perhaps the best way to illustrate the interpersonal cognitive model in practice, with the various domains noted above, is to work through a case example. The details given below have been changed to avoid recognition.

The case of John

John came from a fairly wealthy family. When he was 20 his father died and he gave up college to look after the family business for his mother. Although no longer directly involved, she had clear ideas about how things should be run, and there were frequent clashes and conflicts. John had never felt that close to his mother but had a strong sense of loyalty to his father, and felt a strong sense of responsibility to look after the business and his mother. His core-self emotional experiences around intimacy were very much of wanting closeness but also feeling obligated and controlled when in close relationships. At times he would play the rescuing hero and martyr.

Despite the conflicts, he usually ended up doing what his mother wanted, although he would harbour a lot of unexpressed resentment. This unexpressed resentment was to be a central focus of his later depressions. His first depression arose shortly after leaving college, when he had a strong desire to escape from the family business, sell up and go back to college, but felt unable to do so. The themes of entrapment, obligation, rescuing hero, guilt, submitting to the wishes of others and anger inhibition were the main ones in his depression. So although to external observers he may have seemed a wealthy and high-ranking male, in reality he was living a highly subordinate life, controlled by a sense of duty (see Gilbert 1992a and Sloman et al. 1994 for other examples of the subordinate lifestyle).

He married a person of the same religious background (rather than his own choice, who was from a different religion) to please the family. Although he did not realise it at the time, he came to perceive her as having many similar characteristics to those of his mother. He moved the business to a new town (against his own wishes) because she was unhappy with where she was living, and he thought this would improve things between them. However, this was the beginning of a manic-depressive cycle.

The move had been far more difficult than he had anticipated. He had been working very long hours to re-establish the business and after six months felt exhausted. He felt his wife did not help much and was not that appreciative of his efforts. His inner resentment grew but was not expressed, and the relationship become more distant. This was a big disappointment. One day he went out and spent many thousands of pounds on new machines, putting the family in debt with a 'devil may care' attitude (in fact later it turned out to have been a good move, but at the time was highly impulsive). He began to think that he was going to make 'loads of money' and would impress everyone with his business skill. Within a few days he was admitted to hospital in a hypomanic state, only to collapse into depression a few weeks later:

Paul: When you went off on your spending spree what was going through your mind?

John: Well, I had had this feeling building in me, this anger and I thought 'Why the hell should I go along with all she [his wife] wanted'. It's my business and Dad had worked hard for it. In fact it probably killed him in the end. Still, I was going to make it a real success. I was going to show Mum and my wife what I could do. Yet I also felt a slave to it. So making money was my way out I guess. I don't know. There were so many things starting to buzz in my mind then. It was like something was trying to burst out of me. I wanted to take life by the scruff of the neck and shake it and shake it.

Paul: Was that feeling of 'something wanting to burst out of you' a new feeling for you or had you had that earlier in your life? [The feeling of something trying to burst out of him seemed very important to me, and I have come across this in other depressed patients.]

John: Oh I'd had it before but nothing like that. When I first took over the business I used to have these urges to get away. I wanted to say to Mum, 'Stuff it. I don't want to be here. Sell the business and let's do our own thing.'

Paul: But you never did, eh? Something stopped you.

John: No, I never did. She would have been heart broken. So would Dad. I felt I owed it to Dad and to Mum. She could not have coped with selling up. And I thought I was being really selfish for even thinking it. And I was making a good living. So I tried to convince myself that things were not so bad really.

We see here a number of core themes of entrapment and feelings of obligation played out as the rescuer and martyr. There was clearly a strong wish to escape but also a major block on escaping – guilt. In ranking theory these themes can lead to a subordinate psychology (Gilbert 1992a; Sloman *et al.* 1994). The early life of John had had many guilt experiences mixed with various religious ideas, and he was very vulnerable to intense feelings of being a selfish person. Much of his life had been spent trying to prove that he was not selfish and that he was a good, worthwhile person: a trusted son. But he had got tied up in knots doing it. It also become clear that some of his manic-depressive swings were reactive to intense conflicts with his interpersonal relationships, and arose from his inability to deal with rage and the desire to escape. It was also interesting to note that he suddenly got taken with a way out, which was a grandiose effort to 'make loads of money', bring in a manager and be a back-seat chairman cruising the world. But this grandiose dream was soon to collapse:

John: When I was in the hospital they told me I had this illness called manic depression and I may have to take drugs for the rest of my life. I was devastated. I not only felt I'd failed everyone but I was now significantly flawed, not normal. But inside, part of me felt it was all so unfair. I was so angry and yet so guilty. Every time my wife and I argued she'd say I was 'going over the top' and 'was I taking my drugs?'. I just felt powerless and trapped. When I told her I wanted to sell the business she told me I was being irresponsible and 'what about the children'. And I couldn't decide if she was right or not. I saw life as endlessly worrying about accounts and the staff. That's when I just went to bed and was brought back to hospital and given ECT.

Paul: Sounds like your wife reminded you of conflicts you'd had earlier in your life.

John: I guess so. They [mother and father] always seemed to be right, though. I just felt there was nothing I could do. Duty was the big thing at home.

Sadly he did not receive much in the way of counselling at this time. And when I first saw him (he had had nearly fifteen years of problems by then, and his first marriage had ended), it took a long time for us to become clear about what the core-emotional experiences were and the way rage and escape were common triggering experiences. He was so full of self-blame and feelings of inferiority and shame for his rage that he had a lot of difficulty talking about it. This is not to say he did not have rages, for he did occasionally, but it was very black and white (rage or resentful silence). And angry outbursts were followed by a guilty collapse into depression and fear of the illness.

Despite my best efforts at reassurance and focus on his self-critical style, when he said 'bad things' about his wife or mother (voiced his resentment, which conflicted with his rescuing hero ideals) he would leave therapy and feel worse. When he thought about his anger to them he would also tell himself that he was just trying to let himself off the hook by blaming others (Bowlby (1980) calls this defensive exclusion). When this happened he would often not turn up to the next therapy session. But slowly we managed to draw out the key conflicts. One day when John was feeling hopeless and lost I said:

Paul: You know, John, your life must never really have seemed like you owned it. Your life seems to have been a constant struggle to do what you thought was right. I guess because you feel that caring for others is the morally right thing to do you have constantly sought to do that. But you know sometimes our anger has a real message for us. It is screaming out for something to be heard. What else wants to be heard? If your anger could speak what would it say?

John closed his eyes and the atmosphere in the room began to change. I repeated the idea to him: 'What in you is screaming to be heard?' At this point John started to cry, which made me feel tearful too. Whereas before his crying had the quality of irritation and unfairness in it, this time it felt quite different, as if he were in touch with real despair, with a deep core-self emotional experience. Then he said, still with eyes closed: 'Please let me go. Let me go, please. Let me go. I have tried so hard. I really have. I've nothing left. Please let me go.'

At this point he cried for a long time. I did not intrude on this deeply emotional episode, but sat with him silently sharing his enormous pain of the life that had not turned out as he had wanted; at all the wrong turns and lost opportunities he thought there had been; at all the doubts and confusions. I believe that he was telling me what he had wanted to tell his mother and father but never had. Towards the end of the session I made some observation like:

Paul: This is obviously a very painful struggle for you. And I think it is possibly one of your key emotional struggles; whether to find your own way or obey the wishes of others. But maybe now's the time to think that perhaps you can stop asking permission to be let go. I mean who are you really asking this of? You can see that it is perhaps something inside you that has to keep throwing yourself into the fight to prove yourself, to prove that you are a good and lovable son and acceptable. But maybe you can learn to accept yourself as you are. Your heroic efforts may not actually give you what you want.

John wiped the tears away and gave a dry smile and a nod.

John: Yeah, permission. Always trying to prove something and get the approval – that's me alright.

From that point on the therapy changed. He rarely missed a session and it become the usual hard work of looking at the basic schemas and the inner conflicts, teaching how to be assertive rather than aggressive or silently resentful, how to deal with guilt and self-blame, exploring the feelings of loyalty to his father and so on. We used flash cards, looking at the advantages and disadvantages, and the two-chairs technique. We helped John say to his parents (in role-play) what he wanted to say. After two years he had lowered his drugs intake and was stable. Although he probably did have a biological sensitivity to bipolar illness, it was the psychology that acted on whatever vulnerability there was. Towards the end of therapy he ran into a major crisis that before, he felt, would have put him back in hospital. But although he became mildly sleep disturbed and felt down, he was able to use what he had learned in the therapy, and the depression soon passed without any change in drugs. He was delighted by that and felt he had more control over his depression and hypomanic swings. Indeed, he has had no hypomanic swings to date and is much more in control of his anger.

In ranking theory (Gilbert 1992a, 1993) the bipolar depressed person is caught in a serious conflict and oscillation in the self between the entrapped, inferior, subordinate self and the expansive, dominant, heroic self. I believe that we had been able to connect empathically with John's struggle to be free, that is, to be neither a controlled subordinate nor an expansively heroic dominant. This was a powerful, emotionally corrective experience of acceptance of the impossibility of both positions. The rescuing hero had to be dropped, but that was intensely painful, for it was what had given him his sense of lovableness and basic goodness. Without this experience I wonder if he would have been able to internalise much of the therapy. But this was not an experience that could have happened in the first few sessions, for he needed to learn to trust me to some degree. This is why core-self experiences need to be focused on in regard to their emotional (not just irrational) quality. As MacKie (1982) noted, sometimes it is as important just to be with the patient as it is to be doing things to the patient. The problem can be knowing when to be and when to do.

The social context

People live in highly contextualised worlds of relationships and values (Gilbert 1995). The sense of entrapment can be within these contexts, be they of the workplace or unemployment and poverty, be they of single parents struggling with young children or in unsatisfactory relationships, and the therapist can be empathic to these external constraints. But people can also be trapped within themselves, by values and the tyranny of the shoulds, oughts and musts. As Sperry (1993) points out, therapy is about changing values and not just cognitions. And we are only just beginning to explore how patients internalise new values, and how this can be as much a maturation process as anything else (Layden *et al.* 1993; Mahoney 1990). We have made great strides in treating depression, but there is still much to do in developing our understanding of the therapeutic process.

CONCLUSIONS

Depression is an 'in-the-body' experience, and the therapist tries to connect with this internal experience. Depression often revolves around conflicts that are both internal and external. There are also many kinds of depression that seem to grow out of genuinely difficult social conditions, such as poverty. Shame and the sense of personal inferiority and unworthiness are also common. The therapist's tasks are not only to educate and inform the patients of how they may be stacking things against themselves (for example, by self-blame, black-and-white thinking, and re-enacting negative self–other social patterns), but also to provide emotionally powerful relational experiences that can connect with their inner struggle and core-self emotional experiences.

The new developments in the treatment of depression are, therefore, not only around the techniques of change (such as changing cognitions and behaviours, social skill training, etc.) but also in understanding core-self emotional experiences, and engaging with the associated emotions, containing them and allowing them to be explored. These empathic bridges are crucial not only in healing shame (Kaufman 1989) but in healing many kinds of splits and conflicts.

REFERENCES

Abramson, L.Y., Metalsky, G.I. and Alloy, L.B. (1989) Hopelessness: a theory-based subtype of depression. *Psychological Review 96*, 358–72.

Beach, S.R.H., Sandeen, E.E. and O'Leary, K.D. (1990) *Depression in Marriage*. New York: Guilford Press.

Beck, A.T. (1967) *Depression: Clinical, Experimental and Theoretical Aspects*. New York: Harper and Row.

Beck, A.T. (1983) Cognitive therapy of depression: new perspectives. In P.J. Clayton and J.E. Barrett (eds) *Treatment of Depression: Old Controversies and New Approaches*. New York: Raven Press.

Beck, A.T., Rush, A.J., Shaw, B.F. and Emery, G. (1979) *Cognitive Therapy of Depression*. New York: Wiley.

Bowlby, J. (1980) *Loss: Sadness and Depression. Attachment and Loss. Vol. 3*. London: Hogarth Press.

Brewin, C.R., Andrews, B. and Gotlib, I.H. (1993) Psychopathology and early experiences: a reappraisal of retrospective reports. *Psychological Bulletin 113*, 82–98.

Brown, G.W. and Harris, T.O. (1978) *The Social Origins of Depression*. London: Tavistock.

Brown, G.W., Adler, W.Z. and Bifulco, A. (1988) Life events, difficulties and recovery from chronic depression. *British Journal of Psychiatry 152* 487–98.

Brown, G.W., Bifulco, A. and Harris, T.O. (1987) Life events, vulnerability and onset of depression: some refinements. *British Journal of Psychiatry 150* 30–42.

Brown, G.W., Harris, T.O. and Hepworth, C. (1995) Loss, humiliation and entrapment among women developing depression: a patient and non-patient comparison. *Psychological Medicine 25* 7–21.

Brown, G.W., Bifulco, A., Harris, T.O. and Bridge, L. (1986) Social support, self-esteem and depression. *Psychological Medicine 16* 813–31.

Deitz, J. (1988) Self-psychological interventions for major depression. *American Journal of Psychotherapy XLII* 597–609.

Deitz, J. (1989) The evolution of the self-psychology approach to depression. *American Journal of Psychotherapy XLIII* 494–505.

Ferster, C.B. (1973) A functional analysis of depression. *American Psychologist 28* 857–70.

Fombonne, E. (1994) Increased rates of depression: update of epidemiological findings and analytical problems. *Acta Psychiatrica Scandinavia 90* 145–56.

Gilbert, P. (1989) *Human Nature and Suffering*. Hove: Lawrence Erlbaum.

Gilbert, P. (1992a) *Depression: The Evolution of Powerlessness*. Hove: Guilford Press/Lawrence Erlbaum.

Gilbert, P. (1992b) *Counselling for Depression*. London: Sage.

Gilbert, P. (1993) Defence and safety: their function in social behaviour and psychopathology. *British Journal of Clinical Psychology 32* 131–54.

Gilbert, P. (1995) Biopsychosocial approaches and evolutionary theory as aids to integration in clinical psychology and psychotherapy. *Clinical Psychology and Psychotherapy 2* 135–58.

Gotlib, I.H. and Colby, C.A. (1987) *Treatment of Depression: An Interpersonal Systems Approach*. New York: Pergamon Press.

Greenberg, L.S. and Safran, J.D. (1987) *Emotion in Psychotherapy*. New York: Guilford Press.

Greenberg, L.S., Elliott, R.K. and Foerster, F.S. (1990) Experiential processes in the psychotherapeutic treatment of depression. In C.D. McCann and N.S. Endler (eds) *Depression: New Directions in Theory, Research and Practice*. Toronto: Wall and Emerson.

Guidano, V.F. and Liotti, G. (1983) *Cognitive Processes and Emotional Disorders*. New York: Guilford Press.

Gut, E. (1989) *Productive and Unproductive Depression: Success or Failure of a Vital Process*. London: Routledge and Kegan Paul.

Holmes, J. (1993) *John Bowlby and Attachment Theory*. London: Routledge.

Horowitz, L.M. and Vitkus, J. (1986) The interpersonal basis of psychiatric symptoms. *Clinical Psychology Review 6* 443–70.

Jenkins, J.H., Kleinman, A. and Good, B.J. (1991) Cross-cultural studies of depression. In J. Becker and A. Kleinman (eds) *Psychosocial Aspects of Depression*. Hillsdale, NJ: Lawrence Erlbaum.

Karasu, T.B. (1990) Toward a clinical model of the psychotherapy for depression, II: an integrative and selective treatment approach. *American Journal of Psychiatry 147* 269–78.

Kaufman, G. (1989) *The Psychology of Shame*. New York: Springer.

Klerman, G.L. and Weissman, M.M. (1994) Interpersonal psychotherapy for depression: background and concepts. In G.L. Klerman and M.M. Weissman (eds) *New Applications of Interpersonal Psychotherapy*. Washington, DC: American Psychiatric Press.

Klerman, G.L., Weissman, M.M., Rounsaville, B.J. and Chevron, E.S. (1984) *Interpersonal Psychotherapy of Depression*. New York: Basic Books.

Kohut, H. (1977) *The Restoration of the Self*. New York: International Universities Press.

Layden, M.A., Newman, C.F., Freeman, A. and Morse, S.B. (1993) *Cognitive Therapy of Borderline Personality Disorder*. Boston: Allyn and Bacon.

Lewinsohn, P.M. (1974) A behavioral approach to depression. In R.J. Friedman and M.M. Katz (eds) *The Psychology of Depression: Contemporary Theory and Research*. New York: Halsted Press.

Lewis, M. (1992) *Shame: The Exposed Self*. New York: Free Press.

Liotti, G. (1988) Attachment and cognition: a guide for the reconstruction of early pathogenic experiences in cognitive therapy. In C. Perris, I.M. Blackburn and H. Perris (eds) *Handbook of Cognitive Psychotherapy*. New York: Springer.

Liotti, G. (1993) Disorganised attachment and dissociative experiences: an illustration of the developmental-ethological approach to cognitive therapy. In K.T. Kuehlwein and H. Rosen (eds) *Cognitive Therapies in Action: Evolving Innovative Practice*. San Francisco: Jossey Bass.

MacKie J. (1982) Attachment theory: its relevance to the therapeutic alliance. *British Journal of Medical Psychology 54* 203–12.

Mahoney, M.J. (1990) *Human Change Processes: The Scientific Foundations of Psychotherapy*. New York: Basic Books.

Nathanson, D.L. (1992) *Shame and Pride: Affect, Sex and the Birth of the Self*. New York: Norton.

Newman, J.C. and Goldfried, M.R. (eds) (1992) *Handbook of Psychotherapy Integration*. New York: Basic Books.

Price, J.S., Sloman, R., Gardner, R., Gilbert, P. and Rhodes, P. (1994) The social competition hypothesis of depression. *British Journal of Psychiatry 164* 309–15.

Rehm, L.P. (1988) Self-management and cognitive processes in depression. In L.B. Alloy (ed.) *Cognitive Processes in Depression*. New York: Guilford Press.

Rehm, L.P. (1989) Behavioral models of anxiety and depression. In P.C. Kendall and D. Watson (eds) *Anxiety and Depression: Distinctive and Overlapping Features*. New York: Academic Press.

Rowan, J. (1990) *Subpersonalities: The People Inside Us*. London: Routledge.

Safran, J.D. and Segal, Z.V. (1990) *Interpersonal Process in Cognitive Therapy*. New York: Basic Books.

Schore, A.N. (1994) *Affect Regulation and the Origin of the Self: The Neurobiology of Emotional Development*. Hillsdale, NJ: Lawrence Erlbaum.

Segrin, C. and Abramson, L.Y. (1994) Negative reactions to depressive behaviours: a communication theories analysis. *Journal of Abnormal Psychology 103* 655–68.

Sloman, L., Price, P., Gilbert, P. and Gardner, R. (1994) Adaptive function of depression: psychotherapeutic implications. *American Journal of Psychotherapy 48* 1–16.

Sperry, R.W. (1993) The impact and promise of the cognitive revolution. *American Psychologist 48* 878–85.

Weissman, M.M. and Klerman, G.L. (1994) Recent research and clinical advances. In G.L. Klerman and M.M. Weissman (eds) *New Applications of Interpersonal Psychotherapy*. Washington, DC: American Psychiatric Press.

Williams, M.J. (1992) *The Psychological Treatment of Depression*. London: Routledge. 2nd edn.

Young, J.E. (1994) *Cognitive Therapy for Personality Disorders: A Schema-Focused Approach*. Florida: Practitioners Resource Series. Revised edn.

Young, J.E., Beck, A.T. and Weinberger, A. (1993) Depression. In H.D. Barlow (ed.) *Clinical Handbook of Psychological Disorders*. New York: Guilford Press.

Chapter 12

Smoking cessation counselling
The Stages of Change model

Andy Parrott

INTRODUCTION

Cigarette smoking is the largest single preventable cause of death in the West. The majority of smokers state that they would like to give it up, but generally continue smoking. The Stages of Change model (Prochaska *et al.* 1992, 1993) categorises smokers into several different sub-groups, according to their current attitudes towards smoking. This chapter focuses on the different types of counselling advice that these different types of smoker need (see Table 12.1). Another new perspective for smoking cessation is the finding that smoking does not itself relieve stress; rather, it sets up deprivation effects which smoking then reverses (Parrott 1994, 1995). Stopping smoking does not therefore mean losing a way of coping with stress. Indeed, former smokers report feeling less stressed within a few months of stopping. These two new directions in smoking cessation counselling are discussed below, after introductory sections on cigarette smoking, and smoking cessation.

CIGARETTE SMOKING AND ITS EFFECTS

This section reviews the dynamics of tobacco smoking, and the physiological/psychological processes which underlie nicotine addiction. The average smoker inhales tobacco smoke around 70,000 times each year. This smoke contains hundreds of chemicals, of which three are central to its addictive nature and adverse health effects: nicotine, carbon monoxide and tar. Nicotine is structurally similar to the neurotransmitter acetylcholine, a small chemical which facilitates communication between neurones within the nervous system. Nicotine from inhaled smoke reaches the brain in 7–10 seconds, where it mimics acetylcholine, and influences a range of psychological functions. Smokers often report that smoking is relaxing or pleasurable, whereas deprivation leads to feelings of irritability and tension (Russell *et al.* 1974; West 1993). It is these opposing effects of nicotine and nicotine depletion which make cigarettes so addictive (Parrott 1994, 1995). This addictiveness was noted by the first Europeans to smoke tobacco. When the conquistadors were reprimanded by their commanders for imitating the native American practice of eating smoke, they 'answered that it was not in their power to refrain' (Mangan and Golding 1984: 35).

Nicotine itself has few health consequences, but carbon monoxide and tar have severe effects upon health. The smoke produced by the burning tobacco leaf comprises 4 per cent carbon monoxide (CO). This is readily taken up by haemoglobin in the red blood corpuscles, and leads to a reduction in the oxygen-carrying capacity of the blood. The peripheral circulation therefore becomes impaired, with some smokers developing peripheral artery disease and gangrene. Around five hundred limb amputations are performed in the UK each year for this reason (Royal College of Physicians 1983). The only preventative measure is to give up smoking, and those who do will retain their limbs, due to the improved circulation which accompanies cessation. But those smokers who carry on smoking generally require surgery within months. One notorious medical photograph shows a smoker with all four limbs surgically removed. Yet even with no hands he carries on smoking, with the cigarette fixed onto an ingenious bent-metal-coathanger construction around his neck! The heart is also covered by a multitude of small capillaries, and the reduced oxygen supply leads to the high incidence of cardiac problems in cigarette smokers. Indeed, more smokers are killed by smoking-induced cardiac disorders than by lung cancer (Royal College of Physicians 1983). Peripheral circulation problems lead to sexual impotence in males, reflecting the reduced blood supply to the penis, while pregnant females have more low-birthweight and stillborn babies, due to the impaired foetal blood supply (note: smoking cessation early in pregnancy reduces this; Surgeon General 1990).

If a smoker inhales through a handkerchief, he or she will detect a sticky brown ring of tar. If he or she repeats this test with expired breath, the amount of residue is reduced. The difference represents the tar retained within the lungs (note: this exercise is often useful in practical cessation classes). Many tar constituents are carcinogenic, particularly the nitrosamines. Cigarette smokers therefore often develop cancers of the lung and throat; cigar and pipe smokers tend to develop cancers of the mouth, lips and tongue; while tobacco chewers develop cancers of the gum, lips and jaw. There are around twelve million tobacco chewers in the USA, who tend to place the wad of tobacco in the same spot within their mouth, and this is where cancers often develop (Glover *et al.* 1989). Tobacco chewers tend to develop cancers more rapidly than cigarette smokers. Many 21-year-olds, having chewed tobacco for 8–10 years, need surgical removal of the jaw or lips on the side of the mouth where their tobacco-wad rested. Low-tar cigarettes are now widely available, but since nicotine is delivered into the lungs via tar droplets these cigarettes also provide only limited nicotine. Smokers compensate for this low-nicotine delivery by inhaling more deeply, and smoking more cigarettes. There are therefore only slight health benefits from moving to low-tar cigarettes, although they have led to a sales boon for tobacco companies.

Cigarette smokers therefore often die prematurely. In the UK, tobacco companies need to recruit over 300 adolescents each day in order to replace the adult smokers killed the previous day by cancer, emphysema and cardiac arrest. Around 110,000 smokers in the UK die each year as a result of these chronic diseases (Parrott 1991). However, smoking also affects the health of recent initiates to smoking. Adolescent smokers report higher rates of shortness of breath, phlegm, wheezing, and chest colds, as well as serious lung disorders such as pneumonia. The incidence of these adolescent breathing disorders shows a close relationship with cigarette consumption. In one US report, the percentage of high-school students reporting shortness of breath was: non-smokers, 5 per cent; less than 1 cigarette/day, 13 per cent; 1–10 cigarettes/day, 13 per cent; 10–20 cigarettes/day, 36 per cent; over 20 cigarettes/day, 58 per cent (Surgeon General 1994: 18–23).

Passive smoking, the inhalation of cigarette smoke by non-smokers, is now also recognised as a widespread health problem (National Institute of Health 1993). Nicotine, tar, and carbon monoxide can all be measured in non-smokers exposed to smoke-contaminated air. The children and colleagues of smokers therefore tend to suffer from the same respiratory illnesses as the smokers themselves. In the USA, around 3,000 adult non-smokers die of lung cancer caused by passive smoking each year (National Institute of Health 1993); while the UK equivalent is around 800 deaths annually. Sudden Infant Death Syndrome (cot death) in babies aged between 1 month and 1 year has also been linked to smoking: 'The World Health Organisation estimate that more than 700 USA infant deaths per year are attributable to maternal smoking' (National Institute of Health 1993: 17). School-age children whose parents smoke suffer heightened rates of pneumonia, influenza, colds and days off school due to illness (Royal College of Physicians 1983). Passive smoking increases the incidence and severity of asthma attacks in children, and may also induce new cases (National Institute of Health 1993). Nevertheless, while the average 10-year-old sees smoking as stupid, his or her older sisters and brothers readily succumb to peer pressure. Female adolescents in particular show no signs of reducing their rate of taking up the habit, and currently comprise the prime target for Western tobacco advertising. Worldwide, cigarette consumption remains on the increase.

SMOKING CESSATION

The majority of adult smokers report that they wish they had never started smoking and would like to stop. Around 2–6 per cent of smokers manage to stop on their own; this represents the percentage of smokers who make a firm cessation attempt, remain abstinent for one year, and provide negative biochemical samples. Far higher success rates (50–90 per cent) are often quoted when only a brief period of abstinence is counted as a success (such as 2–8 weeks), or abstinence is not confirmed biochemically. Many commercial programmes give totally misleading success rates this way. Overall, however, around 95 per cent of unaided smokers fail with each cessation attempt, when assessed by strict criteria.

These low success rates have led to a large industry of cessation clinics, public health campaigns, and self-help manuals (Carey et al. 1989; Fisher et al. 1993; Surgeon General 1988, 1990). Viswesvaran and Schmidt (1992) surveyed the findings from 633 different studies, involving over 70,000 subjects. Many cessation programmes were reviewed: education on health problems; relaxation training; social skills training; hypnosis; acupuncture; nicotine replacement (gum, patch); and aversive smoking. Control subjects from the 633 studies reported an average success rate of 6 per cent. Simple physician recommendation to stop smoking generated a slightly higher 7 per cent success rate. Basic counselling coupled with some additional information, such as health education or social skills training, led to greater success (17 per cent). However, the highest quit rates were found with comprehensive multicomponent packages (35 per cent average annual success). This agrees with the Surgeon General's (1988: 459–560) conclusions regarding the efficacy of multicomponent packages. In particular, combined pharmacological and psychological programmes (such as nicotine chewing gum to overcome nicotine withdrawal coupled with skills training to cope with social pressure) led to some of the highest success rates (30–40 per cent). However, even with the most successful schemes, the majority of smokers were smoking again within the year.

SMOKING AND STRESS

Many smokers view cigarettes as a psychological aid which helps them cope with stress, concentrate at work, or generate feelings of pleasure (Parrott 1995; West 1993). Factor-analyses of self-reported smoking motives reveal two main factors. The first represents non-pharmacological motives: psychosocial smoking (in social situations), and sensorimotor aspects (oral/manual manipulation). The second factor represents psychopharmacological motives: addiction, automatic smoking, stress and arousal modulation (Russell et al. 1974). Subsequent research has confirmed this two-factor pattern (Parrott 1994), although scores on the non-pharmacological factor now tend to be low, confirming that smoking in the 1990s is no longer socially desirable. In contrast, scores on the pharmacological motives remain high, confirming that nicotine has retained its addictive properties. Many smokers believe that they will miss these psychoactive 'benefits' if they quit smoking (Warburton 1992). However, a series of recent studies has shown that the psychological changes which accompany smoking largely reflect the reversal of deprivation effects. Thus when smokers give it up they will not lose any 'benefits', but their overall psychological status will improve. This can be illustrated by reference to the relationship between smoking and stress.

The majority of smokers (85 per cent) report that smoking generates feelings of reduced anxiety and stress (Parrott 1994). One interpretation of this is that smoking relieves stress (Warburton 1992). However, closer examination of the empirical data questions this interpretation, since smokers report above-average levels of stress (West 1993). In the UK Health and Lifestyle survey of 9,000 participants, current smokers reported significantly higher levels of daily stress than either non-smokers or *former smokers*. Two longitudinal studies have confirmed that smoking cessation leads to reduced feelings of stress; in each study, successful cessation led to significantly lower levels of daily stress (Cohen and Lichtenstein 1990; Parrott and Craig 1994). Active smoking is therefore associated with high levels of daily stress, whereas cessation leads to reduced stress. The smoking/stress relationship was re-examined by Parrott (1994, 1995), who proposed a new explanatory model, based upon the negative mood effects of nicotine depletion. Regular smokers report irritability/tenseness when they have not smoked recently, but only *average* mood states immediately after smoking (Parrott 1994). The stress relief which follows smoking therefore simply reflects mood normalisation, rather than any real gain. When smokers quit, they stop suffering from the negative mood effects of nicotine depletion between cigarettes. Long-term cessation then leads to improved mood states (Parrott 1995).

Similar patterns were found with both alertness and pleasure (Parrott 1994; Parrott and Patel n.d.). In each case, nicotine withdrawal leads to negative psychological states (impaired concentration and heightened irritation), while the positive moods which accompany the act of smoking (improved alertness and increased pleasure) largely reflect the reversal depletion effects. The main message for smokers is that they will not suffer psychologically in the long term. They may suffer severe craving/withdrawal symptoms for several weeks, but these will diminish over time, and in the long term their daily moods will improve (Cohen and Lichtenstein 1990; Parrott and Craig 1994; Parrott 1995).

THE STAGES OF CHANGE MODEL

Prochaska and DiClemente suggested that the main reason for this high failure rate is that only a few smokers are ready to quit at any one time. They developed the Stages of Change model, which categorises smokers according to their level of preparedness for change (DiClemente 1992; Prochaska et al. 1992, 1993). Five stages were derived from discriminant function and cluster analysis of initial questionnaires (Table 12.1). The first sub-group comprises pre-contemplators, who plan to remain as smokers. They often accept that others are worried about their smoking, but tend to underestimate their concerns. Pre-contemplators sometimes attend cessation programmes, but this tends to reflect pressure from their doctor or partner: 'When precontemplators present for psychotherapy, they often do so because of pressure from others. Usually they feel coerced' (Prochaska et al. 1992: 1103). It is therefore not surprising that they generally fail to quit smoking, although they may briefly change: 'Once the pressure is off, however, they quickly return to their old ways.' Around 40–60 per cent of smokers are at the pre-contemplation stage.

The second major sub-group is contemplators (Table 12.1), who acknowledge that their smoking is a problem, but are not currently planning to change. They struggle with the pros and cons, and weigh the ease of continued smoking against the difficulty of quitting. Around 30–40 per cent of smokers are contemplators. The third group comprises the small number of smokers who are almost ready to give it up (preparation phase). They have recently reduced their consumption, and are currently planning when to give up. Those at the next (action) stage have actually given it up. They often suffer from nicotine withdrawal symptoms, although around 50 per cent of them report that these symptoms are not as severe as they had expected. It should be emphasised that only a small percentage of smokers are at the preparation or action stages (5–15 per cent), although most cessation programmes implicitly assume that all smokers who want to give it up are at these stages (Marks 1993). The fifth and final stage is maintenance. People at this stage last smoked over 3–6 months ago, and no longer experience severe cravings, but are still in danger of relapse.

It should also be noted that the Stages of Change model has important implications for many other areas of behavioural change – heroin and alcohol addiction, assertiveness training and eating disorders – and not just smoking cessation. The core message is that the client's current level of functioning needs to be understood *before* any particular advice is given. Empirical support for the utility of this approach is provided by Prochaska et al. (1993). Four smoking cessation groups were compared, with three being given Stages of Change treatment programmes, while the control group was given the best traditional package. The highest success rates were achieved with an interactive computer-based programme,

Table 12.1 Cigarette smoking and the Stages of Change model

Stage	Attitudes towards cigarette smoking	Smoking cessation counselling/advice
Pre-contemplation	Content as smoker No wish for change	Health information Raise consciousness Assess views of others
Contemplation	Wish to give up smoking – but not yet! Change too difficult	Re-evaluate pros/cons Focus upon successful change in the past
Preparation	Planning for cessation Actively cutting down Set date for quitting	Management strategies Prepare family/friends
Action	No longer smoking May experience craving and nicotine withdrawal	Active coping skills Relaxation training Nicotine gum/patch
Maintenance	Not smoked recently Danger of relapse	Relapse does not indicate failure Learn from relapse

Source: after Prochaska *et al.* 1992

where each subject worked through his or her own programme according to his or her level of preparedness for change. This programme doubled the success rate produced by the control group. However, the Stages of Change model also notes that change can occur in any direction. Just as current smokers can quit, so former smokers may start smoking again. Clients often re-present with the same old problems, whether smoking, overeating, or being bullied in the workplace. However, the client is *not* the same as before, once he or she has experienced change. The therapist should encourage clients to learn from all these recent experiences, and recommence a fresh cycle of change towards the new lifestyle they desire.

CESSATION COUNSELLING FOR PRE-CONTEMPLATORS

DiClemente (1992) admits that therapy with the pre-contemplators is often difficult, but notes that while counselling may not lead to immediate success it may provide long-term seeds for change in the future: 'Pre-contemplators are less open with significant others about their problems, and do little . . . in the direction of overcoming problems. In therapy, these are the most resistant or least active clients' (Prochaska *et al.* 1992: 1109). Four types of pre-contemplation have been described: reluctance, rebellion, resignation and rationalization (DiClemente 1992: 192).

Reluctant pre-contemplators do not see a problem. They are often ignorant about smoking, and fail to acknowledge any adverse effects, either upon themselves or for others. Health information books or videos, practical tasks such as monitoring other people's views about smoking, or role-playing in psychodrama may help them realise that their smoking does cause problems for others. Rebellious pre-contemplators are resistant about being told what to do. They tend to argue against many things, and often show anger or hostility against their partner, doctor or counsellor. DiClemente (1992: 193) recommends that the counsellor should provide alternative choices, which the client may then decide between: 'The real task is trying to shift some of that energy into contemplating change rather than resistance or rebellion.'

The third type of pre-contemplator is overwhelmed by the enormity of the problem of being a nicotine addict. Any change is seen as impossible, and the only hope for the future is to stop youngsters from starting. Therapy for these 'resigned pre-contemplators' might comprise exploring how change has occurred in others, and suggesting areas where they can personally experience change. This might be facilitated by setting small manageable goals (30-minute delay in lighting up each morning), in order to foster self-control skills. The fourth type, the 'rationalising pre-contemplator', has worked out the answers, and can easily explain why they personally are not at risk from smoking. Their father died of lung cancer, but genetically they take after their mother; they work out physically, and this keeps them fit. Rationalisation processes are always difficult to influence, since they have a strong internal logic (like the delusional systems of paranoid schizophrenics). Any logical debate offered by the therapist tends to be incorporated into the egocentric views of uniqueness/correctness in the client. One therapeutic possibility might be to discuss the 'optimism bias', the tendency displayed by most people (except depressives) to have an optimistic belief about their own health (McKenna et al. 1993). However, while rationalising pre-contemplators might agree that other people are too optimistic, they may carefully explain that they happen to be very realistic.

CESSATION COUNSELLING FOR CONTEMPLATORS

When smoking cessation programmes are offered in the workplace, up to 70 per cent of smokers display an interest (that is, most smokers apart from pre-contemplators), but attendance rates then average 5 per cent (DiClemente 1992). Many of these non-attenders are contemplators; they want to give it up, but not yet. Contemplators comprise an intriguing and frustrating type of smoker. They readily admit to the problem, and may be knowledgeable about the perils of smoking, but see giving it up as currently too difficult. The contemplator sees numerous barriers to change, and counselling should foster the process of re-evaluation. The aim should be to help the person face up to his or her own behaviour and its effects on significant others, such as spouse or children. School health education programmes can facilitate this process quite dramatically. Picture the 9-year-old who returns home and asks his or her parents why they smoke, and why they are trying to kill him or her. Parents who face this question find it very difficult to answer, and may experience a rapid re-evaluation of their own smoking behaviour.

Counsellors can also help the client to reconceptualise smoking as a manageable behaviour, and foster the belief in successful change. For instance, many contemplators will have tried to give it up in the past, but their subsequent relapse has strengthened the belief that change is impossible. The therapist can help clients to re-evaluate this 'failure' in a more positive light, to see it as an example of successful change, even if only for a short period. It confirms that they were able to quit, and can therefore do so again. The therapist should then help clients to re-examine the reasons for their past relapse. Did it occur in certain situations, or with particular individuals? If so, how might these problems be handled better in the future? The clients might approach the person who contributed to their previous relapse, and discuss how they might behave differently in the future (that is, to be supportive next time). Or did relapse occur because of environmental stressors? If so, would relaxation training or a different work pattern be useful?

CESSATION COUNSELLING FOR THE PREPARATION STAGE

This is an intermediate state between contemplation and action, and is often quite brief. Smokers should reduce their intake before quitting. Marks (1993) describes a series of simple self-conditioning exercises, through which smokers train themselves to replace automatic smoking with more conscious realisation of the negative aspects of smoke inhalation. Each cigarette is smoked in a totally mindful way, concentrating upon its unpleasant acrid taste, and the deleterious effects upon heart and lungs: 'When eliminating dependency on the drug nicotine, we are talking about de-programming that part of your mind which makes you restless and unhappy when you deny yourself a cigarette' (Marks 1993: 10). The aim is to reduce the desire for nicotine, and so foster a dramatic reduction in cigarette consumption over 7–10 days. Friends and colleagues should also be prepared for the cessation day. The client should plan and practise coping skills, learn relaxation programmes for high-stress situations, or begin a programme of moderate exercise (regular walking, aerobics classes, etc.). The role of the counsellor is to act as guide and support, encourage forward planning, discuss problem situations as they arise, and generally encourage these cessation plans.

Another topic for consideration is whether to use nicotine replacement: nicotine chewing gum or transdermal nicotine patches (Stapleton *et al.* 1995). Cigarette smoking essentially comprises the self-administration of nicotine. The inhalation of burning vegetation is never pleasurable unless it contains a psychoactive substance (cannabis, opium or nicotine). This is why herbal cigarettes are rarely useful as a cessation aid; they are unpleasant to smoke and, incidentally, very unhealthy. When smokers give it up, they generally suffer a range of nicotine withdrawal symptoms. Nicotine replacement (gum or patch) reduces the severity of these nicotine withdrawal symptoms, and leads to a *doubling* of cessation rates (Stapleton *et al.* 1995) (see Figure 12.1; abstinence was biochemically confirmed). The main decision is which device to use. Smokers who feel they need psychomotor gratification may prefer to use nicotine chewing gum. Those with false teeth may prefer the transdermal patch.

Women who experience pre-menstrual tension should plan their giving-up date carefully; a day early in the menstrual cycle may be optimal. Craig *et al.* (1992) compared the ability of mid-cycle females, pre-menstrual females and males to abstain from smoking for two days. Mid-cycle females reported the easiest abstinence, pre-menstrual females had the

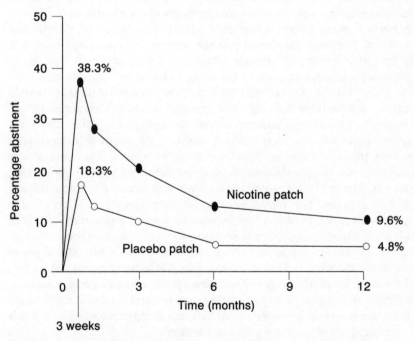

Figure 12.1 Smoking abstinence rates with transdermal nicotine/placebo patches (from Stapleton *et al.* 1995, with permission)

greatest difficulty, and males were generally intermediate. Those females who smoke most during their pre-menstrual phase can be forewarned that relapse may be more likely then. However, any temporary resumption does not indicate 'failure', but simply a brief lapse. They should abstain again immediately after any premenstrual phase relapse.

CESSATION COUNSELLING FOR THE ACTION STAGE

This is the stage when the person actually stops smoking. It therefore represents the most overt and visible type of change. Many people, professionals included, wrongly think that this is the only period of change, and most research has been concerned with it. However, in the Stages of Change model, 'action' is preceded by other equally important changes, for instance in attitudes and behavioural intentions. The type of advice required by each client at this stage will therefore depend on the preparation he or she has gone through beforehand. Well-prepared clients, who have been planning for this stage with their therapist, may need only minimal levels of support and advice. This often occurs when everything progresses according to plan. Similarly, some clients may turn up for their initial appointment having already undertaken the necessary groundwork. They may use the therapist for general confirmation and support. Often cessation progresses so smoothly that it seems like a miracle cure.

However, many clients experience severe difficulties in maintaining abstinence. The therapist should provide support and encouragement, and help the client reinterpret problem situations in a constructive way. Many of those who attempt to give up by using 'willpower' fall into this category. These people believe that they will be successful if they remain steadfast, and confront their cigarette cravings head-on. This approach can be mentally exhausting, and those who try and give up this way soon welcome ideas on how to reinterpret problem situations in behavioural/ cognitive terms in order to develop coping responses. The general aim should be to develop alternative, more constructive ways of living without cigarettes. Marks (1993) provides a number of practical exercises to facilitate this process. For instance, a small-scale change in activity like playing with a set of worry beads may be useful, particularly if these beads were given by a close friend who supports your cessation attempt. Larger-scale alterations in behaviour, such as new activities/hobbies in areas where smoking is less prevalent, might also be necessary. An alternative to the local pub might need to be found, since alcohol is a major contributor to relapse. Perhaps a small group of drinkers could find a landlord willing to set up a non-smoking bar, or a completely smoke-free pub (which might become a strong local attraction).

CESSATION COUNSELLING FOR THE MAINTENANCE STAGE

While the 'action' stage generally lasts 3–6 months, the final 'mainte-nance' phase can spread over many years: 'The real test of change for most problem behaviours, especially the addictive behaviours, is long-term sustained change over several years' (DiClemente 1992: 199). During this period, the new status of being a non-smoker needs to become firmly established. This is not a trivial stage, since relapse occurs in many smokers who have given it up for long periods (Surgeon General 1990). For instance, around 15 per cent of smokers who have remained abstinent for two years relapse again within the next two years (Surgeon General 1990: 595–616). Relapse and relapse prevention have therefore become major topics for cessation research. Information on the long-term benefits of cessation may help the smoker to remain abstinent. All smoking-induced diseases are reduced when one quits. The heightened rate of coro-nary heart disease (CHD) in smokers is reduced by 50 per cent one year after quitting, while after 15 years' cessation the rate becomes similar to that of never-smokers (Surgeon General 1990). Similar improvements occur for lung cancer, stroke and chronic lung disease. Overall therefore: 'Persons who quit smoking before age 50 have one-half the risk of dying in the next 15 years compared with continuing smokers' (Surgeon General 1990: i). Marks (1993) states that if you do relapse and light one cigarette, you should immediately carry on smoking a couple more, until you feel so sick that you cannot smoke any more. Each relapse then becomes a nega-tive rather than a positive experience, and should preclude permanent resumption.

Marlatt (1994) compared traditional Western/medical models of addic-tive behaviours with Eastern/Buddhist approaches. Many Western medical models suggest that you are either a drug user or you are not. Relapse indi-cates failure, and simply confirms that the person is a drug addict. Marlatt suggests that this view is overwhelmingly negative. Instead clients should focus upon the positive aspects of their cessation attempt, and congratu-late themselves for successfully abstaining for a period. They should learn from the situation where they relapsed, and understand why they lit up again. The message is that temporary relapse should *not* lead to long-term resumption. Relapse does not necessarily mean failure. Another topic covered by Marlatt is cravings. These are seen as strong urges, which wax and wane over time. Marlatt uses a number of west-coast Californian images, and craving is equated to surfing. The urge to smoke builds up and strengthens, just as the wave increases in size as it approaches the beach. But eventually the wave breaks, and so too will the urge to smoke. Clients should learn to ride their drug cravings, just as the surfer rides each wave. It is not necessary to give into an urge, since it will dissipate naturally over time.

REFERENCES

Carey, M.P., Snel, D.L., Carey, K.B. and Richards, C.S. (1989) Self-initiated smoking cessation: a review of the empirical literature from a stress and coping perspective. *Cognitive Therapy and Research 13* 323–41.

Cohen, S. and Lichtenstein, E. (1990) Perceived stress, quitting smoking, and smoking relapse. *Health Psychology 9* 466–78.

Craig, D., Parrott, A.C. and Coomber, J.A. (1992) Smoking cessation in women: effects of the menstrual cycle. *International Journal of the Addictions 27* 695–704.

DiClemente, C.C. (1992) Motivational interviewing and the stages of change. In W.R.Millner and S. Rollnick (eds) *Motivational Interviewing.* New York: Guilford Press.

Fisher, E.B., Lichtenstein, E., Haire-Joshu, D., Morgan, G.D. and Rehberg, H.R. (1993) Methods, successes, and failures of smoking cessation programs. *Annual Review of Medicine 44* 481–513.

Glover, E.D., Schroeder, K.L., Henningfield, J.E., Severson, H.H. and Christen, A.G. (1989) An interpretive review of smokeless tobacco research in the United States. *Journal of Drug Education 19* 1–19.

Mangan, G.L. and Golding, J.F. (1984) *The Psychopharmacology of Smoking.* Cambridge: Cambridge University Press.

Marks, D.F. (1993) *The Quit for Life Programme: An Easier Way to Stop Smoking.* Leicester: BPS Publications.

Marlatt, G.A. (1994) Addiction and acceptance. Unpublished. See G.A. Marlatt and J.R. Gordon (eds) (1985) *Relapse Prevention.* New York: Guilford Press.

McKenna, F.P., Warburton, D.M. and Winwood, M. (1993) Exploring the limits of optimism: the case of smokers' decision making. *British Journal of Psychology 84* 389–94.

National Institute of Health (1993) Respiratory health effects of passive smoking. *Smoking and Tobacco Control Monograph* No. 4. Washington, DC: US Government Printing Office.

Parrott, A.C. (1991) Social drugs: effects upon health. In M. Pitts and K. Phillips (eds) *The Psychology of Health.* London: Routledge.

Parrott, A.C. (1994) Individual differences in stress and arousal during cigarette smoking. *Psychopharmacology 115* 389–96.

Parrott, A.C. (1995) Stress modulation over the day in cigarette smokers. *Addiction 90* 237–44.

Parrott, A.C. and Craig, D. (1994) Smoking Cessation Leads to Reduced Stress: Possible Explanations. Paper given at the Annual Scientific Meeting of the Psychobiology Section of the British Psychological Society. Ambleside, Great Britain.

Parrott, A.C. and Patel, J. (n.d.) The Pleasures of Smoking, or the Irritations of Abstinence? Unpublished.

Prochaska, J.O., DiClemente, C.C. and Norcross, J.C. (1992) In search of how people change. *American Psychologist 47* 1102–14.

Prochaska, J.O., DiClemente, C.C., Velicer, W.F. and Rossi, J.S. (1993) Standardized, individualized, interactive, and personalized self-help programs for smoking cessation. *Health Psychology 12* 399–405.

Royal College of Physicians (1983) *Health or Smoking?* London: Pitman Medical.

Russell, M.A.H., Peto, J. and Patel, U.A. (1974) The classification of smoking by a factorial structure of motives. *Journal of the Royal Statistical Society 137* 313–33.

Stapleton, J.A., Russell, M.A.H., Feyerabend, C., Wiseman, S.M., Gustavsson,

G., Sawe, U. and Wiseman, D. (1995) Dose effects and predictors of outcome in a randomised trial of transdermal nicotine patches in clinical practice. *Addiction 90* 31–42.

Surgeon General (1988) *The Health Consequences of Smoking: Nicotine Addiction.* Washington, DC: US Government Printing Office.

Surgeon General (1990) *The Health Benefits of Smoking Cessation.* Washington, DC: US Government Printing Office.

Surgeon General (1994) *Preventing Tobacco Use Among Young People.* Washington, DC: US Government Printing Office.

Viswesvaran, C. and Schmidt, F.L. (1992) A meta-analytic comparison of the effectiveness of smoking cessation methods. *Journal of Applied Psychology 77* 554–61.

Warburton, D. (1992) Smoking within reason. *Journal of Smoking-Related Disorders 3* 55–9.

West, R.J. (1993) Beneficial effects of nicotine: fact or fiction? *Addiction 88* 589–90. (Also the replies: *Addiction 89* 135–46).

Chapter 13

New directions in stress

Delia Cushway

INTRODUCTION

In recent years the fastest growing area of involvement for counsellors has been in the field of stress counselling. In this chapter three important new directions where recent research and practice can inform the work of the counsellor are discussed. First is the umbrella nature and complexity of the stress process itself. If counsellors are to be effective in their work it is important that they should be able to unravel this complex term and its meaning for their clients. Second is the involvement of counsellors in the rapidly expanding industry of stress management for occupational stress. The variety of schemes designed to help employees cope with stress and the effectiveness of such schemes will be discussed. Third is the growing evidence and awareness of the particular stresses faced by counsellors themselves, including how they can be acknowledged and coped with both in training and in professional life. Areas related to stress which have not been included concern post-traumatic stress counselling (see, for example, Hodgkinson and Stewart 1991; Scott and Stradling 1992) and the role of the counsellor in post-incident counselling and psychological debriefing (Parkinson 1993).

THE STRESS PROCESS

Although 'stress' is a popular term that is widely used by both professionals and the general public, its meaning is not always clear. The confusions around the conceptualisation of stress have created problems for researchers and practitioners, since there are wide discrepancies in the way that it is viewed and operationalised. You may like to pause for a moment to consider what the term 'stress' means to you. For example, is it a condition from which the individual is suffering or is it a property of an increasingly complex environment? Alternatively, is stress some, possibly rather vague, combination of both of these? It is likely that your answer will fall into one of these three categories, each of which represents one of the three dominant definitions or models of stress. Counsellors who have a clear working model of the stress process will be more effective in helping their clients understand and work through their difficulties.

If you consider that stress is a condition from which the individual is suffering then you subscribe to the response definition of stress, which considers stress to be a pattern of physiological or psychological reactions exhibited by a person who is under pressure from a disturbing or dysfunctional environment. Thus, in this model, stress is an internal response to external stressors. The major proponent of this stress-as-response definition was Selye (1950). Working from a medical perspective, Selye proposed the general adaption syndrome (GAS), which considered stress to be a non-specific response to any demand made on the individual. This position has been useful for those researchers working from a medical or physiological perspective or those attempting to understand stress-related illnesses, but has been less helpful for those working from an organisational or psychological perspective. For example, if a counsellor's model of stress does not take into account the environmental stressors there may be a danger of unduly pathologising individuals' problems. In order to take psychosocial stress into account, Kagan and Levi (1971) extended this stress-as-response definition to include psychosocial stimuli as causal factors in stress-related illnesses. In this extension of the simpler model, the physiological stress response is viewed as the product of an interaction between the stimulus and the psychobiological programme of the person. The importance of psychosocial stimuli has been highlighted by studies indicating a correlation between negative life events and physical illness (Holmes and Rahe 1967), as well as by the observation of daily stress, or hassles, on somatic health (Delongis *et al.* 1982).

If you consider that stress is a property of the environment then you are subscribing to the stimulus definition of stress, where stress is considered to be a characteristic of the environment that is disturbing or disruptive for the person. In this model, following an engineering analogy, stress is an external force that causes a reaction of strain in the individual. However, a problem with this model is that it is inadequate to explain individual differences in response to the same level of stress. Each of us will react differently to any given stressful event depending on a number of factors, including how subjectively stressful each individual perceives the stressful event to be. Another problem with this model is its assumption that an undemanding (or boring) environment is an ideal one because it is stress free (Cox 1987). Whilst this model, with its emphasis on environmental stressors, is clearly too simple, it has been adopted by a number of researchers (for example, Payne and Firth-Cozens 1987), partly because it is testable. Moreover, it is clearly important to identify the various kinds of environmental condition which are likely to lead to strain for different groups, since this knowledge has significant implications for managers and planners. It is important for counsellors to remember that, while it is crucial to tease out the psychological components of the individual's response to stress, it is unlikely that teaching individuals to cope better is the complete answer to stressful environments. The stress–strain model allows us to incorporate structural and organisational solutions and avoid undue pathologising of the individual.

If you consider that stress is more complex than either of these two models then you are subscribing to the currently favoured transactional model of stress. This model combines the stimulus and response approaches and defines stress as the interaction between environmental stimuli and individual responses (Lazarus and Folkman 1984). In addition to focusing on the continuing relationship, or transaction, between the person and the environment, this approach emphasises intervening psychological processes, such as perception and cognitive appraisal (Cox and Mackay 1985). Stress is considered to occur only when the person perceives an external demand as exceeding his or her capacity to deal with it. Thus, the individual's personal evaluation of the nature of the demand, of the available resources and personal skills, and of the presumed outcomes will determine the stress experience. This transactional model acknowledges both the complexity and the individuality of the stress process and thus avoids some of the criticisms of earlier definitions. The model which follows (see Figure 13.1) is an important one for the counsellor to consider when assessing the nature of the stress process for each individual client.

The model in Figure 13.1, adapted from Payne and Firth-Cozens (1987), acknowledges the stress–strain model by highlighting the position of environmental stressors, but incorporates Lazarus's interactional perspective and includes many of the important elements in the stress process which it is important for the counsellor to consider when counselling for stress problems. Thus, stressors occur in the objective environment. They are

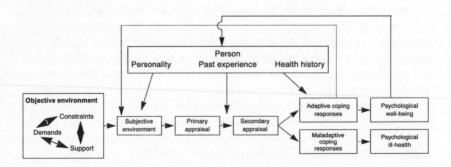

Figure 13.1 Model of the stress process (adapted from Payne and Firth-Cozens 1987)

defined as job demands which may be moderated by constraints and supports to create a balance which determines the stressfulness of the environment. For example, two counsellors working in general practitioner (GP) surgeries may each have the same number of patients to see. However, one counsellor may be working in purpose-built, appropriate accommodation with suitable back-up resources, while the second counsellor may have the constraint of working in unsuitable or inconvenient accommodation with poor receptionist and administrative back-up support. Clearly the second counsellor will be subject to more stress than the first. However, if the second counsellor has a quality relationship with a partner, a good network of friends, and appropriate supervision and support from colleagues and managers, the constraints may be offset by the amount of social support received. A counsellor working in a highly demanding job in a hospice may be able to control resources and constraints more than a counsellor working with less demanding clients in the voluntary sector. This illustrates how it is that people working in very demanding jobs may be less stressed than people working in less demanding jobs. The role of control in ameliorating the effects of stressors has been studied by Karasek (1979) and Fisher (1986). Karasek has developed the demand–discretion model, whereby job stress is considered to be a function of the demands of the job offset by the amount of discretion or control the individual has over the working situation.

The next box in Figure 13.1 indicates the individual's subjective perception of environmental stress. The overall environmental stressfulness, which needs to be accurately assessed by the counsellor, combines with the personality variables, such as perfectionism, as well as the person's past experience and life events to create the subjective environment. These internal variables also need to be assessed by the counsellor. The same objective level of stress can lead to very different subjective perceptions of environmental stress.

The dynamic nature of the stress process is indicated by the appraisal boxes in the centre of the figure. Lazarus (1966) considers that there are two steps in the continual appraisal process. At primary appraisal the individual appraises the degree of subjectively perceived threat or challenge, and at secondary appraisal the individual appraises the coping options and the available resources to decide what actions are appropriate. Both stages of appraisal are influenced by personal characteristics such as the individual's previous experiences. After appraisal the individual needs to take actions, or coping responses, to deal with the situation. The concept of coping will be considered later in this chapter. The final boxes in this figure illustrate the longer-term outcome of the stress process, which, dependent on the adaptiveness of the coping strategies adopted, can be either psychological well-being or physical and psychological ill-health. It is clear that, because of the complexity of the process, the effects of stress may differ in the amount of time they take to become apparent in different individuals.

The transactional model of stress highlights the complexity of what is essentially a process. In order to work effectively with clients, it is important for the counsellor to be able to assess all the elements in the process. Thus the counsellor needs to take into account the objective environmental demands, including supports and constraints, as well as how these are subjectively perceived by the individual. The counsellor needs to assess the individual's contribution in terms of personality, past life experiences, and health history, as well as how the person appraises the situation and his or her available coping resources. The counsellor also needs to assess with the client the adaptiveness, or maladaptiveness, of the coping strategies employed and how these can alleviate or exacerbate psychological distress. What should be clear from this description is that working with stress demands a high level of skill from counsellors, who will need to work very differently with individual clients. Employing a standard stress management package is unlikely to be helpful, and may even be harmful to some stressed individuals. This theme will be pursued in the next section of this chapter, which will examine the implications of recent research for counsellors working in the field of occupational stress.

STRESS MANAGEMENT FOR OCCUPATIONAL STRESS

In recent years stress management has become a rapidly growing industry employing increasing numbers of counsellors. It has helped to put counselling firmly on the map as a valued and relevant activity, and counsellors have not been slow to exploit this opportunity. However, this is an area where practice has moved ahead of research, and if counsellors are to keep their credibility in this field then they need to evaluate the emerging evidence and think clearly about exactly what is effective for whom. Worksite stress management has been defined by Ivancevich *et al.* (1990: 252) as 'any activity, program, or opportunity initiated by an organisation, which focuses on reducing the negative outcomes of these stressors'. There are broadly two types of stress management intervention suggested by the stress management literature (Murphy 1988). The first approach, individual-level intervention, involves enhancing or augmenting the coping responses of individuals, whereas the second type of intervention, known as organisational-level intervention, refers to efforts initiated by management intended to reduce negative outcomes and consequences. DeFrank and Cooper (1987) have expanded this view and produced a framework for describing three levels of stress management interventions and outcomes, which also illustrates interventions or targets for intervention and ways of assessing outcomes at each level (see Table 13.1). As well as the individual and organisational levels, this table shows a third level of intervention, focusing on the interface of the individual with the organisation. For example, one important stressor frequently reported by health professionals is conflict over roles and relationships with other staff (Cushway and Tyler 1994; Tyler and Cushway 1992). Interventions at this level may be evaluated by measuring both subjective changes in individuals, such as job satisfaction, and changes in more objective organisational measures, such as absenteeism.

Stress-management interventions can also be distinguished by their goals. Reynolds and Briner (1994) consider that most stress-management interventions are preventative, and draw a distinction between primary, secondary or tertiary stress-management prevention programmes. These researchers suggest that most stress-management training is primary prevention in that it is directed at individuals who are not presently suffering from stress but at risk, whereas worksite counselling and psychotherapy usually have a different goal in that they aim to treat distressed individuals with a problem or disorder. Thus, individual therapy or counselling is usually either secondary or tertiary prevention. It is important for counsellors planning stress management interventions to be clear about the goals of their intervention as well as how to assess its effectiveness.

Organisational-level interventions

Nearly all of the available literature on stress management (for example, Burke 1993) suggests that individual-level interventions are unlikely to be very effective in reducing occupational stress unless they are accompanied by appropriate organisational responses. However, there have been few reports and evaluations of organisational-level stress-management interventions, although it might be expected that interventions at this level might bring about large benefits for the organisation. Examples of organisational interventions, which have been described by Burke (1993) and Elkin and Rosch (1990), include redefining work roles and reducing work overload, redesigning the working environment and/or the task, establishing flexible work schedules, encouraging participative management, improving career development, providing social support and feedback, and building cohesive teams. Although Burke (1993) concludes that those organisational-level interventions that have been tried have generally had positive results, organisations may have been reluctant to implement them since they can be costly and may involve radical restructuring, for example, by increasing employee participation. However, participants in two recent studies of NHS employees have suggested that better support from, and communication with, colleagues, improved training and more professional recognition and appreciation would all help to reduce stress (Cushway and Tyler 1994; Tyler and Cushway 1992). It is clear that,

Table 13.1 Stress management interventions: levels, types and outcomes

Types of intervention	Outcomes
Individual level:	*Individual level:*
Stress education and monitoring	Physiological measures such as blood pressure
Relaxation/meditation	Anxiety, depression, etc.
Cognitive coping strategies	Psychosomatic complaints
Assertiveness training	Subjective stress
Time management	Subjective psychological well-being
Counselling/psychotherapy	Quality of life
Individual/organisational interface:	*Individual/organisational interface:*
Relationships at work	Job stress
Person environment fit	Job satisfaction
Role issues	Burn-out
Participation and autonomy	Productivity and performance
	Absenteeism
	Turnover
	Health care utilisation and claims
Organisational level:	*Organisational level:*
Organisational structure	Productivity
Working conditions	Turnover
Selection and placement	Absenteeism
Training and development	Health care claims
	Recruitment/retention

Source: after De Frank and Cooper 1987

although some organisational-level interventions will involve substantial financial commitment, others depend not on large cash injections but rather on creating a supportive, creative and positive organisational climate. It is likely that, in order to attract and retain the best employees, successful organisations in the twenty-first century will need to promote a positive and supportive culture.

Individual-level interventions

There is a need to incorporate individual-level interventions into the stress management process, although counsellors need to be aware that there can be ethical problems with selecting the individual alone as the target of change, as this implies that the problem of stress resides primarily with the individual and, thus, that the onus to change lies on the individual. Stress-management interventions targeting individuals should only be carried out in the context of an appropriate response to stress. Cooper and Cartwright (1994) consider that workplace stress audits are an essential part of the process, since it is necessary to gain an accurate picture of the individual organisation and its workplace stressors in order to provide an effective stress-management strategy.

There are broadly two types of individual intervention presently utilised. These are stress-management training (SMT) and individual counselling or psychotherapy. SMT, which is usually carried out with groups of individuals, typically includes a package of techniques aimed at reducing the impact of psychological stress on the individual. There is a wide variety of techniques in use and not all of them will be present in every package. A comprehensive SMT includes the following: normalisation of the experience of stress; education about the nature of stress and its implication for disease; encouraging individuals to recognise and monitor their own stress; and cognitive techniques, based on cognitive restructuring or stress inoculation training, which encourage individuals to adopt a more positive approach towards stressful situations, utilise problem-solving skills, rehearse adaptive coping strategies, and consider their priorities. Time management and assertiveness training are also commonly included in SMT. Thus, SMT includes a complex range of skills, and counsellors running stress-management groups need to be thoroughly versed in the principles and practice of each technique, as well as having skills in the facilitation and management of groups. This is important, since any SMT group may contain a few distressed individuals, and counsellors need to be aware that any intervention can be potentially harmful for some participants, and to know how both to recognise this and to manage the situation if it occurs.

Although stress management is widely used, critics have suggested that it has not been adequately evaluated. An early review of stress-management interventions reported that much of the supporting evidence was anecdotal and indirect (Newman and Beehr 1979). Although the SMT studies have improved considerably, a later review suggests that methodological problems with many existing studies have included the lack of adequate controls, inadequate follow-up periods and inappropriate outcome measures (Murphy 1988). Ivancevich *et al.* (1990) also recommend methodological improvements to future studies as well as more focus on organisation-level interventions. These latter reviews are both more optimistic than the recent picture painted by Reynolds and Briner (1994), who point out that, if SMT participants are mostly an unselected group of non-distressed individuals, then the potential benefits of SMT can only be assessed in terms of prevention of later disorder. These researchers emphasise that, using these criteria, it is presently impossible to assess the efficacy of SMT as a primary prevention strategy. The message for counsellors is that they need to be cautious and to assess the evidence carefully before making grandiose claims for SMT. Although the picture may be one of cautious optimism, it is important for counsellors to consider what is being delivered to whom and for what benefit.

In contrast to SMT, individual counselling or psychotherapy is usually offered to distressed individuals and can therefore be considered to be either secondary or tertiary prevention. It is organised in two ways, either as in-house counselling provision, or as external counselling provision. In-house counselling is set up by the organisation, which employs a counsellor or psychologist to provide personal counselling to its employees on personal or work-related issues. In this case the counsellor is either an employee of the organisation or contracted in to provide the counselling service. Probably the most appropriately organised and effectively evaluated British example is that of the UK Post Office, which employed two counsellors within its Occupational Health Department and demonstrated improvement on many of its outcome measures (Allinson *et al.* 1989). External counselling is usually delivered by contract counselling or by employee assistance programmes (EAPs), which provide a range of welfare, information and support services as well as counselling (Berridge and Cooper 1993). EAPs have been imported from the US and are rapidly growing in Britain. There are advantages and disadvantages of both types of provision, which involve issues such as confidentiality of counselling, and these need to be considered carefully by the employing organisation. Counsellors are also encouraged to assess these schemes carefully before providing their services.

The results from counselling and psychotherapy generally indicate larger and more long-lasting changes in psychological well-being than from SMT (for example, Firth and Shapiro 1986). These writers suggest that the greater changes produced by counselling or psychotherapy probably reflect improvements from the initially greater distress levels of the clients. There is evidence that sickness absence can be reduced (Allinson *et al.* 1989), although there is no evidence that work performance or efficiency is improved. Counsellors are encouraged to heed the caution issued by Firth and Shapiro (1986: 726) that 'Clinical interventions are not designed to help clients cope with impossible or unreasonable work demands, nor are they designed to solve organisational problems.' It is probable that the rapidly increasing provision of counselling by organisations is motivated as much by fear of litigation and the wish to save money as by humanitarian concern for the individual.

STRESS AND COPING IN COUNSELLORS

One of the major new directions in stress has been the growing awareness and literature on the stresses of counsellors themselves. Much research has focused on the stresses of health professionals, in particular nurses and doctors (for example, Payne and Firth-Cozens 1987; Sutherland and Cooper 1990). However, there has also been a growing literature on the stresses of mental health professionals, in particular counsellors and psychotherapists, in both Britain (for example, Dryden 1995; Cushway 1992; Cushway and Tyler 1994) and the US (Norcross and Guy 1995). Of course, counsellors are human too, and will therefore suffer from all the same concerns and life stressors as their clients. Added to this, counsellors choose to expose themselves, day after day, to the emotional and physical pain and suffering of others. It is hardly surprising, then, that the work will have its costs as well as its benefits for those involved. While this section will focus on the negative stress for counsellors, it must be acknowledged that most counsellors and psychotherapists also find their work enormously satisfying (for example, Norcross *et al.* 1993). In order to maximise job satisfaction as well as preventing burn-out, we need to be able to acknowledge and alleviate the stresses. If we are unable to look after ourselves it is unlikely that we will have much of substance to offer to others.

Wounded healers?

As awareness of the stress and burn-out processes has increased, so have questions about why counsellors choose to be involved in such hazardous work. Since the mid-1980s there has been an increasing body of literature investigating the motives of psychotherapists (for example, Guy 1987; Sussman 1992). Although there are considerable methodological problems with researching this area, the consensus in this literature seems to be that an important determinant for becoming a therapist may be a conscious or unconscious wish to make good the unresolved difficulties of early childhood. An investigation of the motives of psychotherapists can be seen to be important from our clients' point of view and not just a piece of unnecessary and self-indulgent navel gazing, since, if the counsellor remains unaware of his or her own difficulties and motivations, the distress may be acted out unwittingly to the detriment of clients. The recent publicity given to the sexual and physical abuse and exploitation of clients gives testimony to this. At the very least, therapeutic effectiveness is hindered. From the point of view of the counsellor, the stresses of the job may combine with personal vulnerabilities and difficult life events to propel the psychotherapist towards personal distress and/or burn-out. It is also true that personal distress can lead the counsellor to be a more sensitive, empathic and effective helper. If counsellors are able to relieve their distress, maybe through training or supervision, then Guy (1987) considers that, although the desire to relieve emotional distress may have motivated the career choice of some helping professionals, it can be functional.

One study compared psychotherapists with family practice physicians and reported finding no significant difference between these groups in prevalence of reported familial psychopathology (Krenek and Zalewski

1993). However, these authors also reported that the presence of a psychi-
atrically disturbed relative within the family of origin and a close
emotional relationship with that relative, coupled with feelings of anger
and guilt towards him or her, were associated with career choice as well as
with self-perceived therapeutic effectiveness and empathy. Another study
of psychotherapists found that over two-thirds of the women and one-third
of the men had experienced some form of physical or sexual abuse (Pope
and Feldman-Summers 1992). While these authors advise caution in interpreting these findings, they do conclude that substantial numbers of
psychotherapists may have suffered from abuse. Elliott and Guy (1993)
found that female psychotherapists reported a higher prevalence of physical and sexual abuse, parental alcoholism or psychiatric history, death of
a family member and greater family dysfunction in their families of origin
than did other female professionals. The literature, at present, is inconclusive. The studies reported above suffer from methodological difficulties
including low response rates and self-selected samples as well as being
self-reported and retrospective. However, the unsurprising finding that
psychotherapists have had as least as much trauma in their early lives as
the general population raises questions about the impact of this on counsellor stress.

How and to what extent psychotherapists resolve their early difficulties
is a complex question. We know that trainee psychotherapists report a
higher level of distress than qualified professionals (Cushway 1992;
Cushway and Tyler 1994) and that reported distress decreases with experience. Qualified psychotherapists report that they feel moderately competent to provide services for victims of abuse (Pope and Feldman-Summers
1992) and the qualified female therapists in the Elliott and Guy (1993)
study reported experiencing less disturbance than women in professions
other than mental health. At present we do not know whether qualified
psychotherapists cope with stress without experiencing as many symptoms and/or whether they are less willing to admit to them. Training is a
crucial time when trainee psychotherapists, maybe for the first time, have
to confront and cope with their own distress. Although this is stressful at
any time, training can cause particular contradictions, since trainees are
expected to become more self-aware and expose their vulnerabilities as a
step towards greater sensitivity. However, trainees are also selected
because of their personal and academic qualities and may therefore have
to live up to this in training and display no weakness.

One problem discussed by Sussman (1992) is that helping professionals
are expected to be strong and invulnerable. Norcross and Prochaska, in
their study of psychotherapists (1986: 110), report: 'psychotherapists are
full of problems we do not expect to find in them. Their problems in living
run the entire gamut of human concerns – abortions, affairs, alcoholism,
divorce, murder of an old friend, family suicide, drug use, a brother on

trial for murder – to name just a few'. Why we should not expect to find these difficulties is unclear. However, it does seem that, paradoxically, the so-called caring professions are remarkably tolerant of sickness, frailty and weakness in their clients, but remarkably intolerant of any human distress or difficulty in their practitioners. Perhaps it is necessary for some psychotherapists to bolster themselves by denying and distancing themselves from the difficulties that are seen in their clients. The attitudes of psychotherapy professionals, though changing recently, can exacerbate the difficulties of practitioners by promoting the macho myth of invulnerability. Thus the difficulties experienced by stressed and burnt-out counsellors can be amplified by the difficulty they may have in acknowledging and accepting their own distress.

The stresses of counselling and psychotherapy

There is a large (mostly US) literature on the stressors facing psychotherapists and counsellors, which has recently been reviewed by Brady *et al.* (1995). Some of the stressors for British psychotherapists working in organisations are similar to those faced by other professionals, such as pressure of workload, lack of resources, conflicts in relationships with other professionals, and poor organisational communication and management (Cushway and Tyler 1994). Those counsellors working in private practice face somewhat different stressors, including time pressures, economic uncertainty, caseload uncertainty and business aspects (Nash *et al.* 1984). Those working in private practice also suffer more from physical isolation, although psychic isolation and loneliness can be a problem for counsellors in all settings and appears to be due to certain aspects of the counselling relationship, such as limiting personal disclosure and sharing, emotional control and restraint, and maintaining confidentiality. Guy (1987) has described the problems for the counsellor of the 'one-way' intimacy of the therapeutic relationship, which can sometimes generalise to family and social relationships. Home–work conflict can be a stressor for many people, but particular problems can be caused by the nature of the counsellor's work. Partners and families can be resentful of the special care and attention apparently lavished on clients, particularly if this highlights any perceived lack of care on the part of the counsellor for them. Counsellors will, of course, have their own life events which can combine with events at work to increase their feelings of stress.

The distress of clients and/or their difficult behaviours have been found to be an important stressor for clinical psychologists (Cushway and Tyler 1994). In particular, suicidal behaviour and aggressive and violent behaviours seem to be the most stressful for the psychotherapist (Deutsch 1984; Farber 1983; Guy *et al.* 1991). Other stressful aspects of distressed and difficult clients are discussed in Dryden (1995). Another stress factor, identified in Britain by Cushway (1992), is that of self-doubt or uncertainty over our own capabilities. Although this is not an unexpected finding to emerge from a study of those in training, 'professional doubt' has also been identified in the US studies of psychotherapists (for example, Hellman *et al.* 1987). We have also found it emerging as a factor in qualified professionals, which is distinct from client distress, indicating that there is a factor connected with the uncertainty and inadequacy counsellors may feel about their effectiveness (Cushway and Tyler 1994; Cushway *et al.* in press). These findings suggest, then, that conducting therapy is an inherently stressful and emotionally demanding activity. Perhaps this is not a surprising finding, since the literature (for example, Dryden and Spurling 1989) suggests that a crucial factor affecting psychotherapy outcome is the therapeutic alliance, implying that effective therapy involves the whole person of the counsellor and is an activity in which he or she is emotionally engaged.

Coping with the stresses of counselling

Counsellors will already be aware of four important strategies that should be built into their practice as a matter of routine. These are: experience; training; supervision; and personal therapy. Their value cannot be over-emphasised for ensuring good practice for clients, as well as for helping to protect the counsellor against stress and burn-out. As might be expected, trainees experience the highest levels of stress (Cushway 1992) and age and experience, as well as lighter caseloads, attenuate work-related stress (Cushway and Tyler 1994; Kwee 1990; Hellman *et al.* 1987; Hellman and Morrison 1987). Clearly, sound initial training in the specific area in which the counsellor is working is paramount. But continuing professional development and training are strongly indicated for ethical reasons to ensure that the counsellor has relevant and up-to-date skills. They will also help to replenish and energise the counsellor as well as help to address professional isolation (Coyle and Goodwin 1992; Segal 1995). All the literature stresses the importance of good and regular supervision (for example, Hawkins and Shohet 1989; Guy 1987), and this is probably the most helpful way that the counsellor can contain and manage the anxiety and self-doubt inherent in therapeutic work with clients. Personal therapy is required by most psychotherapy training courses and recommended by many counselling training courses in Britain. While personal therapy must be essential if the individual experiences much personal distress, the research evidence is inconclusive about its value (Bergin and Garfield 1994; Wheeler 1991). There are certainly many training benefits from experiencing therapy, but from the standpoint of coping with stress there is some evidence that undertaking personal therapy whilst in training can be disturbing (Norcross and Goldfried 1992; Glass 1986). Personal therapy is generally reported to have had positive effects by the majority of psychotherapists and counsellors surveyed (for example, Darongkamas *et al.* 1994; Norcross *et al.* 1992). However, it has also been found to be positively correlated with reported stress, although the direction of causation is unclear (Darongkamas, *et al.* 1994).

The findings on coping suggest that it is ultimately an individual affair, and the approach that has been used by the majority of researchers in the field, which is consistent with this view, is that of conceptualising coping in terms of specific methods and/or foci of coping. The approach I have found most fruitful in my research is that of Billings and Moos (1981), who distinguish three methods of coping. These are: active-cognitive coping, where the individual attempts to manage his or her appraisal of the situation (for example, 'tried to see the positive side'); active-behavioural coping, which refers to the actual behavioural attempts to deal with the situation (for example, 'talked with partner'); and avoidance coping, where the individual attempts to avoid confronting the stressful situation (for example, 'avoided being with people in general'). Studies of trainees (Cushway 1992) and qualified psychotherapists (Cushway and Tyler 1994; Norcross and Prochaska 1986) have produced consistent findings in that active methods are found to be reported most frequently as helpful as well as being negatively correlated with distress, whereas avoidance strategies are correlated with the highest levels of distress. It is possible to say with relative confidence that the coping strategy which is cited by therapists as most effective for them is talking to a partner, friend, or colleague at work. Thus the most frequently reported coping methods are active-behavioural, including talking to loved ones, colleagues or friends, or engaging in sporting, social or leisure activities. Almost as frequently reported are active-cognitive methods, which include active problem solving or planning.

The implication of these findings for counsellors is that they should be encouraged to seek out support. This can be either by the formation of reciprocal support partnerships with peers, or by belonging to a support network or group. It is important that counsellors overcome any of the attitudinal barriers outlined earlier so that they are able to seek out and receive the support they need. This view is confirmed by the consistent research finding, mentioned earlier, of a positive relationship between psychological distress and avoidance coping. Avoidance coping may not always be a negative strategy, since there may be instances where avoiding the problem by various means may be adaptive. For example, if the problem cannot be solved, then a realistic strategy, at least in the short term, may be to get away for a while. However, we have found that where the avoidance coping processes involve the defensive process of denial, they are less likely to be adaptive (Tyler and Cushway 1992). It is possible that covert attitudes and beliefs that, for example, to show weakness is a sign of failure may actually encourage unhelpful denial and the use of maladaptive avoidance strategies.

Self-care: implications for trainers

Adaptive coping and good self-care should start early in professional life. A model for alleviating distress, providing support provision and teaching self-care during training, which was based on a study of stress in trainees (Cushway 1992), has been designed and piloted with clinical psychology trainees. The model, which has been described more fully elsewhere (Cushway *et al.* 1993; Cushway 1996), has five components (see Figure 13.2).

First, and most importantly, the philosophy adopted by trainers should be one that acknowledges and normalises stress. Thus, trainers need to present themselves as human, sometimes vulnerable people and not as superhuman. They also need to model a coping rather than a mastery model. Unless we practise what we preach, our trainees will perceive receiving personal support as a weakness and will fail to incorporate preventive personal support into their working lives. A second principle of the model is that awareness about the importance of self-care should be raised among supervisors, teachers and other qualified professionals. A third principle is that individual level interventions should be carried out in conjunction with an

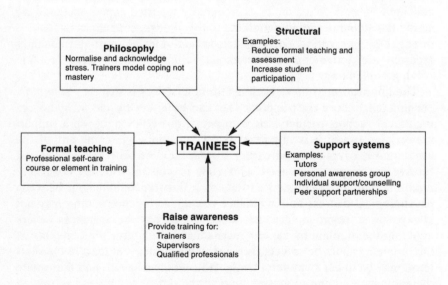

Figure 13.2 Model of support provision during training

appropriate organisational response. Thus, structural alterations to courses designed to modify stress, such as increasing the amount of trainee participation and reducing the workload, also need to be considered. It is helpful if trainees feel that courses are sensitive to their needs. The fourth aspect of the model is a formal teaching component comprising a professional self-care course whereby trainees are taught how to build professional self-care – for example, stress management – into their professional practice.

The fifth component of the model is the support systems themselves. Clearly the type of provision required will depend on the particular training course, but an important principle is that a network of different kinds of support needs to be provided, since individuals have different needs and preferences and can opt to use the methods of their choice. Another important principle of the support systems is that they are voluntary. In the clinical psychology example, trainees are assigned both a personal tutor and an appraisal tutor, have the opportunity to attend a voluntary personal awareness group throughout their training, and are able to access free, individual, confidential support, which ranges from crisis intervention and short-term counselling through to longer-term personal therapy and development. In practice, about 70 per cent of trainees attend the personal awareness groups and about 50 per cent of trainees avail themselves of the individual counselling/therapy provision at some time during their training. Trainees can access the support independently and confidentially, although many do discuss their needs and choices with course staff. This is facilitated if trainees perceive obtaining personal support as a valued and legitimate activity.

The main message to counselling trainers is that they need to be as tolerant and compassionate to their trainees as they are to their clients. In this way our trainees will be more tolerant of their own distress and will learn to take better care of themselves. As well as being of benefit to individual counsellors, it is suggested that this will also benefit the counselling professions and the clients they serve.

If appropriate self-care and stress management are introduced during training, it is hoped that this will foster a constructive perspective and sound habits that will endure throughout the counsellor's professional life. It has already been mentioned that the research evidence suggests the importance of the counsellor obtaining and maintaining a good social support system. This should include a confidant(e), who can be a partner or significant other, and the counsellor will need to organise schedules and obligations to allow for quantity and quality time together. Most people, however, need more than this relationship alone, and there is a need for a network of family members, friends and colleagues. Involvement with a wide variety of people can provide support, a balanced perspective and accurate feedback, and reduce the vulnerability inherent in the investment of a single relationship. Other self-care interventions include a balanced lifestyle that will provide opportunities for leisure, exercise, holidays and relaxation, as well as recognising the need for solitude and privacy.

The inherent stresses of practising psychotherapy can be addressed in a number of ways. Work may be varied by the inclusion of supervision, teaching, research and writing. Contact with colleagues may be fostered by organising support groups, peer supervision, and becoming a member of local, regional or national organisations.

Self-care checklist:

- Become aware of any blocks you may have to acknowledging your own distress.
- Learn to recognise your own sources of stress as well as how you personally respond to stress.
- Regularly monitor your own stress levels.
- Learn and practise appropriate coping strategies.
- Recognise that everyone's ability to cope has a limit.
- Obtain good training initially and throughout professional life in order to continue to develop professionally.
- Obtain good supervision.
- Obtain suitable therapy when appropriate.
- Learn to manage your lifestyle and aim for balance between work and other activities.
- Promote support systems and seek out support; for example, from a confidant(e), support partnerships, support groups or networks.
- Do not carry too large a caseload.
- Vary work and promote contact with colleagues.

It is my view that not to take care of ourselves is both professionally negligent and personally self-neglectful. Counselling as a profession has the potential to be demanding, depleting, discouraging and exhausting to the point of burn-out. However, appropriate coping and self-care enhance the enjoyment of counselling and facilitate taking care of other people. With careful management, counselling is a profession that provides stimulation, satisfaction, recognition, variety, challenge and enjoyment. Besides the growth of clients, it can foster self-growth and self-knowledge.

REFERENCES

Allinson, T., Cooper, C.L. and Reynolds, P. (1989) Stress counselling in the workplace: the post office experience. *The Psychologist 2* 384–8.
Bergin, A.E. and Garfield, S.L. (eds) (1994) *Handbook of Psychotherapy and Behavior Change.* New York: Wiley.
Berridge, J. and Cooper, C.L. (1993) Stress and coping in US organisations: the role of the employee assistance programme. *Work and Stress 7* 89–102.

Billings, A.G. and Moos, R.H. (1981) The role of coping resources and social resources in attenuating the stress of life events. *Journal of Behavioral Medicine 4* 139–57.

Brady, J.L., Healy, F.C., Norcross, J.C. and Guy, J.D. (1995) Stress in counsellors: an integrative research review. In W. Dryden (ed.) *The Stresses of Counselling in Action*. London: Sage.

Burke, R.J. (1993) Organisational-level interventions to reduce occupational stressors. *Work and Stress 7* 77–87.

Cooper, C.L. and Cartwright, S. (1994) Stress management interventions in the workplace: stress counselling and stress audits. *British Journal of Guidance and Counselling 22* 65–73.

Cox, T. (1987) Stress, coping and problem solving. *Work and Stress 1* 5–14.

Cox, T. and Mackay, C. (1985) The measurement of self-reported stress and arousal. *British Journal of Psychology 76* 183–6.

Coyle, A. and Goodwin, M. (1992) Training, workload and stress among HIV counsellors. *AIDS Care 4* 217–21.

Cushway, D. (1992) Stress in clinical psychology trainees. *British Journal of Clinical Psychology 31* 169–71.

Cushway, D. (1996) Stress in trainee psychotherapists. In V.P. Varma (ed.) *Stresses in Psychotherapists*. London: Routledge.

Cushway, D. and Tyler, P. (1994) Stress and coping in clinical psychologists. *Stress Medicine 10* 35–42.

Cushway, D., Tyler, P. and Nolan, P. (in press) Development of a stress scale for mental health professionals. *British Journal of Clinical Psychology*.

Cushway, D., Dent, H., Offen, L. and Howells, K. (1993) Providing personal support at Birmingham: answering the challenge to training courses. *Clinical Psychology Forum 58* 20–3.

Darongkamas, J., Burton, M.V. and Cushway, D. (1994) The use of personal therapy by clinical psychologists working in the NHS in the United Kingdom. *Clinical Psychology and Psychotherapy 1* 165–73.

DeFrank, R.S. and Cooper, C.L. (1987) Worksite stress management interventions: their effectiveness and conceptualisation. *Journal of Managerial Psychology 2* 40–50.

Delongis, A., Coyne, J.C., Dakof, G., Folkman, S. and Lazarus, R. (1982) Relationship of daily hassles, uplifts and major life events to health status. *Health Psychology 1* 119–36.

Deutsch, C.J. (1984) Self-reported sources of stress among psychotherapists. *Professional Psychology: Research and Practice 15* 833–45.

Dryden, W. (ed.) (1995) *The Stresses of Counselling in Action*. London: Sage.

Dryden, W. and Spurling, L. (eds) (1989) *Becoming a Psychotherapist*. London: Routledge.

Elkin, A.J. and Rosch, P.J. (1990) Promoting mental health at work. *Occupational Medicine State of the Art Review 5* 739–54.

Elliott, D.M. and Guy, J.D. (1993) Mental health professionals versus non-mental health professionals: childhood trauma and adult functioning. *Professional Psychology: Research and Practice 24* 83–90.

Farber, B.A. (1983) Psychotherapists' perceptions of stressful patient behavior. *Professional Psychology: Research and Practice 14* 697–705.

Firth, J.A. and Shapiro, D.A. (1986) An evaluation of psychotherapy for job-related distress. *Journal of Occupational Psychology 59* 111–19.

Fisher, S. (1986) *Stress and Strategy*. London: Lawrence Erlbaum.

Glass, J. (1986) Personal therapy and the student therapist. *Canadian Journal of Psychiatry 31* 304–11.

Guy, J.D. (1987) *The Personal Life of the Psychotherapist*. New York: Wiley.

Guy, J.D., Brown, C.K. and Poelstra, P.L. (1991) Living with the aftermath: a national survey of the consequences of patient violence directed at psychotherapists. *Psychology in Private Practice 9* 35–9.

Hawkins, P. and Shohet, R. (1989) *Supervision in the Helping Professions*. Milton Keynes: Open University Press.

Hellman, I.D. and Morrison, T.L. (1987) Practice setting and type of caseload as factors in psychotherapist stress. *Psychotherapy 42* 427–33.

Hellman, I.D., Morrison, T.L. and Abramowitz, S.I. (1987) Therapist experience and the stresses of psychotherapeutic work. *Psychotherapy 24* 171–7.

Hodgkinson, P.E. and Stewart, M. (1991) *Coping with Catastrophe*. London: Routledge.

Holmes, T.H. and Rahe, R.H. (1967) The social readjustment rating scale. *Journal of Psychosomatic Research 11* 213–18.

Ivancevich, J.M., Matteson, M.T., Freedman, S.M. and Phillips, J.S. (1990) Worksite stress management interventions. *American Psychologist 45* 252–61.

Kagan, A.R. and Levi, L. (1971) Adaptation of the psychosocial environment to man's abilities and needs. In L. Levi (ed.), *Society, Stress and Disease*. London: Oxford University Press.

Karasek, R.J. (1979) Job demands, job decision latitude and mental strain: implications for job redesign. *Administrative Science Quarterly 24* 285–308.

Krenek, R.J. and Zalewski, C. (1993) Psychiatric illness in families of mental health professionals: relationship to career choice and self-perceived therapeutic variables. *Journal of Social Behavior and Personality 8* 439–52.

Kwee, M.G.T. (1990) Burnout among Dutch psychotherapists. *Psychological Reports 67* 107–12.

Lazarus, R.S. (1966) *Psychological Stress and the Coping Process*. New York: McGraw-Hill.

Lazarus, R.S. and Folkman, S. (1984) *Stress, Appraisal and Coping*. New York: Springer.

Murphy, L.R. (1988) Workplace interventions for stress reduction and prevention. In C.L. Cooper and R. Payne (eds) *Causes, Coping and Consequences of Stress at Work*. Chichester: Wiley.

Nash, J., Norcross, J.C. and Prochaska, J.O. (1984) Satisfactions and stresses of independent practice. *Psychotherapy in Private Practice 2* 39–48.

Newman, J.E. and Beehr, T.A. (1979) Personal and organisational strategies for handling job stress: a review of research and opinion. *Personnel Psychology 32* 1–43.

Norcross, J. and Goldfried, M.R. (eds) (1992) *Handbook of Psychotherapy Integration*. New York: Basic Books.

Norcross, J.C. and Guy, J.D. (1995) *Leaving it at the Office: Understanding and Alleviating the Distress of Conducting Psychotherapy*. New York: Guilford Press.

Norcross, J.C. and Prochaska, J.O. (1986) Psychotherapist heal thyself. II: The self-initiated and therapy facilitated change of psychological distress. *Psychotherapy 23* 345–56.

Norcross, J., Dryden, W. and DeMichele, J.T. (1992) British clinical psychologists and personal therapy. III: What's good for the goose? *Clinical Psychology Forum 44* 29–33.

Norcross, J.C., Prochaska, J.O. and Farber, B.A. (1993) Psychologists conducting psychotherapy: new findings and historical comparisons on the Psychotherapy Division membership. *Psychotherapy 30* 692–7.

Parkinson, P. (1993) *Post-Trauma Stress*. London: Sheldon Press.

Payne, R. and Firth-Cozens, J. (1987) *Stress in Health Professionals*. Chichester: Wiley.

Pope, K.S. and Feldman-Summers, S. (1992) National survey of psychologists' sexual and physical abuse history and their evaluation of training and competence in these areas. *Professional Psychology: Research and Practice 23* 353–61.

Reynolds, S. and Briner, R.B. (1994) Stress management at work: with whom, for whom and to what ends? *British Journal of Guidance and Counselling 22* 75–88.

Scott, M.J. and Stradling, S.G. (1992) *Counselling for Post-Traumatic Stress Disorder*. London: Sage.

Segal, J. (1995) The stresses of working with clients with disabilities. In W. Dryden (ed.) *The Stresses of Counselling in Action*. London: Sage.

Selye, H. (1950) *Stress*. Montreal: Acta.

Sussman, M.S. (1992) *A Curious Calling: Unconscious Motivation for Practising Psychotherapy*. Northvale, NJ: Jason Aronson.

Sutherland, V.J. and Cooper, C.L. (1990) *Understanding Stress: A Psychological Perspective for Health Professionals*. London: Chapman and Hall.

Tyler, P.A. and Cushway, D. (1992) Stress, coping and mental well-being in hospital nurses. *Stress Medicine 8* 91–8.

Wheeler, S. (1991) Personal therapy: an essential aspect of counsellor training, or a distraction from focusing on the client? *International Journal for the Advancement of Counselling 14* 193–202.

Chapter 14

Working with narratives

John McLeod

INTRODUCTION

One of the defining characteristics of being human is telling stories. People tell stories as a way of making sense of, communicating and sharing their experience of life. In the past, social scientists and psychologists have largely ignored the 'storied' aspect of human conduct in the search for variables and causal factors considered to be theoretically important. Only in recent years has there emerged a movement within social science in the direction of taking stories seriously. Within psychology, some of the landmark contributions to this debate are to be found in the work of Gergen (1988), Howard (1991), Polkinghorne (1988), Sarbin (1986) and their colleagues. Probably the single most influential writer on this topic has been the social and developmental psychologist Jerome Bruner. For Bruner (1986, 1991) there are two distinct ways of knowing. *Paradigmatic* knowing consists of abstract, theoretical models. By contrast, *narrative* knowing comprises the stories people tell about events and experiences. In concentrating their energies on creating paradigmatic ways of knowing, Bruner argues, psychologists and social scientists have not given sufficient attention to understanding the processes of story-telling through which most human experience is transmitted on an everyday basis.

This awareness of the significance of stories has also had an impact in the world of counselling and psychotherapy. In psychoanalysis, Schafer (1980, 1992) and Spence (1982) have argued that the work of an analyst involves helping the clients to reconstruct their life story and discover and create 'narrative truth', the version of the life story that gives sense and purpose to life. Russell (1991) and Viney (1993) have written about narrative therapy from a cognitive-constructivist point of view. Polster (1987) has used the idea of the life story within the context of a humanistic model of therapy. Laird (1989) has evolved a feminist narrative therapy. However, the single most important narrative approach to therapy has emerged from the writings of family therapists such as Gustafson (1992),

Parry and Doan (1994), White and Epston (1994) and Penn and Frankfurt (1994). Narrative ideas have also been employed in such diverse approaches to therapy as Jungian, Ericksonian hypnotherapy and transactional analysis. Indeed, the realisation that counselling and psychotherapy are based to some degree on the telling and sharing of stories is probably a feature in all orientations.

But why does story-telling and 're-authoring' help people troubled by emotional and behavioural problems? At this time, there has been very little research into this question. However, it appears that there are a number of facilitative processes potentially associated with the experience of telling a story to an interested and empathic listener. These can be summarised as:

* the experience of being accepted and 'heard'. This is particularly important when the story being told has been a secret, when the person has been silenced by another, or when the events being recounted are especially painful;
* the opportunity for the client to discover, in the telling of his or her story, that there are different stories that can be told about a life, or an event, therefore opening up the possibility of gaining a wider perspective or choosing a new story to tell or live by. Sometimes this effect is achieved through the client challenging themselves; at other times it is an act of reframing or interpretation on the part of the counsellor;
* using the creation of a narrative account to make sense of a confusing set of experiences;
* the release of emotion that can occur when a story is finally shared;
* the sense of completion and resolution that can accompany finding an ending to a story that has been interrupted by trauma or loss;
* learning that a personal story is not wholly unique, but is similar to the stories told by other people who have undergone similar experiences. This can reduce isolation and induce hope.

These change mechanisms are all based in an appreciation of the significance of the life story as central to personal identity.

The aim of this chapter is to describe some of the methods through which a narrative approach to counselling can be implemented. The list of techniques and strategies offered makes no claim to be exhaustive. Narrative therapy is a rapidly expanding field, and there will certainly be many useful techniques that have been omitted, through either lack of space or lack of knowledge of them. Moreover, it is difficult to fit narrative techniques into discrete categories, because many of the former comprise sophisticated intervention techniques that operate on different levels. The discussion that follows reviews ways of working with narrative in counselling under three broad headings: writing, narrative deconstruction, and healing stories.

WRITING

Many of the basic skills used by counsellors and psychotherapists operate to help the client tell his or her story. Empathic listening and reflection, acceptance, open-ended questions, non-verbal encouragement and an attentive posture all function to create an environment in which the client can describe his or her experience of important events. There are other methods, however, by which the client's narrative can be given a specific focus. One of the main tools that can be used in this sphere is writing.

The value of keeping a personal journal or diary as a means of self-help or self-therapy is widely propounded (Progoff 1975; Rainer 1980). The therapeutic effect of writing about difficult experiences has been studied in a series of experiments conducted by Pennebaker and his colleagues. In one study, Pennebaker *et al.* (1990) randomly divided students who had just entered college into two groups. Those in the experimental group were asked to write for twenty minutes on three consecutive days about their 'very deepest thoughts and feelings about coming to college'. Students in the control condition were asked to write for a comparable period on the topic of 'what you have done since you woke up this morning'. Results showed that students in the experimental condition visited the college health centre less often in the follow-up period than did those in the control condition. In another study, Pennebaker *et al.* (1988) invited students to write for four consecutive days about 'the most traumatic experiences of your entire life', and again found health improvements compared to a control group who had written on a neutral topic. Spera *et al.* (1994) carried out a similar study with unemployed professionals, who wrote about their deepest thoughts and feelings concerning their redundancy, and how their lives had been affected. These participants were re-employed significantly more quickly than were the members of the control condition who had been instructed to write about relatively superficial themes.

In his analysis of the factors responsible for the benefits of this kind of writing, Pennebaker (1993) found that those research participants reporting the biggest gains from writing tended to be those who expressed more 'negative' emotions (anxiety, sadness, loss) in their stories, who used the writing task to develop insight and understanding about their problems, and whose stories became more coherent over time. Pennebaker (1988) suggests that there are four main reasons behind the beneficial effects of writing. First, writing helps the person to reframe and cognitively assimilate a difficult experience. Second, the act of putting an experience into words brings order and coherence to previously overwhelming images. Third, writing externalises the event, with the result that it does not need to be internally rehearsed. This is similar to the process of writing down a shopping list, rather than juggling the items in one's head on the way to the supermarket. Fourth, people have a basic need to express their experience. As long as the experience remains undisclosed and private, neural mechanisms are being used to inhibit self-expression. Long-term inhibition therefore leads to stress-related illnesses. Once the material is disclosed, the ensuing reduction in anxiety and arousal results in health benefits.

It is worth emphasising that, in these experiments, subjects write anonymously. No one reads what they have written, gives feedback, makes interpretations. There are none of the benefits associated with forming a relationship with a counsellor or psychotherapist. The Pennebaker studies demonstrate the value of a minimal narrative intervention, that of writing about traumatic events, and provide evidence that confirms the benefits of diary and journal writing in general.

A quite different approach to using writing can be found in the work of Penn and Frankfurt (1994). The rationale for their approach reflects their observation that:

> Frequently, clients enter therapy with fixed and constricting narratives that provide an articulation of their stance toward the world. They tell their first stories as if they were monologues: single-voiced, absolute and closed . . . they listen to themselves and are unresponsive to others.
>
> (1994: 223)

Penn and Frankfurt use writing as a means of facilitating dialogic, 'many-voiced' conversations. For example, the client may be asked to write accounts of new experiences, memories from childhood, or letters to significant others. These narratives are then read aloud to the therapist, family members or significant others. They find that the writing carried out by the client 'always addresses what has been missing . . . a missing body of feeling that, when included, changes the relationship' (1994: 230).

Asking clients to write about their lives is a technique that has a long history in therapy (Burton 1965; Greening 1977; Lange 1994; Maultsby 1971). For example, personal construct therapists have, since the 1950s, invited clients to write 'self-characterisation' sketches (Fransella 1985).

Writing is a therapeutic tool that can be used by the therapist or counsellor as well as by the client. White and Epston (1990) point out that written communication allows new learning or insight to be kept in a form that enables the person to refer back to a tangible document recording this 'alternative knowledge'. Specifically, White and Epston often write letters to their clients after sessions, summarising their sense of what is happening. They may also write letters inviting family members to participate in therapy, letters of prediction (what they believe will happen over the next six months), letters at the end of therapy, and 'to whom it may concern' reference letters. They help clients to write letters to significant others, 'discharging' them of previous roles and responsibilities. Another of their methods of employing narrative for therapeutic purposes is to create 'alternative' or 'counter-documents', which publicly celebrate personal developments. Examples of these would be the 'Escape from Misery Certificate', the 'Escape from Guilt Certificate' and the 'Breaking the Grip of Sneaky Poo Certificate'. The purpose of these letters and certificates is to contribute to the process of a therapy that aims to help clients to 're-author' their life stories in areas where these stories are destructive or limiting.

There are other important examples of therapist-written narratives. Yalom *et al.* (1975) and Aveline (1986) describe the practice of group therapy leaders sending accounts of group themes and issues to their group members after each session. Within cognitive-analytic therapy (CAT), the therapist prepares a written 'reformulation' of the maladaptive relationship patterns being exhibited by the client, and this document constitutes the basis for much of the therapy (Ryle 1990).

Most of the time, counsellors and psychotherapists engage in various types of conversation with their clients. Introducing writing adds a new dimension to counsellor–client communication. When thoughts and feelings are written down, they may become more structured, organised and purposeful. The written document can serve as a permanent record of significant new thoughts and feelings. It can be shown to other people. And there can be an authority associated with the written word that can be exploited by clients seeking to 're-author' aspects of their own lives. In using written material, it is of course necessary to be sensitive to any difficulties clients may have with literacy and language.

DECONSTRUCTING AND RECONSTRUCTING LIFE STORIES

Counselling and psychotherapy can be understood, at least in part, as involving the experience of telling stories about one's troubles to another person and using this relationship to generate new understanding, new ways of being and acting, and ultimately new stories. From this point of view, the heart of the therapeutic process consists of identifying the stories told by the client, examining the meaning and structure of these stories, and contrasting them with other stories that might be told. This process can be described as one of deconstruction followed by, or accompanied by, reconstruction. The concept of 'deconstruction' has been widely used in post-modern sociology and literary criticism. However, from a therapeutic perspective, it has been defined in the following terms:

> Deconstruction has to do with procedures that subvert taken-for-granted realities and practices; those so-called 'truths' that are split off from the conditions and the context of their production, those

disembodied ways of speaking that hide their biases and prejudices, and those familiar practices of self and of relationship that are subjugating of persons' lives. Many of the methods of deconstruction render strange these familiar and everyday taken-for-granted realities and practices by objectifying them. In this sense, the methods of deconstruction are methods that 'exoticise the domestic'.

(White 1991: 21)

For the counsellor, the task of deconstruction requires being able to 'render strange' the familiar, split-off and disembodied ways of talking about self exhibited by the client during a therapy session. For example, Young and Beier (1982) argue that self-defeating and 'subjugating' life stories are perpetuated through interactions in which the other person responds to the client in a predictable way. Thus, a client who behaves in a caustic or critical manner will evoke negative reactions from other people, which in turn will reinforce his or her definition of self (or story about self) as unlikable and unworthy. If, however, the therapist declines to respond in the predicted manner, opportunities may be opened up for the client to see, as if for the first time, just how strange are the taken-for-granted strategies he or she employs to objectify himself or herself. In the following excerpt from a therapy session, the client is a student seeing a counsellor at a University Counselling Centre, and has two weeks remaining of a time-limited therapy contract:

Client: Well, you know we have only two weeks left in the semester, and I, uh, well, just don't see the point in continuing. I'm sure it's just a waste of time now – since I'll be leaving soon. Maybe we should just stop now.

Therapist: (With exaggeration and a smile) Thank goodness you said something. All I think about is how I could spend my extra hour on Thursday if only you weren't around.

Client: (Laughs) I guess I didn't mean it quite that way. I guess I felt sort of sad about stopping and did not want to prolong the agony.

(Young and Beier 1982: 271)

This brief interaction illustrates one of the ways in which a story can be deconstructed. The opening statement by the client can be understood as a fragment of a story he tells himself about being inadequate ('a waste of your time'). The therapist declines to give the reassurance expected by the client, and in the ensuing moment of uncertainty the client offers another quite different story-line about himself. Now he describes himself as sad and in 'agony' over the ending.

A somewhat different approach to deconstructing client stories has been developed by Luborsky and his colleagues at the University of Pennsylvania (Luborsky et al. 1992, 1994; Luborsky and Crits-Christoph

1990). These therapists propose that all the stories told by clients in therapy express a set of core conflictual relationship themes (CCRTs). By observing, identifying and then interpreting these themes, the therapist can help the client to gain enough insight to begin the process of changing the interaction patterns that correspond to these stories. This model is grounded in a psychodynamic approach, with CCRTs being viewed as equivalent to transference reactions. CCRTs can be identified in stories the client tells about relationships with other people, stories about the therapist, behaviour in relation to the therapist, and dream material. The structure of a CCRT comprises three elements: a wish, response from other, and response from self. Examples of wishes frequently found in client narratives are 'to be close and accepted', 'to be loved and understood', and 'to assert self and be independent'. Typical responses from others are 'rejecting and opposing' and 'controlling', and the most prevalent responses from self are 'disappointed and depressed', 'unreceptive' and 'helpless'. The value of the CCRT formula in deconstructing clients' stories is that it gives the counsellor a means of cutting through the detail of client narratives and focusing on the central life meanings or patterns expressed through these stories. Luborsky (1984) has described an approach to psychodynamic therapy that is based on this kind of narrative understanding.

Narrative deconstruction in therapy has received considerable attention in recent years. Schafer (1992) has depicted all psychodynamic therapy in these terms. Edelson (1993) looks for the elements of the classic Hollywood movie (the protagonist, the antagonist or villain, triggering events, flashbacks) in the stories told by his clients. Berne (1975) uses the favourite fairy story of the client as a means of exploring the 'storied' nature of his or her life. Bagarozzi and Anderson (1989), in similar fashion, ask the client to retell his or her favourite story from novels, films or TV series. Gustafson (1992) has identified categories of story told by clients. White and Epston (1990), and also Russell and Van Den Broek (1992), listen for 'rival' narratives, examples of different types of story told about the same type of event, in the stories recounted by their clients.

The process of narrative reconstruction covers a range of different therapeutic operations and techniques. Most of the uses of writing introduced earlier can be seen as reconstruction strategies, taking as their goal the replacement of repetitive, objectifying stories with new, life-enhancing ones. An important theme in reconstruction is narrative completion. Many clients have undergone experiences that are difficult to talk about at all. Their stories of these experiences are as a result confused, chaotic and unfinished. The work of Wigren (1994) represents a particularly useful approach to narrative completion. In her therapy with clients who had survived trauma, Wigren (1994) found that the circumstances of the trauma had often disrupted their ability to make and share stories of what had happened. For some clients, their network of social relations had been shattered by the traumatic event. What had happened to them was too painful for other people to want to hear. Trauma was also associated with levels of physiological arousal and emotion that made communication and 'making sense' difficult. Traumatic memories were also hard to assimilate at a cognitive level, since the events that had been experienced were 'unbelievable'.

Several methods of facilitating narrative reconstruction have been developed by Parry and Doan (1994). They note that one of the best ways of helping clients create new stories is for the therapist to be sensitive to the strengths and wider meanings expressed by the clients, their 'solutions', rather than becoming fixated on the 'problems' and weaknesses that are presented in sessions. They also observe that it is beneficial for clients constructing new life stories to have access to audiences that will accept and celebrate these stories. Parry and Doan (1994) have published a number of exercises and worksheets that can be used to promote narrative reconstruction along these lines.

Another powerful technique for eliciting new life narratives is the 'miracle question':

> Suppose that when you go to sleep tonight, a miracle happens and the problems that brought you here are solved. But since you are asleep, you don't know that the miracle has happened until you wake up tomorrow. What will be the difference that will tell you that a miracle has happened?
>
> (de Shazer 1988:78)

The 'miracle question' invites the client to take two steps beyond his or her current problems. First, the problems have been solved. Second, the client is to consider the behavioural consequences of the solution. The use of the notion of 'miracle' further impels the client into an imaginary realm, far from his or her troubled life. At the same time, the request to provide as much mundane detail as possible of what would take place in this imaginary future paradoxically leads the client to generate ideas about small changes that could in fact be achievable.

There are two key principles underpinning the work of narrative deconstruction and reconstruction. The first is that this is a joint enterprise, a co-construction negotiated between client and therapist. Second, successful reconstruction or 'reauthoring' involves finding broader perspectives within which the thoughts, feelings and actions of the client can be understood. It is a matter not merely of reframing, of replacing one story with an alternative one, but of constructing a metanarrative which subsumes the pre-existing, troubled stories into a broader framework of meaning. Sometimes, clients create these broader frameworks from local, familiar resources. On other occasions, the theory of psychotherapy held by the counsellor functions as a metanarrative template through which the client reshapes his or her life story (Omer and Strenger 1992). However, the search for potent, higher-level narrative structures has led some counsellors and therapists to look beyond therapy, to seek therapeutic stories in a variety of cultural sources.

HEALING STORIES: EXTERNALLY PROVIDED NARRATIVES

The work with narratives that has been described so far has been fundamentally client-centred, in the sense that it has comprised different approaches to engaging with the stories spontaneously told by clients themselves. There is another strand in narrative therapy, however, which involves supplying clients with stories generated by other people. The clearest examples of this approach are the use of mythic stories by Gersie (1991) and the use of therapist-inspired, 'everyday' stories by Ericksonian therapists (Rosen 1982).

Gersie and King (1990) and Gersie (1991) draw upon a worldwide stock of myths, folk tales and fairy stories in their therapeutic work. Their model is based on working with groups, and employing mythic stories to facilitate the experience of creative 'story-making' in members of the group. For example, in group work with bereaved people, Gersie (1991) has evolved a structure for group sessions which begins with exercises designed to sensitise participants to the theme for the session. The group facilitator then tells the mythic story. Following this event, group members perform expressive tasks relating to the story (such as drawing, clay modelling, writing), share their experiences with other group members, and finally reflect on the material and make connections between the session and their life as a whole. Gersie (1991) intentionally selects stories that are unfamiliar to participants, to enhance the impact and memorability of the tale. These ancient stories supply powerful metaphors that can resonate with the life stories and experience of individual participants.

Ericksonian approaches to counselling and psychotherapy draw upon the theory and practice of Milton H. Erickson, and are informed by ideas from family therapy and hypnotherapy. Erickson himself was a master story-teller, and the therapeutic use of story-telling has remained an essential element in this approach. Many of Erickson's 'teaching tales' have been collected together in a book by Rosen (1982). Lankton and Lankton look upon a teaching story as constituting a 'therapeutic metaphor', defined as: 'a story with dramatic devices that captures attention and provides an altered framework through which the client(s) can entertain novel experience' (1986: 154). However, unlike Gersie (1991), who uses pre-existing myths and folk tales to supply a narrative 'altered framework', Ericksonian therapists construct stories from their own observations of life and their feelings in relation to their client. Rosen writes that 'the best way for the therapist to select stories is through his own free associations . . . by this I mean not only cognitive free associations, but also bodily responses, emotions, perceptions, and, particularly, imagery associations' (1982: 39–40).

A brief example of one of Erickson's teaching tales illustrates some of these themes:

> A lot of people were worried because I was four years old and didn't talk, and I had a sister two years younger than me who talked, and she is still talking but she hasn't said anything. And many people got distressed because I was a four-year-old boy who couldn't talk. My mother said, comfortably, 'When the time comes, then he will talk'.
>
> (Rosen 1982: 58–9)

Many teaching stories may be longer and more complex, but this brief narrative contains some significant therapeutic features. The story has a message, that the unconscious mind can be trusted, or that a person will speak when it is the right time for him or her to do so. The story has dramatic hold: the listener wants to know how the tale will unfold. Humour is used to involve the listener ('still talking but she hasn't said anything'). Finally, the listener is left with a powerful image ('my mother said, comfortably').

These healing stories are not the personal narratives, the client's stories of pain and trouble, that are employed in other approaches, but are drawn from a collective cultural stock of anecdotes, folk tales and myths. A story of this kind offered by a therapist to a client contains, in its import or 'moral', a general lesson to be learned, a broader perspective on whatever issue the client is exploring. However, the meaning of the story is not explicit, nor is it simple. These meanings emerge over time, and the client is able to return to the story on later occasions and find more in it. Bettelheim (1976) has described the ways that children are able to use fairy tales to give meaning to their experiences. The therapist-provided stories employed by Gersie, Erickson and others serve a similar function, of relating current concerns to wider existential dilemmas and developmental tasks.

CONCLUSIONS

Narrative approaches and techniques represent a significant area of development within contemporary counselling and psychotherapy. There are many ideas and methods that open up exciting possibilities for new and effective ways of working with clients. This chapter has focused largely on examples of practical techniques employed by narrative-informed therapists. However, it is important not to lose sight of the basic notion that people express themselves through stories, and that listening for, and to, the story is a powerful means of entering the world of the client.

Using narrative as a framework for therapy involves adopting a philosophical position or 'image of the person' that is distinctively different from currently prevailing psychological models (Sarbin 1986; White and Epston 1990). Narrative knowing is always situated, always views the person as an active, story-constructing agent, always implies an audience, and always understands human action as sequenced, unfolding over time, and with purpose. Working with stories inevitably brings a therapist face to face with the cultural context of the client. Developing ways of understanding stories requires making links between therapy and disciplines such as linguistics, literary criticism, anthropology and cultural studies. Omer (1993a: 59) has suggested that therapists working with stories should be 'endowed with an ability with and sensitivity to words, images, storylines, and dramatic sequences'.

Finally, like any other form of counselling or psychotherapy, narrative approaches have their limitations and dangers. Recently, controversies over the validity of 'recovered' or 'false' memories, particularly in therapy with survivors of child sexual abuse, have highlighted the error of assuming that what Spence (1982) has called 'narrative truth' (the story that has meaning and sense for the client) is the same as 'historical truth' (what actually happened). Another risk in narrative work is that of the therapist becoming committed to an over-simplified version of the client's life story. This is a particular danger in time-limited work, where a counsellor or psychotherapist may arrive at a formulation or 'life sketch' on the basis of only a limited amount of information about the client (Omer 1993b). A third potential hazard is to interpret the narrative approach as comprising an essentially cognitive way of working with clients, as if reauthoring a life story somehow resembled writing an essay. I believe this to be a mistaken view. Stories, the real stories about how one lives, express strong feelings. Listening to such stories requires being open to feelings. Stories are the way we process our emotions, how we move from one feeling state to another. Narrative therapy depends, like most other therapies, on an appreciation of, and an ability to operate within, the relational and emotional world of the client.

REFERENCES

Aveline, M.O. (1986) The use of written reports in brief group psychotherapy training. *International Journal of Group Psychotherapy* 36 477–82.

Bagarozzi, D.A. and Anderson, S.A. (1989) *Personal, Marital and Family Myths: Theoretical Formulations and Clinical Strategies*. New York: Norton.

Berne, E. (1975) *What Do You Say After You Say Hello? The Psychology of Human Destiny*. London: Corgi.

Bettelheim, B. (1976) *The Uses of Enchantment: The Meaning and Importance of Fairy Tales*. Harmondsworth: Penguin.

Bruner, J.S. (1986) *Actual Minds, Possible Worlds*. Cambridge, MA: Harvard University Press.

Bruner, J. (1991) The narrative construction of reality. *Critical Inquiry 18* 1–21.

Burton, A. (1965) The use of written productions in psychotherapy. In L. Pearson (ed.) *Written Communications in Psychotherapy*. Springs, IL: Thomas.

de Shazer, S. (1988) *Clues: Investigating Solutions in Brief Therapy*. New York: Norton.

Edelson, M. (1993) Telling and enacting stories in psychoanalysis and psychotherapy: implications for teaching psychotherapy. *Psychoanalytic Study of the Child 48* 293–325.

Fransella, F. (1985) Individual psychotherapy. In E. Button (ed.) *Personal Construct Theory and Mental Health*. Beckenham: Croom Helm.

Gergen, K.J. (1988) If persons are texts. In S.B. Messer, L.A. Sass and R.L. Woolfolk (eds) *Hermeneutics and Psychological Theory: Interpretive Perspectives on Personality, Psychotherapy and Psychopathology*. New Brunswick, NJ: Rutgers University Press.

Gersie, A. (1991) *Storymaking in Bereavement: Dragons Fight in the Meadow*. London: Jessica Kingsley.

Gersie, A. and King, N. (1990) *Storymaking in Education and Therapy*. London: Jessica Kingsley.

Greening, T.C. (1977) The uses of autobiography. In W. Anderson (ed.) *Therapy and the Arts: Tools of Consciousness*. New York: Harper and Row.

Gustafson, J.P. (1992) *Self-Delight in a Harsh World: The Main Stories of Individual, Marital and Family Psychotherapy*. New York: Norton.

Howard, G.S. (1991) Culture tales: a narrative approach to thinking, cross-cultural psychology and psychotherapy. *American Psychologist 46* 187–97.

Laird, J. (1989) Women and stories: restoring women's self-constructions. In M. McGoldrick, C.M. Anderson and F. Walsh (eds) *Women in Families: A Framework for Family Therapy*. New York: Norton.

Lange, A. (1994) Writing assignments in the treatment of grief and traumas from the past. In J. Zeig (ed.) *Ericksonian Methods: The Essence of the Story*. New York: Brunner/Mazel.

Lankton, S.R. and Lankton, C.H. (1986) *Enchantment and Intervention in Family Therapy: Training in Ericksonian Approaches*. New York: Brunner/Mazel.

Luborsky, L. (1984) *Principles of Psychoanalytic Psychotherapy: A Manual for Supportive-Expressive Treatment*. New York: Basic Books.

Luborsky, L. and Crits-Christoph, P. (eds) (1990) *Understanding Transference: The CCRT Method*. New York: Basic Books.

Luborsky, L., Barber, J.P. and Diguer, L. (1992) The meanings of narratives told during psychotherapy: the fruits of a new observational unit. *Psychotherapy Research 2* 277–90.

Luborsky, L., Popp, C., Luborsky, E. and Mark, D. (1994) The core conflictual relationship theme. *Psychotherapy Research 4* 172–83.

Maultsby, M.C. (1971) Systematic written homework in psychotherapy. *Psychotherapy 8* 195–8.

McKinney, F. (1977) Free writing as therapy. *Psychotherapy 13* 183–7.

Omer, H. (1993a) Quasi-literary elements in psychotherapy. *Psychotherapy 30* 59–66.

Omer, H. (1993b) Short-term psychotherapy and the rise of the life-sketch. *Psychotherapy 30* 668–73.

Omer, H. and Strenger, C. (1992) The pluralist revolution: from the one true meaning to an infinity of constructed ones. *Psychotherapy 29* 253–61.

Parry, A. and Doan, R.E. (1994) *Story Re-Visions: Narrative Therapy in the Post-Modern World*. New York: Guilford Press.

Penn, P. and Frankfurt, M. (1994) Creating a participant text: writing, multiple voices, narrative multiplicity. *Family Process 33* 217–32.

Pennebaker, J.W. (1988) Confiding traumatic experiences and health. In S. Fisher and J. Reason (eds) *Handbook of Life Stress, Cognition and Health*. Chichester: Wiley.

Pennebaker, J.W. (1993) Putting stress into words: health, linguistic and therapeutic implications. *Behaviour Research and Therapy 31* 539–48.

Pennebaker, J.W., Colder, M. and Sharp, L.K. (1990) Accelerating the coping process. *Journal of Personality and Social Psychology 58* 528–37.

Pennebaker, J.W., Kiecolt-Glaser, J.K. and Glaser, R. (1988) Disclosure of traumas and immune function: health implications for psychotherapy. *Journal of Consulting and Clinical Psychology 56* 239–45.

Polkinghorne, D.E. (1988) *Narrative Knowing and the Human Sciences*. Albany, NY: SUNY Press.

Polster, E. (1987) *Every Person's Life is Worth a Novel*. New York: Norton.

Progoff, I. (1975) *At a Journal Workshop*. New York: Dialogue House.

Rainer, T. (1980) *The New Diary*. London: Angus and Robertson.

Rosen, S. (ed.) (1982) *My Voice Will Go with You: The Teaching Tales of Milton H. Erickson*. New York: Norton.

Russell, R.L. (1991) Narrative in views of humanity, science and action: lessons for cognitive therapy. *Journal of Cognitive Psychotherapy 5* 241–56.

Russell, R.L. and Van den Broek, P. (1992) Changing narrative schemas in psychotherapy. *Psychotherapy 29* 344–54.

Ryle, A. (1990) *Cognitive-Analytic Therapy: Active Participation in Change – A New Integration in Brief Psychotherapy*. Chichester: Wiley.

Sarbin, T.R. (1986) The narrative as a root metaphor for psychology. In T.R. Sarbin (ed.) *Narrative Psychology: The Storied Nature of Human Conduct*. New York: Praeger.

Schafer, R. (1980) Narration in the psychoanalytic dialogue. *Critical Inquiry 7* 29–53.

Schafer, R. (1992) *Retelling a Life*. New York: Basic Books.

Spence, D.P. (1982) *Narrative Truth and Historical Truth: Meaning and Interpretation in Psychoanalysis*. New York: Norton.

Spera, S.P., Buhrfeind, E.D. and Pennebaker, J.W. (1994) Creative writing and coping with job loss. *Academy of Management Journal 37* 722–33.

Viney, L. (1993) *Life Stories: Personal Construct Therapy with the Elderly*. Chichester: Wiley.

White, M. (1991) Deconstruction and therapy. *Dulwich Centre Newsletter* Autumn 21–40.

White, M. and Epston, D. (1990) *Narrative Means to Therapeutic Ends*. New York: Norton.

Wigren, J. (1994) Narrative completion in the treatment of trauma. *Psychotherapy 31* 415–23.

Yalom, I.D., Brown, S. and Bloch, S. (1975) The written summary as a group psychotherapy technique. *Archives of General Psychiatry 36* 605–13.

Young, D.M. and Beier, E.G. (1982) Being asocial in social places: giving the client a new experience. In J.C. Anchin and D.J. Kiesler (eds) *Handbook of Interpersonal Psychotherapy*. New York: Pergamon.

Chapter 15

Teaching the principles of unconditional self-acceptance in a structured group setting

Windy Dryden

INTRODUCTION

In this chapter, I will describe an eight-week psychoeducational group in which I teach group members the principles of unconditional self-acceptance. These principles stem from the theory of rational emotive behaviour therapy (REBT), an approach to cognitive-behaviour therapy founded forty years ago by Albert Ellis. The group is the first psychoeducational programme on self-acceptance run on REBT lines that has been conducted in a hospital setting in Britain. As such this constitutes a new development. What follows here is meant to help readers to understand the content and development of such groups. It is not designed to be a group leader's guide.

In the chapter, I will do the following:

1 briefly introduce rational emotive behaviour therapy and outline the REBT concept of ego disturbance;
2 present the principles of unconditional self-acceptance;
3 outline the steps of a self-acceptance group and some of the exercises that I use at each step, and discuss briefly the context in which I run these groups.

REBT AND EGO DISTURBANCE

One of REBT's basic premises is that psychological disturbance stems primarily from the irrational beliefs that we hold about ourselves, others and the world. However, REBT theory holds that the way we feel, think and act are intertwined so that when considering their clients' feelings of depression, for example, rational emotive behaviour therapists will consider not only the beliefs that underpin the clients' depression, but also their behaviour which may serve to perpetuate their depressogenic beliefs.

REBT therapists can, in my view, best be seen as psychological educators, in that they will teach their clients the basic REBT view of disturbance and, once the clients have indicated that they wish to work in this way, will teach them how to identify, challenge and change the irrational beliefs which underpin their psychological problems. For a much fuller consideration of the theory and practice of REBT see Dryden (1995a, 1995b).

Ego disturbance

REBT theory distinguishes between two major types of psychological disturbance: ego disturbance and discomfort disturbance (Dryden 1994). Ego disturbance stems from irrational beliefs related to a person's 'self', while discomfort disturbance stems from irrational beliefs related to that individual's personal domain unrelated to his or her 'self', but centrally related to his or her sense of comfort.

Ego disturbance results when a person makes a demand on himself or herself, others, or the world which is not met, and the person then puts himself or herself down in some way. The following themes are usually involved in ego disturbance:

- failing to achieve an important target or goal;
- acting incompetently (in public or private);
- not living up to one's standards;
- breaking one's ethical code;
- being criticised;
- being ridiculed;
- not being accepted, approved, appreciated or loved by significant others.

Ego-related irrational beliefs are found in a variety of emotional disturbances. Please note, however, that I am not saying that these ego irrational beliefs completely account for the emotions listed below. Rather, I am saying that these beliefs are often found when clients report these emotional experiences. In the following examples, you will note that each of these irrational beliefs contains two elements. First, there is a demanding belief which often takes the form of a 'must', 'absolute should', 'have to' or 'got to'; second, there is a self-downing belief which takes the form of a global negative evaluation of one's total 'self'. REBT theory states that self-downing beliefs are derived from the 'musturbatory' beliefs.

Depression

- 'Because I have failed the test, as I absolutely should not have done, I am a failure.'
- 'Since my partner has rejected me, as he absolutely should not have done, this proves that I am no good.'

Anxiety

- 'If I failed at my upcoming test, which I must not do, I would be a failure.'
- 'If he rejected me as I think he will soon, but which he must not do, I would be no good.'

Guilt

- 'I have hurt the feelings of my parents, which I absolutely should not have done, and therefore I am a bad person.'
- 'I failed to help a good friend of mine. The fact that I did not do what I absolutely should have done proves that I am a rotten person.'

Shame

- 'I have acted foolishly in front of my peers, which I absolutely should not have done, and this makes me an inadequate person.'
- 'I have been having sexual feelings towards my sister, which I absolutely should not have, and the fact that I have these feelings makes me a shameful person.'

Hurt

- 'My ex-girlfriend is going out with my best friend, which absolutely should not happen. Since it is happening, this proves that I am unlovable.'

Anger

- 'You absolutely should not have criticised me in the way that you did. Your criticism reminds me that I am a failure.'

Jealousy

- 'If my husband looks at another woman, which he must not do, it means that he finds her more attractive. This must not happen, and proves that I am worthless.'

Envy

- 'My friend is making better progress than I am in our respective careers. I must have what he has and because I don't this makes me less worthy than I would be if I had what he has.'

UNCONDITIONAL SELF-ACCEPTANCE

As I showed in the above section, ego disturbance occurs when a person makes a global, negative evaluation of his or her total self, which in turn is based on the existence of a 'musturbatory' belief. REBT theory states that the healthy alternative to ego disturbance is based on a set of beliefs founded on the concept of unconditional self-acceptance. In this section I will outline the ten principles that underpin this concept.

1 *Human beings cannot legitimately be given a single global rating.* In the previous section I gave several examples of the ways in which people put themselves down (for example, 'I am a failure', 'I am a bad person', etc.). Each of these examples involves the person giving himself or herself a single global rating. Indeed, the concept of self-esteem frequently advocated by the majority of counsellors and psychotherapists is based on this same principle. Low self-esteem involves the assignment of a single, negative, global rating to a person, and high self-esteem involves the assignment of a single, positive, global rating to the person.

REBT theory argues that it is not possible to give a person a single global rating, be it negative or positive. This is best shown if we define clearly the terms 'self' and 'esteem'. First, let us take the term 'self'. Hauck (1991: 33) has provided a very simple but profound definition of the self. He says that the self is 'every conceivable thing about you that can be rated'. This means that all your thoughts, images, feelings, behaviours and bodily parts are part of your 'self', and all these different aspects that belong to you from the beginning of your life to the moment just before your death have to be included in your 'self'. Now let us consider the term 'esteem'. This is derived from the verb 'to estimate', which means to give something a rating, judgement or estimation. The question then arises: 'Can we give the self a single *legitimate* rating, estimation or judgement which completely accounts for its complexity?' The answer is clearly 'no'. As Hauck (1991) notes, it is possible to rate different aspects of one's 'self', but a person is far too complex to warrant a single, legitimate, global rating.

Even if it were valid to give a person a single global rating – a task which would involve a team of objective judges and a computer so powerful that it could analyse the millions upon millions of data produced by that person – as soon as that global judgement was made, it would become immediately redundant, since that person would continue to produce more data. In other words, a person is an on-going, ever-changing process and thus defies the ascription of a single, static, global judgement.

By contrast, the concept of unconditional self-acceptance does not involve any such rating or evaluation. Rather, accepting yourself involves acknowledging that you are a complex, on-going, ever-changing process that defies being legitimately rated by yourself or by others. However, and this is a crucial point, unconditional self-acceptance does allow you to rate different aspects of yourself. Indeed, it encourages this type of evaluation, since doing this allows you to focus on your negative aspects and do something to improve them without self-blame. Conversely, if you focus on your negative aspects from the standpoint of self-esteem, then you are less likely to change them, because you are sidetracked by giving your 'self' a global negative rating for having these aspects. It is difficult to change anything about yourself while you are beating yourself over the head for having those aspects in the first place.

2 *Human beings are essentially fallible.* REBT theory holds that if human beings have an essence it is probably that we are essentially fallible. As Maultsby (1984) put it, humans have an incurable error-making tendency. I would add that we frequently make more serious mistakes than we are prepared to accept and that we often keep repeating the same errors. Why do this? Hauck (1991) argues that we keep repeating our errors out of stupidity, ignorance or because we are psychologically disturbed. Ellis (1994) noted that humans find it very easy to disturb themselves and difficult to undisturb themselves. Self-acceptance, then, means acknowledging that our essence is fallibility and that we are not perfectible.

3 *All humans are equal in humanity, but unequal in their different aspects.* This principle follows on from the two listed above. If the essence of humanity is fallibility then all humans are equal in their humanity, and since human beings cannot be rated it follows that no human is worthier than any other. This principle reveals rational emotive behaviour therapy as one of the most, if not the most, humanistic of all psychotherapies. However, this principle of parity among humans does not deny that there is a great deal of variation among human beings with respect to their different aspects. Thus, Adolf Hitler may be equal in humanity to Mother Theresa, but in terms of their compassion to human beings, the latter far outscores the former.

4 *The rational use of the concept of human worth.* From the principles discussed thus far, you will see that the concept of human worth is problematic, since it rests on the assignment of a single global rating (worth) to a process (the 'self') which defies such a simple rating. However, a number of clients want to retain the idea of human worth even though it has inherent problems. The main problem with the concept of human worth is that people normally make their worth contingent on variables that change (for example, 'I am worthwhile if I do well in my exams', which implies that if I do not do well then I am not worthwhile). Even if a person fulfils the conditions of worth at any given moment, he or she is still vulnerable to emotional disturbance if those conditions are not continually met.

The only way that a person can apply the concept of human worth in a rational manner is to make his or her worth contingent on one of two constants. First, he or she can say that he or she is worthwhile because he or she is human. Second, he or she can say that he or she is worthwhile as long as he or she is alive. This can be even applied by people who believe in an afterlife ('I am worthwhile as long as I am alive in this life or any future life that I may have'). However, the difficulty with this concept, as Ellis (1972) has shown, is that someone can just as easily say: 'I am worthless because I am alive' or 'I am worthless because I am human.' For this reason, most REBT therapists discourage their clients from using the concept of human worth.

5 *Unconditional self-acceptance avoids errors of over-generalisation.* When people apply the concept of conditional self-esteem they constantly make errors of over-generalisation, or what might be called part–whole errors. In the part–whole error, a person infers that he or she has failed to achieve a certain goal (which represents a part of the person), evaluates this failure negatively, and then concludes that he or she is a failure (which is the whole of the person). In other words, the person rates the whole of himself or herself on the basis of his or her rating of a part of himself or herself. Applying the concept of unconditional self-acceptance to this example, the person would still infer that he or she has failed to achieve his or her goal, and would still evaluate this failure negatively. However, his or her conclusion, that his or her failure proves that he or she is a fallible human being, would be perfectly logical.

6 *Unconditional self-acceptance is based on a flexible, preferential philosophy.* Earlier in this chapter, I pointed out that self-downing beliefs are derived from rigid, 'musturbatory' beliefs, as in Ellis's memorable phrase 'Shouldhood leads to shithood. You're never a shit without a should.' What follows from this is that unconditional self-acceptance beliefs are derived from flexible, preferential beliefs. For example, if you believe that you are inadequate because you acted in a socially inappropriate manner, then this self-downing belief stems from the rigid belief that: 'I must not behave inappropriately in a social context.' A self-accepting alternative belief would involve you accepting yourself as a fallible human being who is not inadequate. This belief in turn would stem from the flexible belief that: 'I would prefer not to act in a socially inappropriate manner, but there's no reason why I absolutely must not do so.'

7 *Self-acceptance promotes constructive action, not resignation.* If we can accept ourselves as fallible human beings, with all that this means, paradoxically we have a much better chance of minimising our errors and psychological problems than if we condemn ourselves for having them in the first place. Such acceptance, then, does not imply resignation, as many

people think. Rather, it promotes our constructive efforts to learn from our errors and minimise our tendency to disturb ourselves. Self-acceptance does this because, as shown above, it is based on a flexible philosophy of desire, in this case a desire to live as happily as possible. This desire motivates us to take constructive action. Conversely, resignation is based on the idea that there is nothing we can do to improve aspects of ourselves, so there is no point in trying. This, then, is the antithesis of self-acceptance.

8 *Unconditional self-acceptance is a habit that can be acquired (but never perfectly, nor for all time).* Behaviour therapists often construe self-defeating behaviour as bad habits that can be broken, and many clients resonate to the idea that self-downing is a bad habit that can be broken. If you want to use the idea of self-downing and unconditional self-acceptance as habits you can do so, but with the following caveats. Be careful to stress that the 'habit' of self-downing can be broken, but never perfectly and not in a once-and-for-all manner. Similarly, stress that unconditional self-acceptance can be acquired, but again never perfectly nor for all time. Emphasise that it is the very nature of fallible human beings to go back to 'self-downing' under stress, even though your client may have worked very hard to break this habit. In doing so you are helping your client to accept himself or herself for his or her lack of self-acceptance.

9 *Internalising the philosophy of unconditional self-acceptance is difficult and involves hard work.* Understanding the concept of unconditional self-acceptance is not that difficult. Internalising a philosophy of unconditional self-acceptance so that it makes a positive difference to the way we think, feel and act most certainly is difficult. Here, it is useful to help clients view the acquisition of self-acceptance as similar to the acquisition of any new skill that has to be learned against the background of a well-ingrained habit that has been over-learned (for example, golf or tennis). As such, acquiring self-acceptance will involve your clients in a lot of hard work; work that has to be done even though clients will experience feelings and tendencies to act that are consistent with their more thoroughly ingrained philosophy of self-downing. This means that clients will have to tolerate a period of 'feeling all wrong' as they strive to internalise a philosophy that makes perfect sense, but is not yet believed. Such conviction comes from repeatedly challenging self-downing beliefs and acting in a way that is consistent with self-accepting beliefs.

10 *Self-acceptance requires force and energy.* The hard work that I mentioned above can be done in two ways. First, it can be done with force and energy, where, for example, clients challenge their self-downing beliefs with a great deal of strength and throw themselves into acting in ways that are consistent with their newly acquired self-accepting beliefs. Second, this work can be done in a weak, 'namby-pamby' fashion. Since

people tend to hold their self-downing beliefs quite rigidly, the latter way of working to acquire a philosophy of self-acceptance will just not work. Thus, it is important to help clients understand the importance of meeting strength with strength or fighting fire with fire. Given this, the more clients use force and energy as they strive to accept themselves, the better their results will be.

RUNNING SELF-ACCEPTANCE GROUPS

I will begin this section by providing a brief outline of the basic assumption that underpins self-acceptance groups. Then I will describe the context in which I run these groups, before providing a session-by-session account of a typical self-acceptance group.

Basic assumption

The self-acceptance groups that I run are based on the idea that the philosophy of self-acceptance can be taught in a structured, educational manner and can be understood by group members in a short period of time. While internalising this philosophy is a long and arduous endeavour which takes a far greater period than the eight weeks over which the group is run, it is possible in this short period to help group members to take the first steps in integrating this philosophy into their belief system.

The context

The context in which a therapy group is run has a decided impact on how it is established and how much impact it has on the well-being of its members. As one colleague complained: 'How can you run a group when every week the chairs are different?' To which I replied: 'Where I work the chairs are the same every week, but the group membership is different!' For I work one morning a week in a private hospital setting where two types of groups are offered: open groups where people come and go and every week the size and membership of the group are different, and closed groups where the same group of clients meet every week for a time-limited period. The self-acceptance groups to be described here are, in my experience, best run as a closed group. If the group were open, I would have to introduce the same ideas every week, and group cohesion would be lost. A closed group means that clients are introduced to the same ideas and the same techniques at the same time, which means that they can help one another in a way that they could not if the group were open.

One issue that does need to be addressed if you work in a private hospital is the timing of clients' appointments with their consultant psychiatrists. Unless you inform consultants of the times of your self-acceptance group and elicit their agreement that they will not schedule appointments during this time, then the group will be disrupted by clients coming back from or going out to see their consultants.

Forming the group

Before you form the group, you need to make decisions about the size of the group, how often it is to meet, and for how long each session. In a private hospital there is the additional constraint that many clients, once they have become 'day patients', do not attend for long periods of time, unless they can afford the high fees or their insurance cover permits long-term attendance. Consequently, my practice is to run a self-acceptance group weekly for one and a half hours over an eight-week period. I have found that a group of between seven and nine clients works best (allowing for one dropout per group).

Since my attendance at the hospital is limited to one morning a week, I do not have the time to interview all the people who wish to join the group. I thus leave the selection of group members to one of the full-time workers at the hospital who know the nature of the group and the types of client who will benefit most from it. These are people whose problems are mainly ego-related, who have had previous exposure to REBT or cognitive therapy, and who agree with the idea that dysfunctional beliefs are at the core of psychological disturbance. In addition, group members need to commit to weekly attendance over the life of the group and be prepared to put into practice what they learn from the group; for example, by the regular completion of homework assignments.

A session-by-session outline of a self-acceptance group

Session 1

Introductions

The members of the group and I introduce ourselves to one another.

Clarifying the preconditions for attendance

Here, I stress that the group is for people whose problems are to do with negative attitudes towards the self and that weekly attendance is expected from all. I also explain the usual rule of confidentiality for group members and elicit members' willingness to comply with this rule.

Who wants high self-esteem?

I normally begin a self-acceptance group by asking members who amongst them would like to have high self-esteem (or feel better about themselves). Virtually everyone raises his or her hand. I then ask each member to indicate what would raise his or her self-esteem. The kinds of answer I get are:

- doing well at work;
- being a better mother;
- being loved;
- living up to my principles;
- doing voluntary work.

Teaching the principles of unconditional self-acceptance

Before I deal with the responses to the question: 'What would raise your self-esteem?', I then spend most of the first session teaching the ten principles of unconditional self-acceptance outlined in the first half of this chapter. After teaching each point, I pause for questions and observations from group members.

Another look at self-esteem

After I have finished teaching the ten principles of self-esteem, I ask the group members to reconsider their answers to my question: 'What would raise your self-esteem?' I help them to see that the items in their responses do not serve to raise their self-esteem, but are desirable things to have or achieve in their own right. I show them that self-esteem is contingent upon doing well at work, being loved, etc., and if they were to do poorly at work later or lose the love of a significant person, for example, their self-esteem would plummet. Helping group members to understand that the concept of self-esteem is the cause of their problems and not the solution is very liberating for most.

Homework

Virtually all the members in my self-acceptance groups have been exposed to REBT or cognitive-behaviour therapy and therefore are familiar with the important role that homework assignments have in the therapeutic process. Since it is beyond the scope of this chapter for me to deal with cases where group members do not do their homework assignments or modify them in some way, I refer the interested reader to Dryden (1995b).

    The first homework assignment that I suggest that group members carry out before the second group session is to read Chapters 1 and 3 of Hauck's (1991) book on self-acceptance, *Hold Your Head Up High*. Chapter 1 outlines the problems that occur when people do not accept themselves, and Chapter 3 presents the principles of self-acceptance. As such these chapters serve as a reminder of the material covered in the first session. I suggest that, while reading the material, group members make a note of points that they disagree with or are unsure of for discussion the following week.

Session 2

Reviewing homework

It is an important principle of REBT that if you set a homework assignment then you review it the following session. So at the beginning of this session (and all subsequent sessions) it is important to review what the group members did for homework. In doing so, I correct any misconceptions that group members display in their reading of the chapters in Hauck (1991).

Goal setting

At this point, the group members are ready to consider what they can achieve from the group and what they can not. I point out that my role is to teach them both the principles of self-acceptance and some techniques to help them to begin to internalise this philosophy. What I can do is to help them begin the journey towards self-acceptance. In eight weeks, I cannot help them to complete it. Given this I ask them to set suitable goals for the group. 'What', I ask, 'would they have achieved by the end of the eight weeks which would show them that they had begun the long and arduous journey towards self-acceptance?' I encourage members to divide into smaller groups and to make their goals as realistic and specific as possible. I ask one group member to make a written note of everybody's goals, which I then photocopy and distribute at the end of the session so that everybody has a copy of the goals of each member.

Dealing with a specific example of the target problem

I ask group members to choose a specific example of a situation in which they considered themselves to be worthless, inadequate, bad, etc. I then ask each member in turn to talk about the experience briefly to the rest of the group. After the person has finished relating the experience, I use the ABC framework of REBT to help him or her assess it, where A stands for the activating event, B for his or her 'musturbatory' and self-downing beliefs, and C for his or her major, disturbed, negative emotion and/or self-defeating behaviour.

Homework

For homework, I ask each group member to use the ABC framework to analyse another example of 'low self-esteem'.

Session 3

Reviewing homework

At the beginning of the session, I check each person's ABC assessment and offer corrective feedback where relevant.

Teaching disputing of ego irrational beliefs

A central task of group members in a self-acceptance group is to learn how to dispute their 'musturbatory' and self-downing irrational beliefs. Thus, I devote the bulk of this session to teaching this core skill. As DiGiuseppe (1991) has shown, disputing involves group members asking themselves three different types of question of their irrational ego beliefs: (1) Are they consistent with reality?; (2) Are they logical?; (3) Do they yield healthy results? As I showed in the first half of this chapter, the answer to these questions is 'no' when they are applied to self-downing beliefs (see Dryden (1994) for a full discussion of why 'musturbatory' beliefs are also inconsistent with reality, are illogical, and yield unhealthy results for the individual concerned).

Disputing also involves helping group members to construct preferential and self-accepting beliefs as healthy alternatives to their irrational ego beliefs. I therefore spend a good deal of the third session helping group members to construct rational ego beliefs.

Homework: identifying and disputing irrational ego beliefs in specific situations

Armed with their new skill of disputing irrational ego beliefs and constructing alternative rational ego beliefs, group members are now ready to put it into practice in their everyday lives before the next session. This forms the basis for the homework assignment for that week.

Session 4

Reviewing homework

I begin the fourth group session by reviewing the previous week's homework assignment and offering corrective feedback as before.

Teaching the rational portfolio method

As mentioned above, disputing irrational beliefs is a core client skill in REBT in general and in self-acceptance groups in particular. As I have recently shown (Dryden 1995c), the purpose of disputing in the present context is to help group members understand why their irrational ego beliefs are irrational and why their alternative rational ego beliefs are rational. Once group members have understood this point, they need additional help to enable them to integrate this understanding into their belief system, so that it influences for the better the way they think and feel about themselves and the way they act in the world. Helping them to develop a rational portfolio of arguments in favour of their rational ego beliefs and against their irrational ego beliefs is the cognitive technique that I use to initiate this integration process.

Having introduced the idea of the rational portfolio, I suggest that group members spend about twenty minutes in the session developing their own portfolio of arguments. Then I ask them to work in two small groups reviewing one another's arguments and suggesting additional arguments. During this time, I act as consultant, listening to the small-group discussion, offering feedback on the arguments developed, and being available as a trouble-shooter if either of the groups gets stuck.

Homework

For homework I suggest that group members review and add to the arguments that they have developed for their rational portfolio. I also suggest that they make a particular note of any arguments about which they have objections, reservations or doubts or which they do not find persuasive.

Session 5

Reviewing homework

I begin the fifth session by reviewing the previous week's homework, paying particular attention to arguments about which group members have objections, doubts or reservations or which they do not find persuasive. I initiate a group discussion on these arguments and intervene to correct misconceptions or to provide additional explanations to help dispel these doubts, etc., and to make their rational arguments more persuasive.

Teaching the zig-zag technique

As noted above, it is common for people to respond to their own rational arguments developed in favour of a self-accepting philosophy with what might be called irrational rebuttals; that is, arguments which cast doubt on the concept of self-acceptance and which in fact advocate a return to the philosophy of self-downing. The zig-zag technique formalises this debate between the irrational and rational 'parts' of the person and gives the person practice at defending his or her rational ego belief against his or her own irrational attack. This technique helps group members to integrate their rational ego beliefs into their belief system.

In the zig-zag technique, the group member begins by writing down a rational ego belief and rating his or her degree of conviction in this belief on a 0–100 rating scale. Then he or she responds to this belief with an irrational argument, which he or she then rebuts. The group member continues in this vein until he or she has responded to all of his or her attacks and can think of no more. He or she then re-rates his or her degree of conviction in his or her rational ego belief, which is usually increased if the person has used the technique properly.

Once I have taught the group members the rudiments of this technique, I ask them to carry it out on their own in the session. I stress the importance of keeping to the point, since it is easy for the person to get sidetracked when using this technique. As group members do this task I go from person to person ensuring that all they are doing it correctly and, in particular, keep the focus of the debate on their target rational ego belief (see Dryden (1995c) for an extended discussion of the zig-zag technique).

Teaching tape-recorded disputing

Tape-recorded disputing is similar to the zig-zag method, but here group members put the dialogue between their rational and irrational ego beliefs on tape. In addition to emphasising once again that it is important to keep to the point while using this method, it is useful to stress that group members respond to their irrational attacks with force and energy. It should be explained that since people often hold their irrational ego beliefs very strongly, weak rational responses will have little lasting effect on irrational attacks. It is useful to give the group members some examples so that they can discriminate between weak and forceful disputing (see Dryden (1995c) for an extended discussion of tape-recorded disputing).

Homework

Tape-recorded disputing is a good homework assignment to set at this point, but it is important to establish first that group members all have access to tape-recorders. If not, suitable arrangements should be made for them to gain such access. In addition, I usually suggest that group members read and note any objections to Chapter 4 of Hauck (1991), which considers the importance of behavioural methods in the development of self-acceptance. This will be the focus of the next two group sessions.

Session 6

Reviewing homework

In checking group members' tapes, it is important to pay particular attention to their ability to stay focused on the target beliefs and to the tone they use during disputing, and feedback should be given accordingly on these two points. As with other reading material, particular emphasis should be given to group members' reservations about the place of behavioural methods in developing self-acceptance.

Providing a rationale for the conjoint use of cognitive and behavioural methods in real-life settings

REBT theory states that behavioural methods have a central role to play in the therapeutic change process. Unless group members act on their rational ego beliefs, the benefits that they will derive from the group will ultimately be minimal. However, the power of behavioural techniques is best harnessed when they are used conjointly with cognitive methods designed to give group members the opportunity to practise their rational ego beliefs in a real-life setting.

Negotiating behavioural-cognitive tasks

After you have provided group members with a rationale for the conjoint use of behavioural and cognitive techniques, it is important to encourage them to agree to set one or two behavioural-cognitive tasks, which they can implement as homework assignments before the next group session. These tasks should preferably be related to group members' goals.

Teaching rational-emotive imagery

Rational-emotive imagery (REI) is an evocative technique designed to give group members practice in strengthening their rational ego beliefs in the face of negative activating events (As). In self-acceptance groups I suggest the use of REI as preparation for the implementation of the behavioural-cognitive techniques discussed above. Once group members have set a behavioural-cognitive technique, I ask them to imagine a worst-case scenario, which constitutes the A in an ABC episode, and to identify and get in touch with an ego-related, disturbed negative emotion (such as hurt). Then, while they are still imagining the same negative A, I ask them to change their emotion to a self-accepting, healthy negative emotion. As I have noted elsewhere (Dryden 1995c), group members achieve this by changing their irrational ego beliefs to rational ego beliefs (see Dryden (1995c) for a fuller discussion of REI).

Homework

For homework, I suggest that group members practise REI three times a day for a few days before implementing their behavioural-cognitive tasks.

Session 7

Reviewing homework

In checking group members' use of REI, you need to make sure that they did, in fact, change their irrational ego beliefs to their rational alternatives rather than change the negative activating event to something more positive. In reviewing their behavioural-cognitive tasks, you need to ensure (1) that they actually faced the situation that they wanted to confront or acted in the manner planned, and (2) that they practised thinking rationally while doing so.

Agreeing other behavioural-cognitive tasks

If members were successful in implementing their behavioural-cognitive assignment, then it is important to capitalise on this success by negotiating two additional behavioural tasks. Encourage group members to choose tasks that are challenging but not overwhelming for them. However, if any group member struggled with his or her initial behavioural-cognitive task, then you will have to be less adventurous in the next such assignment you negotiate with that person.

Explaining and agreeing shame-attacking exercises

Shame-attacking exercises involve group members acting in a so-called 'shameful' manner and accepting themselves as they do so. They should attract attention to themselves without alarming others, breaking the law, or getting themselves into trouble at work. Examples of good shame-attacking exercises are as follows:

- wearing different coloured shoes;
- asking to see a three piece suite in a sweet shop;
- singing off-key in public;
- asking for directions to a road one is already in.

I suggest that group members do at least one shame-attacking exercise before the last group session.

Homework

The last set of homework assignments is as described above. In addition, I ask group members to come to the last session prepared to talk about what they have achieved from the group and to give feedback about their experience of being in it.

Session 8

Reviewing homework

For the last time, I check on group members' homework assignments and give corrective feedback as usual. Group members are usually keen to learn about one another's shame-attacking exercises, and this generates a sense of fun which, in my opinion, is quite suitable to the ending of a group of this educational nature.

The self-acceptance quiz

In the spirit of fun and to assess what group members have learned, I ask them to complete in writing a short written quiz (see Table 15.1). Why not take the quiz yourself to see what you have learned from this chapter?

Evaluating progress and eliciting feedback on the group

I then ask group members to relate what progress they have made towards self-acceptance and whether or not they have achieved their goals. I also ask them to give feedback on the group experience, my way of running it, and how it might be improved. Since all group members are involved in other groups in the hospital and many are also in individual psychotherapy, it has not been possible for me to carry out formal research into the effectiveness of self-acceptance groups.

Table 15.1 Self-acceptance quiz

GIVE REASONS FOR EACH ANSWER.

1. Having the love of a significant other makes you a more worthwhile person.
   True or False?

2. If someone you admire is better than you at an important activity, he or she is a better person than you.
   True or False?

3. If you fail at something really important, you are not a failure, but a fallible human being.
   True or False?

4. You can give a human being a single global rating which completely accounts for them.
   True or False?

5. Someone who rapes a small child is wicked through and through.
   True or False?

6. Mother Theresa has more worth than Adolf Hitler.
   True or False?

Helping group members to maintain and extend their gains

The final task that I ask group members to do is to develop a list of ways of maintaining and extending the gains that they have made from participating in the group (see Dryden (1995b, 1995c) for a fuller discussion of these two points). I stress to them that they have taken the first few steps along the road to self-acceptance, and that how far they go along this road will be largely dependent on the amount of work that they are prepared to do on themselves, using the tools that I have taught them during the group. On this point, I wish them well and we say our goodbyes.

REFERENCES

DiGiuseppe, R. (1991) Comprehensive cognitive disputing in RET. In M.E Bernard (ed.) *Using Rational-Emotive Therapy Effectively*. New York: Plenum Press.

Dryden, W. (1994) *Invitation to Rational-Emotive Psychology*. London: Whurr Publishers.

Dryden, W. (1995a) *Preparing for Client Change in Rational Emotive Behaviour Therapy*. London: Whurr Publishers.

Dryden, W. (1995b) *Facilitating Client Change in Rational Emotive Behaviour Therapy*. London: Whurr Publishers.

Dryden, W. (1995c) *Brief Rational Emotive Behaviour Therapy*. Chichester: Wiley.

Ellis, A. (1972) *Psychotherapy and the Value of a Human Being*. New York: Institute for Rational-Emotive Therapy.

Ellis, A. (1994) *Reason and Emotion in Psychotherapy: A Comprehensive Method of Treating Human Disturbances*. New York: Birch Lane Press. Revised and updated.
Hauck, P. (1991) *Hold Your Head Up High*. London: Sheldon Press.
Maultsby Jr, M.C. (1984) *Rational Behavior Therapy*. Englewood Cliffs, NJ: Prentice Hall.

Chapter 16

Parenting education and support

Hetty Einzig

INTRODUCTION

> Modern parenthood is too demanding and complex a task to be performed well merely because we have all once been children.
>
> (Mia Kellmer Pringle 1975, cited in Pugh *et al.* 1994: 235)

As counsellors most of us will recognise the primacy of the damage caused to our clients by their early experiences of inadequate or harmful parenting. Traditionally, counsellors and psychotherapists have been in the business of 'picking up the pieces', attempting to repair some of the damage of these early years in a variety of ways. Increasingly, however, those with a counselling training and background are recognising the importance of preventive intervention and are starting to explore areas of proactive work or 'psychoeducation'. One such area of work that is attracting their attention is the field of parenting education and support.

Parenting is a delicate area for intervention of any kind, fraught with sensitivity, charged with emotion and often guilt. In the UK we tend to regard parenting as a solely private matter, and intervention as intrusion. But we know that abusive parenting produces abused children, many of whom in their turn will abuse themselves, their children, or those close to them. We know now also that confident parenting can produce confident children, and that 'good enough' parenting – that much over-used term – can be more than good enough. So the challenge is how to intervene in this process to optimise the conditions, skills and opportunities for all parents to have the chance to provide 'good enough' parenting for their children.

The model of family life most parents will follow unconsciously or consciously is the one they were brought up in. But the world has changed radically from the one that shaped our parents' views and the model may no longer work or be appropriate. Since World War II we have seen the disintegration of stable communities, the breakdown of a shared value system, and the loss of a common sense of place and purpose. These have all undermined the traditional authority and security of the family as a communal enterprise. Religion, another cohesive force, has changed in practice: while religious fundamentalism may be growing, the church as a community focus has declined.

Separation, single parenthood and remarriage are creating different types of family – the number of children living with a lone parent almost doubled between 1979 and 1991 (Utting *et al.* 1994). Greater cultural and ethnic diversity bring new mores and influences. Technological advances, changing work patterns and greater mobility bring new challenges and demand adaptability.

Being a parent is a lot harder today than it was. While child-hostile, 'Victorian' parenting styles have been challenged and rejected, so now too have the unstructured, no-rules styles that flourished in the 1960s. Rules and norms have given way to uncertainty.

Economically things have changed for parents too: dual-earner families have increased from 43 per cent to 60 per cent in the last 20 years, but one in four children are being brought up in families where there is no breadwinner. The number of children living in poverty has increased from one in eight in 1979 to one in three in 1991 (Utting *et al.* 1994). Unemployment has increased and many incomes have barely kept pace with inflation. At the same time, during the 1980s in particular, we have witnessed the replacement of community values and relationships by individualistic and commercial ones, thus stripping the family activities of caring, parenting and mutual support of their dignity and social value.

Poverty, poor housing, unemployment, commercial pressures to consume and lack of community amenities are all major factors in family breakdown and the quality of parenting. At the same time, parents are expected to take the blame for all ills and have been newly under attack in recent years by the government and the media: single mothers, absent and feckless fathers, parents who abdicate responsibility, or who discipline too much or not enough.

The Eurobarometer Survey of 1990, 'The Family and Desire for Children' (EC 1990), revealed that the overwhelming moral commitment for most Europeans (96 per cent) is to the family. But whereas all other European countries see the most important role for families as 'bringing up and educating children', less than one in four in the UK endorsed that view. In contrast, most UK respondents felt that the most important role of the family was 'to provide love and affection'. The UK's romantic view of marriage gives it the second highest marriage rate in Europe (after Portugal), but it also has the second highest divorce rate (after Denmark). And the evidence showing the damage caused to children by divorce has gathered to a point difficult to ignore.

These statistics reflect a confusion and ambivalence about marriage, parenting and children in Britain that is all too apparent, and will also have its effect on family life. Indeed, the number of women opting out of parenthood is rising with a projection of approximately 20 per cent of women born in the 1960s, 1970s and 1980s remaining childless. Among other reasons for this, the author suggests, is the lack of support we give families in the UK (Condy 1995).

Despite the nine-month gestation, becoming a parent is sudden and it is forever. For most it is a joy but also a responsibility. The couple has become a family. Both mother and father will have to reassess their concept of themselves as individuals, and the couple must start the un-settling process of renegotiating the terms of their relationship – this more or less from day one, with little understanding of what to expect, with less sleep, with no preparation, and while coping with the constant physi-cal and emotional needs of an entirely dependent new being. Most people start out loving their child and wanting to be good parents but, as the statistics show, parents today are feeling increasingly under pressure, disheartened and confused.

For some the shock is irreparably damaging. Based on his seven-year study of 250 couples in Penn State who were followed from the third trimester of pregnancy with their first child, Jay Belsky concludes that one in two marriages goes into decline after the baby's arrival (Belsky and Kelly 1994).

It is astonishing that we expect in-service training for all new jobs that involve complex skills, but that we assume that parenting will come natu-rally. Parenting is a multilevel, multiskill task that changes as rapidly as the child develops, and as new children are born, or the family structure alters.

WHAT IS PARENTING EDUCATION AND SUPPORT?

'Parenting education' describes a range of teaching and support pro-grammes which focus on the skills, feelings and tasks of being a parent. These are aimed at mothers-to-be, couples, fathers, single parents, same-sex couples, children of all ages, adolescents and young adults. The term 'parenting education' distinguishes the activities it describes from 'parent education', which usually means preparation for parenthood: parentcraft classes which prepare the mother-to-be for labour, deliv-ery and baby care, and focus on the medical and physical aspects of giving birth and caring for the newborn. Parenting education is aimed at people of all ages, focusing on communication and personal relation-ship skills above all else.

Parenting education in Britain today tends to reject the didactic approach of the child-care expert in favour of an approach which values parents' own abilities. Rather than 'what to do' and 'how to do it' this approach teaches communication and relationship skills, along with providing information to encourage the making of informed and conscious choices, and teaching on specific topics (such as child development, sex education, inoculation, pain relief or feeding). It tends to include and encourage fathers, emphasise an understanding and tolerance of individuality within the family, an acceptance of emotions, both painful and joyous, and an acceptance and understanding of the baby/child's separate needs, development and forms of expression.

Parenting support is usually, but not always or solely, an integral part of parenting education. It has been found that parents supporting each other, usually in the form of on-going groups (facilitated or self-help), is key in helping parents deal with the powerful emotions of being parents (Webster-Stratton and Herbert 1994). The effect is to lower anxiety and raise confidence, thereby making them more open to exploring difficulties and considering new ways of parenting. With the support of their peers and the secure holding provided by a skilled facilitator (also usually a parent with additional training), parents realise they are not alone.

The defensiveness and reactive behaviour often displayed in consultation with 'experts' (paediatricians, health visitors, social workers, child psychotherapists) that springs from the unconscious or semiconscious fear of being a 'bad' parent, and of being found out in that failure, tends to dissipate in these types of group. Parents can become involved in learning and change without feeling stigmatised.

The myriad different parenting education and support schemes tend to share some or all of the following aims and approaches:

- raising parents' self-esteem and confidence in their parenting;
- emphasising the importance of the parents' relationship with each other;
- emphasising and reinforcing the satisfaction and value of parenting;
- introducing and cultivating the concept of 'good enough' parenting;
- emphasising and supporting the needs, development and individuality of the child as well as the parent;
- recognising that parents are the child's first teachers;
- giving parents the opportunity to reflect on the ways they were parented and how these get passed on to their own child;
- helping parents assess their ways of parenting and consider other, perhaps more effective ways.

Further common threads are: the kinds of subjects tackled (such as crying, sleeping, feeding, sibling rivalry, discipline, school problems, anger, fears, violence, etc.); the relationship and communication skills taught (such as listening, challenging, negotiating, expressing needs, tolerance of difference, etc.); and a willingness to examine 'what gets in the way' (such as what it is, individually and collectively, that stops us being competent parents).

Many schemes have a strong person-centred orientation, while others are informed by a psychodynamic model, and still others are behavioural in character. Many combine elements from all three, blending exploration and discussion with some direct teaching or suggested task where appropriate. In terms of style the facilitator may use self-disclosure, humour, metaphor and a range of other personal touches to create a relaxed, 'we're all in this together' atmosphere, and get away from the expert/patient syndrome which has been found to be disabling for many parents.

At present, parenting education is provided by a tremendous variety of different agencies and at many different points of intervention. There are countless schemes around the country, some aimed at 'at-risk' families, others for 'ordinary' parents who want to raise their coping skills and awareness of family interaction; some are run through churches and other faith communities, in schools, health centres and family centres, through community education programmes and the Open University. The majority are run by organisations in the voluntary sector. There are education packs for adolescents for use in schools and youth groups, and there are groups for parents of teenagers, of stepchildren, of children with special needs, and so on. It is currently estimated that parenting education and support reaches approximately 60,000 parents per year, that is, about 8 per cent of eligible parents (those with children under 18) (Smith 1995).

Most of the preventative programmes that flourished during the 1980s were born essentially of the personal growth and psychotherapy movement in the United States, and incorporate some of its 'here-and-now' techniques into a more psychoanalytic model of parenting with success. Re-enactment and enactment, reframing and positive connotation, defining the problem and establishing a goal and an action plan may all be used at different times by different programmes. These techniques are familiar ones in a range of counselling models.

Parenting education and support are very much about equipping people with the knowledge to anticipate problems and the skills to solve or manage them. By providing a combined emphasis on feelings and skills, on interpersonal exploration and factual information, they effectively empower people to approach the multilevel task of parenting with confidence.

The following list of programmes is not fully representative, or exhaustive, but will give, I hope, a flavour of the diversity and richness of the field. Further details can be obtained from the Parenting Education and Support Forum (see end of chapter).

• *Parent Network* was started in 1986. It provides education and support for parents through its group-based programme, Parent Link. The aim is to develop self-awareness and self-confidence, and parents receive handbooks on the topics covered. Informal groups usually continue, and they may do follow-up modules on sibling rivalry, anger management, living with teenagers, etc. Over two hundred Parent Link co-ordinators operate in around thirty local areas, and well over five thousand people have attended a Parent Link programme.

- *Exploring Parenthood* is based in London and runs a number of different courses for parents, many of them targeted at specific groups. For example, Parents Against Crime is for parents whose children are in trouble with the law, and there are groups for foster parents and step-parents, and for ethnic minorities, amongst others.
- *HOMESTART* is the largest national organisation providing outreach work, support, friendship and practical help to families (usually with children under 5) under stress, in their own home.
- *Parentline* offers telephone counselling, advice and information to all parents nationwide.
- *Parents Anonymous* is another telephone help line (similar to the Samaritans), run by parents, for those in danger of physically abusing a child.
- *NEWPIN* runs its personal development programme, which combines peer group support, individual counselling and group therapy, at 20 local centres. They work primarily with parents suffering from depression and feelings of isolation, and their aim is specifically to break the repetitive cycle of destructive family behaviour. Founded in 1985, NEWPIN takes many referrals from the social services, and outcomes have shown that once the parent joins the programme no child has ever been taken into care or returned to the 'at-risk' register.
- *PIPPIN* (Parents in Partnership – Parent Infant Network) started in 1991 and is a structured, preventive education and support programme which complements traditional antenatal classes. Its aim is to support the development of positive early family and parent–child relationships. It starts around the fourth month of pregnancy, specifically includes fathers, and has a four-phase, seventeen-session course, plus a home visit. Groups usually continue after the course finishes.
- Fifteen schools participated in the *Parentwise (Birmingham)* programme in 1993, with a further fifteen involved in 1994/5. Each school developed three courses, according to the needs and wishes of the parents, offering them the opportunity to develop personal skills and enabling them to support their children's education at all levels.
- *Effective Parenting Programme* is a school-based programme designed to support parents in their parenting role, providing a forum to share experiences, fears and anxieties, pool practical tips and learn about child development. Intended to bridge the gap between home and school, it aims to raise both parents' and children's self-esteem.
- The *Veritas* parenting programmes are flexible self-help courses organised by schools, health visitors, churches and other community groups, using the audio and video tapes and other course materials provided.

The aim is to enable parents to communicate better, and develop a growing sense of responsibility, with their children. Worldwide, 1.7 million copies of the programme have been sold, and it is estimated that almost 200,000 parents in the UK have experienced it since 1986 (Smith 1995).

SKILLS AND TRAINING FOR FACILITATORS
OF PARENTING EDUCATION

In their comprehensive book *Confident Parents, Confident Children*, Pugh *et al.* (1994) identify the skills necessary for facilitators of parenting education: they need to be skilled in handling groups; be skilled in communicating; have counselling skills; and value what individuals bring to the group (see also Parr 1995).

Specific training is provided by a few of the parenting organisations, although this might range from a one-day induction to the kind of in-depth training provided, for example, by PIPPIN or Exploring Parenthood. Training should cover: relevant knowledge (of child and human development, family patterns, local resources, etc.); skills in working with individuals and groups on sensitive issues; the ability to examine their own attitudes, values and feelings in respect of family life; and a sensitivity to others' point of view (Pugh *et al.* 1994: 89).

Much of this the counsellor receives in an in-depth counselling training, and it seems that counsellors are and could be particularly appropriate facilitators if they can acquire the necessary group skills and relevant information and knowledge. As there is no one group of professionals who can claim a monopoly on parenting education, perhaps counselling training organisations could consider adding an optional module of parenting education and support to their core training.

Two points are key in this respect. One is the different nature of the contract that counsellors have with their clients and parenting education facilitators have with their group. The parallels between running a counselling and a parenting support group are very strong – indeed, where parents are distressed or in crisis, there may appear to be little distinction between the two. Counsellors are trained to encourage depth of process in their clients, the exploration of painful feelings, the working through of issues and relationship difficulties, and even sometimes catharsis or abreaction. However, in most cases, lengthy, in-depth exploration, personal process and working through in the group would not be appropriate in a parenting education group. Just as the nurse using counselling skills to support a troubled patient must know his or her boundaries and limitations, so the counsellor working with a group of parents must be skilled at setting boundaries, and keeping in focus the fact that they have come to explore their role as parents: this is the contract. The iceberg model is useful in this context: you need to know a lot more than you actually manifest in order to know where and how to set the limits of the exploratory process. Given that much of the material around parenting is emotionally highly charged, counsellors are particularly well placed, due to their in-depth training, both to allow and to contain this material safely.

The second point is the extent to which the counsellor is able to shed the status of expert, clinician, healer or Earth Mother, and truly facilitate or 'guide' the group in a spirit of equality. To the extent that counsellors are able to do this and truly value and highlight the skills the group and its individuals bring, they will empower the group and rekindle the parents' confidence in fulfilling their task with consciousness and compassion – for themselves as much as for their children.

BREAKING THE CYCLE OF DEPRIVATION

Many parents are isolated in our society, through different cultural norms, poverty, lack of education, language, or having moved away from family or friends, and many more feel isolated by the way our society relegates parenting and particularly mothers to the second division. Isolation and confusion as much as hormones contribute to the high levels of post-natal depression in this country: 50–70 per cent of mothers get the baby blues, with 15 per cent diagnosed as postnatally depressed (of whom 25 per cent go on to develop chronic severe depression) (Child Psychotherapy Trust 1993, cited in Parr 1994).

The effects of a depressed mother on even a very young infant have been observed by Lynne Murray, amongst others: infants of depressed mothers form insecure attachments and show delays in cognitive development tasks when compared to controls. The negative impact of this on the child's personal, educational and psychological development can be severe (Murray 1992). The depressed mother in a sense isolates herself from her infant, who in turn appears flat, unresponsive, isolated. A negative feedback loop of physical and emotional isolation is created. One of the key elements of parenting education and support is to cut through this cycle of isolation by helping parents to join existing networks and create new ones through the group. Murray has shown that a variety of brief (eight-week) therapeutic interventions can have a positive impact in the treatment of maternal depression and also on infant development (Murray 1993). As yet no comparable research trials have been done using the intervention of group work.

Up to 10 per cent of British children and young people have a psychological problem – this rises to 25 per cent in the inner cities. Research shows that these problems can persist into adulthood and in turn impair their ability to be good parents (Parr 1994). Depressed, vulnerable, abused parents have lower empathy with and tolerance of children's needs; are more likely to use punishment, particularly physical, excessively and unpredictably, and to use discipline erratically, too severely or not at all; and have inappropriate expectations of children's developmental capabilities. They are also at higher risk of role reversal, of expecting children to meet their, adult, needs (Bavolek 1990; Parr 1994; Utting et al. 1994; etc.). And it has been shown that family breakdown may have a delayed effect on children, leading to mental illness or even suicide later in life (Parr 1994).

And so the 'cycle of deprivation' continues. This concept was introduced in a report in the early 1970s by the then Secretary of State for Social Services, Sir Keith Joseph, to refer to the way personal, psychological and social problems interact and persist from one generation to another. It was influential, along with a succession of other reports, in highlighting the role of education in supporting parents to break that cycle. The initiatives that flourished during the 1970s were targeted at low-income groups in very deprived areas, within the framework of adult and community education, the Open University, family centres, etc. Unfortunately, many were cut in the 1980s.

The parenting education and support organisations that developed in the voluntary sector, in part to fill this gap, were aimed, necessarily in the first instance, at parents who could pay for courses, but also as part of therapeutic programmes for parents experiencing severe difficulties. These programmes benefited from being untainted by the attitude, endemic within the state health and social services, that individuals must identify themselves with a problem and seek help from an expert. This casts people in an inadequate or passive role rather than as people able to identify their needs and seek ways to meet those needs (De'Ath 1988).

EFFECTIVENESS AND EVALUATION OF PARENTING EDUCATION AND SUPPORT

It costs about £34,000 to keep a child in residential care for a year, and a place in a secure unit costs £100,000 (Audit Commission 1994). NEWPIN can work with a family in crisis for one year at a total cost of £2,200. Other programmes cost similarly little: £490 per family under stress for HOMESTART, £100 per family for a seventeen-week programme with PIPPIN, £16 per call for Parentline, £70 per parent for a thirteen-week programme with Parent Network, £35 per family in a special theme group at Exploring Parenthood, £33 for the teaching pack of the Children's Society, £8 per parent for the Veritas materials and course, and so on (Einzig 1994). The implications of this are clear and highly in favour of preventive intervention.

Parenting education facilitators are likely to behave as friendly 'guides'. They might make use of a range of techniques to encourage the

sharing of family stories and insight into their impact, to foster communication skills and the valuing of what each person brings to parenting.
Some programmes, like PIPPIN, will invite the babies, once born, and
subsequently the growing toddlers, to share in the group process as
'extended family members'.

Encouraging parents to include their babies in this semi-structured
learning environment can have a profound effect on the ease of all the
relationships within the group. Watching video-taped material of the
groups in action, it is notable that the toddlers are less attention-seeking of
their parents than might otherwise be the case, and relate with easy intimacy to the other adults in the group and to each other. The group
members do not appear to experience their own adult needs as clashing
with those of their infants but exhibit flexibility in attending to both,
moving fluently from contributing to the discussion to serving their own
or other children's needs and back again without tension or irritation
(Dunnigan and Einzig 1994).

More formal evaluation research is still in its early days in this field. As
with counselling, comparative studies are very difficult to mount, since
there are so many factors involved in behavioural and emotional change
that it is hard to prove that parenting education is the key factor. However,
there is a wide body of American and British research which shows
that, while environment, school and peer-group pressure exert their influence on the growing child, at least as powerful an influence on social
behaviour and educational achievement is parenting (Utting *et al.* 1994;
McCord 1990; etc.). Between birth and the age of 16, children spend less
than 15 per cent of their waking time in school; thus parents are responsible for 85 per cent of their time (Alexander and Clyne 1995).

Carolyn and Peter Cowan of the University of California have conducted longitudinal studies into the impact of a first baby on the couple
relationship, and into the effects of the transition to parenthood on the
child in terms of social adjustment and educational achievement. Their
model combines a number of variables from both parents, and shows that:

> a negative path from more depressive symptoms in the parents, to more
> marital conflict, to less parental control [leads to] more externalising in
> the child. This combined model accounts for an impressive 65 per cent
> of the variance in preschool children's externalising [aggressive]
> behaviour.
>
> (Cowan *et al.* 1991:96)

Further to this, using their complex multiple measures on the couple in
pregnancy they find they can predict 30–37 per cent of the variance in the
couple's co-parenting style with their children of 3½ years old. These are
then correlated with ratings of the child's behaviour at 5½ years at kindergarten:

we find family conditions occurring long before the child enters kindergarten predict the child's academic and social adaptation to school . . . [with an] impressive continuity . . . between parents' adjustment to the transition to parenthood and their children's later adjustment to the demands of elementary school.

(Cowan and Cowan 1991: 98–9)

The Cowan research broke new ground by dividing their sample into two groups, one receiving parenting education and support on the birth of the first child, the other acting as a control. The two groups were followed for four years:

18 months after giving birth 12.5 per cent of the new parent couples without an intervention had separated or divorced. The marriages of all of the parents who had participated in a couples group during their transition to parenthood were still intact . . . When the children were between 3½ and 4 years of age, the rate of separation and divorce in the non-intervention families had increased to 15 per cent and the first couple from the intervention sub sample had separated.

(1991: 101)

At about this stage it seems that the notably positive effects of intervention start to wane, which would suggest that 'booster shot' interventions would be advisable.

Parents want the kind of support and learning offered by the parenting education programmes. The 1992 Health Education Authority review of antenatal services records parents' dissatisfaction with existing services and lists their requests: they want to be listened to, they want opportunities to share their feelings and anxieties, they want information to enable them to make their own choices for their baby and themselves, and they want fathers involved more (Combes and Schonveld 1992).

In the United States, parenting education programmes are well established. For example, Stephen Bavolek's Nurturing Programs, which focus on abusive families, have been running for ten years. Evaluation has shown that the reabuse rate is as low as 7 per cent (Bavolek 1990).

It is clear now from the collective research that parenting education and support impact positively on the mental and emotional health of the parents and therefore on the healthy development of the child. Some research has shown that results are better from facilitated group work than from one-to-one or couple counselling with parents, and they last longer (Webster-Stratton and Herbert 1994).

QUESTIONS AND CONCLUSIONS

As parenting education and support becomes more widespread, the demand for them grows, the number of agencies involved in their provision expands, and a number of issues become more pressing. What kind of training is needed, and how much? How can standards be maintained, and how do we recognise those who have done an in-depth training as distinct from those who have had a few hours' induction? There are no immediate answers to these thorny problems, and no doubt the debate that is just starting will still be raging years from now.

In terms of prior training, those facilitating parenting skills courses come from a range of different disciplines, but most have an educational psychology or health visitor background, with the second largest group coming from teaching and social work (Smith 1995). It is interesting that, despite the prime importance of counselling and group skills in this context, it appears that counsellors are not yet operating in this field in identifiable numbers. Perhaps stimulated by this variety of backgrounds, the question of professional identity is starting to feature in seminars and discussions: who and what are 'parent educators', and where do they fit within the range of social workers, health visitors, teachers, midwives, psychologists and counsellors with whom they interface and often collaborate? What are their professional status, their values and ethical base, their system of accountability? And who gives them a mandate to do this work?

Another question that is voiced is whether all facilitators should be, or should have been, parents themselves. In other words, are paraprofessionals (parents with a modicum of training) more successful in working with parents than professionals, and what are the implications of this? What also is their role seen from the point of view of society: to encourage conformity and acquiescent citizenship, or to empower parents to demand better services for their families and their children?

These and other issues are just beginning to be discussed, as the field starts to be mapped and the momentum of public and government attention draws practitioners together to meet and talk with increasing frequency. They are not so different from the issues that counsellors also continue, increasingly, to grapple with.

We are now in the throes of major transitions in the counselling profession, and at the threshold of others. The area of 'primary prevention' or 'proactive intervention' is one such threshold. The area of 'psychoeducation' is another. It would seem that the message from a number of quarters is that counsellors must respond more directly to the needs and demands of ordinary people, and of the 'market place', as well as operate more fully within a wider social context, if counselling is to flourish as we approach the turn of the century. Parenting education and support crosses traditional boundaries between education and health care. It also has the particular resonance and power that comes from an essentially grass-roots development: a fast-growing range of individual or barely networked projects linked by a common need and hunger for change. It will be interesting to see if parenting education and support, like the feminist movement, which rose from similar beginnings (groups of women talking to each other), can develop the collective muscle to effect real and lasting political change in the status of parenting and the family in this country.

It is a key element of the future development of parenting education and support that it becomes accepted for its preventive benefits and is not simply targeted at families at risk. A crude but instructive analogy can be made with a vaccination drive. To wipe out measles or diphtheria, what the immunologists call 'herd immunity' must be created: a high proportion of the population must be vaccinated. The same is true for social change. A climate must be created in Britain in which parenting is valued, in which we recognise that parenting is not instinctive but learnt, and that parents need support in bringing up the next generation – the children that constitute society's future. Everybody should have access to a wide range of models of parenting education and support, offered at a range of different points of intervention.

With the current and inevitably increasing focus on cost saving in health care, counsellors too are being forced to consider issues of cost benefit, evaluation, diversification and integration. Prevention, education and self-help are fast becoming key areas of research and development within a transforming National Health Service. The concept of the patient has given way to that of the client/consumer, with the correlation of being able to seek or purchase ways to get one's needs met. If the profession wishes to establish itself firmly within this new-look NHS, then counsellors can no longer afford to ignore the trends and transformations already afoot in health care and within their own discipline.

'It is generally agreed that the impact of parenting is felt throughout one's lifetime and for succeeding generations. No other form of human interaction can boast such power and longevity' (Bavolek 1990, cited in Pugh *et al.* 1994: 11). If we accept the truth of this statement, and there must be few counsellors who do not, then one of the most fundamental, challenging and effective arenas of preventative health care must lie in parenting education and support.

Further information from: Parenting Education and Support Forum, NCB, 8 Wakley Street, London EC1V 7QE. Tel: 0171 843 6099.

REFERENCES

Alexander, T. and Clyne, P. (1995) *Riches Beyond Price: Making the Most of Family Education*. Leicester: NIACE.
Audit Commission (1994) *Seen But Not Heard: Developing Community Child*

Health and Social Services for Children in Need. London: HMSO.

Bavolek, S. (1990) *Parenting: Theory, Policy and Practice*. Research and Validation Report of the Nurturing Programmes. Wisconsin: Eau Claire, Family Development Resources Inc.

Belsky, J. and Kelly, J. (1994) *The Transition to Parenthood: How a First Child Changes a Marriage*. London: Vermilion.

Combes, G. and Schonveld, A. (1992) *Life Will Never Be The Same Again: Learning To Be a First Time Parent*. A review of antenatal and postnatal health education. London: HEA.

Condy, A. (1994) Factsheet 18 for the United Nations International Year of the Family. London: Family Policy Studies Centre.

Condy, A. (1995) Choosing not to have children. *Family Policy Bulletin* (April) 2–3.

Cowan, C.P. *et al.* (1991) Becoming a family: marriage, parenting and child development. In P.A. Cowan and M. Hetherington (eds) *Family Transitions*. London: Lawrence Erlbaum.

De'Ath, E. (1988) Families and their differing needs. In E. Street and W. Dryden (eds) *Family Therapy in Britain*. Milton Keynes: Open University Press.

Dunnigan, B. and Einzig, H. (1994) *PIPPIN*. Short film describing the PIPPIN programme. London: Artemis Trust.

EC (European Commission) (1990) The Family and Desire for Children. Brussels: EC.

Einzig, H. (1994) Briefing on Parenting Education and Support. For the United Nations International Year of the Family. Unpublished.

Mansfield, P., Collard, J. and McAllister, F. (forthcoming) *Person, Partner, Parent*. London: Macmillan.

McCord, J. (1990) Long-term perspectives on parental absence. In L. Robins and M. Rutter (eds) *Straight and Devious Pathways from Childhood to Adulthood*. Cambridge: Cambridge University Press.

Murray, L. (1992) The impact of post-natal depression on infant development. *Journal of Child Psychology and Psychiatry 33* (3) 543–61.

Murray, L. (1993) The impact of post-natal depression on infant development: a naturalist study and a treatment trial. Presentation at the IPA Conference on Psychoanalytic Research, 12/13 March, London.

Parr, M. (1994) Towards a Humanistic/Integrative Approach to Parent Infant Counselling and Supporting Men and Women in the Transition to Parenthood. Unpublished masters dissertation. Regents College School of Psychotherapy and Counselling, London.

Parr, M. (1995) Support for Couples in the Transition to Parenthood. PhD forthcoming. University of East London.

Pugh, G., De'Ath, E. and Smith, C. (1994) *Confident Parents, Confident Children: Policy and Practice in Parent Education and Support*. London: National Children's Bureau.

Seaburn, D., Landau Stanton, J. and Horwitz, S. (1993) Core intervention techniques in family therapy process. In R.H. Mikesell *et al.* (eds) *Family Psychology and Systems Therapy*. Washington, DC: American Psychological Association.

Smith, C. (1996) *Learning To Be Parents: A Survey of Group-Based Parenting Skills Programmes*. London: National Children's Bureau.

Utting, D. (1995) *Family and Parenthood: Supporting Families, Preventing Breakdown*. York: Joseph Rowntree Foundation.

Utting, D., Bright, J. and Henricson, C. (1994) *Crime and the Family: Improving*

Hetty Einzig

Childrearing and Preventing Delinquency. London: Family Policy Studies Centre.

Webster-Stratton, C. and Herbert, M. (1994) *Troubled Families, Problem Children: Working with Parents, A Collaborative Process*. London: Wiley.

Part III

Counsellor education and training

Chapter 17

Multiculturalism

Jenny Bimrose

INTRODUCTION

Multiculturalism is now well established as relevant to the theory and practice of mainstream counselling. It has, however, been slower to engage interest and commitment in the United Kingdom than in the United States, where it originated over two decades ago. Reasons for this are varied but, since the term 'multiculturalism' misleadingly implies ethnicity, it probably (in part) relates to the relative sizes of the ethnic minority populations of the two countries. In the UK ethnic minority populations are estimated to be 4.7 per cent of the overall population (Labour Force Survey 1988–1990, quoted in Jones 1993: 12), compared with the USA where they are estimated to be 24.4 per cent (US Bureau of the Census 1990, quoted in Bernal and Castro 1994: 797). Consequently, there may appear to be less of a practical, moral and ethical imperative in the UK for counsellors to adopt this approach. Kareem and Littlewood (1992: 5) argue that the relative 'psychotherapeutic neglect' of minority groups in Britain can be attributed to the fact that 'the United States, unlike Britain, has considered itself explicitly as a country of immigrants'.

Irrespective of the stage of development or degree of acceptance, multiculturalism is a counselling approach which deserves – and increasingly demands – the attention of counselling practitioners, policy makers, trainers and researchers. Since the broad definition of the term 'multiculturalism' embraces a wide range of social variables or differences such as gender, sexual preference, disability and social class as well as ethnicity, the approach described by this term clearly has relevance for every client presenting for counselling in the UK. This chapter will examine its meaning and origins, discuss the current stage of its development, and consider future directions.

ORIGINS AND MEANINGS

Difficulties which relate to the inconsistent and confusing use of language around the concept of 'multiculturalism' are increasingly being acknowledged and discussed by writers in the area. For example, Pedersen states that 'the concept of multiculturalism has been defined and described in a great variety of ways . . . sometimes even within the same article!' (1991a: 5). And Ivey *et al.* state that 'there is no fully satisfactory set of terms that describes the vast array of multicultural experience comprising our world' (1993: 6). They define the term 'multiculturalism' in the broad sense, being clear that adopting a multicultural perspective must go beyond ethnic/racial difference to gender difference, socio-economic status, sexual preference, physical issues, and so on. Pedersen is more precise in his definition of multiculturalism, arguing that 'culture' should be defined to include 'demographic variables (e.g. age, sex, place of residence), status variables (e.g. social, educational, economic), and affiliations (formal and informal), as well as ethnographic variables such as nationality, ethnicity, language, and religion' (1991b: 7). By using this wide, and exact, definition of culture, he argues that the concept becomes generic to all counselling relationships, which emphasises the need for counsellors to deal effectively with the complex interaction of multicultural differences presented by individual clients.

The urgent need for a broad yet precise definition of the term has arisen from the somewhat ad hoc nature of the development of multiculturalism. Current interest in this approach for counselling is attributed to the racial civil rights movement in the United States in the 1960s and 1970s (Helms 1994: 162), which was concerned with the equal and fair treatment of all citizens in every sphere of society. Amongst other issues, the movement stimulated research into the usage of counselling services by ethnic minority groups. From his review of the literature, Pine (1972) discovered a disturbing view of counselling held by minority groups. They reported counselling to be a 'waste of time' and that 'counsellors do not accept, respect, and understand cultural differences; that counsellors are arrogant and contemptuous; and that counsellors don't know how to deal with their own hangups' (1972: 35). Sue and Sue summarise the findings of other research carried out in the 1970s which revealed that not only did minority groups under-use mental health services, but that minority clients terminated counselling/therapy at a rate of approximately 50 per cent, compared with a termination rate of less than 30 per cent for white clients (1990: 7).

As a consistent picture of dissatisfaction with counselling services on the part of ethnic minority clients emerged, explanations were sought. The most compelling and widely accepted was the critique of counselling practice as an ethnocentric activity. Many authors, for example, Pedersen (1983: 177), Raubenheimer (1987: 229), d'Ardenne and Mahtani (1989:

Preface), LaFromboise and Foster (1989: 115), Sue and Sue (1990: 8), and Ivey *et al.* (1993: 1) have argued that mainstream counselling and psychotherapy are white, middle-class activities that operate with many values and assumptions which are fundamentally different from those of other client groups. They are ethnocentric or 'culturally encapsulated' (Wrenn 1985), holding at their centre a notion of normality derived from white culture, which is irrelevant to and has the potential for alienating them. Since this explanation is also relevant to other client differences such as gender and socio-economic status, the discussion of 'culture' quickly broadened to include a whole range of other contextual factors.

After the definition of the problem and the identification of an acceptable explanation, responses or proposed solutions rapidly developed which sought to address this particular critique of mainstream counselling approaches. Many of these responses or alternative counselling approaches developed in parallel, and not in a coherent fashion which took account of each other. The result was a plethora of competing, often under-developed 'multicultural' counselling approaches advocating various methods of responding to types of 'cultural' or client difference in appropriate 'culturally aware' ways.

Bimrose (1993) proposed a framework for making sense of the bewildering array of these alternative approaches, which consists of a threefold categorisation. This focuses on the relationship of counselling approaches to the social context and distinguishes between individualistic, integrationist and structuralist approaches. 'Individualistic' refers to counselling approaches which separate an individual's need for help from his or her social context. One of the central ideas of the existential-humanistic tradition (and therefore a major influence in the development of counselling theory and practice) is that individuals are able to determine their own destinies. Thus, control is seen as lying within the individual. Society's response (for example, racism and sexism) to individual characteristics which are beyond the individual's control (for example, ethnicity and gender) is not regarded as a primary responsibility of the counselling process.

In contrast, 'integrationist' refers to the rapidly increasing counselling perspectives which propose that an understanding of society's response to individual difference (social context) must be integrated into counselling practice. This category includes those approaches which have focused on particular aspects of individual difference such as culture (for example, Ivey 1994; Brislin and Yoshida 1994; Locke 1992; Sue and Sue 1990) or gender (for example, Chaplin 1988; Walker 1990; Good *et al.* 1990) and their social consequences. They have developed new training and practice responses which take account of these differences in various ways as part of the counselling process. Also within the category 'integrationist' would be grouped counselling approaches which advocate an understanding of individuals within systems (for example, Egan and Cowan 1979; Holland 1992).

Finally, 'structuralist' refers to approaches which emphasise the structures within society (for example, political, economic and social) which create the circumstances giving rise to individual distress that requires counselling. These approaches question the legitimacy of current counselling or therapy practice at the individual level as an appropriate response to individual distress, and advocate fundamental structural change (for example, Woolfe 1983; Smail 1987).

Thus, having begun with a grave concern about the relevance of mainstream counselling to ethnic minorities, 'multiculturalism' has, over the past two decades or so, developed into a significant movement which both incorporates a wide range of client differences affecting clients' worldviews and life chances, and provides a variety of counselling responses. Pedersen (1991b) proposes that 'we are moving toward a generic theory of multiculturalism as a "fourth force" position, complementary to the other three forces of psychodynamic, behavioural and humanistic explanations of human behaviour' and claims that 'a multicultural perspective has changed the way we look at counselling across fields and theories' (1991b: 6).

CURRENT STAGE OF DEVELOPMENT

'Multiculturalism' has now come of age. A review of the literature reveals three trends which indicate that this 'fourth force' has reached its stage of establishment. First, the rapid development of new approaches to cultural difference is beginning to give way to a critical review of existing approaches. Second, attempts are beginning to be made to develop the means to measure and evaluate practitioners' competence and professional effectiveness as multicultural counsellors. Third, attention is being directed at developing effective training, which is one of the main means of achieving counselling competence in multiculturalism. These three trends will now be discussed in turn.

Critiques of existing approaches

Critiques of existing multicultural approaches are developing apace. One of these relates to the assumptions underlying various approaches. A notable example relates to the notions of 'sensitivity' and 'awareness'. Seminal texts in the area of improving intercultural or cross-cultural competence emphasise the need for increased sensitivity or awareness on the part of the counsellor (for example, Brislin and Yoshida 1994: 5; Sue and Sue 1990: 166) as a prerequisite for effective practice. The underlying assumption is that such increased sensitivity and awareness will automatically improve counselling effectiveness. Ridley *et al.* (1994) question this, arguing that the concept has not yet been satisfactorily defined, guidelines on how to operationalise the concept have not yet been developed, and the means to measure whether it has been achieved do not yet exist. Their contention is that 'these flaws are fatal because they hamper application of the construct, destroying its usefulness for multi-cultural counselling, training and research' (1994: 125).

Even more fundamental, Sundberg and Sue question whether 'the fact that the client and counsellor differ in cultural background makes for differences in the effectiveness of the counselling' (1989: 336). They identify five assumptions underlying certain models of multicultural counselling as appropriate areas for research. These are that interculturally effective counselling will take place when:

- mutual understanding of the purpose and expectations of counselling exists;
- the counsellors' intercultural understanding and communication skills are developed;
- intercultural attitudes and skills are developed;
- the client's external environment is understood and taken into account in the counselling process;
- the counsellor understands and is able to distinguish between those elements of counselling that are universal to all clients (for example, counsellor tolerance of anxiety in the client) and those that require a culturally specific response (for example, Western-oriented counsellors and clients are more likely to be individualistic in their attributions than Third World counsellors and clients).

Other critiques are concerned with the potentially diluting effect of multi-culturalism as an approach embracing too many social differences. Helms argues that:

whereas multiculturalism may be a useful construct for encouraging discussion about matters of culture in society in general, it is virtually useless as a scientific construct. In particular, the lack of specificity about which aspects of individual diversity are appropriately subsumed under the rubric of multiculturalism has contributed to considerable confusion in theory, research, and practice.

(1994: 162)

If this dilution is to be halted, more rigour must be applied in the use of cultural – in particular racial – constructs. Strawbridge (1994) is also critical of the diluting effect of multiculturalism on counselling practice. She argues that the recognition of cultural difference and increased sensitivity does not address 'the exploitative and oppressive power relations endemic within white society' and that a much more radical approach is required nearer to 'anti-racism', focusing more on an understanding of power relationships within society (1994: 5).

One final example of the emerging critiques of multiculturalism concerns itself with the different developmental assumptions of the approach compared with another popular emerging counselling trend – brief therapy. Steenbarger (1993) develops a model of multicontextual counselling which, he argues, reconciles these two important new trends in counselling. He identifies the fundamental contradiction of the two models of counselling: one which locates problems within clients and advocates the treatment of individuals, and the other emphasising the social context and system intervention. This particular critique draws attention to the need to reconcile apparently irreconcilable new trends in counselling, stating that 'brief multicultural work does not need to be an oxymoron and, indeed, may represent a desirable and needed addition to counselling repertoires' (1993: 13).

Measurement and evaluation of multicultural competence

Related to the critiques of assumptions underlying multiculturalism is the recognition of the need for measures of this type of counselling competence. Ponterotto et al. (1994) provide a useful review of four new instruments that have been designed to assess this. They are the Cross-Cultural Counselling Inventory – Revised (CCCI–R), the Multicultural Counselling Awareness Scale: Form B (MCAS:B), the Multicultural Counselling Inventory (MCI) and the Multicultural Awareness, Knowledge, Skills Survey (MAKSS). Their main conclusion is that 'multicultural instrumentation is in its infancy with regard to empirical validation' (1994: 321). They caution against its use in training before more extensive research and development is carried out. Since three of these four measures are 'self-report' instruments, they also identify the need to develop methods for supervisor evaluation of multicultural counsellor competence.

All the four instruments reviewed by Ponterotto et al. (1994) used a framework of multicultural competencies based on Sue and Sue's threefold categorisation of skills, knowledge and awareness (1990). In the development of one of these four instruments, the MCI, the originators set out to investigate whether there were more dimensions than these three to multicultural competence. One additional factor was found, 'Multicultural Counselling Relationship'. In their inventory, this item consisted of eight items referring to 'the counsellor's interactional process with the minority client, such as the counsellor's trustworthiness, comfort level, stereotypes of the minority client and worldview' (Sodowski et al. 1994: 142). Sufficient evidence was found to support the claim that this was a significant factor along with skill, awareness and knowledge, and though the need for more validation of the measure is acknowledged, it is claimed that effective multicultural training must incorporate this element (Sodowski *et al.* 1994: 145).

Multicultural training

A central theme in the multicultural literature is the need for change in counsellors in order for them to become 'multiculturally skilled counsellors'. Such changes implicate counsellor training, so perhaps not surprisingly, increasing attention is being paid to the type and quality of training available in this area. D'Andrea and Daniels (1991) discuss various approaches to training currently being used in the United States in counsellor education programmes. They propose four development stages for training programmes regarding multiculturalism:

1 The 'culturally entrenched' stage, where little discussion related to the needs of minority groups is encouraged, and core conditions of counselling such as genuineness, empathy and respect are regarded as sufficient to allow counsellors to transcend differences occurring between clients and themselves;
2 the 'cross-cultural awakening' stage, where cultural differences are acknowledged, but where training focuses implicitly or explicitly on between-group similarities, and an emphasis is placed on skills training in developing empathy and positive regard with their clients – and little else;
3 the 'cultural integrity' stage, where various types of cross-cultural counselling courses are integrated into course provision (for example, cross-cultural communication skills and knowledge of ethnic minority populations);
4 the 'infusion' stage, where an integrated curriculum ensures that multicultural counselling goals are embedded into all elements of the course.

Evaluation of the effectiveness of training is also beginning to take place. One method is the investigation of the competence of those who have completed such training. Allison *et al.* (1994) present the findings of a postal survey which examined levels of competence in providing services to thirteen categories of clients from ethnic and diverse groups. Of 292 respondents who had completed doctoral programmes in clinical, counselling and school psychology, 96 per cent reported high levels of competence when counselling European Americans, compared with much lower numbers of respondents who indicated competence with most of the minority ethnic and diverse groups examined (for example, 37 per cent reported high levels of competence in counselling African Americans, 64 per cent with the economically disadvantaged and 35 per cent with gay men). Bimrose and Bayne (1995) similarly conducted a postal survey of qualified and practising counsellors. They too found high levels of discomfort reported by counsellors working with diverse client groups (for example, 57 per cent reported discomfort based on gender and 46 per cent reported discomfort based on ethnicity).

FUTURE DIRECTIONS

The need for a multicultural approach to counselling is not in question. There is general agreement amongst writers in the area that further research and development work is required to establish it more firmly as a rigorous and respectable counselling approach. Several future directions for multicultural counselling are suggested.

Competencies have already been identified for counselling the ethnically different (Sue and Sue 1990). It is now necessary to establish the extent to which these competencies may be common to, and different from, those needed for the effective counselling of clients from other social groups (for example, gender, social class, sexual preference). In addition to the development of the competency element of effective multicultural counselling, attention needs to be given to the development and validation of appropriate 'process' models. Ivey *et al.* propose a five-stage decisional model for counselling ethnically different clients (1993: 76). Chaplin proposes a 'feminine' rhythm model for counselling, as an appropriate model for both female and male clients, which is different from what she regards as the 'masculine' control model characterising mainstream counselling approaches (1988: 4). Are these necessary and, if so, are they adequate? Do other types of process model need to be developed for use with other types of client?

Effective training methods and programmes need to be developed which will enable the operationalisation of these 'cultural' competencies and process models. Alongside this goes the need for further investigation of the relationship between the acquisition of cultural competence on the part of the counsellor and positive outcomes for clients. And of course, the means for reliable evaluation of the culturally competent counsellor need further development.

More coherence in the overall development of multiculturalism is emerging as research builds upon previous research. Fundamental to all of the new developments is the need for a unifying theoretical framework using clearly defined concepts.

CONCLUSIONS

Multiculturalism in counselling is here to stay. It exhorts counsellors to take more account of the social context from which their clients present for counselling, and within which they are located. Counselling has traditionally shied away from becoming 'political' by working beyond the individual with systems and structures. However, there seems to be growing acceptance within the profession that this position is no longer tenable. For example, Sue and Sue (1990: 24) state:

> For too long we have deceived ourselves into believing that the practice of counselling and the data base that underlie the profession are morally, ethically, and politically neutral. The results have been . . . provision of an excuse to the profession for not taking social action to rectify inequities in the system.

Multiculturalism is an approach to counselling that provides those counsellors who feel that traditional counselling practice in some way falls short of client expectations with a means for continuing within their profession by adopting an approach different from any previously existing. What remains to be seen is the extent to which the more radical element of the movement, lobbying for more 'systems change' from counsellors, wins the arguments over those adopting a more moderate approach which advocates work within systems.

REFERENCES

Allison, K.W., Crawford, I., Echemendia, R., Robinson, L. and Knepp, D. (1994) Human diversity and professional competence: training in clinical and counselling psychology revisited. *American Psychologist 49* (9) 792–6.

Bernal, M.E. and Castro, F.G. (1994) Are clinical psychologists prepared for service and research with ethnic minorities? *American Psychologist 49* (9) 797–805.

Bimrose, J. (1993) Counselling and social context. In R. Bayne, and P. Nicolson (eds) *Counselling and Psychology for Health Professionals*. London: Chapman and Hall.

Bimrose, J. and Bayne, R. (1995) A multicultural framework in counsellor training: a preliminary evaluation. *British Journal of Guidance and Counselling 23* (2) 259–65.

Brislin, R.W. and Yoshida, T. (1994) *Improving Intercultural Interactions: Modules for Cross-Cultural Training Programs*. Thousand Oaks, CA: Sage.

Chaplin, J. (1988) *Feminist Counselling in Action*. London: Sage.

d'Andrea, M. and Daniels, J. (1991) Exploring the different levels of multicultural counselling training in counsellor education. *Journal of Counselling and Development 70* 78–85.

d'Ardenne, P. and Mahtani, A. (1989) *Transcultural Counselling in Action*. London: Sage.

Egan, G. and Cowan, R.M. (1979) *People and Systems: An Integrative Approach to Human Development*. Pacific Grove, CA: Brooks/Cole.

Good, G.E., Gilbert, L.A. and Scher, M. (1990) Gender aware therapy: a synthesis of feminist therapy and knowledge about gender. *Journal of Counselling and Development 68* (4) 376–80.

Helms, J.E. (1994) How multiculturalism obscures racial factors in the therapy process: comment on Ridley *et al.* (1994), Sodowsky *et al.* (1994), Ottavi *et al.* (1994), and Thompson *et al.* (1994). *Journal of Counselling Psychology 41* (2) 162–5.

Holland, S. (1992) From social abuse to social action: a neighbourhood psychotherapy and social action project for women. In J.M. Ussher and P. Nicolson (eds) *Gender Issues in Clinical Psychology*. London: Routledge.

Ivey, A.E. (1994) *Intentional Interviewing and Counselling: Facilitating Client Development in a Multicultural Society*. Pacific Grove, CA: Brooks/Cole.

Ivey, A.E., Ivey, M.B. and Simek-Morgan, L. (1993) *Counselling and Psychotherapy: A Multicultural Perspective*. Boston: Allyn and Bacon. 3rd edn.

Jones, T. (1993) *Britain's Ethnic Minorities*. London: Policy Studies Institute.

Kareem, J. and Littlewood, R. (eds) (1992) *Intercultural Therapy: Themes, Interpretations and Practice*. Oxford: Blackwell Scientific.

LaFromboise, T.D. and Foster, S.L. (1989) Ethics in multicultural counselling. In P.B. Pedersen, J.G. Draguns, W.J. Lonner and J.E. Trimble (eds) *Counselling Across Cultures*. Honolulu: University of Hawaii Press. 3rd edn.

Locke, D.C. (1992) *Increasing Multicultural Understanding: A Comprehensive Model*. Newbury Park, CA: Sage.

Pedersen, P. (1983) The cultural complexity of counselling. *International Journal for the Advancement of Counselling* 6 177–92.

Pedersen, P.B. (1991a) Introduction to Part 1: A conceptual framework. *Journal of Counseling and Development* 70 (1) 5.

Pedersen, P.B. (1991b) Multiculturalism as a generic approach to counselling. *Journal of Counseling and Development* 70 (1) 6–12.

Pine, G.J. (1972) Counselling minority groups: a review of the literature. *Counselling and Values* 17 35–44.

Ponterotto, J.G., Rieger, B.P., Barrett, A. and Sparks, R. (1994) Assessing multicultural counselling competence: a review of instrumentation. *Journal of Counseling and Development* 72 316–22.

Raubenheimer, J.R. (1987) Counselling across cultural borders in South Africa. *International Journal for the Advancement of Counselling* 10 229–53.

Ridley, C.R., Mendoza, D.W., Kanitz, B.E., Angermeiier, L. and Zenk, R. (1994) Cultural sensitivity in multicultural counselling: a perceptual schema model. *Journal of Counseling Psychology* 41 (2) 125–36.

Sodowski, G.R. *et al.* (1994) Development of the multicultural counselling inventory: a self-report measure of multicultural competence. *Journal of Counselling Psychology* 41 (2) 137–49.

Smail, D. (1987) *Taking Care: An Alternative to Therapy*. London: Dent.

Steenbarger, B.N. (1993) A multicontextual model of counselling: bridging brevity and diversity. *Journal of Counseling and Development* 72 8–15.

Strawbridge, S. (1994) Towards anti-oppressive practice in counselling psychology. *Counselling Psychology Review* 9 (1) 5–12.

Sue, D.W. and Sue, D. (1990) *Counselling the Culturally Different: Theory and Practice*. New York: Wiley.

Sundberg, N.D. and Sue, D. (1989) Research and research hypotheses about effectiveness in intercultural counselling. In P.B. Pederson, J.G. Draguns, W.J. Lonner and J.E. Trimble (eds) *Counselling Across Cultures*. Honolulu: University of Hawaii Press.

Walker, M. (1990) *Women in Therapy and Counselling*. Milton Keynes: Open University Press.

Woolfe, R. (1983) Counselling in a world of crisis: towards a sociology of counselling. *International Journal for the Advancement of Counselling* 6 167–76.

Wrenn, C.G. (1985) The culturally encapsulated counsellor revisited. In P. Pedersen (ed.) *Handbook of Cross-Cultural Counselling and Therapy*. Westport, CT: Greenwood.

Chapter 18

Feminism and counselling

Janice Russell

INTRODUCTION

In 1983, Luise Eichenbaum and Susie Orbach stated with confidence that 'The women's liberation movement has given us a totally new way to understand women's psychology' (1983: 3). In developing their own psychodynamic mode of feminist psychotherapy, they crystallised a widespread optimism that such understandings could inform the therapeutic help available to women in the Western world. Further, they hoped that this would be a part of a political process which would further the goals of feminism. I would argue that despite considerable achievements, this optimism has not been largely realised. The major contention of this chapter will be that in post-modernity, the discourse of feminism, of which feminist psychology is one strand, has become marginalised within the practice and theory of counselling. In the form of a value which informs practice, I would say that feminism remains almost invisible except within 'specialised areas'. Further, within the discourse of counselling – that is, the language, theories, symbols and practices which make counselling what it is – there is a danger that the profession of counselling will, in the wake of others, become increasingly male dominated as it gains status. Whether this perspective is an astute perception or the product of paranoia is not my point. Rather, I am suggesting that there needs to be continued debate and inclusion of these issues in the development of counselling.

I began counselling in 1978, well before the days of professionalisation. I worked in a woman-oriented setting and was fortunate to receive excellent supervision from women who were themselves feminists. My understanding of women's issues has long been located in a conviction that they are society's issues, women's and men's alike. We exist in relation to each other. I am also a sociologist, and I believe that interdisciplinary perspectives are invaluable to the future of counselling. And I am a woman, charged with the responsibility to raise a daughter and a son to the best of my ability in a world which offers them different choices because of their genders. These, then, are the perspectives from which I write.

I hope this chapter will be something of a polemic. I aim to take the reader on a brief journey through the feminist possibilities. I would like to question why these are not more integrated into our practice. I cannot hope to cover all arguments, though I will try to summarise many. I hope readers are stimulated to raise their own arguments and to expand the gaps that I will inevitably leave. I will end the chapter by making some suggestions as to how counsellors and the profession of counselling might begin to bring the rich knowledge gathered through feminism to bear on the theory and practice of counselling.

TERMINOLOGY

Before discussing the historical contribution of feminism to counselling, I will offer a brief note on the term feminism. There is available some excellent and informative work on the debate as to what feminism is. In this context, I am using it to represent a perspective, a way of construing the world, our experiences and the possibilities which we see for the future. It is a perspective which defies rigidity, while genuinely affording value to women's experience as of central importance and worth. It is a perspective which acknowledges that women and men may come to think, speak and act differently on the basis of those experiences. Feminism is a way of seeing the world which works towards helping women take an equal place in society, both in their social situations and in the formation of knowledge which informs social practices.

Within this framework, I am not concerned to identify one specific model of 'feminist counselling'. Rather, I would contend that feminism is a perspective based on a set of values, and that to integrate it into the counselling world is not a matter of proposing a particular method or technique (Chaplin 1988: 2; Walker 1990: 73). It needs to inform our discipline within all aspects of practice and development. We need to see a feminist presence and knowledge at all layers, and within all branches, of the profession.

I use the term 'counselling' to refer to a process of therapeutic help which represents a specific social practice. I am aware that this is a potentially contentious view and that there is currently much debate on the similarities and differences between counselling and psychotherapy. My choice of terminology represents my sociological self. As I have elaborated elsewhere (Russell 1993), I would say that all these processes have in common that they are 'talking cures', that they have in mind an understanding of 'a healthy self', and that they embrace the notion of self-determination. My intention is to capture their commonality of social function, not to conflate their theoretical differences.

It is worth noting at this point that the terminology employed above reflects a tendency in counselling to suggest an individualist model of mental health and illness. This is not so overt as within psychiatry, but it does exist. There is, for example, the notion of a 'fully functioning' or 'self-actualising' self which is common to Rogerian approaches and underpinnings, and which originates with the work of Abraham Maslow. While this is ostensibly a move away from explicit concepts of mental health and illness, it can continue to locate the responsibility for malaise within the individual. This can be dangerous if it is conceived that the individuals are the sole root of their own problems. Individuals may be helped to respond in different ways to external situations, but we must recognise that structural situations exist which create the malaise in the first place. I personally adopt the view that individuals have potential to fuel internal resources to cope with external situations, but also that the status quo surrounding individuals may be oppressive and destructive to their well-being. Locating responsibility for all the problems encountered by women within themselves is dangerous, as it leads to the adaptive model of mental health where women are seen to be neurotic in some way if they do not accept the social structures around them.

HISTORICAL OVERVIEW

Historically, then, I would suggest that the contributions of women's thinking to counselling psychology go back far beyond the 'second-wave' feminist movement as suggested by Eichenbaum and Orbach. The work of Karen Horney, for example, proposed radical insights into women's psychology within a paradigm which acknowledged the interaction of the individual and social construction of self (Westkott 1986). Horney argued strongly against Freudian theories which relied so heavily on primal instinct, substituting instead an understanding that cultural factors were instrumental in the creation of psychic malaise. Her theories of neurosis placed women's development firmly in a context where those cultural factors were devaluing to women, and fraught with contradictions and constrictions. Horney's ideas were revolutionary, and it is perhaps no accident that her theories have not survived with the same impact as those of her male counterparts within the psychoanalytic movement, itself heavily male dominated.

The work of Melanie Klein has fared more successfully in informing future developments, certainly in the revival of object relations theory and its reformulations (Eichenbaum and Orbach 1983; Dinnerstein 1976). The theoretical basis of Klein's work remains more ego focused than that of Horney's, and it may be argued that culturally it was and remains less contentious to the societal status quo than the work of Horney. It may be noted that Klein's work and its derivatives place tremendous emphasis on the role of mothering. While this has been seen as a useful conceptualisation by some feminist therapists, it may also be seen as an oppressive perspective, as the behaviour of the mother towards the child becomes the paramount site of exploration. Although this is wonderfully woman centred in some respects, and although reformulations profess to locate the individual within a cultural context (Chodorow 1978), it is also highly problematic. Such theories may actually be collusive with an oppressive status quo, where women are perceived as having primary responsibility for the psychic well-being of their children. This leaves women with an enormously powerful role, where unrealistic expectations may fuel guilt and inappropriate responsibility for the development and actions of their offspring. The role of mother demands a traditional obligation which may be seen as antithetical to feminism. Moreover, as Segal (1987) has pointed out, the term 'mother' refers to a somewhat stereotyped, middle-class version of this particular role.

By the 1970s, several feminists had made crucial challenges to the concept of personhood. Bear in mind here that the concept of personhood is crucial to the philosophies and psychological theories which inform counselling, although rarely is the received concept overtly discussed or challenged from within the discipline. Contextually, Betty Friedan had captured the plight of women in post-war society, a situation where popular psychology had played a central part in their oppression (Friedan 1963). Kate Millett had identified that an oppressive social context would inform ego development (1969: 55). Broverman and Broverman (1970) published their classic study on the different models of mental health applied to women and men by practitioners of both sexes. Phyllis Chesler (1972) had challenged the social construction of women's madness and the purpose and effectiveness of so-called treatments.

In 1976, Jean Baker Miller identified the need to develop new ways of understanding the psychology of women, an understanding central to developing appropriate therapeutic help. She crystallised the central challenge:

> In recent years it has become apparent that women must create new conceptions of what it means to be a person if they are to change the day-to-day workings of their lives. When women seriously resist the old internal and external proscriptions and demands they have to find new conceptions to live by.
>
> (1976: 48)

In other words, the process of liberation for women would entail a whole new way of looking at self. Carol Gilligan made further contributions to the debate with her estimable documentation of the different modes of representation which women and men adopt, and their implications for both everyday life and the construction of morality (1982, 1986). Gilligan's approach is striking also for integrating feminist notions of empowerment in the research processes which inform her theoretical standpoints. Such integration is rare in the mainstream profession in Britain.

CONTEMPORARY FEMINIST CONTRIBUTIONS

Over the decades of the 1980s and 1990s to date, several innovations have been made in the therapeutic arena. Luise Eichenbaum and Susie Orbach were instrumental in developing a specific model of psychotherapy, and in introducing a new forum for working in the form of the London Women's Therapy Centre. Several such centres are now in operation, spanning perspectives from eclectic models of counselling to pure, long-term psychotherapy. Rape crisis centres were set up from the mid-1970s onwards, embracing a perspective which emphasised the rights of a woman to her own body and exploding many of the myths around sexuality. More recently, some Women's Aid refuges, long familiar with the value and relevance of the use of counselling skills in their work, have begun to debate the inclusion of individual counselling in their practice. It has been argued that the use of individual counselling is seen as antithetical to the nature and values of Women's Aid (Perry 1993: 21). At least two refuges in the north-east have recently fought for funding for the appointment of individual counsellors, and one is now in post. Family Service Units have also pioneered women's counselling projects (Perry 1993: 31–4).

We have seen further innovations born of women's experience. Joyce Chaplin (1988) has developed what she calls a 'rhythm model' of counselling to inform her work, very much concerned with the interconnectedness of self and social context. She identifies seven stages of the counselling process, and highlights issues of power and control throughout. In the States, Mary Ballou and Nancy Gabalac (1985) produced a cohesive model of feminist counselling which identifies stages of 'harmful adaptation' in a woman's life, and specific tasks of counselling to help women validate their experience and regain self-determination. Their model is provocative and highlights dilemmas associated with feminist counselling, as one of their principles is that inevitably the client will be encouraged to embrace feminist principles. The major issue of contention in this model is the question of whether such a principle is compatible with a philosophy of self-determination, or whether it represents the imposition of one set of values over another. Even if the latter is the case, it might be suggested that the self-empowerment inherent in feminism offers the saving grace. There is undoubtedly room for debate here, given that counselling is located within ethical and moral systems. The practice of counselling already gives rise to ambiguities and contradictions if we accept that the client's value system, without reference to morality, is of paramount importance, a philosophy well entrenched

within counselling. Currently, if the value system of the client is tradi-
tional-patriarchal, there is little challenge as long as he or she is not
overtly abusive. This may be seen as being collusive with a morality
which is oppressive, and in this context we cannot too easily dismiss the
requirement that the client embraces feminism. Further exploration of this
issue is not possible here, but needs noting as of central importance.

It may be argued that much progress has been made by the approaches
and settings described above. It is not my intention to trivialise their
impact on the people with whom they work directly, or to deny them any
influence. In structure and in status, however, I would still argue that
feminist approaches remain marginalised not only by the way their theoretical contributions are received, but by the way their work is structured.
It is important to note that most projects specifically concerned with feminist counselling are funded from the voluntary sector, and under constant
pressure to negotiate, justify and secure such funding. Their existence is
precarious. In this sense, they are not recognised as having mainstream
value. Janet Perry highlights one instance where, due to the success of
counselling interventions with a group of abused women, the funding for
the project was withdrawn and reallocated to providing counselling for
men who perpetrated sexual abuse (Perry 1993). This throws the continual
tension of such projects into sharp relief.

IS COUNSELLING ANTITHETICAL TO FEMINISM?

There is some ambiguity as to whether or how the influence of feminist
counselling has served the wider cause of feminism, as it can be argued
that the practice of individual counselling is antithetical to the empowerment of women. This argument may be extended to suggest that the practice of counselling is influential to the construction of the self as
individualist and self-serving. If this is so, then oppressed groups of
people will not benefit from the overall development of counselling as a
social practice.

I have already stated that some organisations and groups have struggled
with the dilemma of whether individual counselling is useful to the aims
of feminism. The point is made that counselling brings with it a whole
new language, whether through concentrating on feelings to the exclusion
of all else, or in the mind-game arena where one person's perception is
given analytic status as a 'projection' rather than being valued for what it
is. It has also been suggested that counselling might undermine the
strengths of the 'collectiveness' of lesbians, and that it has a depoliticising
and conditioning effect (Mercy 1990). The case for and against the value
of therapy for lesbians remains hotly debated (Perkins 1992; Brown
1992).

Celia Kitzinger and Rachel Perkins (1993) argue vehemently, albeit selectively, against the use of counselling for lesbians. I am in great sympathy with many of their arguments. They draw attention to the dangers of interpretive therapies, where real societal and cultural problems are rephrased in the language of therapy, and thus become conceptualised as the problem of the individual. They also write eloquently on the pervasiveness of the language of therapy in everyday expression, thus affecting the construct of the political and the moral. Within this frame, the political becomes the personal. Kitzinger and Perkins end their anti-psychology work forcefully:

> Most of us are adequate human beings who do not need 'safety' so much as 'freedom'. And on those occasions when we are not able to cope on our own, we can take care of each other. We do not need psychology. Psychology is, and always will be, destructive of the lesbian/feminist enterprise. Without psychology, we can, like millions of others, bear the limits, contradictions, vulnerabilities and burdens of our humanity. Without psychology, we can build lesbian communities, lesbian ethics, and lesbian politics.

> (1993: 201)

Where therapy is the kind of interpretive enterprise described by Kitzinger and Perkins, then I would have to extrapolate their argument and agree that it would be largely antithetical to the values of feminism. My worst fantasy about the impact of therapy is, and has been for many years, that the therapeutic process produces therapised clones for whom introspection and the feelings mode are paramount, to the exclusion of individual spontaneity, intellectual ability, and political awareness and activism.

However, I do take issue with the linear vision which Kitzinger and Perkins produce. It seems ironic that both these women wish to be prescriptive to others from a position where they have studied psychology in a highly specific context, that is, within the echelons of academia. It is all very well to profess from such a standpoint that lesbians *should* be able to help and support each other. In the ideal world, as Smail (1987) has suggested, all human beings, not only specific categories, would support each other through natural and contrived life events. Counsellors would be redundant.

However, this is not currently the case. Having had the enriching experience of working as a counselling trainer with survivors of the Iraq/Kuwait war, and currently with Bosnian refugees, it is clear to me that there are times when a counselling interventionist approach is useful to groups surviving oppression. While I have tremendous faith in the resources of individuals to survive the greatest odds, I also believe that there are times when their resources are depleted, and if an external, formal helping approach can be useful and expedient, then it seems an ideological privilege to reject the value of counselling per se. In the situations I work in, I have not seen evidence of counselling reducing the political to the personal. On the contrary, the alleviation of distress and the replenishing of internal resources can serve to enable individuals to pursue the political.

I do not say this without reservation. Although I am interspersing the terms 'counselling' and 'therapy' from a functionalist perspective, I know that I do in fact make major distinctions within those activities which might best be described as around essentialist notions of the self. In my work with clients from my own and other cultures, I have been acutely aware of helping them to develop strategies which are responsive to cultural and personal notions of self, and which recognise that those might be discrepant. Such a view informs my conceptualisation of the potential of counselling and feminism being compatible, whatever the sexual and political preferences of the individuals concerned.

There are two areas which it is crucial to recognise if this is to be the case. One is that, as stated, valuable counselling should be a process whereby individuals are aided to develop their own notions of self and development, not to receive the sorts of poor interpretation which Kitzinger and Perkins cite so profusely. Nobody, not just specific categories of people, should be subject to the sort of poor 'therapy' which they describe. My own perspective is constructivist, and although I accept notions of authenticity, I reject strongly the notion of the 'real' self, or indeed fixed interpretive theories of personality development. Second, a major element of my own understanding and practice of counselling, which seems to be omitted from Kitzinger and Perkins' analysis, is that counselling is a prospective activity which at its best helps people to empower themselves to take some control over how they shape their lives. In a feminist context, this is entirely compatible with development of political awareness and activity, and challenging very real oppressive situations.

Many more issues exist around this area. It has long been questioned whether male counsellors can work with female clients (Chesler 1972). There is increasing acknowledgement that counsellors are powerful and can be exploitative of their clients through the abuse of either the power in the relationship, or the power of the psychological theory (Russell 1993). How do sexism and heterosexism enter this arena? There is room for much more debate, debate which personally I would like to see as integral to mainstream teachings and development.

THE COUNSELLING WORLD

In a context of such rich debate and development, it pays to wonder why this area is not more central to the world of counselling. I contended at the outset of this chapter that feminism is marginalised to specialist areas.

One of the examples of this is in which theories remain dominant in the counselling world. Let us examine a typology of the major theorists who are likely to inform teaching courses. At the counselling skills and qualities level, we are likely to look at Carl Rogers, Gerard Egan and Richard Nelson-Jones as classic core texts. Within counselling at progressive levels, we might move to different approaches and aspects of the counselling relationship whose rudiments were developed by Fritz Perls, Albert Ellis, George Kelly, Eric Berne, Carl Jung and, of course, Sigmund Freud. Latterly, innovative theories have come from David Groves, Richard Bandler and John Heron. Central psychological theories which inform practice include the work of Erik Erikson, Aaron Beck and Abraham Maslow. There will be more, but I guess the point is made.

I know that there are women in there, notably Alice Miller and Melanie Klein. And even with such disparate numbers of male–female influence, my point is not just to make a gender count. If feminism is a perspective based on certain values, then men too can be feminists. Conversely, I want to avoid the trap of 'woman equals feminist'. And I do not want to diminish the work of innovators such as Fay Fransella and Peggy Dalton (1990), who have adapted and developed Kelly's work so wonderfully and with an eye to its value for work with women. I also want to recognise the increasing value afforded to the work of Dorothy Rowe, Emmy van Deurzen Smith, Brigid Proctor, Francesca Inskipp and Moira Walker, to name some of the women who have made an impact as practitioners and writers within the mainstream counselling forum.

Three central points do need to be made, however. First, where do the central theories which inform counselling emanate from? In the case of Erikson, for example, we know that his whole theory of the stages of human development was based on his research into a limited number of case studies on young men. Kohlberg, similarly, based his whole theory of moral development on a sample of young men. In these cases, male experience is used to represent human experience. Second, whose interpretations inform the theories? It is well documented that Freud denied huge chunks of female experience as he developed his theoretical standpoints. What is less well researched is how other theorists' gender has influenced their interpretation. If Gilligan's findings are taken seriously, then we may argue that the male interpretation of the events before him may represent only one way of looking at the picture. And finally, where are the feminist counselling models? Usually, if included at all, it is my experience that they are options rather than central texts. In other words, the representation of theories within counselling is dominated either by studies of male experience or by male interpretation of experiences. This last may be extended to the interpretations of process in the therapeutic encounter as well as to theories of human development.

Another question is that of who dominates within the major publications available to counselling. Published books and journals represent another means as to how discourses are produced. Who are the major influences currently? My observation is that again, in terms of generic theory or principles, the market seems to be male dominated, certainly in editorial terms, unless the subject is one of those deemed to be a specialism.

This is even more apparent in books on research. As counselling becomes more professionalised, so it becomes increasingly taught to higher academic levels. Simultaneously, as the profession grows, so it becomes more interested in learning through evaluation. Research is becoming ever more important. A count through a recent publicity brochure showed that over 95 per cent of the texts were written or edited by men. Moreover, the word 'feminist' simply did not appear in the indexes, let alone the chapter headings.

Equally important is the question of how knowledge gains status. I have been fascinated to note how the idea of new paradigm research (Reason and Rowan 1981; Reason 1988), where people are co-operative subjects rather than faceless objects, is becoming adopted by the mainstream. My fascination is fuelled by having encountered a decade ago some of the founding principles of such research in the work of feminists of the calibre of Ann Oakley and Janet Finch, to name but two. These researchers were concerned to make research a collaborative, ethical, reflexive and informative process, in both its collection and its dissemination, yet the richness of their work is rarely mentioned save in acknowledgement. Somehow, feminist perspectives remain marginalised again. This is not exclusive to the counselling world, but it seems especially important that in a profession which espouses the values of equality and empowerment, the practice should not be collusive with a patriarchal status quo. It is not enough to acknowledge the value of women and feminist practitioners. This leaves the road open to a situation where women excel at the 'hands-on' caring aspects of the profession, while the discourse of counselling is produced by men. There is a danger here of replicating traditional roles in the production of knowledge.

CONCLUSIONS

So, what is to be done? Theoretically, it could be argued that it should be enough for counsellors to embrace the values of non-exploitation embedded in professional codes of ethics, the notions of unconditional positive regard and of empowerment for both clients and colleagues, and all will be well. Unfortunately, even were we all to be blessed enough to exercise these values unerringly, life is rarely so simple. There are structural as well as theoretical issues at stake in the production of knowledge. To include feminist values and bodies of knowledge within the discourse of counselling is the concern of the whole profession as a body and in the way it represents itself and develops. This has implications for the profession's need to explore both its theoretical bases and its discursive practices to integrate feminism as a value rather than to marginalise it. I do not profess to have all the answers, and the following comments are designed to provoke thought, not to act as a blueprint. Doubtless there are gaps in my thinking and approach. It does strike me, however, that there are several foci for change.

Counselling courses

It seems to me that counselling education could put much more emphasis on its philosophical foundations and its theories of self, with due consideration of the context of their development. This should then be open to being presented alongside alternative theories of self and relationship as proposed by such theorists as Jean Baker Miller and Carol Gilligan. How compatible or not are these with the views of Rogers and Maslow?

I would also suggest that the exploration of the dynamics of gender issues should be integral to counselling courses, rather than a sideline which interested tutors or students might introduce. How do gender dynamics influence the counselling relationship? What implications does it have that much of counselling relies on values and attributes which have been seen to be traditionally 'female', such as the expression of feeling, the offering of warmth? How does the traditionally 'male' forum of the cognitive fit in here, and do we need to integrate more of this?

Alongside frameworks such as Egan's, I would like to see the inclusion of feminist paradigms such as those of Chaplin (1988) and Ballou and Gabalac (1985), and to examine how their stages of change might inform each other. And it would be useful to review book lists, to make the sorts of text described here integral to reading rather than to be dragged out for the chosen project.

There is another point here in terms of not only how to integrate existing theory, but how to make opportunities for study and generation of theory more accessible to women. The practice of counselling is still female dominated, although as it becomes more professionalised, this is in process of change. It is still not easy for women to concentrate on academic pursuit, as many combine it with domestic responsibility. My most striking example of this is in literally writing my last book in an understair cupboard at home while having full responsibility for the care of two children. An enlivening experience, and one of my ambitions is to produce a feminist text which captures the interspersion of intellectual thought with domestic interruption. It would go something like:

> The generation of discourse remains male dominated ... *Mam, I haven't got any clean knickers . . . Have you looked in the washing basket . . .*

and issues of power in the production of knowledge are paramount.

And so on. One woman I know combines her study to masters level with a full-time job and prime responsibility for the running of her household – with nine children.

Changing this status quo is a vast task. It would be helpful, however, for counselling courses and academic institutions to give more consideration to making access easier through provision of child care and other strategic facilities which remain important and unresolved many years on from 'second-wave' feminist initiatives. Women without support and facilities remain excluded from the possibility of gaining status and influence through activities such as research and writing.

Codes of ethics and practice

Much work has been done on the codes of ethics and practice within professional bodies. It could yet go further. The British Association for Counselling (BAC), for example, has as yet no supported policy document on equality of opportunity. It is also important that ethical committees find ways to be truly accessible to women, indeed to all user groups. I was struck in my research into sexually exploitative behaviour (Russell 1993) by how apprehensive women were of approaching ethical committees for fear of not being believed or being seen as neurotic.

Accreditation

The voluntary sector and the 'barefoot' counsellor need to be included within the professionalisation process. I am delighted to see that a third avenue for accreditation has recently been introduced by BAC which will go some way toward this aim. I would also like to see a competence-based assessment procedure adopted on a wider scale (Russell and Dexter 1993), for the reason that this would enable those in the voluntary sector, many of whom are women, to have their skills, experience and competence acknowledged. This view raises contentious issues. The main point relevant to this work is that this approach entails structure and hierarchy which become potentially oppressive. It is essential that the principles of equality of opportunity are embedded in such a process (Bond and Russell 1993).

Reflexivity

Finally, as a professional body, it is incumbent on counsellors to reflect constantly on their practice from the point of view of sexism and heterosexism. Reflexive practice is a value well inhered within the adoption of supervision. Perhaps we need to be thorough in the consideration of our own attitudes and values. I invite the interested reader to consider your own responses to the following questions and statements:

- I believe that women are more caring than men.
- I believe that men are more logical than women.
- I believe that women are equal to men in every way.
- I have a considered understanding of how cultural contexts may affect women and men differently.
- I am familiar with feminist models of person development.
- I have an understanding of the impact of women's reproductive systems on their life cycle.
- I have explored the impact of gender dynamics on counselling practice.

The list could go on, and I do not include it to elicit a version of 'political correctness'. The point is rather to stimulate some self-challenge on the issues under review, and for practitioners to consider what their values, understandings and interests are.

The worst scenario that could happen in ignoring these issues is that the counselling world colludes with the adjustment model of mental health and with women's unequal position in society (cf. Broverman and Broverman 1970; Kitzinger and Perkins 1993). The new direction is to amalgamate some of our learnings from previous pitfalls (for example, through the developments of the early psychoanalytic institutes), to recognise the importance of feminist theory as a part of mainstream counselling, and to initiate practices and codes which enable us to develop an integrated and anti-sexist approach.

REFERENCES

Baker Miller, J. (1976) *Towards a New Psychology of Women*. Harmondsworth: Penguin.
Ballou, M. and Gabalac, N. (1985) *A Feminist Position on Mental Health*. Springfield, IL: Charles Thomas.
Bond, T. and Russell, J. (1993) Report on Ethical Standards and Equality of Opportunity in Advice, Guidance and Counselling. London: Department of Environment.
Broverman, I.K. and Broverman, D.M. (1970) Sex-role stereotypes and clinical judgements of mental health. *Journal of Consulting and Clinical Psychology 34* (1) 1–7.
Brown, L. (1992) While waiting for the revolution: the case for a lesbian feminist psychotherapy. *Feminism and Psychology 2* (2) 239–53.
Chaplin, J. (1988) *Feminist Counselling in Action*. London: Sage.
Chesler, P. (1972) *Women and Madness*. New York: Doubleday.
Chodorow, N. (1978) *The Reproduction of Mothering*. London: University of California Press.
Dinnerstein, D. (1976) *The Mermaid and the Minotaur*. New York: Harper and Row.

Eichenbaum, L. and Orbach, S. (1983) *Understanding Women*. Harmondsworth: Penguin.

Fransella, F. and Dalton, P. (1990) *Personal Construct Counselling in Action*. London: Sage.

Friedan, B. (1963) *The Feminine Mystique*. Harmondsworth: Penguin.

Gilligan, C. (1982) *In a Different Voice: Psychological Theory and Women's Development*. Cambridge, MA: Harvard University Press.

Gilligan, C. (1986) *Mapping the Moral Domain*. Cambridge, MA: Harvard University Press.

Kitzinger, C. and Perkins, R. (1993) *Changing our Minds*. London: Onlywomen Press.

Mercy, J. (1990) Out of the closet . . . and onto the couch. *A Queer Tribe 5*.

Millett, K. (1969) *Sexual Politics*. London: Virago.

Perkins, R. (1992) Waiting for the revolution – or working for it? A reply to Laura Brown and Katherine Sender. *Feminism and Psychology 2* (2) 258–61.

Perry, J. (1993) *Counselling for Women*. Buckingham: Open University Press.

Reason, P. (ed.) (1988) *Human Inquiry in Action: Developments in New Paradigm Research*. London: Sage.

Reason, P. and Rowan, J. (eds) (1981) *Human Inquiry: A Source Book of New Paradigm Research*. Chichester: Wiley.

Russell, J. (1993) *Out of Bounds: Sexual Exploitation in Counselling and Therapy*. London: Sage.

Russell, J. and Dexter, G. (1993) Ménage à trois: accreditation, NVQs and BAC. *Counselling 4* 266–9.

Segal, L. (1987) *Is The Future Female?*. London: Virago.

Smail, D. (1987) *Taking Care: An Alternative to Therapy*. London: Dent.

Walker, M. (1990) *Women in Therapy and Counselling*. Milton Keynes: Open University Press.

Westkott, M. (1986) *The Feminist Legacy of Karen Horney*. New Haven, CT: Yale University Press.

Chapter 19

Accreditation of prior learning

Jenny Bimrose

INTRODUCTION

A radical restructuring of the current system of vocational qualifications is under way in the UK. The Lead Body for Advice, Guidance, Counselling and Psychotherapy was established to define competencies and set standards for new National Vocational Qualifications (NVQs) and Scottish Vocational Qualifications (SVQs) in the occupational areas identified by its title. Counselling's professional body, the British Association for Counselling (BAC), has made a significant commitment to the development of these qualifications. 'BAC is putting considerable effort into the development of the NVQs in Counselling on behalf of their members so as to ensure a quality product' (*Counselling* 1995, *6* (2) 101). In addition, the BAC scheme for Recognition of Counsellor Training courses includes proposals for accreditation of prior learning (APL). It is within this context that the process of APL can be regarded as a new trend in counselling. 'Since APL involves the assessment of individuals against outcome-specified standards, it lends itself to extensive use in the new vocational qualification frameworks of NVQs in England and Wales and National Certificate in Scotland' (Employment Department 1990: 3).

This chapter will explore the origins and some of the features of APL. It will describe the stages involved in the process of APL and discuss some of the practical and ethical issues that may arise in counsellor training.

WHAT IS APL?

APL refers to the notion that people learn most effectively by 'doing'. This is not a new concept. For example, Lewin (1951), Kolb (1984) and Schon (1987) all stressed the importance and value of experiential learning to human growth and development. APL has developed these ideas by establishing the principle that the learning arising from experience should be formally recognised, or credited. There are a number of different abbreviations currently in usage, all describing aspects of the same process. The most common ones are APL, APEL (assessment of prior experiential learning), APA (accreditation of prior achievement), RPL (recognition of prior learning), PLA (prior learning assessment) and APEAL (accreditation of prior experience achievements and learning). This variety of terms can be confusing, but they all relate to the idea that an individual's knowledge and skills can be formally credited, irrespective of where or how they were obtained (BTEC 1990).

Although the practice of APL is relatively new in the UK, Simosko (1992: 13) discusses evidence for various forms of accreditation of prior learning being used as long ago as fifth-century China, and in Europe during the Middle Ages (with the guild system). Moreover, elements of practice are currently used in various contexts – in education, training and employment – without the label 'accreditation of prior learning'. For example, during selection interviews, interviewers may try to establish whether applicants are competent in a relevant area for which they do not have any formal qualifications. Equally, interviewees may present examples of their achievements in different media at interview, in an attempt to impress the selector. In 'APL language', this is the equivalent of presenting a range of evidence to demonstrate particular competencies.

NVQS AND APL

The National Targets for Education and Training, which were launched by the Confederation of British Industry (CBI) and have been endorsed by government, aim to upgrade the nation's qualifications. They focus on the whole population, with different targets set for young people and adults. For the adult workforce ('lifetime learning') they are as follows:

- by 1996, all employees should take part in training or development activities;
- by 1996, 50 per cent of the workforce will be aiming for NVQ/SVQs or units towards them; by 2000, 50 per cent of the workforce will be qualified to at least NVQ/SVQ III (or equivalent); by 1996, 50 per cent of medium to larger organisations will be 'Investors in People'.

('Competitiveness: Helping Business to Win',
Cmnd 2563, May 1994: 31)

It was the White Paper 'Working Together – Education and Training' (Department of Employment 1986) which stated that vocational qualifications in the UK needed to be reformed. Subsequent to the White Paper, the National Council for Vocational Qualifications (NCVQ) was established to lead this reform. Government has financed the development of new occupational standards vocational qualifications through the NCVQ. One notable feature of the process has been that the development has been led by employee representatives, not educationalists and trainers as has so often been the case previously. Employee representatives have been required to form themselves into groups called Industry Lead Bodies (ILBs). Once an ILB has developed the standards that best represent its occupational area, it develops qualifications based on those standards. The NCVQ then approves these qualifications, if the qualifications meet NCVQ's own standards of quality (Simosko 1992).

The assumption underlying the changes is that the economic competitiveness of the country will be increased by improving the level of qualifications of the nation's workforce, though how the workforce acquires these qualifications seems to be of less importance. Since the requisite capacity does not exist within current education and training provision to meet the targets set, alternative means are needed. The NCVQ, together with the Scottish Vocational Education Council (SCOTVEC) and a number of awarding bodies, have endorsed the concept of APL (Simosko 1991) as a legitimate part of the process of upgrading qualifications. Indeed, as Hodkinson (1995) points out, much of the early development work relating to APEL in the UK took place with the NCVQ.

COUNSELLING, APL AND NVQS

After a period of lengthy negotiation with professional bodies, employers and practitioners, and after field trials had been conducted, the national standards for advice, guidance and counselling were finally endorsed by the relevant Lead Body (1995). To contribute to the process of negotiation, BAC set up a BAC NVQ Liaison Group which 'ensures that BAC representatives on the Lead Body all speak from an informed position on BAC policy' (*Counselling* 1995, 6 (2) 101). The first release of standards which have been endorsed by the Lead Body does not include mediation, advocacy, psychotherapy or therapeutic counselling (including couples work), which are subjects for further standards development. (Lead Body 1995: para. 2.2).

The process of agreeing these standards was difficult and lengthy, partly because of the lack of agreement relating to definitions both of advice, guidance and counselling and of the relationship between them. The Lead Body reported in their newsletter (March 1993: 2) that 'there is considerable inconsistency in definition and function of advice, guidance and counselling', and that a recent feasibility study which they had undertaken had been 'haunted by difficulties with terminology and definitions'. Nevertheless, there now exists a set of national standards for this broad and complex occupational area. These will make APL more attractive and possible, because they are accessible and transparent to all. They will be used as the base from which NVQ qualifications in counselling will be developed. For instance, a number of qualifications in counselling should be available in the early part of 1996 (Lead Body newsletter August

1995: 1). Once these qualifications are available for counselling, individuals will be able to map their competencies against the requirements for a particular qualification.

STAGES IN THE APL PROCESS AND SOME IMPLICATIONS FOR COUNSELLING

Accounts of the different steps in the process of APL vary slightly, but it is possible to identify 'key' stages. First, the individual must decide what qualification he or she wishes to claim credit for, and which recognised body will accredit the learning. The body which will award NVQs in counselling has not, at the time of writing, been selected. Currently, therefore, most APL is offered by colleges of further and higher education, and universities. Some employers, professional bodies and training organisations (for example, the Local Government Management Board) also offer APL for some occupational areas. Since APL is still relatively new in the United Kingdom, it is not offered by all education and training organisations, and even within one organisation, like a university or college, APL may be offered for only a limited number of its courses. So for counselling, as for many other occupational areas, the choice is limited to those educational and training providers who may currently offer APL. However, once the accrediting body has been selected, it is possible (and likely) that there will be a rapid expansion of centres awarding NVQs in counselling and offering APL too.

Second, the individual identifies the particular learning outcomes or competencies he or she wishes to present for assessment. There is a difference between the identification of prior learning (Stage 2) and organising it into forms appropriate for assessment (Stage 3). The identification of prior learning comes through systematic reflection on experience. The individual then reviews his or her experiences, selects those where something was learned, and writes a clear statement about what it was. The national standards for counselling which now exist provide a framework for this stage. Of course, in addition to confirming competence, this process of 'mapping' may also reveal lack of competence. The process of APL does not in itself assist the individual in addressing any lack of competence, and individuals are left to organise any training required.

The third stage in the APL process is the collection and collation of evidence to support the statements of what was learned. Having identified the competencies for which credit is to be claimed, evidence must be gathered, and structured in a form suitable for assessment – usually in a 'portfolio'. A portfolio in this context is a portable collection of evidence, usually presented in a 'bound folder' (Simosko 1991: 31). It is the portfolio which is submitted for assessment, and which forms the basis for the award of the qualification. The accrediting body may provide written guidelines and offer support for an individual assembling his or her portfolio. Constructing a portfolio will take time (often months, sometimes years) to complete.

However, the nature of the evidence necessary for inclusion in these 'portfolios' may prove particularly problematic for counselling. Since NVQs are designed to demonstrate competence in the workplace, the evidence demonstrating this competence must be drawn from the workplace. Simulation of situations is not permissible, and the extent to which assessors may infer competence (without direct observation) is limited. It may, therefore, prove problematic to find sources of evidence which both satisfy the requirements of the accrediting body (when selected) and do not compromise the counselling (and/or supervisory) relationship.

Two types of evidence can be used in the APL process: direct and indirect. Direct evidence is evidence produced by the candidate. Examples may include client case notes, an interview record, an audio/video tape recording, a personal log of a counselling session, or an evaluative commentary on the candidate's own practice of counselling. Indirect evidence is evidence produced by someone else, but relating to some aspect of the competence of the candidate. Examples may include feedback from formal supervision with 'witness testimony' from a supervisor, records of supervision sessions, reports and a policy statement.

Generally, direct evidence is considered stronger than indirect evidence, but both are useful in developing portfolios. It is likely that in constructing portfolios, candidates will need to use a combination of direct and indirect evidence to support their claims to credit.

The individual wishing to make the claim for credit is responsible for the first three stages of the APL process outlined above. Finally, the portfolio is submitted to the accrediting body for assessment, and the awarding body decides whether the evidence provided is sufficient to merit the award of the qualification sought.

ADVANTAGES AND DISADVANTAGES OF APL

APL can benefit both individual and organisation. It provides formal, external recognition for an individual's accomplishments, which can be important for self-esteem and for the credibility of the employing organisation. Time may be saved – it can be quicker to gain a qualification using APL, though this is not always the case. On a formal course of study, individuals are sometimes required to cover ground with which they are already familiar. This can be avoided. The process itself can be beneficial to the individual, by helping to develop a reflective approach to practice. This has been identified as the most important benefit of APEL in higher education. 'Thinking through, organising and presenting their case, making their claim to have mastered certain knowledge and skills is excellent education' (CNNA 1988: 5). Finally, APL has proved an important vehicle for widening access to education, particularly higher education (Evans and Turner 1993).

There are, however, also disadvantages. Since it is relatively new, the process of APL is generally unfamiliar and can be difficult to grasp. For those used to the more traditional methods of assessment, adjusting to the requirement to identify and articulate 'learning outcomes' for which credit is to be claimed, then selecting the evidence and method of presentation to support a claim for learning, can prove challenging. And it is not only the individuals wishing to claim credit who are likely to be unfamiliar with the process. Educators, trainers and work-based supervisors supporting and assessing those wishing to claim credit may lack experience of APL and may have to 'learn alongside' their candidates. This can, of course, result in a positive experience for all concerned – but may not. Training support has been identified as critical for APL, and for the successful embedding of NVQs (Blackman and Brown 1992). The process is likely to require time, personal effort and perseverance. By its very nature, APL requires a high level of organisational skill and self-direction on the part of those claiming credit. If such skills and qualities are absent, the individual may flounder. There is also invariably a financial cost, which will vary according to the accrediting body and the type of qualification sought. Lastly, the process can clearly discriminate against people who have experienced unemployment (Blackman and Brown 1992), or who have been away from employment for long periods.

Various misconceptions have also grown up around APL. Often it is assumed that it is quick, cheap and easy. In practice, it is rarely any of these things. A potential candidate for APL was disappointed and angry when I explained what would be involved: 'I thought I could get a qualification for just turning up.' On reflection, he decided to take a more traditional route to qualification.

CONCLUSIONS

APL is an innovative and radical concept which challenges traditional thinking and practice around methods of assessment and accreditation. A process which has grown out of the development of NVQs, APL is now recognised in its own right, and is gradually gaining acceptance within education and training. Perhaps its strongest appeal is its ability to assist in the widening of access and enhancement of equal opportunities relating to education and training.

Yet it presents something of a paradox for counselling. As counselling is an occupational area which employs a significant proportion of unqualified but competent people, APL is the mechanism which could facilitate accreditation in a way which emphasises and safeguards professional standards. It is, however, also a process which – without adequate training support and careful quality control – could damage the very standards it has the potential to improve.

Additionally, it presents a challenge for counselling and counsellor training. Important ethical issues (for example, relating to the confidentiality of the client–counsellor, counsellor–supervisor relationship) need in some way to be resolved so that the evidence necessary to demonstrate the competence of the counsellor can be collected and presented for assessment. It is, however, here to stay, and counselling's best interest will undoubtedly be served by a speedy resolution of these dilemmas and the establishment of good practice.

REFERENCES

Blackman, S.J. and Brown, A. (1992) Constraints upon portfolio development in the accreditation of prior learning. In J. Mulligan and C. Green (eds) *Empowerment through Experiential Learning: Explorations of Good Practice.* London: Kogan Page.

BTEC (Business and Technician Education Council) (1990) The Accreditation of Prior Learning (APL): General Guideline. London: BTEC Publications.

CNAA (Council for National Academic Awards) (1988) Assessment of Prior Learning. Development Services Briefing No. 4. London: CNAA.

Department of Employment (1986) White Paper: Working Together – Education and Training. London: HMSO.

Employment Department (1990) Accreditation of Prior Learning: A Training Agency Perspective. Sheffield: Employment Department.

Evans, N. and Turner, A. (1993) *The Potential of the Assessment of Experiential Learning in Universities.* London: Learning from Experience Trust and Employment Department.

Hodkinson, P. (1995) An Overview of NVQ Issues. Paper presented at the Conference Reviewing NVQs: The Way Forward, Further Education Research Association, University of Warwick, 19 May.

Kolb, D. (1984) *Experiential Learning.* Englewood Cliffs, NJ: Prentice Hall.

Lead Body (Advice, Guidance, Counselling and Psychotherapy Lead Body) (1995) First Release of Standards by the Advice, Guidance, Counselling and Psychotherapy Lead Body. Welwyn: AGC and PLB.

Lewin, K. (1951) *Field Study in Social Science.* New York: Harper.

Schon, D. (1987) *Educating the Reflective Practitioner.* San Francisco: Jossey Bass.

Simosko, S. (1991) *APL: A Practical Guide for Professionals.* London: Kogan Page.

Simosko, S. (1992) *Get Qualification for What you Know and Can Do.* London: Kogan Page.

Chapter 20

New directions in supervision

Francesca Inskipp

INTRODUCTION

I would like to suggest that the exciting new direction for supervision is that it is moving to becoming a discipline in its own right, moving away from being tied to a specific counselling orientation, developing theory and frameworks that separate it from counselling, using some of the same but some different skills. Alongside this, there is an increasing demand for a high standard of supervision to help develop and maintain good standards of counselling. What are the influences that energise this movement?

At the time of writing (1995) counselling has a public profile unimagined even ten years ago, and as the number of training courses multiply, producing a myriad of counsellors for the public, the issue of quality control and accountability is vital. Counselling is a private activity and supervision is the main, and possibly the only, way that the counselling profession can monitor the work of its members and endeavour to ensure a competent and ethical service to the public.

So how is supervision responding to this responsibility? Prior to 1988, counsellors became supervisors by having enough experience to oversee other counsellors' work; they usually took on their new role by modelling their supervision on that which they had received, and often supervising using counselling values and assumptions. Now it seems as if supervision is 'coming of age', maybe struggling with moving from adolescence to adulthood. In the last ten years there has been an upsurge, driven in three ways: (1) by initiatives from the British Association for Counselling (BAC); (2) by the emergence of training for supervisors; and (3) by publications on supervision. Each of these has probably increased the momentum in the others.

INITIATIVES BY BAC

In accordance with its aim of seeking to raise standards of counselling, BAC has been formative in promoting new developments in supervision.

In 1984 BAC in its Code of Ethics and Practice for Counsellors said: 'Counsellors monitor their counselling work through regular supervision by professionally competent supervisors and are able to account to clients and colleagues for what they do and why' (BAC 1984: para. 3.3). In 1990, an amended Code stated: 'It is a breach of the ethical requirement for counsellors to practise without regular counselling supervision/consultative support' (BAC 1990: para. B.3.1). This is a much stronger statement. The 1990 Code also gave a whole section (B.3.1–3.6) to issues of supervision/consultative support, confirming that supervision is seen by BAC as the method by which ethical standards of counselling and accountability to the public are maintained.

In 1988, BAC published a Code of Ethics and Practice for the Supervision of Counsellors (BAC 1988b), derived from the Code for Counsellors, which defined the purpose, nature, responsibilities and models of supervision. At the time of writing (1995) this Code is in the process of being revised to be more specific for supervision, so highlighting again its separation from counselling.

During this period a process for the accreditation of individual counsellors was set up. This requires the applicant to have been in regular supervision for a minimum of three years and to submit a supervisor's report. Also in this time, a process for the recognition of training courses for counsellors was developed. For a course to be recognised, students had to include a minimum of 100 hours' work with clients and receive at least one hour of supervision for every eight hours of counselling. In 1988, BAC published a *Counselling and Psychotherapy Resources Directory* (BAC 1988a), and counsellors and psychotherapists who wished to be listed here had to confirm that they were in on-going supervision.

All of these actions created a demand for more supervisors and in that same year, in order to raise standards of supervision, BAC set up a scheme for the recognition of supervisors. This required that supervisors should be experienced counsellors, have had a minimum of two years' supervising counsellors, and have done some training in supervision. To gain recognition, supervisors have to write an account of their philosophy and theory of counselling and of supervision, submit an analysed audio or video tape of a supervision session, and attend a day when they do a live supervision session with another applicant, are in turn supervised, and are questioned on their practice and how it matches their submitted paper work on theory and philosophy. Assessment on the 'live' day is done by two peer assessors who have already been through the process; there are clear criteria which have been refined as the recognition has progressed. In March 1995 there were 54 recognised supervisors and some concern about why more candidates were not coming forward. As a result, a decision was taken to revise the scheme.

In 1994 BAC took part in the development of National Vocational

Qualifications (NVQs) for counselling supervisors. The formulating of performance criteria has necessitated supervisors from different counselling and psychotherapy orientations coming together to discuss, work out and agree these criteria. When, and if, these criteria are eventually agreed and put into practice, this may provide an alternative route for qualification.

SUPERVISOR TRAINING

The recognition scheme asks for training in supervision, and since its start it has been noticeable that courses for training supervisors have begun to spring up around the country. Courses range from masters degrees containing a module on supervision, through diplomas requiring two years' part-time training, to certificates requiring around 80–100 hours' training and practice. Alongside these there are also weekend and day workshops on specific areas in supervision. Some training is specifically tied to one theoretical orientation, but other courses offer training in frameworks which cross different counselling theories. The development of training has raised more debate on how supervisors should be trained and what content should be included. This debate is helping to define the skills, knowledge and attitudes additional to, or different from, those of the counsellor.

PUBLICATIONS ON COUNSELLING SUPERVISION

The third upsurge is the steady stream of publications on supervision appearing in Britain. Before this there had been very few British publications, and we had to rely on American literature for theory and research. These were prolific but not entirely applicable, as supervision in the States is only mandatory for counsellors in training. The American writing and research are therefore on that area, whereas supervisors in the UK need to be able to supervise experienced counsellors as well as trainees, and need training and theory for both. However, the training of supervisors has been influenced by the work of Stoltenberg and Delworth (1987) on developmental stages of supervisees. They identified different needs of trainees at different stages, and although there is some criticism that this framework can be too rigidly applied, it can help supervisors to be aware of the differing learning needs of the counsellors, and to match the supervision to these needs. It has also encouraged the formation of some theory on the developmental stages of supervisors and how these might be matched with developmental stages of supervisees.

Another American writer, Elizabeth Holloway (1992), has run workshops and taken part in conferences in the UK. Her publications have been influential in promoting a task and role model of supervision, and in introducing a model for the supervision of supervisors.

In 1985 Patrick Casement's *On Learning from the Patient* was published, in which he describes a process for developing an 'internal supervisor'. This is a way for the analyst to monitor himself or herself in interaction with the patient, and so to develop techniques more specifically related to the individual patient.

In 1988 Brigid Proctor's 'Supervision: a co-operative exercise in accountability' appeared. This opened the issues of joint responsibility and defined three tasks of supervision:

1 normative – taking responsibility for standards and ethics;
2 formative – sharing responsibility for the development of the counsellor in skills, knowledge and understanding;
3 restorative – providing opportunities for discharge and recharge of batteries.

Later in 1988 Brigid Proctor's and my three audio tapes and two booklets on skills for supervisees and supervisors appeared (Inskipp and Proctor 1988). We think we broke new ground in suggesting that counsellors could be more proactive both in taking responsibility within supervision and in developing skills to prepare for and use it; we suggested that this was an important area to include in counsellor training. We followed this in 1994 by producing an open learning resource Part I, consisting of a book and two audio tapes, *Making the Most of Supervision* (Inskipp and Proctor 1994), which developed our ideas in more depth and promoted the idea of supervision as a shared responsibility, carefully contracted between supervisor and supervisee. Part II, *Becoming a Counsellor Supervisor*, followed in 1995. Brigid also produced a video and training manual, *Supervision: A Working Alliance*, which looked at the importance of making clear contracts for the shared responsibilities and promoted ideas for the training of supervisors.

In 1989 Hawkins and Shohet's *Supervision in the Helping Professions* was published. This promoted a process model of supervision across orientations, and provided a framework of six different ways of focusing in session. They stressed the need for commitment from both supervisor and supervisee alike, and provided guidelines and options for them both.

In 1990 Gaie Houston's *Supervision and Counselling* appeared. This gave clear and concise ideas, especially on group supervision.

In 1991 Dryden and Thorne edited *Training and Supervision for Counselling in Action*, which contained a chapter on the training of supervisors and another on the supervisory relationship as the key issue in supervision.

In 1994 Feltham and Dryden's *Developing Counsellor Supervision* was published as a practical guide for supervisors. In the Introduction the authors say:

Since counsellor training in Britain still predominantly follows the historical influence of the psychoanalytic and person-centred traditions, what has been written and what is presented in supervision training often emulates these influences. We hope in this book to bring some balance from the eclectic, integrative and cognitive-behavioural orientations which have been steadily gaining ground in Britain.

(Feltham and Dryden 1994: ix)

This seems to demonstrate a trend in the literature – and in many training courses – that supervision is moving away from being tied to a specific counselling theoretical orientation and is developing frameworks and theory which can be used across different orientations.

Also published in 1994 was Page and Wosket's *Supervising the Counsellor: A Cyclical Model*. The authors say in the Preface:

[Supervising] is no longer perceived as an activity which can be bolted on to the profession of counselling and psychotherapy and something at which any half decent counsellor could make a reasonable attempt. Supervision has earned the right to be considered as a *distinct discipline* (my emphasis) and can now justly claim to be taken seriously by researchers, theorists and practitioners.

(Page and Wosket 1994: ix, my italics)

The authors suggest their cyclical model of five stages – contract, focus, space, bridge, review – is 'a unifying supervision framework which can be used by practitioners from a broad range of counselling orientations' (1994: ix).

Two further books are Elizabeth Holloway's *Clinical Supervision: A Systems Approach* (1995) and Michael Carroll's *Counselling Supervision: Theory, Skills and Practice* (1995b).

All this, I think, heralds the dawn of a new discipline.

WHAT ARE THE NEW DIRECTIONS?

Supervision across theoretical orientations or focused on one

Debatable issues are:

• working in one orientation;
• working across orientations.

Working in one orientation

Points made in favour of this are that trainee counsellors need supervision to induct them into the core model in which they are being trained, and may become confused if they are supervised in another model. Experienced counsellors need the supervisor to understand their frameworks and help them develop their own way of working.

Working across orientations

The proponents of this approach say that training courses are moving towards integrative and eclectic models which require integrative supervision. Experienced counsellors can benefit from broadening their way of working – no model has been proved to be sufficient for all clients. Individual and group supervisors may have counsellors working on different theories and need to be able to translate language and concepts across theories.

Influences which promote broadening and integration

These include not only developments in supervision training and the publication of training ideas, but also BAC initiatives which bring together experienced counsellors, trainers and supervisors from across orientations to work on tasks together – developing Codes of Ethics, recognition procedures, etc. It seems as if by working on these tasks counsellors are able to explore similarities and differences in theory and philosophy openly, and find common ground and common language in order to share and use each other's ideas.

Differences from counselling

There is a movement towards models of supervision which stress tasks, roles, skills and relationships which are different from counselling. What are these additional skills, knowledge and attitudes, beyond 'clinical' knowledge and skills, which the supervisor will need to develop?

A relationship

The first is a relationship in which responsibilities and assumptions are clearly defined. Clear contracting of the differing roles and responsibilities, both at the inception of the relationship and in on-going reviews, can build an alliance where responsibilities for the development of ethical competence and confidence in the supervisee are shared. The only responsibility and authority which the supervisor must hold is if the supervisee is unaware of, or unwilling to acknowledge, his or her own incompetence or unethical work – and this authority needs to be acknowledged in the contracting. John Rowan in a recent workshop defined supervision as 'a passionate joint inquiry'. This, I think, suggests a collegial relationship, different from the therapeutic relationship between counsellor and client, which may be more familiar but which carries different assumptions.

Bernard (1994), writing on 'Clinical Supervision: Impending Issues', says:

> While supervisors emerged from the apprenticeship model, they were bound to rely on their skills as therapists in their work with supervisees. As such, they were inclined to focus on the supervisee's vulnerabilities as the center of supervision. By contrast, educational models look at the supervisee as an eager learner . . . Theories of psychotherapy were developed to deal with intransigent problems. Resistance was to be expected. Education . . . does not assume resistance. Rather education challenges the cutting edge of the supervisee's ability.

Stenack and Dye (1983), studying what supervisees want and do not want from supervision, found that they tend to dislike intrusive supervision focused mainly on exploring their internal processes, in which they are made to feel 'client' rather than colleague. The supervisor does need to be aware of the possible vulnerability of the counsellor in presenting his or her work and himself or herself, especially in a group.

The supervisor by reason of experience and role acceptance has more power and authority in the relationship, but I would argue that supervision needs to be an 'adult–adult' relationship, and any transference or counter-transference as it arises needs to be brought into the open and worked through. One important difference, highlighted I think by the 'process' model of supervision (Hawkins and Shohet 1989), is the open sharing by the supervisor of his or her internal processes as he or she works with the supervisee. As a counsellor he or she may be more cautious about what he or she shares with a client. If the supervisor sees the counsellor as a 'learner', a change of view requires different knowledge and skills.

Adult learning

Supervisors need a knowledge of how adults learn, differences in learning styles, and what helps and hinders learning. There is useful material on this in Bayne (1995). Supervisors need skills to be able to use the knowledge to create the best learning environment for this specific supervisee – and to change as the developmental needs change.

Developmental needs

Knowledge of the developmental needs of counsellors is needed, and the ability and flexibility to use this. Much research in the USA has focused on exploring different needs of supervisees as they develop, defining four specific stages, each requiring different skills and knowledge from the supervisor. As mentioned above, because their supervision is almost entirely concerned with trainees, this theory is more applicable in the USA than the UK, but it has stimulated the building of frameworks in the UK for working with trainees in different stages and with experienced counsellors as they develop. Carroll (1995a) has shown that supervisors indicate very strongly that they are aware of the developmental needs of supervisees and adapt their interventions and roles accordingly; however, their supervisees did not experience any changes in the supervisor's way of working over two years. One study showed that supervisors did change their tasks over time, but in no orderly fashion that would indicate a connection between learning needs and supervisory task (Carroll 1995a). This study took place before the surge in supervisor training, and maybe this is one skill which will develop with training.

Contracting

Skills and ability to make clear contracts are needed to clarify responsibilities, tasks, roles, learning agendas and practicalities, especially for supervising trainees and for working in an agency or organisation.

Assessment

The supervisor needs skills and knowledge to be confident about evaluation, assessment and report writing. One difference between counselling and supervising is the need to evaluate and judge. Supervision cannot be unconditional, but many supervisors are not clear where the boundaries lie between 'good enough' and 'not good enough', and are unwilling to pass judgement. This is partly a 'counselling' attitude, and there is probably ambiguity on what is 'good counselling'. A further problem is that many supervisors have no experience of assessment by agreeing criteria and setting learning goals, and may not be clear on differences between ongoing evaluation and final assessments. Report writing needs clarity of purpose, ability to review, and ability to give and receive regular feedback with the supervisee. It also needs an openness to explore power issues in the relationship.

Technical skills

The assumptions and theories of the supervisor affect the way the supervisee presents. If the supervisor is looking for unconscious processes, he or she wants spontaneous presentation; if the supervisor wants to help the supervisee learn from what he or she has actually done he or she needs an accurate presentation – an audio or video tape to work from. Many courses are requiring students to record their work with clients on audio tape and use this in supervision – and there is still a lot to learn on the best ways of doing this. Are supervisors flexible enough to work with a variety of ways of presenting?

Experienced counsellors are also finding tape-recording helpful for their learning and development, and there is now much less resistance to this mode of working. Rogers (1980: 138) wrote:

> I was at last able to scrounge equipment for recording my and my students' interviews. I cannot exaggerate the excitement of our learnings as we clustered about the machine that enabled us to listen to ourselves, playing over and over some puzzling point at which the interview clearly went wrong, or those moments in which the client moved significantly forward.

Technical advances in recording and in other fields – such as telephone with viewing – may open new ways of doing supervision. Interpersonal process recall (IPR) techniques are also a valuable addition to supervision.

OTHER DEVELOPMENTS

Supervising in a multicultural, multi-ethnic society

This is an area in which developments urgently need to take place, including exploration of issues relating to gender and to oppression generally in supervision. Some research (Thompson 1991) with supervision trainers showed that although there was an awareness of the need for training for supervisors in this, very little was done on training courses: it was fitted in as an extra rather than being integral to the course. BAC supervisor recognition did not include these areas in its criteria for assessment, and there is little mention of them in supervision training writings. Maybe BAC needs to set up a conference or workshops to explore and exchange training possibilities. This highlights the importance of the next point.

Research and development on supervision training for supervisors

Research projects are beginning to appear in Britain. In this changing field with possibilities for exciting developments, research should establish what is needed, what works, and how ideas can be disseminated.

The context

How does the context affect the role and tasks of the supervisor? I will discuss the supervision of trainee counsellors on Diploma courses, and then supervision in organisations.

Supervision of trainee counsellors on Diploma courses

There are a number of issues around this:

- *Who should supervise*? Should trainees be supervised by staff on the course, either specially employed as supervisors, or part of the teaching staff? If not, how does the course assess the on-going development of competence of the trainee with clients? If the course is of one theoretical persuasion, must all supervisors be supervising on this theory?
- *Assessment for qualification.* Should supervisors be responsible for assessing trainees' work with clients? If not, how else can it be assessed? How does this affect the role of the supervisor? If supervisors are external to the course, how are standards of assessment equated?
- *Integrative courses.* It is suggested that supervision is the main way trainees can be helped to integrate across theories; therefore supervision should be given priority time on the course, and 'teaching' may be a large part of the supervision task. How does this affect the role? Should supervision be by staff employed on the course? Can this role only be taken by outside supervisors if they are closely associated with the content and methods of teaching on the course and meet regularly with the staff?
- *Training to make the most of supervision.* This is beginning to happen in several training courses, and as this develops it could produce new ways of working for both supervisor and supervisee.

Supervision in organisations

There is an increase in the number of counsellors employed in a range of diverse organisations – general practitioner (GP) surgeries, National Health projects, industrial and professional firms, educational institutions. Within many organisations there are also people required to take on counselling as part of another role – nurses, welfare officers, social workers, managers, etc. – and they may need counselling supervision beyond their normal managerial supervision.

The BAC Code of Ethics says:

> Counsellors who have line managers owe them appropriate managerial accountability for their work. The counselling supervisor role should be independent of the line manager role. However where the counselling supervisor is also the line manager, the counsellor should also have access to independent consultative support.

> (BAC 1992: para. B.3.3)

Organisations may understand supervision in very different terms, and it is therefore important for counsellors and supervisors working for organisations to have clarified for themselves frameworks of supervision, from which they can explain and contract clearly the purposes and boundaries of counselling supervision, and how it may relate to any managerial supervision. This clarity is helped by good supervision training where organisational issues can be explored and anticipated.

Accountability, complaints and legal issues

It is not clear what responsibility a supervisor may hold for a supervisee who has had an official complaint made against him or her. Legally he or she cannot be held responsible. In a recent discussion with supervisors from different orientations who had differing views on how much recording they expected from supervisees, and how much recording they did themselves, it was suggested that it could be important if a complaint was brought that the counsellor and supervisor could confirm that the issue had been discussed at supervision; it was therefore important for supervisors to keep at least minimum records of clients and issues discussed, especially ethical issues.

Group supervision

A new direction in my work with Brigid Proctor has been in designing and running courses in creative group supervision. There has been very little theory developed on group supervision, which has often been seen just as individual supervision done in a group.

Three things have emerged from developing group supervision. First, the kind of group supervision can vary on a continuum from individual supervision done in a group, with group as audience, to peer-group supervision, where all members are responsible for supervising and being supervised by each other. We have identified four kinds of groups:

1 *Supervision in a group*. Here the supervisor supervises individuals in turn, and the other members are audience. The supervisor has two main roles: supervisor and manager of the structure.
2 *Participative group supervision*. The supervisor supervises, members learn how to and are encouraged to participate. The supervisor has four roles: supervisor, manager, group facilitator and 'teacher' of supervision.
3 *Co-operative supervision*. The supervisor facilitates the members in progressively supervising each other. The supervisor's main role is group facilitator, group 'teacher' and supervisor.
4 *Peer supervision*. Members supervise each other and negotiate structure, leadership, roles and responsibilities.

Each group requires different contracting for the roles and responsibilities so that members – and supervisors – have clear expectations about how the tasks will be performed.

Our second finding was that the group supervisor needs extra skills and knowledge of the group process, and the ability to use the process to build a safe and challenging climate. Engaging in the group process enables members to practise skills, especially 'immediacy' skills, which help their work with clients.

Third, creative group supervision can provide opportunities for professional and personal development which outweigh those of individual supervision. It could be not just economically useful, but a preferred option.

Professional development of supervisors

The welfare of the client demands the professional and personal development of the counsellor, and this can only be maintained if the supervisor is also concerned with his or her professional development. Counselling as it spreads is changing. Students on courses may be more in touch with new developments than experienced supervisors are, who, because they exercise influence in supervision, may be a retrograde force. To prevent this, they have an obligation to keep up to date and be in touch with new ideas.

CONCLUSIONS

These are some of the issues which I see as important. If supervision is in its adolescence, this may be a time of energetic growth – and some struggles to find an identity. It may be exciting and demanding for its counselling parents!

REFERENCES

BAC (British Association for Counselling) (1984, 1990, 1992) Code of Ethics and Practice for Counsellors. Rugby: BAC.

BAC (1988a) *Counselling and Psychotherapy Resources Directory*. Rugby: BAC.

BAC (1988b) Code of Ethics and Practice for the Supervision of Counsellors. Rugby: BAC.

BAC (1990) *The Recognition of Counsellor Training Courses*. Rugby: BAC. 2nd edn.

Bayne, R. (1995) *The Myers-Briggs Type Indicator: A Critical Review and Practical Guide*. London: Chapman and Hall.

Bernard, J.M. (1994) Clinical Supervision: Impending Issues. Unpublished paper. Fairfield University, CT.

Bond, T. (1993) *Standards and Ethics for Counselling in Action*. London: Sage

Carroll, M.F. (1995a) The Generic Tasks of Supervision: An Analysis of Supervisee Expectations, Supervisor Interviews and Supervisory Audio-Taped Sessions. Unpublished dissertation, University of Surrey.

Carroll, M.F. (1995b) *Counselling Supervision: Theory, Skills and Practice*. London: Cassell.

Casement, P. (1985) *On Learning from the Patient*. London: Routledge.

Dryden, W. and Thorne, W. (eds) (1991) *Training and Supervision for Counselling in Action*. London: Sage.

Feltham, C. and Dryden, W. (1994) *Developing Counsellor Supervision*. London: Sage.

Hawkins, P. and Shohet, R. (1989) *Supervision in the Helping Professions*. Milton Keynes: Open University Press.

Holloway, E. (1992) Supervision: a way of teaching and learning. In S.D. Brown and R.W. Lent (eds) *Handbook of Counseling Psychology*. Chichester: Wiley. 2nd edn.

Holloway, E. (1995) *Clinical Supervision: A Systems Approach*. London:Sage.

Houston, G. (1990) *Supervision and Counselling*. London: Rochester Foundation.

Inskipp, F. and Proctor, B. (1988) *Skills for Supervising and Being Supervised*. St Leonards-on-Sea: Alexia Publications.

Inskipp, F. and Proctor, B. (1994) *Making the Most of Supervision*. Twickenham: Cascade.

Inskipp, F. and Proctor, B. (1995) *Becoming a Counsellor Supervisor*. Twickenham: Cascade.

Page, S. and Wosket, V. (1994) *Supervising the Counsellor: A Cyclical Model*. London: Routledge.

Proctor, B. (1988) Supervision: a co-operative exercise in accountability. In M. Marken and M. Payne (eds) *Enabling and Ensuring*. Leicester: National Youth Bureau and Council for Education and Training in Youth and Community Work.

Rogers, C.R. (1980) *A Way of Being*. Boston: Mifflin Co.

Stenack, R.J. and Dye, H.A. (1983) Practicum supervisor roles: effects on supervisee statements. *Counselor Education and Supervision 23* (21) 157–68.

Stoltenberg, C. and Delworth, R. (1987) *Supervising Counsellors and Therapists: A Developmental Approach*. London: Jossey Bass.

Thompson, J. (1991) Issues of Race and Culture in Counselling Supervision Training Courses. MSc dissertation, University of East London.

Chapter 21

Towards the construction of a model of counselling
Some issues

Ian Horton

INTRODUCTION

What is a model of counselling? Relatively little has been written on its necessary elements. Although so many approaches to counselling have been spawned by the numerous theories of personality, several theorists have argued that a model of counselling (or psychotherapy) is not the same as a theory of personality (for example, Mahrer 1989: 30). Nevertheless, there is no consensus on what actually constitutes an adequate model. There has been an apparent reluctance to put as much energy into theory construction as has been devoted to empirical fact finding (McLeod 1994), but it is possible to discern a growing interest in theory construction, especially within the integrative lobby (Beitman 1994). This chapter seeks to promote this tentative new direction.

The chapter first discusses briefly the importance of theory in counsellor practice and training and highlights some of the issues in the development of integrative paradigms. It goes on to identify some of the concepts and principles that have been put forward as contenders for inclusion in the construction of a model of counselling. Finally the chapter outlines a basic training model that incorporates these elements and provides an open system framework that allows for the progressive assimilation of theory.

IMPORTANCE OF THEORY IN PRACTICE

Counselling involves theory. Counselling interventions and strategies are not employed in a vacuum, although the theoretical rationale and basic assumptions may not necessarily be fully articulated or understood (Lebow 1987: 3). Each intervention provides a working microtheory (Greenberg *et al.* 1994). Even a simple reflection of feeling or paraphrase of meaning is underpinned by some theoretical rationale that defines the purpose and intended impact on the client. Counsellors offer to intervene in the lives of their clients. It can be argued that if they expect to be taken seriously then they must also expect to be able to explain what they are doing and why they are doing it. They must be able to provide a plausible account of the sometimes complex and subtle processes with which they are working and most importantly, of how their proposed intervention relates to these processes. The case for the importance of theory is easily made in this way. Few people would argue that counsellors should be permitted to tamper with processes which they have not made a serious attempt to understand. However, if the function of theory is to enable counsellors to articulate 'what they are doing and why they are doing it' then it would seem important to put the emphasis on what Orlinsky *et al.* (1994) refer to as 'therapeutic operations', rather than on personality theories and the aetiology of psychological problems. This idea will be developed later in the chapter.

IMPORTANCE OF THEORY IN COUNSELLOR TRAINING

Dryden *et al.* (1995) put forward a persuasive argument for the importance of theory as an essential component of professional counsellor training. Their views reflect those of the British Association for Counselling (BAC). The BAC scheme for the formal recognition of counsellor training courses – established in 1988 – requires that courses provide a coherent and in-depth training in a specific 'core theoretical model'. The scheme also requires that students are able to compare and contrast their core model with other approaches (BAC 1990). The United Kingdom Council for Psychotherapy (UKCP) and the British Psychological Society (BPS 1993) have recently published their own training requirements. The UKCP imply rather than make explicit a requirement for training in a particular orientation, and also state that there should be an 'introduction to a range of psychotherapies and counselling so that trainees may have an awareness of alternative treatments' (UKCP 1993). The BPS take a different view. They require students to 'understand a broad range of theoretical frameworks and have a detailed knowledge of at least two distinct theoretical approaches' (BPS 1993). The inference is that the BPS encourage students to understand the process from a variety of theoretical perspectives and *ipso facto* to work within whatever theoretical frame seems most appropriate for the particular client – irrespective of any potentially conflicting philosophies or values.

An increasing number of counsellor training courses with integrative core models are applying for BAC recognition. Where there are no well-articulated, published exemplars of the particular approach, courses are required to submit a full description of the approach being advocated (BAC 1993). BAC panels debate long and hard over judgements on what constitutes an adequate (integrative) model. The criteria defy any easy consensual operational definition.

PROLIFERATION OF THEORIES

Clearly, the development of new approaches to counselling and attempts to combine diverse ideas is not a new direction. It has been something of an enduring preoccupation that has captured the imagination of at least some counsellors for many decades. Norcross and Greencavage (1994: 4) review various surveys which indicate that between 1959 and 1986 the number of different schools of counselling or psychotherapy rose from 36 to over 400. By the mid-1980s, dogmatic commitment to exclusive or single theories seemed much less common, and what was variously referred to as 'creative synthesis', 'syncretism', 'multimodalism' and 'eclecticism' was widely recognised as a major position in terms of adherents (Brabeck and Welfel 1985). Today the more common and seemingly more respectable term is 'integration'. Despite Stiles *et al.*'s (1993: 115) claim that 'it has become increasingly apparent that the existence of pure theory is a myth', the often heated controversy and debate over the issues and implications of new and combined theories continue unabated.

The growing network of divergent paths towards combining ideas and techniques is undoubtedly in part a reaction to the confusion, fragmentation and discontent with the proliferation of approaches. It has resulted in a new direction which is producing many new 'integrative models', destined to become the fixed or pure-form approaches of tomorrow. This serves only to exacerbate a situation in which both consumers and practitioners are confronted by staggering 'over-choice'.

Lambert and Bergin (1994: 181) from their review of research evidence suggest that counselling and psychotherapy are overall and in general beneficial. However, despite the enormous increase in both the quantity and quality of research – the volume of research findings has more than doubled over the last ten years (Orlinsky *et al.* 1994) – it has not been possible to demonstrate the superiority of one approach over any other, although the efficacy of some approaches has been demonstrated in response to specific presenting problems. Furthermore, some aspects of the therapeutic process (such as therapeutic alliance) have been shown to have very strong positive associations with outcome (Bergin and Garfield 1994). It is this association between aspects of the process and positive outcome, common to all or most approaches, which provides the rationale for a new direction that seeks to unpack therapeutic packages and examine the active ingredients.

APPROACHES TO THEORY CONSTRUCTION

There is a major new direction towards the integration of diverse techniques and concepts into broad, comprehensive and pragmatic approaches to counselling that avoid allegiances to narrow theories or schools of thought (Lambert and Bergin 1994). The central tenet is the need to start by examining the components of a model. Only in this way is it possible to clarify *what* it is that can be integrated with *what*. Beitman (1994: 205) suggests that in the past, new approaches have largely been the product of inductive reasoning: that is, they follow from particular cases and clinical experience. He cites Rice and Greenberg, who argue that a major limitation of this bottom-up approach to theory construction is that it inevitably lags behind clinical innovation until that is sufficiently used by practitioners to justify controlled evaluation, and that in any case existing research is inadequate to support even the well-established theories, let alone new models. Beitman puts forward an eloquent plea to 'stop exploring psychotherapy integration and start defining the principles of integration' through a process of theory-derived, top-down deductive reasoning. This starts with the development of general, higher-order constructs and principles, which can then be applied to particular cases (Beitman 1994: 226). Such an approach to theory construction requires a model that defines the components of a theory.

MODELS OF THEORETICAL COMPONENTS

There have been several isolated attempts to define the components of a theory. Nelson-Jones (1985: 131) suggested four components, which can be summarised as:

1 basic assumptions;
2 an explanation of how both functional and dysfunctional feelings, thoughts and behaviours are acquired;
3 an explanation of how they are perpetuated or sustained;
4 practical suggestions for changing and modifying dysfunctional feelings, thoughts and behaviours that are internally consistent with the preceding elements.

The first three components comprise the essence of a theory of personality. However, the links between a personality theory and the methods of treatment derived from it are tenuous at best (Fonagy and Higgett 1984), and it is not clear just what strategies and interventions accurately interpret a theory, or what constitutes internal consistency. Some cognitive-behavioural approaches and new developments in counselling, such as solution-focused brief therapy (George *et al.* 1990), in which it is assumed that attempts to understand the cause of the problem are not necessary or even useful and that problems do not represent underlying pathology, would be found lacking if this model of a theory were accepted.

Neimeyer (1993: 141) describes the components of a model of 'theoretically progressive integration' that seeks to elaborate what he sees as a coherent theory of therapy, that attempts to provide both a conceptualisation of and a direction for clinical practice. Neimeyer describes the structure of psychotherapy theories in a diagram of three concentric circles around the core metatheoretical or philosophical assumptions, and moving outwards from 'formal theory' about the nature of human development, through 'clinical theory' that provides an organising framework for therapeutic interventions, to the outer circle of 'strategies and techniques'. He sees it as highly improbable that epistemologically incompatible systems will ever converge to yield a unified system to guide clinical practice. Neimeyer suggests that the optimal circumstances for theoretical integration are compatibility of the core metatheory. However, he acknowledges that functional integration may also take place at the level of clinical theory, strategies and interventions.

An earlier attempt to define the components of a theory was put forward by Mahrer (1989). He starts from the premise that a theory of counselling (or psychotherapy) is not the same as a theory of personality. Mahrer emphasises what Neimeyer describes as 'clinical theory' and, like Beitman (1990), seems to regard counselling as a practical endeavour, intended to help people to change. Mahrer's seven components can be summarised as:

1 useful material to be elicited from the client;
2 how and what to listen for;
3 explanatory concepts to describe presenting problems and targets for change;
4 therapeutic goals and directions of change;
5 general and more specific principles of change;
6 strategies, techniques and procedures;
7 what strategies to use under what circumstances.

Although Mahrer describes the various components in greater depth than has been found elsewhere in the literature, it is still difficult to arrive at an operational definition that satisfactorily distinguishes between several of them (Bayne *et al.* 1994: 151).

Beitman (1994: 204) suggests that in the past, theory has 'tended to obfuscate what actually transpires during the therapy hour', and that the theoretical components should be described more simply. He claims that it is possible to identify general principles of psychotherapy integration that reach beyond the content of specific schools. The assumption here is that these principles provide the basic components for any model of counselling.

COMPONENTS OF A THEORETICAL MODEL

This part of the chapter examines the possible components of a model. It is concerned with the active ingredients of all or most approaches to counselling or psychotherapy. Lazarus (1990) quotes London, who observed that 'However interesting, plausible and appealing a theory may be, it is techniques, not theories, that are actually used with people.' Lazarus argues that any evaluation of the effectiveness of counselling, therefore, is always an evaluation of what the counsellor actually does to implement his or her particular philosophy and formal theory.

Four components are presented here. They would be an integral part of any model of counselling at the level of clinical theory and strategies. The assumption is that while a particular model may not interpret these components in the same way as presented here, a working model needs to make explicit the position it adopts on each component.

Process structures and themes

Beitman (1994: 211) writes that 'there is a pressing need for the identification of conceptual structures that will provide students and practitioners with grounding and direction'. Two therapeutic structures (stages and contracting) and three core themes (content, relationship and reflection) are outlined here.

Stages

The assumption is that it is possible to conceptualise the process through which the counsellor and client work together in terms of broadly defined developmental stages. The stages provide a framework for intervention and are characterised by stage-related goals or tasks, which need to be achieved at one stage as a prerequisite of forward movement and change. This assumption is supported by recent research findings. Orlinsky *et al.* (1994) present a generic model of input, process and outcome stage variables and identify a new direction for research into the sequential flow of events both during and across sessions. They discuss the research findings concerned with the temporal aspects of the process, and the relation of outcome to the differential effects of the achievement of stage-related goals. The findings suggest that it is important to achieve particular process goals at particular stages in the process.

While the process stages are temporally related, with individuals progressing over time from one to the next, straightforward linear progression is rare and a cyclical pattern is more common as the dynamics of the relationship develop, new issues emerge, and goals are evaluated and often redefined.

The stages may be defined simply as the beginning, middle and end of the process (Bayne *et al.* 1994; Mearns and Thorne 1988). Alternatively they may provide a more complex structure such as the stages of engagement, pattern search, change and termination (Beitman 1990). The basic concept of process stages that serve to link goals with strategies can be found elsewhere (for example, Stiles *et al.* 1993; Egan 1990; Brammer *et al.* 1993; Ivey *et al.* 1987; Trower *et al.* 1988; Clarkson 1989; Tracey 1989; Lang *et al.* 1990). A complementary model of process stages has been proposed by Prochaska (1984). This identifies the stages of a client's readiness to change, and related interventions and strategies appropriate to the goals for each stage.

Therapeutic contracting

The provision of any particular arrangements or mode of therapeutic contract seems to show no consistent relation to outcome (Orlinksy *et al.* 1994). However, ground rules are an essential part of the coun-sellor–client relationship and contribute to those aspects of the process that do have a strong positive association with outcome (such as client co-operation and the quality of client participation). Contracting occurs on two levels. The first is concerned with such issues as length, frequency, duration, privacy, confidentiality and so on. These issues can be especially important to contain some clients and ensure stability of counselling arrangements. At the other level, the development of a therapeutic plan enables the counsellor and client to move towards a common under-standing of what they are trying to achieve together. 'If you don't know where you're going, you'll probably end up somewhere else' (Campbell 1974), and if you have no sense of where you are going, how will you know when you get there? Aspects of contracting such as the initial target for change, goal consensus, clarity of client expectations, client role preparation, readiness and suitability have been shown as key variables associated with beneficial outcomes (Orlinsky *et al.* 1994).

Content and therapeutic operations

Contained within the boundaries of the therapeutic contract and running through the process stages are a number of developmental and goal-related core themes. The 'content' theme describes the tasks and the thera-peutic operations and strategies that are employed to process client presenting problems and issues through the various stages.

A model of counselling would need to make explicit the position it adopts on the importance of human development and the nature and func-tion of explanatory frameworks for the origin and maintenance of prob-lems. Theories of counselling hold radically different views on this matter. Some theorists believe that the notion of psychological cause is philo-sophically problematic and may be an illusion (for example, Beitman 1994; Egan 1990; Lazarus 1990; de Shazer 1988). Nevertheless, Frank (1971) asserts that the provision of new perspectives or information on the nature and sometimes on the origin of the problem is associated with positive outcome, irrespective of the exact content of the explanation, as long as it is experienced by the client as plausible and useful. Beitman (1994: 215) postulates that people are predisposed to seek causes for their problems, presumably because they believe that understanding the origin will lead to solutions. However, he is critical of many psychological explanations that do not offer any account of how problems are perpetuated or any clear directions for change. He presents a list of eleven 'causal atheoretical explanations that suggest how to change'. These explanatory frameworks offer potential for integration.

Relationship

The therapeutic relationship is a core theme that helps to structure the process and provide a potential vehicle for content. The strongest evidence linking process to outcome – independent of any particular therapeutic school – concerns the therapeutic alliance or the quality of the bond between counsellor and client (Orlinsky *et al.* 1994). The development of an effective working relationship is often seen as a prerequisite for client learning. It is developed and maintained at various levels: the real, professional and transferential (Greenson 1967). The client 'self–observer alliance' is an essential practical element of the relationship through which clients talk about their thoughts, feelings and behaviours (Beitman 1994). The dynamics of the relationship, or what may be happening within both the counsellor and the client and between them, may provide a window on the client's presenting problem. In this way the relationship relates directly to the content theme (Horton 1993).

Reflection

This core theme operates at two levels, one outside the counselling relationship, the other within it. The first concerns the counsellor's reflection on clinical problems and therapeutic issues through supervision. I have written elsewhere of the importance of supervision as an integral, albeit complementary part of the counselling process (Horton 1993). Davis (1989) provides a useful checklist for reviewing and evaluating conceptual ability, clinical performance and personal learning through supervision. The other level of reflection that is within the process is both covert and overt. It may involve the counsellor's 'internal supervisor' (Casement 1985) to help 're-capture the internal stream of consciousness' (Barker 1985: 155). This is the counsellor's own emotional reaction – his or her thoughts, feelings and fantasies in response to the client – as a tool for listening (Horton 1993). This process is compatible with any orientation that accepts the utility of examining inner experience. Overt reflection within the process involves the counsellor and client in review and evaluation of therapeutic plans, progress, methods and intended outcomes at each stage.

General principles of change

This component of a model is concerned with basic assumptions that underpin the process of change. Beitman (1994: 221) presents seven principles, which are adapted here.

Identify a focus or target for change

This identifies potential areas for intervention, including thoughts, feelings, behaviours, system dynamics and levels of change. Initial intervention is often at the level of symptom or situational problems. The progressively deeper levels move from maladaptive cognitions and interpersonal conflicts to systems or family conflict and intrapersonal conflict (Prochaska and DiClemente 1992). This and other models recognise that the areas and levels are interrelated and that change in one may result in changes in others. Hallam (1992) supports this view when he suggests that counsellors need to employ a technology that respects the views and responds to the needs of clients at a multiplicity of levels.

Assume the client is responsible for change

Most approaches accept that counsellors can only facilitate change and cannot make changes for their clients or make their clients change. A client's readiness to change provides a firm predictor of outcome and may be used to determine process goals and the related strategies and interventions (Prochaska and DiClemente 1992).

Utilise client resources

Problems change and people help themselves without the benefit of counselling through a variety of techniques and strategies that are in fact common to counselling. Counsellors need to build on clients' strengths and resources and enable them to utilise existing ways of coping (Haley 1973; Ivey *et al.* 1987; Horowitz 1994). Indeed, some new directions in brief counselling are based entirely on encouraging 'problem-free talk', and working with instances of deviation from the presenting problem situation, when things are not so bad, and with what clients actually do to enable them at least to survive (de Shazer 1988; O'Hanlon and Weiner-Davis 1988).

Explore and confront resistance to change

Some clients come reluctantly to counselling and frequently drop out, and most exhibit some resistance to change because it involves the loss of what is familiar. There are often secondary gains or pay-offs from even painful situations that serve to perpetuate the problem. People vary in their level of reactance or tendency to resist external efforts to influence, which they experience as limiting their range of choices.

Recognise systemic influences

Counsellors need to take account of a client's cultural history and social context variables (such as gender, race, family) that may both contribute to the client's problem and in turn be affected by any change in the client. The ultimate purpose is to accomplish the basic tasks of counselling, which involve defining the problem, communicating empathy and respect, achieving a status that will allow the counsellor to help the client, finding appropriate ways of managing or resolving the problem, helping the client to implement learning, and ending in such a way that counselling will be considered a viable option for the client in the future (Bernard and Goodyear 1991: 203).

Facilitate learning and new perspectives

Counselling is intended to help clients change. This inevitably involves learning to think, feel and behave differently. People appear to have radically different ways of learning (Bayne 1995: 125) that need to be recognised and explicated in any comprehensive model of counselling (Wallace 1986).

Encourage application and generalisation of learning

It is not enough for clients to learn how to think, feel and behave differently in the counselling room if it does not make a difference to their life outside. Some clients in some situations may need help to apply and generalise their learning.

Process of change

A model of counselling needs to include some explanation of the process of change. Stiles *et al.* (1990) describe an integrative process model that explains the way in which problematic experiences are assimilated into schemas developed in the therapeutic interaction through a series of predictable stages. It does not prescribe any particular theoretical approach or method to produce the sequence of change. The model identifies 'assimilation' as the process common to all theoretical approaches, and draws concepts from developmental psychology and all the main schools of counselling. The concept of a 'schema' is used as a generic term for a well-organised and familiar pattern of ideas, experiences, behaviours and feelings, into which the problematic experience is gradually assimilated. It is central to a number of new directions in counselling (Bricker *et al.* 1993; Horowitz 1994; Padesky 1994) and provides a potential common language for the integration of clinical theory and techniques. Stiles *et al.* (1990) sees the counselling relationship as having its own developmental sequence, which is in itself therapeutic and also provides a vehicle for assimilation.

A complementary perspective on the process of change can be found in control process theory (Horowitz 1994).

Mechanisms of change

Alongside any description of the process of change must be some account of how change actually occurs. A model of counselling needs to identify the factors that facilitate client change. Although particular orientations tend to emphasise specific mechanisms of change, it seems likely that common therapeutic factors are present in most forms of counselling. Research findings provide no clear evidence on the differential contribution of what must remain the various hypothesised therapeutic variables. Nevertheless, there is empirical support for a range of mechanisms of change (Bergin and Garfield 1994). Garfield (1992: 185) describes the common mechanisms as:

1 relationship between counsellor and client;
2 emotional release or catharsis;
3 provision of some rationale, explanation or interpretation of psychological problems;
4 reinforcement of client resources and strengths;
5 exposure through
   a) desensitization to problems in an understanding and accepting climate;
   b) facing or confronting what is being avoided;
6 information or skills training.

Similarly, Prochaska and DiClemente (1992) present a list of ten atheoretical and separate mechanisms of change that are particularly relevant for producing change at different stages of the process.

CONCLUSIONS: A BASIC TRAINING MODEL

This model incorporates the basic structures and themes identified in the previous section. It is an integrative process model that is intended to provide both a conceptualisation of the counselling process and a direction for clinical practice that does not try to undermine the integrity of different approaches. It is a working model of the process that provides an organising framework for integrating concepts and strategies from other approaches. Alternatively, it can stand alone as an integrative skills approach to counselling. The model provides a map of the process through which the counsellor and client work together. It provides guidelines intended to help counsellors articulate what they are doing and why they are doing it.

The model does not imply any one theory of personality or human development. Psychological problems are regarded as multidimensional and seldom attributable to one source, situation or factor. It is assumed that people are too complex to be explained by any one theory and that social context plays an important part (Brammer *et al.* 1993; Fonagy and Higgett 1984; Cormier and Cormier 1991). There are many equally valid yet different routes to the same destination. Clients need to be helped to identify their goals or desired outcomes, which can then be achieved through a variety of strategies (Mahalik 1990). Bernard and Goodyear (1991: 195) cite Smith, who referred to the 'myth of sameness' as the error of many counsellors who espouse a single approach and are convinced that it is generic and can be applied to individuals of varying backgrounds, personality types and presenting problems. Perhaps the key question is whether you fit your approach to the client or the client to the approach. Arguments for a flexible integrative approach are well documented elsewhere (for example, Lebow 1987; Norcross and Goldfried 1992; Dryden and Norcross 1990).

This basic training model is conceptualised as a matrix of stages (see Table 21.1), which provides the structure through which each of the inter-related relationship, content and reflection themes are sequentially developed. Each theme is characterised by the need to achieve particular process goals or tasks at each stage. The developing relationship between the counsellor and client is the first theme. In Stage 1, the tasks are to build the relationship, establish rapport and the working alliance, facilitate client self-disclosure, and clarify boundaries and the client role. In Stage 2, the therapeutic climate and working alliance are maintained. Work continues within the boundaries and contract to develop and, where appropriate, to use the dynamics of the relationship as a basis for motivation and learning. Stage 3 is concerned with seeking resolution of issues around ending.

The second theme is the content of the client's problems and the related

Table 21.1 Overview of a basic training model

Theme	Stage 1 tasks	Stage 2 tasks	Stage 3 tasks
1 Relationship	Establish	Maintain and use	End
2 Content	Assess problem and resources	Facilitate learning and change	Consolidate and apply
3 Planning	Develop therapeutic plans and client goals	Monitor and revise; reflect on process	Evaluate process and outcomes

therapeutic operations. In Stage 1, the task is one of problem identification through understanding the client's world view and experience, exploration of precipitating events, antecedents, social context and problem intensity, and assessment of client strengths and resources. The counsellor may develop a tentative clinical formulation of the nature, origins and ramifications of client problems in a way that suggests a target for change. Stage 2 is concerned with facilitating learning and change. The tasks are to search for patterns and key themes, affirm and where possible use the client's unique strengths and ways of coping, determine desired outcomes, and work towards new perspectives, deeper self-awareness, and learning different ways of thinking, feeling and behaving. Stage 3 focuses on consolidating learning and change through helping the client to apply and integrate change into new ways of being or living, and through identifying obstacles and ways of sustaining and expanding change.

The third theme running through each stage is reflection and therapeutic planning. In Stage 1 the contract and therapeutic goals are negotiated. Two types of goal are recognised as equally valid and interrelated: those concerned with helping the client to discover solutions or ways of managing immediate problems more effectively, and broader goals of growth, deeper awareness and self-actualisation (Brammer *et al.* 1993). In Stage 2, the tasks are to monitor and where necessary revise therapeutic plans and client goals and also to reflect on and evaluate process. The final stage of the reflection and therapeutic planning theme is concerned with ending and evaluation. The tasks are to clarify and contract ending procedures; to review what has been achieved, why change has happened, what still needs to be achieved, what may happen in the future to anticipate potential stresses and identify ways of coping with them and to evaluate the nature of the counselling relationship (Bayne *et al.* 1994: 58–60).

The model makes a distinction between strategies and skills. Strategies are ways of achieving particular tasks, while skills are the behaviours - interventions or responses - for actually doing so. For example, the task of establishing a working alliance is partially achieved by communicating the 'core qualities', while the strategy is implemented by using the skills of active listening. The strategies and skills are essential tools, which provide a set of logical and practical guidelines, but they are not an end in themselves. Rather, they need to be integrated into counselling through the quality of the relationship.

To achieve competence to practise as an integrative or eclectic counsellor, it is important first to emphasise the development of skills for establishing and maintaining the therapeutic relationship (Beutler and Consoli 1992). Active listening skills and a solid foundation in relationship-oriented strategies should be acquired. Only subsequently should specific techniques be emphasised. Thereafter, training should concentrate on developing a working knowledge of the integrative process model; the principles, process and mechanisms of change; and the explanatory, causal frameworks that contain suggestions for targets of change.

The basic training model is an open systems framework which allows flexibility in approach, is readily adapted to diverse client populations, remains open to potential changes and research findings, and can be tailored by counsellors to match their own personal styles.

REFERENCES

BAC (1990) The Recognition of Counsellor Training Courses. Rugby: BAC. 2nd edn.

BAC (1993) The Recognition of Counsellor Training Courses Scheme. Guidelines for Integrative and Eclectic Courses. Rugby: BAC.

Barker, C. (1985) Interpersonal process recall in clinical training and research. In F.N. Watts (ed.) New Developments in Clinical Psychology. New York: Wiley.

Bayne, R. (1995) The Myers-Briggs Type Indicator: A Critical Review and Practical Guide. London: Chapman and Hall.

Bayne, R., Horton, I., Merry, T. and Noyes, E. (1994) The Counsellor's Handbook: A Practical A–Z Guide to Professional and Clinical Practice. London: Chapman and Hall.

Beitman, B. (1990) Why I am an integrationist (not an eclectic). In W. Dryden and J.C. Norcross (eds) Eclecticism and Integration in Counselling and Psychotherapy. Loughton: Gale Centre.

Beitman, B.D. (1994) Stop exploring! Start defining the principles of psychotherapy integration: call for a consensus conference. Journal of Psychotherapy Integration 4 (3) 203–28.

Bergin, A.E. and Garfield, S.L. (eds) (1994) Handbook of Psychotherapy and Behavior Change. New York: Wiley. 4th edn.

Bernard, J.M. and Goodyear, R.K. (1991) The Fundamentals of Clinical Supervision. Needham Heights, MA: Allyn and Bacon.

Beutler, L.E. and Consoli, A.J. (1992) Systematic eclectic psychotherapy. In J.C. Norcross and M.R. Goldfried (eds) Handbook of Psychotherapy Integration. New York: Basic Books.

BPS (1993) Membership and Qualifications Board Training Committee in Counselling Psychology. Guidelines for the Assessment of Postgraduate Training Courses in Counselling Psychology. Leicester: BPS.

Brabeck, M.M. and Welfel, E.R. (1985) Counseling theory: understanding the trend towards eclecticism from a developmental perspective. *Journal of Counseling and Development 63* 343–50.

Brammer, L.M., Abrego, P.J. and Shostrom, E.L. (1993) *Therapeutic Counseling and Psychotherapy*. Englewood Cliffs, NJ: Prentice Hall. 6th edn.

Bricker, D.C. and Young, J.E. (1993) *A Client's Guide to Schema-Focused Cognitive Therapy*. New York: Cognitive Therapy Center/ATID Publications.

Campbell, D. (1974) *If You Don't Know Where You're Going, You'll Probably End Up Somewhere Else*. London: Argus Publications.

Casement, P. (1985) *On Learning from the Patient*. London: Tavistock.

Clarkson, P. (1989) *Gestalt Counselling in Action*. London: Sage.

Cormier, W.H. and Cormier, L.S. (1991) *Interviewing Strategies for Helpers*. Pacific Grove, CA: Brooks/Cole.

Davis, J. (1989) Issues in the evaluation of counsellors by supervisors. *Counselling 69* 31–7.

de Shazer, S. (1988) *Clues: Investigating Solutions in Brief Therapy*. London: Norton.

Dryden, W. and Norcross, J.C. (eds) (1990) *Eclecticism and Integration in Counselling and Psychotherapy*. Loughton: Gale Centre.

Dryden, W., Horton, I. and Mearns, D. (1995) *Issues in Professional Counsellor Training*. London: Cassell.

Egan, G. (1990) *The Skilled Helper – A Systematic Approach to Effective Helping*. Pacific Grove, CA: Brooks/Cole. 4th edn.

Fonagy, P. and Higgett, A. (1984) *Personality Theory and Clinical Practice*. London: Methuen.

Frank, J. (1971) Therapeutic factors in psychotherapy. *American Journal of Psychotherapy 25* 350–61.

Garfield, S.L. (1992) Eclectic psychotherapy: a common factors approach. In J.C. Norcross and M.R. Goldfried (eds) *Handbook of Psychotherapy Integration*. New York: Basic Books.

George, E., Iveson, C. and Ratner, H. (1990) *Problem to Solution*. London: BT Press.

Greenberg, L.S., Elliott, R.K. and Lietaer, G. (1994) Research on experiential psychotherapies. In A.E. Bergin and S.L. Garfield (eds) *Handbook of Psychotherapy and Behavior Change*. New York: Wiley. 4th edn.

Greenson, R.R. (1967) *The Technique and Practice of Psychoanalysis*. Vol. 1. New York: International Universities Press.

Haley, J. (1973) *Uncommon Therapy*. New York: Norton.

Hallam, R. (1992) *Counselling for Anxiety Problems*. London: Sage.

Horowitz, M.J. (1994) States, schemas and control: general theories for psychotherapy integration. *Clinical Psychology and Psychotherapy 1* (3) 143–52.

Horton, I. (1993) Supervision. In R. Bayne and P. Nicolson (eds) *Counselling and Psychology for Health Professionals*. London: Chapman Hall.

Ivey, A.E., Ivey, M.B. and Simek-Downing, L. (1987) *Counselling and Psychotherapy: Integrating Skills, Theory and Practice*. Englewood Cliffs, NJ: Prentice Hall. 2nd edn.

Lambert, M.J. and Bergin, A.E. (1994) The effectiveness of psychotherapy. In A.E. Bergin and S.L. Garfield (eds) *Handbook of Psychotherapy and Behavior Change*. New York: Wiley. 4th edn.

Lang, G., Van der Molen, H., Trower, P. and Look, R. (1990) *Personal Conversations – Roles and Skills for Counsellors*. London: Routledge.

Lazarus, A. (1990) Why I am an eclectic (not an integrationist). In W. Dryden and J.C. Norcross (eds) *Eclecticism and Integration in Counselling and Psychotherapy*. Loughton: Gale Centre.

Lebow, J.L. (1987) Developing a personal integration in family therapy: principles for model construction and practice. *Journal of Marital and Family Therapy 13* (1) 1–14.

Mahalik, J.R. (1990) Systematic eclectic models. *Counseling Psychologist 18* (4) 655–79.

Mahrer, A.R. (1989) *The Integration of Psychotherapies – A Guide for Practicing Therapists*. New York: Human Science Press.

McLeod, J. (1994) *An Introduction to Counselling*. Buckingham: Open University.

Mearns, D. and Thorne, B. (1988) *Person Centred Counselling in Action*. London: Sage.

Neimeyer, R.A. (1993) Constructivism and the problem of psychotherapy integration. *Journal of Psychotherapy Integration 3* (2) 133–58.

Nelson-Jones, R. (1985) Eclecticism, integration and comprehensiveness in counselling theory and practice. *British Journal of Guidance and Counselling 13* (2) 129–39.

Norcross, J.C. and Goldfried, M.R. (1992) (eds) *Handbook of Psychotherapy Integration*. New York: Basic Books.

Norcross, J.C. and Greencavage, L.M. (1994) Eclecticism and integration in counselling and psychotherapy: major themes and obstacles. In W. Dryden and J.C. Norcross (eds) *Eclecticism and Integration in Counselling and Psychotherapy*. Loughton: Gale Centre.

O'Hanlon, W. and Weiner-Davis, M. (1988) *In Search of Solutions*. New York: Norton.

Orlinsky, D.E., Grawe, K. and Parks, B.K. (1994) Process and outcome in psychotherapy – *noch einmal*. In A.E. Bergin and S.L. Garfield (eds) *Handbook of Psychotherapy and Behavior Change*. New York: Wiley. 4th edn.

Padesky, C.A. (1994) Schema change processes in cognitive therapy. *Clinical Psychology and Psychotherapy 1* (5) 267–78.

Prochaska, J.O. (1984) *Systems of Psychotherapy: A Transtheoretical Analysis*. Homewood, IL: Dorsey Press. 2nd edn.

Prochaska, J.O. and DiClemente, C.C. (1992) The transtheoretical approach. In J.C. Norcross and M.R. Goldfried (eds) *Handbook of Psychotherapy Integration*. New York: Basic Books.

Stiles, W.B., Shapiro, D.A. and Barkham, M. (1990) Research directions for psychotherapy integration. In J.C. Norcross (ed.) Research Directions for Psychotherapy Integration: A Roundtable. *Journal of Psychotherapy Integration 3* 91–131.

Stiles, W.B., Elliott, R., Firth-Cozens, J.A., Llewelyn, S.P., Margison, F.R., Shapiro, D.A. and Hardy, G. (1993) Assimilation of problematic experiences by clients in psychotherapy. *Psychotherapy 27* (3) 411–20.

Tracey, T.J. (1989) The stages of influence in counselling. In W. Dryden (ed.) *Key Issues for Counselling in Action*. London: Sage.

Trower, P., Casey, A. and Dryden, W. (1988) *Cognitive-Behavioural Counselling in Action*. London: Sage.

UKCP (1993) Training Requirements Information Sheet. London: Regent's College.

Wallace, W.A. (1986) *Theories of Counselling and Psychotherapy: A Basic Issues Approach*. Boston: Allyn and Bacon.

Chapter 22

Beyond denial, myth and superstition in the counselling profession

Colin Feltham

INTRODUCTION

I will briefly explain my personal position in relation to this title and chapter, followed by a view of various problems within the profession and finally how they might be addressed. I take myth to mean 'fictitious narrative', and superstition to be 'unreasoning awe or fear, . . . a tenet, scruple, habit, etc., founded on fear or ignorance' (*Shorter Oxford English Dictionary* 1983). As for denial, 'some parts of us are difficult to look at or "own" and we may therefore deny their existence or their full significance' (Bayne *et al.* 1994: 43). I am suggesting as new directions: (1) a general change of attitude, allowing for the legitimacy of serious questioning of fundamental counselling ideology; (2) the injection into training of a specific critical component; (3) the recognition within counselling institutes and authorities of their own fictions, philosophical oppressions and other 'shadows'.

The field of counselling surely has its share of unconvincing theories, terminological obstacles, unnecessary rituals and institutionalised opinions masquerading as knowledge. I believe the essence of counselling to be, like certain religious and philosophical endeavours, intimately related to truth seeking and salvation seeking. Like religion, counselling and psychotherapy probably generate as many problems as they solve, and they certainly create a great deal of myth and superstition. If we directly compare the clergy with the counselling profession, I would say that the existence of sanctioned priests creates the false impression and belief that they are closer to God than others. Likewise, a counselling profession creates an illusion that sanctioned counsellors know more about human nature and are necessarily more skilful listeners and helpers than others. Certainly it is a commonly drawn conclusion that people who spend many years in psychoanalysis and analytic training must in some way be closer to profound human truths, and/or possess far greater self-knowledge, than others. Doubt is cast on such conclusions by, among others, Maeder (1989) and Masson (1991).

It seems probable that the founders of religions, as of new psychothera-peutic systems, are genuinely intent on discovering new (or perennial but freshly experienced) truths and transmitting these to others. Probably, they are indeed in closer touch with God, mystical experience, the Unconscious or whatever, at least temporarily. But inevitably, it seems, a process of corruption sets in, whereby initial raw contact with new and profound discoveries is imperceptibly converted into dogma and institu-tionalisation. The closest I have personally come to any understanding and holistic experience of profound truths has been through the writings of Krishnamurti in particular, but also those of mystics generally. I have also had a number of experiences across the years, sometimes in therapeuti-cally oriented groups, which belong to the realm of the profoundly authentic and apparently unrepeatable (by any effort or method), in which personal problems lessen, dissolve or take on new perspectives (Cohen and Phipps 1979). I would refer to this realm as 'holistic', except for the reservation that this word has become an empty cliché. The core problem-atic issue here is that priests, philosophers, counsellors and others invari-ably attempt to systematise, colonise and bureaucratise that realm and to license themselves as its gate-keepers.

So, I regard counselling itself as problematic because it holds forth the promise that there is a method, or methods, whereby people will be reli-ably helped towards that realm. (It may be a myth of my own that there is such a realm, of course!) It seems to me that a few people are helped dramatically, a few are not helped or are harmed, and the vast majority are probably helped modestly. When they are helped, we still do not really understand exactly how counselling has helped them, although the weight of current evidence suggests that success rests mainly on non-specific relationship factors (concern, love, presence). Just as the existence of God is problematic, so the existence of an Unconscious is problematic. Priests and counsellors may know something that others do not, or their training and standing may simply create illusions of greater knowledge. It may indeed be the case, as has often been put, that any therapeutic potency possessed by priests and healers is due to their own and their clients' beliefs in sanctioned myths (which may be known as theological or thera-peutic rationales).

The degree to which counselling is nebulous and problematic is, I think, widely denied by practitioners. Counselling is a relatively new or still evolving profession and much of its success may depend on the uncritical enthusiasm of practitioners. It follows that critiques of coun-selling are generally not welcomed by counsellors, and indeed their validity is frequently denied out of hand. I suggest that they often have considerable validity and that we should consider taking them into the heart of our training, as put forward by Samuels (1993). Substantial critiques include those put forward by Szasz (1978), Clare and Thompson

(1981), Dryden and Feltham (1992), Spinelli (1994), Howard (1995) and Feltham (1995). In addition, Heaton (1993) suggests that philosophical scepticism has a central part to play in psychotherapy and counselling, and McNamee and Gergen (1992) present critical post-modernist perspectives on the talking therapies.

THE CORE THEORETICAL MODEL

The United Kingdom Council for Psychotherapy (UKCP) and the British Association for Counselling (BAC) require that training courses to be validated must adhere to an identifiable theoretical model or tradition. Accreditation criteria also stress the importance of a core model. This may refer broadly to psychoanalytic, humanistic or integrative models, for example, or to specific cases of person-centred, Gestalt, transactional analysis or other singular models. The argument advanced for the importance of a core theory is as follows. Although there is no evidence that any one approach is in practice superior to another, it is essential that trainees receive in-depth training in one main approach so that they possess a set of practical competencies and coherent grasp of theory that can be applied to their clinical work. Even though they may later question, modify or reject their initial training model, they must have this grounding. The core model should be capable of offering explanations of the causes of psychological distress, perpetuating factors, rationale for interventions, contraindications, and so on (Dryden 1990). Beyond the training period, too, there are many counselling agencies which act like exclusive clubs and will not employ counsellors unless they share the agency's theoretical orientation.

I have come to wonder if the idea of a core model is a myth born out of the anxieties of professionalisation and failure to apply tests of logic and efficacy. It is also important to ask 'Who says that a core theoretical model is essential?' Is it unanimously agreed by all practitioners that formative training must rest on a core model? It is not, since I, for one, dispute it, and I know of others who do too, if only privately. Also, I am told that in Canada, for example, such hullabaloo about core models is virtually absent. Has insistence on a core model been decided by a quango of experts? (If so, who?) Has it been decided democratically by a majority vote? (If so, how, when, and so on?) What criteria for judgement did this majority employ? Is it supported by weighty research evidence? By common sense? Is it axiomatic? Certainly those therapists whose reports of their formative influences were analysed by Norcross and Guy (1989: 227–8) considered the core knowledge presented within their original training as of minimal importance.

Many I have spoken to claim not to belong to any distinct approach (including eclectic or integrative), and even to dislike such labels altogether, yet tacitly it is acknowledged that it is difficult to admit to this openly. Yet, is there any evidence at all that this group of 'agnostics' is any less clinically effective than groups of purists? I doubt it. When I have discussed this matter with people who strongly believe in the need for a core theory, their reply is invariably an assertive, even dogmatic, 'You've just got to have a thorough grounding in one coherent approach', in a tone which echoes the 'You've just got to eat your greens because they're good for you/it's obvious/don't be so immature as to question this!' kinds of familiar childhood injunction.

One can easily envisage a training course which honestly, even polemically, embraces the pluralistic embarrassment of the current counselling and psychotherapy scene from the outset. Samuels (1993: 321) asks us to recognise that 'the whole field is riddled with rhetoric' and that 'starting at the beginning is no guarantee of comprehension'. The counter-argument is that trainees will become confused and therefore ineffective if they are not given a thorough ABC-style introduction to one model and its associated techniques. Does this not betray an image of trainees as rather child-like and incapable of intellectual discrimination? Wheeler (1993) argues that a sound theoretical framework is essential in training and that integrationists or eclectics may later choose to utilise what they have learned from different thorough trainings: eclectic dabbling, in this view, is likely to lead to clinical ineffectiveness. Samuels's pluralistic view challenges this and asks us to consider that it is perhaps more honest, truer to reality and even ultimately more clinically effective to base training on a pluralistic and polemical view. We do not know that psychoanalysis, for example, is truer to reality or more clinically helpful than psychosynthesis, cognitive-behavioural therapy or any other model: subjectively, many practitioners strongly *believe* this to be the case and insist that it *is* the case. But in fact it is altogether unproven.

CONFIDENTIALITY

Something we can all agree on is the necessity, perhaps even sacredness, of confidentiality. What is counselling if not a private, professional, preciously boundaried activity? Clients cannot discuss their innermost concerns, they cannot disclose their peccadilloes, their vulnerability and pain, unless they are absolutely sure they can trust the counsellor. Counselling resembles the religious confessional. Well, suppose that we begin to inquire into the meaning, reality and limits of confidentiality?

Now, most counsellors agree on, and in theory always inform clients of, two caveats to confidentiality. Supervisors must have access to some information about their supervisees' clients and, when group supervision is employed, several of the counsellor's colleagues inevitably hear details about clients (probably with surnames, at least, omitted). Trainers, researchers and writers are also frequently privy to clinical material, which is often shared with colleagues. All such information should always be shared only after clients' explicit agreement and/or it should be disguised beyond recognition. Confidentiality is stretched in all these ways, and may also be challenged or breached in cases of suspected danger to self or others. In theory, counsellors do not divulge anything to their non-supervisory colleagues, partners or close friends, but there is of course no way to police this. When dwelt on, these many grey areas surely puncture the myth of watertight confidentiality.

Is rigid confidentiality always in the best interests of the client? Consider this example. A woman telephones a counsellor and says that her doctor suggests she gets some stress counselling. She describes certain symptoms, including muscular spasms. The counsellor says she wants to check on these symptoms before arranging a counselling session, but she is not quite sure where to turn. Her supervision is not due for another two weeks and this case is not an emergency warranting phone calls to the supervisor, who, anyway, has very little medical knowledge. The counsellor, as is her wont, mentions this case to her husband, whose profession is paramedical. By chance, he has recently read about a neurological disorder in a magazine, the symptoms of which correspond to those described by the client. The counsellor does a little research and relays the results to the client, who subsequently returns to her doctor, asks for further investigations, and has it confirmed that her condition is not psychogenic but dystonia, a neurological disorder. But for the counsellor's technical breach of confidentiality, the client would have gone along for an indefinite number of sessions of ultimately fruitless stress counselling. A fortuitous diagnosis helped the client when obsessional confidentiality would have led nowhere. For some clients, absolute confidentiality may be more important than even the alleviation of their distress, but I suspect that there are many who would gladly give permission to the counsellor to consult *anyone* who might help them.

Confidentiality creates or confirms a sense of specialness. The client is unique, her circumstances and problems are unique and uniquely fascinating, and she would be easily identified if talked about. Now, all counsellors – and certainly anyone who has participated in group therapy – must know that most problems are balefully common, that many human plights are universal. One of the most common and perhaps unhelpful fantasies generated by clients is that they are uniquely crazy, sinful, awful, bedevilled, victimised and irredeemable. Many busy counsellors will admit to confusing one client with another occasionally in their own minds, precisely because tales of woe are often quite similar. Perhaps in fostering clients' beliefs in their uniqueness we inadvertently perpetuate counter-therapeutic attitudes: confidentiality by its very nature may create a distorted fantasy world. Indeed, many sociologically informed critics of counselling point to its socially dangerous tendency to play down what is universal (Rose 1989; Newman 1991; Hillman and Ventura 1992; Smail 1993).

I have known some clients to say 'Oh, there's nothing very confidential about anything in my life.' This can be interpreted as a lack of self-worth or a disingenuous game. It can, however, be regarded as a simple truth. It can mean 'I have nothing to hide.' Paradoxically, the condition of confidentiality in counselling may sometimes reinforce the sense of isolation that causes so much sickness in the first place: if we could set about re-establishing trusting communities, we might confidently entrust our vulnerabilities to each other, instead of only to designated experts. In fact, when people confess to their sins, defects or foibles in religious, mutual aid or consciousness-raising groups, they are doing just this. Interestingly, many who choose to exhibit their problems and secrets publicly, for example on television, often seem to gain greatly by doing so (Dryden 1992: 76–87). I am not advocating the abandonment or dilution of confidentiality but recommending that we continually question our most prized precepts, including confidentiality, in order to rescue them from becoming mere myths or superstitions.

SUPERVISION

It is the proud boast of counsellors in Britain that quality is assured by regular clinical supervision of practitioners for the duration of their professional lifetime. Supervision now has an identity quite separate from counselling itself, from training and personal therapy. Like confidentiality, supervision is one of the central defining characteristics of professional counselling. It separates the charlatans from the reputable and offers protection to clients. It has come to sound like an absolutely, undebatably good practice; indeed, by the BAC it is considered essential. But is it?

Traditionally in Britain, clinical psychologists, many psychotherapists and psychoanalysts have not formally been required to receive regular supervision. In the USA, supervision is for the most part not mandatory beyond a certain period of training. We have to ask: are unsupervised or irregularly supervised clinical practitioners offering an inferior or dangerous service? If they were, would we not have heard about it by now? One can only guess that the vast majority of clients seen by unsupervised or irregularly supervised practitioners have not in fact received substandard treatment and have not been abused. British counsellors, obliged to receive regular supervision, are either not to be trusted without it, or are perhaps offering a superior service. Presumably, counsellors abuse their clients less and are more clinically effective, overseen as diligently as they are. It is an unpalatable conclusion, but one we must consider, that

supervision of counselling, in spite of its appeal to the sense of professionalism, may actually make little difference compared with unsupervised
practice. It may well be interesting, reassuring and momentarily stimu-
lating for counsellors themselves, of course. Even to write this triggers off
fantasies of being disbarred from the counselling profession, since supervision has become a central, defining feature of counselling, and possibly
a superstition that may not be challenged at all. Let us remember that to
challenge is not automatically to condemn or denigrate but to open up
fundamental debates.

I have myself written about the benefits and methods of supervision,
but this does not preclude the possibility of questioning whether it is in
fact essential. It seems subjectively and professionally like a good idea,
and a practice which can do nothing but good, but it should not be immune
from criticism. Supervision cannot guarantee to eradicate or even reduce
the abuse of clients, since supervisors cannot practically police their
supervisees' actual contacts with clients; anyone determined to exploit
clients can easily conceal this from a supervisor. Parks (1992) offers interesting examples of therapists and supervisors regarded as abusive or
unhelpful by clients and supervisees. As for the question of supervision
enhancing effectiveness, a kind of collusion in supervision is, I think,
actually likely where supervisor and supervisee closely share beliefs and a
core theoretical model. How likely is it that in a psychoanalytic supervisory dyad, for example, the possible ineffectiveness of that model in
certain cases will be examined? Instead of a counsellor being in regular
supervision with the same supervisor, might it not be a better practice for
the counsellor to seek out consultancy specifically related to his or her
particular clients at any one time? Could not a professional, trouble-
shooting hot-line be established, offering expert and tailored consultancy?

Finally, consider one of the central ironies in all this: that regular supervision for counsellors is *mandatory*. You do not have the option to use
supervision if and when you consider it optimal. It may be that the very
regularity of supervision inclines it towards a ritual, like church attendance, which may be helpful sometimes, but sometimes will simply be a
ritual. The same can be said for mandatory personal therapy for trainees.
Limitations of space prevent further exploration of this subject, but I am
constantly surprised at the ferociousness with which many counsellors
and therapists uncritically declare lengthy therapy for trainees (or even
qualified and experienced practitioners) to be imperative. There is no hard
evidence that such therapy is essential, but there is plenty of passionate
conviction. Gellner (1985) gives a philosopher's analysis of these very
issues.

BOUNDARIES

One of the most commonly used terms in counselling is 'boundary'. A defining characteristic of counselling is the discipline with which counsellors observe certain boundaries. Counselling is not socialising, befriending or friendship. It is not advice-giving, advocacy or control of clients. Counsellors should not engage in sex with clients, nor should they disclose too much, if any, personal information about themselves to clients. Each counselling session has strict time boundaries. If the client arrives late, this is clinically significant. If the counsellor allows the session to run over time, this is indicative of bad practice and probably of some counter-transferential phenomena. Sessions should probably be fifty minutes long for all clients and they should preferably be at the same time each week. There are some frame management theorists who argue that it is crucial that everything in the clinical environment should be consistent (same time, same room and so on). Some counsellors believe that absolutely no physical contact should take place between themselves and clients and that there should be no small talk at all. However liberal the counsellor or counselling orientation, boundaries are always considered important, if not sacrosanct.

Arnold Lazarus, in a chapter entitled 'Dos and don'ts and sacred cows' (in Dryden 1991), attacks many of the prized injunctions and superstitions of the counselling and therapy professions. Agreeing that prohibitions against sexual contact and aggressive and demeaning behaviour should be maintained as virtual 'taboos', Lazarus goes on to challenge injunctions against advice-giving, self-disclosure, socialising, providing therapy for friends or family members, and accepting gifts or favours from clients. While agreeing that certain ground rules are necessary in counselling, Lazarus argues that the highly individual needs of clients oblige us to place a premium on flexibility. The boundary between counselling and socialising might be profitably stretched or challenged, then, if the client's progress were enhanced by a dinner or game of tennis together. Lazarus admits to engaging in just such judiciously considered socialising at times. Even more contentious has been the celebrated case of Brian Thorne's quasi-sexual encounter with a client for well-described therapeutic reasons (Thorne 1987). Also extremely challenging on the subject of therapeutic boundaries and the ethics of mutuality is the work of Heyward (1994).

Now, it is easy to insist that absolutely non-negotiable boundaries always protect clients, but they may also inhibit creative manoeuvres in counselling in certain instances. I am unsure whether the traditions of meeting clients in our room or office (not in their homes), sitting on chairs (generally not lying down together, walking or adopting other positions), are necessary, or simply unquestioned habits. Several colleagues have confirmed my own observation that therapeutic progress is often made when the counsellor finds himself or herself travelling in a car with a client or engaging in activities which are familiar, everyday, and not eyeball-to-eyeball encounters of the traditional counselling kind. Freud, of course, sometimes analysed a client or colleague during a walk together, and the title of 'ambulatory psychotherapy' presumably bestows some legitimacy on this practice.

The same holds true for time boundaries. Some clients benefit from prolonged sessions, others seem to have difficulty with the traditional fifty-minute-long hour. So, I believe that we must continually review the usefulness or counter-productivity of our professional boundaries. It is already true, of course, that many humanistic therapists sit or lie on the floor; the experiential psychotherapist Alvin Mahrer reclines side by side on reclining chairs with clients; and classical psychoanalysts have always sat behind their clients. The fruitful trend towards various models of time-limited therapy, from single-session therapy, the 'two plus one' model and cognitive-analytic therapy (sixteen sessions), to brief intermittent therapy across the life cycle, has emerged from questioning the traditional psychotherapeutic model of necessary years of therapy. Look out, however, for the myths generated by this brief therapy trend (Zeig and Gilligan 1990).

OTHER CONSIDERATIONS

The question of what is myth and superstition may be applied at every level and stage of counselling. Is training necessary, for example? Lazarus (1990) has asked whether in certain cases training counter-productively destroys the natural abilities possessed by some trainees. Some research has suggested that untrained counsellors may perform as well as or even better than trained counsellors (Durlak 1979; Hattie *et al.* 1984). We are still in the dark about who makes a good or excellent counsellor and who does not, but it is quite possible that it might be more important to identify the characteristics of the 'born counsellor' and to attract such people into counselling than to churn out thousands of 'wannabes'. Are our current training traditions optimal or do they need to be radically revised?

Why do we perpetuate the myth of counselling as a non-directive enterprise dedicated to enhancing the client's self-determination, when in fact counselling ideology is full of strongly held beliefs and injunctions? The novelist Fay Weldon has argued that counsellors have spawned an attitude of psychological or emotional correctness: we must own our feelings, be genuine, spontaneous, assertive, self-actualising, etc. Such attitudes have been satirised by Weldon in her novel *Affliction* (Weldon 1994). Kegan (1994) asks whether such psychotherapeutic demands have not actually added stress to many people's lives (in ways which parallel, perhaps, the guilt- and fear-inducing tendencies of much religion). We like to regard ourselves as agents of empowerment but avoid looking too closely at our abuses of power (Guggenbühl-Craig 1971). Wood (1983) has suggested, similarly to Szasz, that problems in living are unavoidable challenges that should not be interpreted as a form of psychological disturbance to be labelled and treated by experts.

Why do we perpetuate the myth of a real division between counselling and psychotherapy? If we wish to maximise the help available to clients, should we not rationalise the (in many ways) rival professions of clinical psychology, counselling psychology, counselling, psychotherapy and psychiatry? (See Pilgrim and Treacher (1992) on this latter point.) Why do we tolerate the proliferation of schools of therapy and the psychobabble that goes with it? Are the emerging forms of eclecticism and integrationism really addressing the needs of clients or are they substituting new myths for old? (Haphazard syncretism, for example, is ineffective – or heretical – according to the new orthodoxy of the integrationists.) If most of our current evidence about the process and outcome of counselling suggests that the quality of the relationship is at the heart of healing and change, what does this imply for approaches which emphasise techniques? If, on the other hand, Lazarus is correct (in Dryden 1991) when he says that we need to address clients' presenting problems in a straightforward way, by using carefully selected interventions, then the relationship is not to be perceived as central. The field is indeed, as Samuels (1993) has told us, ridden with opinions and polemics. Why deny it?

CONCLUSIONS: NEW DIRECTIONS

I should like to see counsellors taking on board serious critiques of the profession. Such critiques do not constitute an inconvenient fly in the ointment but alert us to our own self-deceit as counsellors who, however much self-awareness work we may have done, remain fallible human beings. Kottler (1993: 181–205) confronts unflinchingly the 'lies we tell ourselves'. We should not be concerned only with the psychopathological resistances and shadow side of our clients or (in personal therapy) with our own, individual pathology and psychological wrinkles. We should also be concerned – perhaps more concerned – with the shadows within, and cast by, the profession we are busily promoting. Such concern could be aired at the level of the professional authority (BAC) and also within training. Trainees should not be treated like children who cannot yet be told that Father Christmas does not exist, and whose questions about religion, sex and death must be answered cautiously, if at all. (In the context of existential theology, this challenge has already been taken on by, among others, Ranke-Heinemann (1992).)

The new direction that counselling should take (and I use the word 'should' precisely because it is superstitiously forbidden in counsellor training!) is to place serious critiques of and objections to counselling on the agenda. Many of the references given in this chapter would provide the basis for a training module, for example. Perhaps counselling and psychotherapy authorities (BAC, UKCP, British Confederation of Psychotherapists, British Psychological Society, etc.) and training institutes should seriously consider building in imaginative mechanisms for responsibly analysing and owning their organisational shadows, as suggested by many Jungians (Stein and Hollwitz 1992).

Counselling has a special responsibility to promote and nurture truthfulness and to identify, confront and reduce untruthfulness, because many personal problems originally derive from dishonesty and disabling myths and rituals in families, organisations and society generally. Also, counselling is ultimately part of the cure or part of the problem, and if myths or untruths are propagated in counselling, if counsellors are reluctant to question the precious shibboleths of the profession, then we become problem creators and energy wasters. Are we as an emerging profession denying the existence of our collective myths while busily engaging in individual myth-busting rituals? If we could stop denying that counselling is deeply problematic and at risk of becoming a new religion or pseudoscience, we could perhaps see it more as a tentative moral force in society and a fallible healing method. There is no easy way to formulate this new direction, but giving it greater space and respect within our conferences and training would be a beginning.

REFERENCES

Bayne, R., Horton, I., Merry, T. and Noyes, E. (1994) *The Counsellor's Handbook*. London: Chapman and Hall.

Clare, A.W. and Thompson, S. (1981) *Let's Talk About Me: A Critical Examination of the New Psychotherapies*. London: BBC.

Cohen, J.M. and Phipps, J.-F. (1979) *The Common Experience*. London: Rider.

Dryden, W. (ed.) (1990) *Individual Therapy: A Handbook*. Milton Keynes: Open University Press.

Dryden, W. (1991) *A Dialogue With Arnold Lazarus: It Depends*. Buckingham: Open University Press.

Dryden, W. (1992) *The Dryden Interviews: Dialogues on the Psychotherapeutic Process*. London: Whurr.

Dryden, W. and Feltham, C. (eds) (1992) *Psychotherapy and its Discontents*. Buckingham: Open University Press.

Durlak, J.A. (1979) Comparative effectiveness of paraprofessional and professional helpers. *Psychological Bulletin 86* (1) 80–92.

Feltham, C. (1995) *What Is Counselling?: The Promise and Problem of the Talking Therapies*. London: Sage.

Gellner, E. (1985) *The Psychoanalytic Movement*. London: Paladin.

Guggenbühl-Craig, A. (1971) *Power in the Helping Professions*. Dallas, TX: Spring Publications.

Hattie, J.A., Sharpley, C.F. and Rogers, H.J. (1984) Comparative effectiveness of professional and paraprofessional helpers. *Psychological Bulletin 95* 534–41.

Heaton, J.M. (1993) The sceptical tradition in psychotherapy. In L. Spurling (ed.) *From The Words Of My Mouth: Tradition in Psychotherapy.* London: Routledge.

Heyward, C. (1994) *When Boundaries Betray Us: Beyond Illusions of What is Ethical in Therapy and Life.* San Francisco: HarperCollins.

Hillman, J. and Ventura, M. (1992) *We've Had a Hundred Years of Psychotherapy and the World's Getting Worse.* San Francisco, CA: HarperCollins.

Howard, A. (1995) *Challenges to Counselling and Therapy.* London: Macmillan.

Kegan, R. (1994) *In Over Our Heads: The Mental Demands of Modern Life.* Cambridge, MA: Harvard University Press.

Kottler, J.A. (1993) *On Being a Therapist.* San Francisco: Jossey Bass.

Lazarus, A.A. (1990) Can psychotherapists transcend the shackles of their training and superstitions? *Journal of Clinical Psychology 46* 351–8.

Maeder, T. (1989) *Children of Psychiatrists and Other Psychotherapists.* New York: Harper and Row.

Masson, J. (1991) *Final Analysis: The Making and Unmaking of a Psychoanalyst.* London: HarperCollins.

McNamee, S. and Gergen, K.J. (eds) (1992) *Therapy as Social Construction.* London: Sage.

Newman, F. (1991) *The Myth of Psychology.* New York: Castillo.

Norcross, J.C. and Guy, J.D. (1989) Ten therapists: the process of becoming and being. In W. Dryden and L. Spurling (eds) *On Becoming a Psychotherapist.* London: Routledge.

Parks, J. (1992) *Shrinks: The Analysts Analyzed.* London: Bloomsbury.

Pilgrim, D. and Treacher, A. (1992) *Clinical Psychology Observed.* London: Routledge.

Ranke-Heinemann, U. (1992) *Putting Away Childish Things.* San Francisco: HarperCollins.

Rose, N. (1989) *Governing the Soul: The Shaping of the Private Self.* London: Routledge.

Samuels, A. (1993) What is a good training? *British Journal of Psychotherapy 9* (3) 317–23.

Smail, D. (1993) *The Origins of Unhappiness: A New Understanding of Personal Distress.* London: HarperCollins.

Spinelli, E. (1994) *Demystifying Therapy.* London: Constable.

Stein, M. and Hollwitz, J. (eds) (1992) *Psyche at Work: Workplace Applications of Jungian Analytical Psychology.* Wilmette, IL: Chiron.

Szasz, T. (1978) *The Myth of Psychotherapy.* New York: Syracuse University Press.

Thorne, B. (1987) Beyond the core conditions. In W. Dryden (ed.) *Key Cases in Psychotherapy.* Beckenham: Croom Helm.

Weldon, F. (1994) *Affliction.* London: Flamingo.

Wheeler, S. (1993) Reservations about eclectic approaches. In W. Dryden (ed.) *Questions and Answers on Counselling in Action.* London: Sage.

Wood, G. (1983) *The Myth of Neurosis.* London: Macmillan.

Zeig, J.K. and Gilligan, S.G. (eds) (1990) *Brief Therapy: Myths, Methods and Metaphors.* New York: Brunner/Mazel.

Name index

Abramson, L.Y. 139, 144
Adams, C.D. 67
Afield, W.E. 113
Alexander, T. 229
Allen, L. 45
Allen, T. 43
Allinson, T. 176
Allison, K.W. 243
Anderson, S.A. 194
Armstrong, D. 102
ASC (Association for Student
   Counselling) 25, 26
Association for Counselling at Work 6,
   12, 13
Association for Pastoral Care and
   Counselling 26
Audit Commission (1994) 228
Aveline, M.O. 91, 192

BAC (British Association for
   Counselling) 5, 9, 11, 12, 13, 22, 25,
   116, 261, 266–7; AGM (1993) 73;
   Annual Conference (1991) 11; Annual
   Report 1992/3 10; Code of Ethics and
   Practice 18, 66, 269; Management
   Committee 16; Membership Survey
   (1993) 20; publications ((1984) 269;
   (1986) 18; (1988) 121, 269; (1990)
   269, 282; (1992) 18, 277; (1993) 18,
   23, 52, 60, 282); Research Workshop
   (1995) 82; training 18, 268, 299
Bagarozzi, D.A. 194
Baker Miller, J. 250, 257
Balint, M. 97, 98
Ballou, M. 251, 257
Bandler, R. 255
Barker, C. 80, 81, 83, 87, 288
Barkham, M. 82, 83, 84, 87, 88

Bates, C.M. 45
Bavolek, S. 228, 230, 232
Bayne, R. 243, 274, 285, 286, 290, 293,
   297
Beach, S.R.H. 139
Beck, A.T. 39, 139, 145, 255
Becker, T. 55
Beehr, T.A. 175
Beier, E.G. 193
Beitman, B. 284, 285, 286, 287, 288,
   289
Belsky, J. 222
Berger, M. 46
Bergin, A.E. 180, 283, 284, 291
Bernal, M.E. 237
Bernard, J.M. 274, 290, 292
Berne, E. 194, 255
Berridge, J. 113, 176
Bettelheim, B. 133, 197
Beutler, L.E. 294
Billings, A.G. 181
Bimrose, J. 239, 243
Binder, J.L. 39
Blackman, S.J. 266
Bond, T. 58, 61, 258
Boot, D. 99
Bowlby, J. 139, 141, 148
BPS (British Psychological Society) 6,
   12, 13, 23, 25, 282; publications
   ((1993) 282; (1995) 60, 129)
Brabeck, M.M. 283
Brady, J.L. 179
Brammer, L.M. 287, 292, 293
Brewin, C.R. 141
Bricker, D.C. 291
Briner, R.B. 173, 175
Brislin, R.W. 239, 240
British False Memory Society 128, 129

Subject index

Bold page numbers indicate main text entries